Dwight Frye's Last Laugh

DWIGHT FRYE'S LAST LAUGH

An Authorized Biography

by
Gregory William Mank
James T. Coughlin
Dwight D. Frye

Luminary Press
Baltimore, Maryland

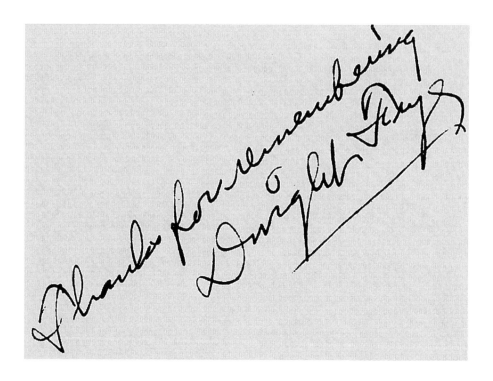

ISBN 1-887664-11-4
Library of Congress Catalog Card Number 96-76713
Manufactured in the United States of America
Printed by Sheridan Books, Fredricksburg, VA
First Printing by Midnight Marquee, Press, Inc., 1997
Second Printing by Luminary Press, a division of Midnight Marquee Press, Inc.,
    June 2003

DEDICATION

To my loving mother, Jane,
for nurturing my appreciation of old films
and encouraging me to pay attention to the character players.
—JTC

To
Randye Cohen
(1952-1995)
who hosted the November 7, 1993,
commemoration honoring Dwight Frye
in Montclair, New Jersey,
and who put me in contact
with Dwight D. Frye

And to
DeWitt Bodeen
(1909 - 1988)
—GWM

Dwight Frye as the haunted Renfield in *Dracula* (Universal, 1931).

Table of Contents

Dwight Frye's Last Laugh

Prologue

> "I can't die with all those lives
> on my conscience!
> All that blood on my hands!"
> — Dwight Frye as Renfield in *Dracula* (1931)

For over 50 years, a ghost has been haunting cinema and theatre history.

Of course, in theatrical canon, ghosts are not uncommon. Indeed, in the horror genre, in which this actor made his indelible mark, they fairly abound. Hollywood is supposedly full of the amok spirits of restless movie bogeymen — often reported in the most colorful of circumstances.

Karloff's ghost, in the star's old private apparel of top hat and "wickies" (i.e., elastic swim trunks), smoking a cigarette, haunting his old Mexican farmhouse high in Coldwater Canyon, and playing with his pet pig, Violet... Lugosi's, smoking a cigar in his bombproof, earthquake-proof Hollywood Hills mansion, dramatically conducting a spectral band of Hungarian Gypsies, weeping at the rhapsodies as they serenade the star until dawn... Lionel Atwill's, sporting a Santa Claus suit, cavorting in his Pacific Palisades hacienda where he hosted that infamous Yuletide "orgy" which crippled his career...

Our Ghost, however — who worked with all the aforementioned gentlemen — is different: he enjoyed no true fame during his movie career. There was no sense of celebrity. Surely none was evident at his funeral in 1943, after the 44-year-old man had suffered a fatal heart attack after long nights of working at an aircraft factory and longer days of seeking bits in the movies.

Indeed, so far as Dwight Frye knew on the night he died, he had no fans at all.

The Ghost visits the most poetic place (in movie fans' imaginations, at least) he could: the back lot of Universal City, California. There, over 65 years ago, a coach drove down a hill to a little village set — opening the film *Dracula*. It was where Dwight Frye began his most famous performance: Renfield, slave to Lugosi's vampire king; the lunatic "fly eater," whose chilling, four-note laugh was (in the words of Denis Gifford, in *A Pictorial History of Horror Movies*) "the most spine-chilling sound in the talkies."

The Ghost wishes to see this site again.

The Universal City of 1997, however, startles the Ghost. He remembers the studio as "Little Europa" (as it was nicknamed in his day), the kingdom of Carl Laemmle and his madly hypochondriacal son Junior; a pastoral movie factory, cradled in the giant mountains of the San Fernando Valley itself, almost as much a never-never land as Dracula's Borgo Pass. But today, though the location is the same, the ambiance is

The back lot of Universal City, California in the 1920s.

otally different. Universal City is a gargantuan conglomerate, ranking with Disney World and Disneyland as one of the world's great tourist attractions, its tour trams carrying millions of tourists annually; there's even a Universal City, Florida.

Reluctantly, the Ghost boards a tram, undetected by the camera-clicking crowds. Soon they ride by the hill from *Dracula*, but tour guide and passengers seem oblivious to the spot where horror history was made. It had been a memorable experience filming *Dracula*, which was completed somehow, despite the seeming colossal indifference of director Tod Browning. Yet the Ghost appreciated Browning—who, after all, had personally selected him for what would be his most famous movie role.

He remembers Bela Lugosi—how could he forget him? The Ghost had acted with Bela on Broadway in 1926/27 in *The Devil in the Cheese*, barely getting to know the imperious Hungarian during the play's five-month run. On the set of *Dracula*, Lugosi had been almost as strange as the vampire he was playing: swirling the cape he would be buried in, roaring "I *am* Dracula!" at his reflection on a soundstage mirror. Yet the Ghost admired such dedication; indeed, he had worked in rather the same fashion. As one of his Broadway leading ladies from the 1920s would remember seven decades later, Dwight Frye had been "the original 'Method' actor."

He remembers poor Helen Chandler, whom the Ghost had admired as a Broadway compatriot; he realizes how she was, during *Dracula*, under the real-life spell of alcohol. And Edward Van Sloan, as Prof. Van Helsing: he was a real friend, one of the few the Ghost had during his Hollywood sojourn—and one who had remained loyal to Dwight Frye's family, for years after Frye's death...

The cast of *Dracula* (Bela Lugosi, David Manners, Dwight Frye, Edward Van Sloan, Helen Chandler), contributors to the legendary Hollywood horror history.

The tram drives through the old European Village, nestled under the Gothic, purple mountains which loom over Universal. The Ghost instantly recognizes the old set, although it has burned down time and again (and has been rebuilt over and over) throughout the decades: it's the Tyrolean village where the villagers lit their torches and pursued Karloff's Monster in 1931's *Frankenstein*. The Ghost had played Fritz, the hunchbacked dwarf-assistant to Colin Clive's anguished Dr. Frankenstein; Fritz, who sadistically tortured the Monster with whip and torch.

He affectionately remembers the summer of 1931 and the happy filming of *Frankenstein*. The Ghost always admired Jimmy Whale, Universal's "ace" director with his cigar and Byronic poses; Whale had made *Frankenstein* a morality play and had encouraged the Ghost to inject comedy into his hunchbacked role. Dwight Frye had always been proud of that bit where, on the stormy night of the Monster's creation, he took time from hobbling up the watchtower laboratory steps—and swiftly adjusted his sock.

There was Colin Clive, as Dr. Frankenstein: a fraught, chain-smoking Englishman, who was in life Dr. Jekyll and Mr. Hyde—Jekyll when he was sober. How delicately Whale had worked with Clive, using coffee and patience to make his Frankenstein as romantic as possible, to keep "Hyde" from peeking through the performance...

And, of course, there was Boris Karloff.

Boris Karloff, in 1931's *Frankenstein*, gave an almost religious touch to the Frankenstein Monster that Dwight Frye, a very religious man, had appreciated.

"...As though man was deserted by his God," Karloff had said of his heartbreaking Monster; indeed, there was an almost religious touch to the actor's Frankenstein Monster that Dwight Frye—a very religious man—had appreciated. The Ghost had felt closer to this dark, charming Englishman than any of the "horror men" with whom he had worked. He admired the beauty of Boris' performance, his bravery and endurance under all that Jack P. Pierce makeup—and had laughed at the sight of "the Monster," sprawled on the set in a beach chair, smoking a cigarette and making sly jokes as he enjoyed a cup of tea.

Karloff, Whale, Clive and (again) Van Sloan: all had been fascinating to work with that summer. The Ghost was proud of *Frankenstein*—and of his movie status as the first victim of the most celebrated movie monster of all time.

The Ghost becomes aware that the tram has stopped; the guide is giving a little talk on *Dracula* and *Frankenstein*. So they *do* remember, the Ghost realizes; the tram passengers are listening as if the guide were talking about beloved fairy tales. The films were so long ago, both released in 1931: the vampire king in time for Valentine's Day, the Monster delivered by Christmas. He hears the names of Lugosi and Karloff. For those two, there had been riches, glory and Hollywood folklore.

For Dwight Frye—"fly eater," "hunchback" and brilliantly convincing actor—there had been bitter typecasting.

For a moment, the pain and frustration he'd felt so deeply in his lifetime creep back into the Ghost's consciousness. He yearns to flee Universal for someplace where he can stand prouder.

In a blink, he finds himself in New York City.

Twenty-five hundred miles away from Hollywood... the New York theatre district. It was here that Dwight Frye had made his Broadway debut in 1922, the same year that Barrymore had played Hamlet, that Jeanne Eagels had played Miss Sadie Thompson. At age 23, Dwight Frye had won the acclaim of America's most sophisticated critics—hailed as "a future Barrymore."

Yet this, too, is a startling sight. The Selwyn Theatre, where, as the derby-sporting, piano-playing, white slaver villain of *Puppets*, he'd stolen the show from Fredric March and Miriam Hopkins, is now a movie house on 42nd Street. The Fulton Theatre, where he danced and sang "Bongo on the Congo" in *Sitting Pretty*, and the Bijou, where he won lavish reviews in *Rita Coventry* and *The Love Habit*, have fallen together in a multi-theatre demolition to make way for a hotel. The lifelong Christian Scientist winces at the garish prostitutes who stalk the theatre district. How different they are from the "jazz baby" ladies of the Roaring '20s, in their Paris frocks and bonnets and opera pump shoes, who elegantly sashayed to the theatres during his New York heyday...

The Ghost is thrilled to see the Booth Theatre, on 45th Street, where Dwight Frye made his Broadway bow as a comic burglar in *The Plot Thickens*. Then there is the Belasco, where Frye played a villain from Hell, named "Alfons the Spider," in the legendary *Mima*. The Molnar morality play had been a Broadway spectacular, in which Hell's monstrous machinery collapsed apocalyptically before an awestruck audience, eight times a week. It was produced by the great David Belasco, whose ghost allegedly haunts the theatre which still bears his name. Indeed, a party of actors went "ghostbusting" in 1995, penetrating Belasco's long-boarded-up quarters high in the theatre, but the Spirit had refused to show. Frye's Ghost doesn't blame him.

He moves up Broadway, past theatres housing giant, pyrotechnically dazzling musicals like *Miss Saigon* and *Les Miserables* and *The Phantom of the Opera*. In the West 60s, he sees a dazzling white compound, not there in his lifetime: Lincoln Center. It features various theatres and attractions and a Performing Arts Library, with files on plays, movies and actors—including Dwight Frye.

Beyond Lincoln Center, the Ghost heads toward Central Park. He stops at a building at 44 West 69th Street, where Dwight, his actress/dancer wife Laura and his very devoted mother had operated a tearoom in the late 1920s. He had loved both women deeply, just as they had loved him; and he had loved the theatre, and had admired the stage personalities who used to frequent this tearoom. It's a very special spot to him for another reason as well: he looks up at the top floor, and realizes that, in the late 1960s, his own son, Dwight, had lived in the same building while he was assistant director and an actor in the original production of *Man of La Mancha*. (Omniscience is a wonderful thing, the Ghost decides.)

He walks along Central Park, turning at the Dakota (where Karloff had lived, high in the eaves, late in his life)... He walks down West 72nd Street, and stops at #166. It was here he spent his newlywed days and nights with his wife Laura. She acted with him in stock, before and after their marriage; gentle, happy, devoted, she understood his drive and tolerated his temper. And she was a very affectionate mother to their son, Dwight David, whom they called "Buddy." In those days, Laura had looked out the window of their apartment and across the street to the luxurious "Ansonia," dreaming that she and Dwight would live there one day; during the first year of their marriage, almost anything seemed possible.

"...Dreams coming true" was the wire Dwight had sent his parents in 1923, exultant as he won Broadway acclaim and joined the world of the theatre. Then Hollywood had baited him—and the dream became a nightmare.

And suddenly—in a snap—he's back again in Hollywood.

Surely there are other "haunts" the Ghost would prefer: Denver, where he won acclaim in his teenage years as a concert pianist; Spokane, where he first met Laura, and where their son was born. Or the Colonial Theatre in Pittsfield, Massachusetts, where Frye played dozens of roles in stock—and which today is a paint store. Or any of the dozens of major cities where he toured in vaudeville, sang and danced in musical comedy, and played stock.

Perhaps the early stock years were the best. Not as thrilling as Broadway celebrity, of course, but indulging the dream that had led Dwight Frye to become an actor—"... that I may play different parts—different characters from life!" In stock he had... the George M. Cohan song and dance role in *The Little Millionaire*... an American Indian... a romantic Chinese poet... and even a "strutting, arrogant Negro" (acted in blackface), with Dwight playing the piano, singing "Tucky Home" and winning (as one Spokane critic reported) "numerous encores."

Yet he's back in Hollywood; once more at Universal, where James Whale had set Dwight's bravura loose again in his mad, masterpiece sequel, *Bride of Frankenstein*. Frye was funny and frightening as Karl, the murdering graverobber—assisting Colin Clive in creating Elsa Lanchester's female monster, and being hurled off the tower laboratory by Karloff's wonderfully amok Monster. Whale had made no real attempt to disguise Colin Clive's "Hyde" side this time, and the actor drank himself to death two years later. There was some sad consolation in that, thought the Ghost; at least Dwight Frye wasn't the first actor in *Frankenstein* to pass to the other side.

The Ghost had acted in each Universal *Frankenstein* sequel produced in his lifetime. He'd been cut from *Son of Frankenstein*, which had given ample footage to Karloff (in his final performance as the Monster) and Lugosi as old Ygor, as well as Basil Rathbone as the son of Dr. Frankenstein and Lionel Atwill as one-armed Inspector Krogh. Maybe if Jimmy Whale (who had cast Frye in several of his films, including *The Invisible Man* as a reporter) had directed *Son of Frankenstein*, rather than Rowland V. Lee, Frye's footage would have remained...

He was back in a bit as an angry villager in *The Ghost of Frankenstein* with Lon Chaney, Jr. as the Monster, and Lugosi once more as Ygor. And *Frankenstein Meets the Wolf Man*—Chaney, Jr. as the Wolf Man, and old Lugosi stomping about as the Monster—not only had given Frye some good dialogue (again as a nervous villager), it was one of his very few films of the 1940s to give him billing.

James Whale had set Dwight's bravura loose again in his mad, masterpiece sequel, *Bride of Frankenstein*.

The Ghost had even visited Universal for Majestic's *The Vampire Bat*; the Poverty Row studio had leased Universal's Frankenstein village. *The Vampire Bat* had cast him as Herman, the bat-petting village idiot with a Renfield laugh. His co-stars were Lionel Atwill, Fay Wray and Melvyn Douglas. A strange man, Atwill, thought the Ghost; he'd been a great Broadway matinee idol of the 1920s, yet he *liked* playing in these horror films — even the bad ones...

The Ghost roams through the now-humbled empires of MGM, Warner Bros., Columbia, RKO. Dwight Frye had acted for all these studios. Indeed, he ultimately had played in almost 60 films.

Yet he had coped with a colossal career downfall. The curse of *Dracula* and *Frankenstein* had cruelly reduced him to a bit player, often without billing. Only horror offerings such as *Dead Men Walk*, produced by lowly PRC in the year of Frye's death, provided decent screen time. His role: Zolarr, a vampire's slave (a la *Dracula*) who happens to be a hunchback (a la *Frankenstein*). Shot in six days, *Dead Men Walk*'s most frightening feature was how sadly Dwight Frye had aged in the decade since *Dracula*.

Profits from *Dead Men Walk* had helped PRC to buy the old Fine Arts Studio on Santa Monica Boulevard. The Ghost seeks PRC—and is amused to see that the old headquarters of this studio, which had exploited him so shamelessly in *Dead Men Walk* (as it had so many other actors in so many negligible films), is now a 24-hour towing service.

Of course, 20th Century-Fox still stands, where Frye was set to portray Newton Baker, Secretary of War, in *Wilson*: a part he'd passionately hoped would rescue the shocking collapse of his career—and a role which death prevented him from playing.

And inevitably, the Ghost ventures up Beachwood Drive, to the old, Spanish-style house in the hills, under the famous Hollywoodland sign. The "land" has long since fallen down, and the landmark no longer lights up with thousands of bulbs, as it did when he first came to the movie colony. 2590 North Beachwood Drive, which defiantly still stands, was his last home, as he worked Douglas Aircraft's graveyard shift as a tool designer by night and haunted casting offices by day.

Here in this little house, Dwight Frye—once Broadway's proud "future Barrymore," now Hollywood's miserably typecast hunchback—had spent his last days and nights. Here he restlessly had played piano and painted. Here he shared his precious little free time with a wife who herself was now working as a department store clerk, but did all she could to soothe her husband's fear and bitterness; and a 12-year-old son, puzzled by his father's temper tantrums, who only years later became fully aware of the financial worry, the career woes and the true anguish his father was suffering.

It was this house Dwight Frye had left on the Sunday evening of November 7, 1943, never to return.

The Ghost passes the Pantages Theatre on Hollywood Boulevard, where he'd taken Laura and "Buddy" to the movies that night; he'd wanted to celebrate his landing the role in *Wilson* with his family. The Pantages' second feature had been *Sherlock Holmes Faces Death*, which afforded Frye glimpses of the old *Dracula* crypt and *Frankenstein* village. For Universal, they had served as convenient, pre-built backdrops in this "B" thriller. For Dwight Frye, they were reminders of the roles that had warped his career—flashed before him just moments before his fatal heart attack.

The old Hollywood Receiving Hospital, where Dwight Frye was pronounced dead, is history. Also long-gone is the mortuary, out on the Sunset Strip, where, at the funeral, his son had touched his face and kissed him.

There is, of course, Forest Lawn Memorial Park, Hollywood's most famous cemetery. Forest Lawn policy dictates that its caretakers give no assistance to those tourists seeking the graves of such legends as Jean Harlow, Errol Flynn, Walt Disney, Lon Chaney, Sr., Clark Gable and Carole Lombard (who are entombed side-by-side).

However, those same caretakers usually don't recognize the name of "Dwight Frye" as a Hollywood great. Checking the directory, they helpfully send those fans seeking the grave to a very high hill, where a small marker commemorates the "Loved Husband, Father, Son" who rests there.

The Ghost, standing on the slope, wonders for a moment about his legacy. Perhaps he's just another figure in the apparently "cursed" repertory of Hollywood horror history. Like Lugosi, with his drug addiction and miserable last days... or Atwill, bitterly raving on his death bed about his sex scandal... or even Jimmy Whale, who, in his sardonically elegant way, had dressed in a favorite suit to drown himself.

Yet, at the same time, the Ghost marvels that fans, over half a century after his forlorn death, come to Forest Lawn to pay him tribute. And the tributes have been growing steadily, sincerely, affectionately, for decades.

In a time overview, the Ghost reviews *Shock! Theatre*, a television sensation of the late 1950s, which resurrected interest in Dwight Frye as *Dracula* and *Frankenstein* all over again.

There are the horror magazines... the 1970s Alice Cooper recording "The Ballad of Dwight Fry(e)" (which Cooper still performs, attired in a strait jacket).... his cult figure status... and Peter MacNicol's superb, affectionate take-off on Dwight Frye's Renfield in Mel Brooks' 1995 Christmas release, *Dracula: Dead and Loving It.*

There has been the video age, and the Universal/MCA release in 1991 (the 60th anniversary of *Dracula* and *Frankenstein*) of beautifully restored video copies of the classics.

And, perhaps most movingly, Dwight Frye's ghost visits the Famous Monsters Convention in Crystal City, Virginia, Memorial Day Weekend, 1993. There, he sees his son, having carried on the family's show business legacy as an actor and producer, sitting on a ballroom stage, along with the son of Bela Lugosi, the daughter of Boris Karloff, and the grandson of Lon Chaney, Jr. All are participating in a panel as fans, packed into the giant ballroom, award them a thunderous ovation.

Someone in the crowd asks Dwight's son to imitate his father's famous Renfield laugh. He politely declines: "I don't know how to do it!"

The Ghost fully realizes now that he has fans, who love him and his work, and how much they care! And six months later—November 7, 1993, the 50th anniversary of his death—the Film Society of Montclair, New Jersey, hosts an official tribute to Dwight Frye.

"My father would have been stunned," said his son, who was guest of honor. "He would never have believed this. He would have been deeply moved."

For a once-forlorn ghost, it has been an amazing journey. He realizes he is taking his place alongside legendary horror stars Karloff, Lugosi, and Chaneys Sr. and Jr.

And, in spite of being so deeply moved, Dwight Frye can now enjoy the last (Renfield) laugh.

A 1918 portrait of Frye taken in Denver at the outset of his stage career.

Dwight Frye's Last Laugh

Chapter One
Life Upon the Wicked Stage

> My dad was an actor who really relished what
> he did. He would not have been happy, I think,
> doing anything else.
> —Dwight D. Frye

Charles Fry, Kansas farmer, and his devoutly religious wife, Ella, knew very little about actors.

They had never traveled to New York, where, in 1899—the year their only child was born in Salina—Maude Adams would star in *Romeo and Juliet*, Mrs. Fiske would play *Becky Sharp*, and Mrs. Leslie Carter would score as *Zaza*.

And they knew little (and cared less) about the pioneering motion picture business, soon to sprout amidst the orange groves of a pastoral California town called Hollywood.

The only first-hand knowledge that 28-year-old, Ohio-born Charles and his 27-year-old, Virginia-born wife Ella had of theatre in America were the stock companies, which sometimes eked their woebegone way to Salina. As was the custom in the plains states, a tent would be pitched in a cornfield, and actors would perform, often in turn-of-the-century melodramas. It was still the era of the villain in the cape and top hat, cackling as he tied the heroine to the railroad tracks, the hero leaping to the rescue in a blast of tinny piano fanfare—all before flickering candlelit footlights.

These actors would herald their way into a town like Salina, treating themselves to a parade, just like the circus would do. But usually, they enjoyed far less respect than the clowns, or acrobats or even the menagerie. When the actors came to town, good people took their teenage daughters off the streets. Wives mandated that their husbands not pass the hotel or boarding house where the company's leading lady might be lodging. Folk reminded each other that it was an actor who shot Lincoln. Ladies even took their cooling pies off windowsills; they feared the actors might steal them.

"One hundred years ago," says their grandson, "it was considered a sin to go on the stage." Surely, in early 1899, as Charles and Ella were expecting their first (and fated to be only) child, they never imagined their offspring was destined for a career in the theatre. And it was a pretty safe bet that, among the books in the farmhouse, Ella Dodd Fry—who was a lifelong, deeply devout Christian Scientist—did not keep a copy of either Mary Shelley's *Frankenstein*, or Bram Stoker's recently published *Dracula*.

On Wednesday, February 22, 1899, the baby boy was born; Ella, for all her Christian Scientist beliefs, had no problem with Dr. J. E. Miller serving as attending physician.

The name of the newborn son: Dwight Iliff Fry. Ella took the name Iliff from Tennyson's *Idylls of the King*.

When the boy was very young, the Frys left their Kansas farm, moving to Denver, Colorado. They were a very close family. Over 20 years later, on April 15, 1922, Dwight would wire this "Easter greeting" to his parents:

> May this Easter bring you both the joy I wish you.
> We three can be thankful for our small reflection
> of that love which has conquered through the ages.
> My love for you is everlasting.
>
> Your Boy

From a very young age, Dwight showed a flair for the arts; he also kept a scrapbook, which survives today in the possession of his son. There clippings record Dwight Fry's first notices — as a very gifted pianist. Schooled in both piano and voice, Dwight had determined by age nine that he would become a concert pianist. Young Dwight's mentor was Mr. Frederick Schweiker of Denver's Western Institute of Music and Dramatic Art. Dwight practiced his piano four hours a day at age nine, eventually building up to eight hours daily by his late teens. The earliest performance-related item in Dwight's scrapbook is a program from a recital given by Schweiker's pupils, dated May 12, 1913; Dwight, listed seventh, performed Mozart's "Sonata in F." As the years went by, Dwight became more prominently featured in these ensemble recitals, playing works by Chopin, Grieg, Liszt and other masters. On October 9, 1914, Dwight gave his first solo recital, at the age of fifteen. His proud mother (whom he always called "Muzzie") sent news of her son's talent to her hometown newspaper in Virginia, which reported:

> We are handed clippings from a Denver newspaper
> which speak in the highest terms of the ability of
> master Dwight Iliff Fry, a lad of fifteen years, who
> recently gave a recital in the Y.M.C.A. building.
> *The Denver Post* says "Master Fry performs on the
> piano... and has been referred to as the 'boy pianist'
> of Denver. He is one of the youngest musicians of
> Denver who possesses such a remarkable talent."
> The boy prodigy is the son of Mrs. Ella Dodd Fry,
> a Lexington girl.

Other clippings refer to the boy pianist as "a musical genius," adding, "We hope and predict for him a great future in his chosen work, music."

Master Dwight Fry gave many solo recitals, playing the works of Beethoven, Schubert and Mozart, et al. On Friday evening, April 7, 1916, in a departure, he appeared in West Side High School's Annual Oratorical Contest, performing "The Making of a Criminal"; he also played the piano that evening — Mozart's "Turkish March," with several violin-playing peers. Dwight took part in the Oratorical Contest the following year too, April 13, 1917, delivering "Keep Your Eye on Uncle Sam." It was a timely selection—the United States had just entered World War I.

However, the musical genius and the budding orator found his real love when, on June 1, 1917, with seven other members of West Side High School's senior class, he appeared in the school play, *The Honeymoon*. Dwight played Cedric Haslam, son of a "well-known authoress," in the three-act play. He had grown increasingly enamored of acting since he'd started attending every Monday night performance of the Denham Stock Company since its inception in the fall of 1913; now he was hooked. After graduating from West Side High School in 1917, Dwight Fry decided to pursue a career as an actor.

His parents were shocked.

> Dwight Frye virtually touched off a bombshell in his straight-laced family tree when he chose the stage and screen for his lot... the Dwarf of Universal's eerie *Frankenstein* came from a long line of farmers and ancestors whose professions were far removed from the "deplorable" art of acting.
>   —from the pressbook for *Frankenstein* (1931)

By 1917, the acting profession in the United States had become a bit more "legitimate" since the days when those melodramas had played Salina. New York's Broadway was aglow with artists that year: John Barrymore was strangling brother Lionel nightly in *Peter Ibbetson*; sister Ethel was starring as *The Lady of the Camelias*. Sigmund Romberg's lush operetta *Maytime* was reducing audiences to tears, while the *Ziegfeld Follies of 1917* boasted W. C. Fields, Fannie Brice, Eddie Cantor and Will Rogers. Also making his Broadway debut in 1917, in the Jack the Ripper play *The Lodger*, was a British matinee idol named Lionel Atwill.

Hollywood was blossoming, too. Charlie Chaplin, Mary Pickford and Douglas Fairbanks were the top attractions. For Carl Laemmle's Universal City, John Ford was directing Harry Carey in shoot-'em-up westerns; for Paramount, Cecil B. DeMille was burning Joan of Arc at the stake in *Joan the Woman*; and D. W. Griffith had left his giant "Babylon" set looming over Sunset Boulevard in the wake of his 1916 classic, *Intolerance*.

The major work for actors, however—and the stepping stone to Broadway and the movies—were the stock companies. Troupes flourished across the country; directors selected plays to fit their resident company, which featured a leading lady, leading man, ingenue, juvenile, second man, second woman, comedy leads and a villain. One actor who, in 1917, was acting with a variety of stock troupes in Canada and western America—often sporting the top hat and cape of the villain—was a British exile who called himself Boris Karloff. In fact, in 1917, the year Dwight Fry graduated from Denver's West Side High School, Boris Karloff came through Colorado in the Billee Bennett stock company's production of *The Virginian*, en route to Los Angeles.

Stock company trouping was an erratic life—and a perilous one. Cyclones, epidemics, business managers who absconded with the bankroll—all these and more snuffed companies out of existence overnight. Those actors who survived in such work often did so in a world of grimy rooming houses, nearly-missed trains, frequent backstage scandals, over-age and tightly corseted ingenues, over-age and bewigged leading men, hasty marriages, bitter divorces, collapsing makeshift scenery, horrible old theatres, dismal dressing rooms, and hostile audiences who really did throw fruits and vegetables at the players when displeased.

It was a life, all too often, of severe deprivation. Indeed, after the aforementioned Mr. Karloff became a major star, he would bury, in the rose garden of his Coldwater Canyon farm, the cremated remains of old stock company cronies who had died without funds for a respectable funeral.

Charles and Ella Fry were wary of "Life Upon the Wicked Stage" (as the song would go in *Show Boat*). Being somewhat unsophisticated, they were suspicious of such a risky way of making a living—and they pressed for Dwight to accept a nice, stable secretarial position at a Denver business firm. As the obedient son, he did so, meanwhile studying with Denver's famed drama coach, Margaret Fealy (whose pupils had included Douglas Fairbanks and Lynne Overman), and each week seeing a different play presented by the Denham Stock Company.

Meanwhile, at the suggestion of Margaret Fealy, the impresario of the Denham took note of young Dwight Fry—and invited him to join the company.

The producer/director/personal manager of the Denham Theatre of Denver was O. D. Woodward. In the 1,732-seat Denham, Woodward presented romance, melodrama, farce, comedy and westerns—as well as Christmas fantasies and Easter religious pageants. The best seat in the house cost seventy-five cents.

It was a new show beginning every week at the Denham—and 10 performances: every night (including Sunday), along with Wednesday, Saturday and Sunday matinees. The Summer of 1918 found the Denham accenting comedy and farce (with some "musical specialties" tossed in for good measure). The leading lady was the versatile Hazel Whitmore; the leading man was Emmett Vogan, later a Hollywood character actor. Coincidentally, Vogan (a close friend of Dwight and his family) would appear with Dwight 25 years later in the latter's last two films, *Hangmen Also Die!* and *Dangerous Blondes*.[1]

June 16, 1918: 19-year-old Dwight Fry played his first documented professional role, "Richard Daunton," at the Denham Theatre in *The Man from Mexico*. Even at this very early time, Dwight had his pride: when it appeared he would play only minor roles, Dwight left the company, telling Woodward he would (as he later told the *New York Telegraph* in 1925) "...wait until you have something better for me." Heeding his parents' advice, Dwight enrolled in the summer business program at the University of Colorado at Boulder. He was there less than two months when he received word from Woodward (via Ella) that the Denham company juvenile had gone to fight in the latter stage of World War I.

Dwight leapt at the opportunity to replace the juvenile, left college at once—and added the "e" to his last name as he rejoined the troupe. He felt "Frye" would look better in print.

He acted at the Denham Stock Company (in presumably "better" roles) in such plays as *Captain Rackett* (as Hobson, who sings "Florida Moon"). Dwight's last role of that first season was Gerald Holmes in *A Bachelor's Romance*, which closed September 28, 1918.

It was also the final performance of Woodward's Denham Stock Company. After nearly six years of almost continual production, Woodward had decided to seek new pastures. During his time in Denver, Woodward had set up his own movie studio, using his stage players and producing at least 18 films. Based on a clipping in Frye's scrapbook, it's likely that Dwight acted in some of these films, although no titles have yet surfaced.

In his first season of stock, Dwight had persevered. And he pasted this clipping in his scrapbook regarding his portrayal of Rufe Waters in the Kentucky feud saga, *Salomy Jane*:

> Dwight Frye showed a gain in mastery of his part this week and will no doubt in time lose the forced and unnatural eagerness which has marked his work thus far.

Spokane, Washington, Saturday night, November 23, 1918: just days after the World War I armistice, 600 people were turned away as a standing-room-only crowd (with standees) applauded "the celebrated crook drama," *Cheating Cheaters*, the premiere performance of the Woodward Players. O. D. Woodward had come to Spokane, braving the national flu epidemic, with his "house staff" and company of 15 players.

"We had a splendid trip from Denver and everybody arrived in the best of health," Woodward had told reporters upon his arrival in Spokane in late October—during a flu quarantine. "There isn't a sign of influenza in the whole company, and we will be ready to open just as soon as the ban is lifted." The ban would last for three weeks.

Meanwhile, with bravado, Woodward renamed Spokane's American Theatre (at Trent and Post Streets) the Woodward Theatre, festooned the house with fresh paint, gilt and new red carpets and made sure the papers knew of his leading lady Miss Hazel Whitmore and leading man Robert Brister (replacing the originally announced Emmett Vogan). The company juvenile: Dwight Frye. A few days before the opening, Woodward, determined to let no chance for publicity pass by, dispatched Dwight and fellow company member Josephine Genaro to sing at the Spokane Ad Club luncheon.

The Saturday night opening was a "triumph." The receptive crowd greeted Miss Whitmore with "a profusion of flowers" at the curtain calls. Dwight played Antonio Verdi, reprising a role he'd played with the Denham Stock Company. "Dwight Frye, the juvenile, was a particular favorite," noted one Spokane critic, "and contributed a piano solo."

Yet the Woodward Players seemed "jinxed." Lingering fear of influenza hurt the box office; business manager Walter Arington battled Woodward. All seemed lost when Arington quit—and took half of the company with him. Yet the remaining Woodward Players rode out the storm, Dwight Frye loyally playing a season that ran from the opening of *Cheating Cheaters* through the April 19, 1919 performance of *The Blue*

Envelope. Acting a different play every week, for the usual 10 performances, rehearsing whenever possible for the new show to come—Dwight played in all but three of the twenty-one plays presented that season. Among his roles: "Diamond Willie" in *The Master Mind*; Obadiah Odlum, "...the village undertaker who looks for business everywhere" in *Sis Hopkins*; Philip Mason in *The Thirteenth Chair* and Abijah Flagg in *Rebecca of Sunnybrook Farm.*

Spokane audiences took the actors to their hearts. The French farce *Mam'zelle*, "a hilarious holiday frolic" that the Woodward Players performed for New Year's Eve of 1918, offered Hazel Whitmore in black harem costume, doing a snake dance (without the snake), Josephine Genaro performing a buck and wing dance that "stopped the show" and Dwight, playing at the grand piano. According to a clipping in his scrapbook, Dwight "was encored, receiving a quintet of floral tributes."

The season was an exhausting, exciting, challenging experience. For Dwight (who was noted to be "the youngest man in the company"), it was an adventure that gave him continual chances to act, hear applause and perfect his craft.

"His heart and soul are in his work," noted a Spokane newspaper.

———————————

At the close of the season, Dwight Frye took off for Chicago, where he played in Edward Dubinsky's production of *The Dangerous Age*. He next headed for New York. As he later wrote in an article for the *The Spokesman-Review* of Spokane:

> Then I came east to try my luck on Broadway.
> I was a little presumptuous, believe me, for just
> the desire to be on Broadway is not enough—
> experience and ability must be the background.

In a sense, Dwight did get "on Broadway" at this time. The date: August 14, 1919. The venue: vaudeville.

———————————

"May your children grow to be acrobats!"

It was the famous "Gypsy curse" of vaudeville—acrobats occupying the bottom level in the hierarchy of the crazy world of comics, singers, tap dancers, leggy chorus girls, ventriloquists with their dummies and magicians with their rabbits and pigeons and sawed-in-half lady assistants. Vaudeville was a circus on a theatre stage, serving as training ground of later legends like Jack Benny, George Burns, the Three Stooges and the Marx Brothers.

Dwight's sketch was called *The Magic Glasses*, "A Speculation in Specs" by Frances Nordstrom; Dwight played the "Poor Man," with Ray L. Royce ("The Doctor"), C. Elliot Griffin (the "Rich Man") and Mary Johnson, aka Mrs. Jack Norworth (as "The Girl"). "Time—Yesterday, To-day, To-morrow; Place—Just Around the Corner," noted the playbill. It was just one part of a vaudeville extravaganza that offered such attractions as the De Wolf Girls (Georgette and Capitola) in the musical sketch "Clothes, Clothes, Clothes"; Moss and Frye ("popular darkey funsters"—the Frye no relation to

Dwight) and Nonette ("The Fascinating Gypsy Violinist and Singer"). The 39-week tour of the Keith Vaudeville Circuit began at the Crotona Theatre in New York City, going as far north as Montreal, as far west as Texas and as far south as Georgia; it finally closed May 27, 1920 at the Academy Theatre in Norfolk, Virginia.

It may be tough for fans of *Dracula* and *Frankenstein* to imagine Dwight Frye in straw hat and seersucker suit, singing, dancing and bouncing comedy one-liners at a blonde. Yet, such was the basic scenario as Dwight began his new act for the Pantages Vaudeville circuit: *Girls Will Be Girls*, with Dwight as Bob. It opened June 28, 1920 in Colorado Springs, moved to Pueblo and then to El Paso, Texas, where a critic described the act:

> *Girls Will Be Girls* was a 20-minute musical tabloid
> with two principals and a chorus of four; it contains
> a few good lines, a catchy number, "My Recipe
> for Love," some risqué gowns, and a blonde that
> is easy to look at.

Girls Will Be Girls died on the night of July 9, 1920, in El Paso, lasting less than two weeks. Dwight, the easy-to-look-at blonde and their cohorts were once again scrambling for work. So was a comic who had followed *Girls Will Be Girls* on the bill, with his monologue, "Just a Young Fellow Trying to Get Along": future radio star Fred Allen.

Then came *La, La, Lucille*. This musical comedy with book by Fred Jackson, music by no less than George Gershwin and lyrics by Arthur J. Jackson and B. G. De Sylva (who was destined to become a top Broadway showman and, in the early 1940s, chief of Paramount Studios) originally had opened at Broadway's Henry Miller's Theatre on May 26, 1919, with Jack Hazzard as leading man. It had played 104 performances, and had been closed in New York for a year by the time Dwight auditioned for this "third company" of the show—and won the male lead. *La, La, Lucille* presented Betty Burke in the title role; Dwight played her husband, John Smith; the plot found the "devoted young couple" forced to divorce in order to inherit a fortune. Dwight performed in five musical numbers—soloing on "The Best of Everything" (backed by the chorus) and duetting with Miss Burke in "From Now On" and "The Ten Commandments of Love."

It was a disaster. The critic in Stamford, Connecticut headlined the review *Ha, Ha, Lucille*, and wrote:

> Indifferent leads augmented by a chorus of some
> half dozen "girls," in gowns as passé and lifeless
> as they themselves, coupled with a weak plot...
> make *La, La, Lucille* quite the worst production that
> anyone has had the audacity to put on here.

Apparently the nightmarish rehearsals had resulted in new cast members being rushed in—including Dwight. He was so new to the show, in fact, that the cast list in the Stamford review listed one "Leon Cunningham" in Dwight's role (Dwight scribbled in the name "Frye" in the clipping he pasted in his scrapbook). The amazed and appalled critic in Stamford described the debacle:

> Even had the principals known their lines—which they most assuredly did not, being repeatedly prompted in a stage whisper that carried to the farthermost points of the theatre and bringing on each occasion a response of laughs, jeers and handclapping from gallery to floor—*La, La, Lucille* would have fallen down most miserably on her chorus.

A New Bedford critic, catching the same performance, suggested *La, La, Lucille* have its name changed to *Ain't It Awful*. The critic also noted that Frye (referred to again as "Mr. Cunningham") "did his best to put energy in his part," despite a "hoarse" voice. At any rate, the play bravely carried on; by the time it reached the Grand Opera House in Pottstown, Pennsylvania in late September, the advance publicity was hyping Frye ("inimitable in his farce methods"), as well as insisting that those chorus girls that the Stamford critic had lambasted were in fact "the prettiest, daintiest, singing and dancing girls on the stage."

La, La, Lucille somehow held together for about 10 weeks.

As 1920 ended, Dwight read everything he could about the Broadway performances that had made history that year, such as John Barrymore's *Richard III*, and Lionel Atwill's *Deburau*.

Great parts were what he wanted to play. Broadway was where he wanted to be.

———————

In the wake of *La, La, Lucille*, Dwight joined the Myrkle-Harder repertory company, touring the northeast. Now it was twelve shows a week—a matinee and night performance Monday through Saturday—in a repertory including *Polly with a Past*, *Civilian Clothes*, *Dawn O'the Mountains*, *39 East*, *Blind Youth* and *The Unkissed Bride*. Dwight was barnstorming with the Myrkle-Harder company in Cortland, New York come Christmas Eve of 1920, and telegraphed his parents in Denver:

> My love to you both and always know that your boy is ever thinking of you and loving you. Merry Xmas and Happy New Year to All
> —Dwight

Dwight carried on the remarkable 12-shows-per-week engagement with Myrkle-Harder for 30 weeks. About two years later, in an interview with *The New York Times*, he would cryptically describe his Myrkle-Harder adventure thusly: "short and terrible."

At this point, having toured vaudeville in *The Magic Glasses*, "died" in El Paso in *Girls Will Be Girls*, faced the debacle of *La, La, Lucille,* survived his "short and

Dwight Frye's Last Laugh

The Colonial Theatre of Pittsfield, Massachusetts where Dwight opened the season with *Adam and Eva.*

terrible" sojourn with Myrkle-Harder and lived a Gypsy life on trains and out of suit-cases, Dwight received an offer that allowed him — at least temporarily — to put down roots again. It came from the Colonial Players of Pittsfield, Massachusetts, the smallest city in the United States with a repertory stock company. Dwight later expressed his major attraction to stock work which, in light of his later Hollywood typecasting, is retrospectively touching:

> As I shall always say, the fascination of playing in stock is predominant with me and the ever-pres-ent reason for being an actor, or for my being an actor, is that I may play different parts — different characters from life!

It was May of 1921, and he was 22 years old. "It was here that the fate star began to center a ray or two upon me," wrote Dwight, "although at the time I didn't know it."

———————————

The Colonial Theatre of Pittsfield, Massachusetts had officially opened September 28, 1903, with the Bostonians' production of the opera *Robin Hood.* Over the years, John and Ethel Barrymore, Paderewski and even Sarah Bernhardt had put in appear-ances at the Colonial.

Samuel and Nathan Goldstein (who owned and operated a number of New England theatres) offered a varied bill of fare at the Colonial: silent films to opera in the winter, touring theatrical and musical companies, and, in the late spring and summer, a stock company.

Colonial Theatre
Pittsfield, Mass.

WEEK COMMENCING

Mon. Eve., May 23rd

Colonial Players

OFFERING AS THEIR INITIAL PRODUCTION

ADAM and EVA

THE PLAYERS

ALFRED SWENSON   RUTH AMOS

BOB McCLUNG

WM. MELVILLE

ELEANOR CARLETON

MARIE HODGKINS

DWIGHT FRYE

BYRON C. IRVING

LOLA JAMES   ALBERT AMEND

In Denver and Spokane, Dwight had played ten performances a week; with Myrkle-Harder, he had played twelve; at the Colonial, he performed eleven. There were no shows Sunday, and only an evening show Monday, but for every other day of the week, there was a 2:10 matinee and an 8:10 evening performance. Rehearsals for the following week's show would begin Tuesday morning and continue Wednesday, Friday and Saturday, usually from 10 a.m. to 12:30 p.m.; Thursday was put aside for "rest and study." The performers barely had time to lunch prior to makeup and costume

Dwight Frye's Last Laugh

preparation for the matinee. Once a play had closed Saturday night, cast and crew could enjoy a day off Sunday before meeting again Monday, at 1:00 p.m., for a final run-through of the new show.

Such was the demanding routine that Dwight Frye signed on for with the Colonial Players.

Once again, Dwight was company juvenile; his fellow players had varying levels of experience and degrees of talent. The leading man was Alfred Swenson, whose greatest acting fame would come in radio, where he starred in *The Adventures of Captain Diamond* (1932). Leading lady of the Colonial Players was Ruth Amos, who would sporadically appear on Broadway in such plays as *A Tree Grows in Brooklyn* (1951) and be active in radio and the early days of television.

May 23, 1921: the Colonial Players opened the season with *Adam and Eva*, with Dwight in the role of Clinton DeWitt. It was a new play every week that spring and summer for Dwight; the plays ranged from farce (*Up in Mabel's Room*); to the Henry Blossom and Victor Herbert musical *The Only Girl*, which permitted Colonial patrons to enjoy Dwight as lawyer John "Fresh" Ayre, soloing "All By Myself" and performing in numbers like "Connubial Bliss" and "When You're Wearing the Ball and Chain"; to *Smilin' Through*, the weeper by Jane Cowl and Jane Murfin (under the pseudonym of Allan Langdon Martin), which featured Frye as Willie Ainley, the family's choice to marry the heroine (Ruth Amos)—who has other ideas; to the juvenile role of Jimmy Bean in *Pollyanna*; to the Chinese lover Song Sing in the Oriental drama *The Love of Su Shong*.

Meanwhile, as Dwight concluded his Colonial engagement, his old impresario, O. D. Woodward, was in trouble. The Woodward Players of Spokane had fallen upon hard times; *The Spokesman-Review* had gone so far as to lambaste the Woodward company as "...some of the worst players Spokane has ever seen in stock." Woodward sent an SOS to his erstwhile juvenile, who came cross-country to rejoin the troupe.

Woodward fought for a comeback for his 1921/1922 Players. He brought back Miss Hazel Whitmore (who had endeared herself to Spokane audiences by playing 405 straight performances); the leading man was Rodney Hildebrand. Emmett Vogan, former leading man in Denver and Dwight's good friend, later joined the company.

The Spokane press would serenade the returning Dwight with praise throughout the Woodward Theatre's 1921/1922 season, with such accolades as "Idol of Woodward Theatre Fans," "Dwight Frye Star at Twenty-Two," and "Probably the youngest juvenile lead in the west." Woodward prepared to open his season by showing off his actors at the Spokane Chamber of Commerce weekly luncheon, where, according to a newspaper clipping, Dwight "was given a rousing ovation after he had entertained with a song, accompanying himself at the piano, and responded with an encore." *Smilin' Through* was the season opener, and Dwight said:

> While I was traveling about I often thought of
> how good it would seem to be back in Spokane,
> and when I stepped off the train at the union
> station a week ago everything looked just as I
> pictured it. I imagined that Spokane people had

Woodward Theatre

WEEK BEGINNING SUNDAY MATINEE, SEPTEMBER 4, 1921

MR. O. D. WOODWARD
Presents

The Woodward Players
Including
MISS HAZEL WHITMORE
MR. RODNEY HILDEBRAND
—in—

"THE GIRL IN THE LIMOUSINE"

A Farce Comedy by Wilson Collison and Avery Hopgood, as Produced by
A. H. Woods at the Globe Theater, New York City.

Production Staged under the Personal Direction of Mr. O. D. Woodward.

———o———

CAST OF CHARACTERS

Tony Hamilton	Rodney Hildebrand
Dr. Jimmie Galen	Dwight Frye
Freddie Neville	Charles Fletcher
Kargan	Smith Davies
Benny	Wm. T. Holden
Riggs	Richard Mack
Giles	William Dills
Betty Neville	Hazel Whitmore
Lucia Galen	Laura Lee
Bernice Warren	Virginia L. Brown
Aunt Cicely	Margaret Robinson

SYNOPSIS

ACT I—The Bed Chamber.
ACT II—The Same. A few minutes later.
ACT III—The Veranda. A few minutes later.

forgotten all about me in my three years' absence. I was never so surprised or elated as when the audience applauded at my first entrance. I went down to my dressing room feeling like I had conquered the world and the whole city of Spokane was not big enough for me that night.

Dwight enjoyed some showcase roles in Spokane between September, 1921 and February, 1922. The press found him comically "ridiculous" as Lord Valentine Foxwell, "a gilded youth," in *Merely Mary Ann*, and splendidly "despicable" as the worthless criminal son of an Irish washerwoman in *Kindling*.

One of the top hits of the season was *Come Seven* (12/19/21). Spokane audiences went wild over this show, which the Woodward Players performed in blackface. Dwight was Florian Slappey, "the 'slick' Negro swell," playing the piano for Emmett Vogan (who sang "Mammy") and soloing himself on "Tucky Home." His song was the hit of the show, the audience demanding (and receiving) encores.

"Frye has sort of a gingerbread finish," noted one Spokane critic, "and does fine work."

Dwight again played Song Sing, "the young poetic Chinese lover," in *The Love of Su Shong* (January 2, 1922)—judged by the Spokane press as "another personal triumph for the juvenile." He concluded the 24 weeks in early February with the Woodward Players in *A Woman's Way*, which also marked the Spokane farewell for Emmett Vogan and Hazel Whitmore. After the departure of the three Spokane favorites, fortune would nose dive for the O. D. Woodward company throughout the balance of the season.

For Dwight, the most memorable aspect of his Spokane return had been the company's ingenue—a petite, brunette actress and dancer who, in the eyes of a late 1920s movie fan, might have resembled a sweet Louise Brooks. She used the stage name of Laura Lee; her real name: Laura Mae Bullivant.

Laura was a Spokane native, daughter of Dr. and Mrs. James Bullivant. Years later, for *The Spokesman-Review*, Dwight would write this remembrance of meeting his future wife:

> ...while I was in Spokane my second season, I met there in the company a young lady—a young lady who was compelled (according to the play, the author, the director) to have love made to her by the juvenile, namely me. In order to earn her salary, she must have me make love to her. In order to earn mine, I began. It was not difficult, I hasten to add, so week in and week out... we got paid for it and the management seemed satisfied.

Laura Lee and Dwight acted together in many plays, including *My Lady Friends*, as characters caught up in "a stormy love affair."

> That was the beginning! Romance had us in its throes. We were under its spell. Then something called fate appeared and separated us. I was poor—we were both young—and too naively sensible—we made up our minds we must be sensible! Sensible is an awful thing to make up your mind to be!... I had to make money—we both had our careers—we were too young to know—anyway, we called fate's bluff and separated.

For Dwight, the most memorable aspect of his Spokane return had been the company's ingenue Laura Mae Bullivant.

In 1928, Dwight would marry Laura in New York City—by which time he had become a major actor. In 1922, however, his future looked bleak. While his personal reviews had been excellent, general audience and critical reception to the Woodward Players of Spokane had become vociferous. Woodward had even managed to toss Marguerite Motie (aka "Miss Spokane") on the stage, in a desperate bid for business; it didn't work. The troupe disbanded after a disastrous performance of *Over the Hill*.

Dwight wasn't there for the final indignities; he'd taken off for the Woodward Theatre in Seattle, Washington. There he acted in 11 plays in 11 weeks, commencing with *A Woman's Way* (2/18/22), concluding with *Stop Thief* (4/30/22).

The engagement introduced Dwight to another player: Alexis Luce, whom the Seattle press hailed as "an actor of great personal charm... He has poise, masculine strength and a cultivated style which is too often lacking on our stage."

Luce, about 15 years older than Dwight and Laura Bullivant, soon became friends with both. Almost 25 years later—after Dwight's death—he would marry Laura.

May, 1922: "at liberty" (the actor's euphemism for being unemployed), Dwight came home to Denver. In spite of his many glowing reviews, he was unduly depressed about his several theatrical (mis)adventures. He actually contemplated giving up acting and trying to regain his old business position. However, encouragement came from a surprising source: his parents. Once strongly opposed to Dwight's theatrical career, they now encouraged their son to pursue his dream and persuaded him to return to Pittsfield for another season with the Colonial Players.

After a matter of only two weeks, Dwight took a train across the country and rejoined the Colonial Players for their 1922 Summer Stock season.

Alfred Swenson was still the Colonial's leading man. However, there was a new leading lady: Edna Preston, a superb actress with a predominately Canadian background, whose future long-range career would encompass radio, television and several Broadway appearances. Dwight's son remembers that Edna Preston and her husband Jimmy Coots remained good friends with his father and eventually with his family for many years.

On May 29, 1922, the Colonial Players' summer season began with *Cornered*, set in the "Pekin Pleasure Palace" of Hell's Kitchen, New York City. Dwight's role: Nick Martin, "the Dope," who (according to *The Berkshire Eagle*) "...in his every twist and turn and mannerism was the typical slave to the craving." He was "Benny the Duck" in *Three Wise Fools*, then played Fred Hammond in *The Nightcap*.

Buddies (6/19/22) deserves special mention. The Colonial Players' first musical of the 1922 season took place in Normandy just after the WWI armistice, with Dwight as doughboy Sonny—mixed up in romantic intrigues and singing "The Wail of the Tale of the Long, Long Trail," "My Indispensable Girl," and "To Be Together is the Main Thing" (the latter two songs with Phyllis Gilmore).

After *Buddies*, Dwight played Native American Maniteekwa in *The Storm*, set in the Pacific Northwest and featuring a sophisticated (for the time) forest fire sequence; in the farce *Twin Beds*, he was Andrew Larkin, a newlywed with a suspicious wife.

"...a young man who was giving the best in him all of the time, no matter how discouraging the circumstances" was how Dwight was described by Mrs. John Hutton—an heiress to the investment fortune of E. F. Hutton and a fan of Dwight's from the previous season. Mrs. Hutton had been trying to persuade a Broadway producer to come and see Frye in Pittsfield. The producer: a tall, stocky, balding, 36-year-old "slow-talking Kansan" named Brock Pemberton. He had produced the 1920 Pulitzer Prize-winning play *Miss Lulu Bett*; in 1944, he would produce another Pulitzer Prize winner: *Harvey*.[2] Finally succumbing to Mrs. Hutton's entreaties, the very busy

DWIGHT FRYE
Juvenile Man—Colonial Players

Mr. Frye will be remembered for his work with the Players last summer. He closed with the local company in August and made a jump to Spokane, Wash., for an engagement with the Woodward Stock company. From Spokane he went to Seattle where he closed the season. Mr. Frye then made another cross country jump in time to join the Colonial company. Dwight claims that he is satisfied to stay in the East in the future.

Entire Week, July 3rd
A HOLIDAY WEEK OFFERING—THE ROLLICKING FARCE.

"TWIN BEDS"

THE BEDS USED ON THE STAGE IN THIS PRODUCTION WILL BE GIVEN AWAY FREE SATURDAY EVENING, JULY 8TH.

Pemberton took the train from Manhattan to see *Twin Beds*—unfortunately missing the first act, in which Dwight had his best scenes. Nevertheless, Pemberton saw enough of Frye to become thoroughly interested in his future. The following week, Pemberton came to see *The Broken Wing*—a play about a flyer who crashes his plane into the house of the Mexican girl who loves him. The plot was outrageous but Dwight's portrayal of American lawyer Sylvester Cross so impressed Pemberton that he offered him a long-term Broadway contract.

> In those days, actors were signed to theatrical contracts and would do play after play for the same producer. It was in 1922 that Brock Pemberton, a Broadway producer, went up to Pittsfield, saw my father in a stock company and signed him to a contract virtually on the spot.

—Dwight D. Frye

Dwight, elated by his great fortune, kept up his furious pace as a Colonial player. After closing in *Shavings* (as Leander Babbitt, the son of the village skinflint, and in love with the daughter of the big-hearted banker), Dwight and other cast members took a rare and brief hiatus, embarking on a short weekend trip to Edna Preston's camp in Lake George, New York. However, they were back at the Colonial bright and early Monday for the final rehearsal of *The Net*. As patrons arrived for the opening night of *The Net*, *The Colonial Chatter*, published by the Players, featured this notice:

> Dwight Frye has not been mentioned of late in these columns, but we were waiting for the big news—Dwight has signed for a Broadway production. Brock Pemberton is the producer and the play will be *In Honor's Name*. Thus another Colonial favorite advances to the front.

Dwight acted with the Colonial Players in three more shows before heading to Broadway. *Nightie Night* was a farce, with Dwight as Philip Burton, "Cub brother-in-law" to Billy (Alfred Swenson).

George M. Cohan's *The Little Millionaire*, the Colonial Players' second musical of the season, really gave the Broadway-bound Dwight a chance to strut his stuff. He enjoyed the starring role of Robert Spooner, which Cohan himself had played on Broadway. Robert and his father Henry (John McCabe) are both obliged to be married in order to satisfy the conditions of the late Mrs. Spooner's will. Dwight was the central figure in three musical numbers in the first act ("The Little Millionaire," "New Yorkers" and "The Old Flag"), and two in the third act ("Wonderful Girl" and "Come to My Bungalow," the latter with Edna Preston), in addition to the penultimate song, "The Wedding," with most of the company.

Dwight's final 1922 appearance at the Colonial came in *The Love Bandit*; he played the gambling brother of Amy Van Clayton (Edna Preston).

So, as summer neared a close, Dwight Frye bid adieu to the Colonial Players and went to New York to prepare for his New York debut. When he would return to the Colonial in the Summer of 1923 for a special guest engagement, it would be as a

Dwight Frye as young composer Patrick Delaney with Dorothy Francis in *Rita Coventry* at the Bijou Theatre.

Dwight Frye's Last Laugh

Chapter Two
Broadway—1922

O what a rogue and peasant slave am I!
Is it not monstrous that this player here,
But in a fiction, in a dream of passion,
Could force his soul so to his own conceit,
That from her working all his visage waned...
—*Hamlet*, Act II, scene 2

It was one of the most glorious years in the history of the American theatre.

Broadway, 1922... the year that John Barrymore played a magnificently mad Hamlet, portraying Shakespeare's sad prince for 101 performances (thus breaking Edwin Booth's 100-performance record)... when Jeanne Eagels first played Miss Sadie Thompson, Somerset Maugham's infamous whore of the tropics, in John Colton's *Rain*.

Will Rogers topped the bill in *The Ziegfeld Follies of 1922*. W. C. Fields headlined *George White's Scandals*. Musicals abounded, all proclaimed with rapturous copy in *The New York Times'* theatre directory: *Blossom Time* ("Greatest Musical Hit of Ages!"), *Marjolaine* ("The Musical Triumph!"), *The Blushing Bride* ("Showered by a first night audience with demonstrations of delirious delight!")...

Melodramas were very popular. *The Cat and the Canary* was a hit at the National Theatre, featuring Henry Hull (destined to star as Universal's *Werewolf of London* in 1935); it concerned a conspiracy to drive a pretty heroine insane, so she may not inherit that gloomy old Hudson estate, Glencliff Manor. *The Monster* (advertised as "a merry thriller") was playing at the 39th Street Theatre; it starred Wilton Lackaye (who had played Svengali in the 1915 film of *Trilby*) as mad Dr. Gustave Ziska, who traps visitors in his spooky house, practices vivisection and shocks the hero in an electric chair. And there was *The Bat*—"sensation of New York and London," which, the Morosco Theatre promised, "Keeps Standees on Tips of Their Toes." All three thrillers would translate to the movies.[3]

The movies were thriving, too, along Broadway, offering such 1922 attractions as Douglas Fairbanks as *Robin Hood*, Valentino in *Blood and Sand*, the Gish Sisters in D. W. Griffith's *Orphans of the Storm* and Erich von Stroheim in *Foolish Wives*.

Yet the New York theatre—America's most elegant fusion of glamour and art—reigned supreme. It was still the era of the great impresario and the great star; hence, David Belasco was presenting Lionel Atwill as *The Grand Duke*, Arthur Hopkins was offering Pauline Lord as *Anna Christie* and Ziegfeld was glorifying Marilyn Miller as *Sally*. Indeed, Broadway was not only the place to see the great performances of the day; it was the place to *be* seen as well.

The young, attractive, "jazz baby" sophisticate female of 1922 would affect her best finery as she applauded the opulence of Ziegfeld, the divine madness of Barrymore or the brazen dramatics of Jeanne Eagels. She would dress elegantly, starting with her light, four ounce, $5 Netheralls corset ("The Follies girls are wearing 'em," revealed Gimbel's advertisement). Attached to the corset's garters could be a pair of black silk stockings, with lisle soles and tops, available for $1.75 a pair at Lord & Taylor on Fifth Avenue; she then might slip into her buckled, black satin "opera pump" high heels ($10.75 per pair). She perhaps covered the foundation with an "Imported Paris Frock," which Franklin Simon was selling for $29.50, and add a $5, 32 inch-long pearl necklace. Finally, she could adorn herself with what was New York's fashion rage that fall (and possibly her most expensive piece of clothing, ranging from $28 to $55): an original, broad-brimmed, "Chapeau Nouveau de Paris." The hat was certain to endear her to the fashion-conscious in the theatre—if not the poor soul who had the sad fortune to sit behind her.

Her escort could be dashing in his own right—in his new, $35 Kuppenheimer suit and a silk-lined derby which Macy's offered on sale that fall for $2.98. Of course, the couple couldn't go out for an after-dinner drink (at least by conventional means); it was the era of Prohibition.

Nevertheless, Broadway was at a Roaring '20s apex; no world perhaps attracted more dramatic dreams—or such melodramatic failures. After midnight on September 5, 1922, two ladies who had passionately desired to belong to Broadway's elite won notice in *The New York Times* by attempting suicide. One was a 20-year-old from Detroit who, once "sustained by dreams of becoming a great actress," gave up by swallowing veronal and bromides in her apartment at 645 Madison Avenue. As she became unconscious, she dropped her cigarette and set her bed afire. The other, a 32-year-old widow who also wanted stardom, swallowed veronal (apparently the barbiturate of popular choice) in a Broadway taxi cab. She had made at least one previous attempt at killing herself.

On the date that both these young ladies botched suicide attempts, Dwight Frye made his Broadway debut.

The Plot Thickens, originally an Italian farce, offered this slapstick scenario:

Ennui-suffering millionaire Adonis Duckworth (Edwin Nicander) pays big money to movie director Benjamin Playfair Jones (John Thorn) to stage some "excitement, romance and adventure" in his life. "Make the world a bucking bronco for me!" exhorts Duckworth. He proceeds to laugh away at a variety of surprises which visit his Long Island estate, thinking they're all the doing of the movie director and his actors; the audience, of course, knows they are the real thing. The surprises included "boudoir complications" with Duckworth's French fiancee (Remy Carpen, whom the *Tribune* called "a refreshing debutante from Paris"; this Pemberton "discovery" lapsed into her native French often in the farce—apparently to the delight of the audience), a night in jail and a father-and-son pair of comic burglars. Playing the papa burglar, Mike Sheehan, was Dallas Welford; playing Mike Sheehan, Jr., was Dwight Frye.

Alexander Woollcott, the most famous and feared critic on 1920s Broadway, was in the Booth Theatre the night of September 5, 1922, as the curtain rose for Dwight Frye's Broadway debut in *The Plot Thickens*. Woollcott (who became the inspiration for "Sheridan Whiteside" in Kaufman and Hart's *The Man Who Came to Dinner*) judged

The Plot Thickens in his *New York Times* review to be "...mostly mirthless..." However, the great man added:

> Indeed, it is only the ancient and artful Dallas Welford and his young accomplice in the burglary interludes who play in the right key—the accomplice being excellently managed by one Dwight Frye. The burglars are amusing enough, father and son, the former very sentimental and paternal, the younger—Junior, he's called—frequently whining "Oh papa," as he goes rifling and filching about under the scientific eye of the old jailbird...

Indeed, Welford and Frye were the hits of the show as Dwight made his whining cry of "Oh, Papa!" one of the funniest sounds of the Broadway season. However, critical consensus was that Pemberton had directed the comedy at too slow a pace, and *The Plot Thickens* was a misfire—lasting only 15 performances.

Nevertheless, Dwight Frye, at age 23, had made his Broadway bow. He had collected a variety of good reviews to paste into his scrapbook. And another entirely different play and role were waiting in the wings for Dwight Frye.

> Owing to the very special nature of Pirandello's *Six Characters in Search of an Author*, opening tonight at the Princess, the engagement will be limited to four weeks and morons will be refused admission.
> —opening night notice, *The New York Times*, October 30, 1922.

It was Brock Pemberton's way of throwing down the gauntlet to New York audiences; a comically arrogant challenge to support his unusual new production. As Alexander Woollcott would synopsize *Six Characters in Search of an Author*:

> The scene, you see, is just the bare stage of a theatre, where a chunky little manager is directing rehearsals of *The Bride's Revenge* with the old standbys of his stock company in the leading roles. Then suddenly, without warning, there file in through the stage door six portentous figures—a gray-haired and garrulous old beau; a lovely, tempestuous young girl; a tragic woman, heavily veiled in black; two small children and a frost-bitten young man.
> Their spokesman explains that they are six characters invented for a play by a dramatist who,

Six Characters in Search of an Author: **The stars assembled in the middle include Margaret Wycherly, Constance Lusby, Ashley Buck, Florence Eldridge, Moffat Johnston and Dwight Frye as The Son.**

despairing of ever seeing them sympathetically embodied by the average run of actors and mistrusting the commercial theatre as a place which would permit their destinies to be worked out, prefers just to let them drift up his chimney like the idle smoke from the pipe on which he was pulling when he invented them. He never wrote the play at all and there they were, adrift in a difficult world, as real as Falstaff or Sancho Panza... as real and as changeless and as immortal.

How they persuade the manager to put them into a play, how they treat him as a murderer when he seeks to alter or soften their destinies to please the dread public and how they war constantly with the dreadful actors who are to embody and wrench them all out of shape—all this is worked out in an astonishingly dramatic and telling play...

This Pirandello play was a potpourri of incest, adultery and suicide. The Stepdaughter turns to prostitution, the Little Girl drowns herself in a fountain, the Boy (the illegitimate one) shoots himself as the only legitimate Son bitterly comments on their tragedy. Pemberton had carefully selected an unusual cast:

For the "heavily-veiled" Mother, Pemberton cast Margaret Wycherly, who had created the role of the mystic in *The Thirteenth Chair*, starring in the original 1916

Dwight Frye's Last Laugh

Broadway production and touring in it for years. (Miss Wycherly also starred in Tod Browning's 1929 MGM film of *The Thirteenth Chair*, with Bela Lugosi as the Inspector.) Moviegoers remember Margaret Wycherly best as the recipient of James Cagney's mad mother love ("Top of the world, Ma!") in Warner Bros.' *White Heat* (1949).

Winning the role of the "tempestuous" Step-daughter was Florence Eldridge, who came to *Six Characters in Search of an Author* direct from *The Cat and the Canary*, in which she'd created the role of damsel-in-distress Annabelle West. Miss Eldridge had made her New York debut as a chorus girl in *Rock-a-Bye Baby* (June, 1917); the very gifted actress would marry Fredric March in 1927, and together they would act in such films as *Mary of Scotland* (1936) and such Broadway plays as *The Skin of Our Teeth* (1942), *Years Ago* (1946) and *Long Day's Journey into Night* (1956). In 1922, however, Miss Eldridge was still a promising newcomer, who (within theatre circles) was known to have a peculiar habit: acting onstage, she reputedly would wear—aside from her stockings—no underwear.[4]

And, for the "frost-bitten" young Son, Pemberton cast Dwight Frye. Reportedly, Pemberton had asked Dwight to read the role in rehearsals, until the originally cast actor arrived from Chicago; he read the part so impressively that he won it. The actor spoke of his role in an interview:

> He's an interesting figure, that boy—even a pathetic one, in spite of his weakness. The egotism and false pride with which his creator has endowed him will not permit him to accept his family. The three illegitimate children and their mother—who, as they keep reminding him, is his mother, too—seem an unendurable stigma to him... Yes, he's an interesting figure, that bitter and thwarted boy.

The play faced its first audience at the Beechwood Theatre, Scarborough-on-Hudson, on October 27, 1922. Pemberton then gave the show a test of fire—performing it before the prison populace of Sing Sing! (Actually, Sing Sing was a safe place to preview a play—there were no critics, and no reviews.) On October 30, 1922, *Six Characters in Search of an Author* opened at Broadway's Princess Theatre, heralded by Pemberton's "moron warning." The result was a surprise hit; surpassing its four-week limited engagement, the play ran 137 performances (a very respectable and profitable run for 1922), and won excellent reviews—including praise for Dwight Frye. As Alexander Woollcott wrote:

> ...There really should be several words for Mr. Frye, a newcomer this season, who is not the most imposing looking actor we have ever beheld, but whose voice has the true dramatic quality and whose two brief appearances this fall have marked him as one coming down out of the Berkshires, of all places, with a talent worth watching.

The aesthetic, philosophical nature of *Six Characters...* put off some critics (morons?). Overall, it was a great success. Interestingly (considering the religious background of Dwight and his mother), *The Christian Science Monitor* called the play "one of the freshest and most original productions seen for a long time past."

It was a wonderful time for Dwight Frye. Laura Bullivant, whom he had romanced in Spokane, was now in New York, working as a dancer; they renewed their relationship. And, as Dwight reported to the Princess Theatre each night for *Six Characters in Search of an Author*, theatre history was happening all about him. On November 7, 1922, Jeanne Eagels opened in *Rain* at Maxine Elliott's Theatre; on November 16, 1922, John Barrymore had his opening night as *Hamlet* at the Sam H. Harris Theatre.

Far less heralded, or successful, was a play that opened at the Greenwich Theatre on December 20, 1922—*The Red Poppy*. Making his official Broadway debut in this play, as Fernando, the Spanish Apache dancer, was a Hungarian émigré named Bela Lugosi. The play collapsed after 14 performances. Lugosi personally collected some lavish reviews—but no salary.

Meanwhile, the surprise and fear that Charles and Ella Fry had felt about their son becoming an actor had long since turned to deep pride. At Christmas of 1922, the 23-year-old Broadway actor sent this telegram home to Denver:

> With these Holiday Greetings I Send the Greatest Love in the World to you Both God Bless You as Your Boy Does
>
> —Dwight

Rita Coventry was a comedy about a glamorous, vainglorious opera diva. This title character (Dorothy Francis) merrily seduces and abandons lovers—until the right man enters the play. The right man: Patrick Delaney, a piano tuner and struggling composer, whose joy and naiveté enchant the diva and the audience. Dwight Frye left *Six Characters in Search of an Author* to accept the role of Patrick Delaney in this new Brock Pemberton production, which opened February 19, 1923 at Broadway's Bijou Theatre.

The next morning, Dwight Frye was established as a major Broadway actor. Kenneth Macgowan, later a major Hollywood producer (1933's *Little Women*, 1935's *Becky Sharp*, 1938's *In Old Chicago*, 1939's *Young Mr. Lincoln*, 1941's *Man Hunt* and many more) was then drama critic of *The New York Globe*. He wrote:

> ...along toward the middle of the second act there enters a most salutary figure—a real character and a fresh character. It is a young piano tuner who composes music, and wears ragged suits and a self-opinionated air. There is no rubber stamp for this fellow—so far. This part gains a great deal from being played most engagingly by Dwight Frye, the elder son in *Six Characters in Search of an Author*. He does many little things with great

Young Patrick Delaney stares pensively, after opera star Rita Coventry has made him her protégé.

care. He entrances the audience, and convinces the critical. When the prima donna begins to talk to the piano-tuner, *Rita Coventry* begins to perk up. If he were the central figure the play would be a rather remarkable piece.

It was bad news for Dorothy Francis (who played Rita Coventry) but great news for Dwight. "So the mantle of stardom really falls where it wasn't intended, on Dwight Frye," wrote Anita Block in *The Call*. "...his acting here ranks among the best we have seen this season."

Coincidentally, that same night, Laura Bullivant opened in a vaudeville show at Broadway's Palace Theatre. As she wrote in her diary:

> 2/19/23: Opened at Palace—great success—everyone very happy. Dwight opened in *Rita*

A portrait of Dwight Frye from *Rita Coventry.*

Coventry —Bijou—I caught last 2 acts—D was
marvelous—hit of show.
    2/20/23: Had breakfast with D—we had great
time reading criticisms.

A special bonus for Dwight (and for theatre patrons) was that *Rita Coventry* allowed him to display his skill at the piano playing ("very appealingly") compositions by
Deems Taylor. Impresario Walter Damrosch, whose daughter Leopoldine had a small

role in *Rita Coventry*, was said to have remarked during opening night intermission that, before long, Dwight Frye would be the greatest comedian of the era.

"Dwight Frye, as the piano tuner, was simply a joy all the way through," wrote Alan Dale of *The New York American*. "It was a refreshingly clever performance, and one that couldn't have been duplicated."

As *Rita Coventry* ran for 24 performances, perhaps no testimonial placed Dwight Frye's work into perspective as did this notice from New York critic Stephen Rathbun. In reviewing the 1922/1923 season, Rathbun wrote:

> For our midseason honor list we name John Barrymore for his Hamlet; Jane Cowl for her Juliet; Rudolph Schildkraut for his acting in *The God of Vengeance*; Jeanne Eagels for her acting in *Rain*; Helen Menken for her acting in *Seventh Heaven*; Haidee Wright for her Queen Elizabeth in *Will Shakespeare*; Dwight Frye for his portrayal of Patrick Delaney, the piano tuner-composer, and for his playing of Deems Taylor's "incidental music" in *Rita Coventry*; Rapley Holmes for his Joe Heran in *Rain*; Ivan Moskvin for his Luka, the pilgrim in Gorki's *The Lower Depths*; Mme. Knipper-Tchekova for her Masha in Tchekhoff's *The Three Sisters*; Morris Gest, because he brought the Moscow Art Theatre to New York; and Otto Kahn, patron of the arts, because he is Morris Gest's good angel and is helping to make Mr. Gest's dreams come true.

So, Dwight Frye, via his third Broadway play, found himself listed alongside Barrymore, Jeanne Eagels and Jane Cowl as one of the top ten actors on Broadway. His future seemed limitless. Surely Brock Pemberton thought so. On February 28, 1923 — nine days after Dwight had opened in *Rita Coventry*, and six days after his 24th birthday — the proud young actor joyfully sent this telegram to his parents in Denver:

> Have Signed Five Year Contract With Pemberton
> Everything Going Fine Letter Explaining No More
> Worry Dreams Coming True My Love
> —Dwight.

Kendall Evans' portrait of Dwight Frye circa 1923.

Dwight Frye's Last Laugh

Chapter Three
Dreams Coming True

Dwight Frye again shows himself as a brilliant young actor.
—Heywood Broun, in his review of *The Love Habit* (1923)

His rise was remarkable.

On March 25, 1923—about one month after Dwight Frye's 24th birthday—the Sunday drama section of *The New York Times* heralded front page cartoons of three Broadway stars: Lionel Atwill (starring in Belasco's *The Comedian*); Paul Muni Weisenfreund (later known as Paul Muni, and playing in the Yiddish Art Theatre's *Anathema*); and Dwight Frye—featured in *The Love Habit*.

Billed as "The Frenchiest of French Farces," *The Love Habit* immediately followed *Rita Coventry* at the Bijou Theatre March 14, 1923. Florence Eldridge starred in the new Brock Pemberton show as Nadine Morand, the "pretty and winsome" Paris heroine; and Dwight was featured as Max Duvelleroy, described in various reviews as "the foppish little Parisian boulevardier" and "a blackmailing dancer." Once again, Alexander Woollcott sang Dwight's praises:

> He is extraordinarily amusing... playing with
> infinite relish the role of a dressy little Parisian
> blackmailer and gigolo... there really might be
> a special paragraph for the horrid lifelikeness of
> the creature from Montmarte that Mr. Frye plays
> with his inky, oily black sideburns reaching down
> to accentuate a kind of evil pallor, like the white
> of a flounder's belly or the white of those things
> you find scampering over the black, damp earth
> under a rock.

Dwight's Max delighted in his insidious behavior. His "tag line" throughout *The Love Habit* was, "Am I not an unmitigated cad?"

In a 1927 interview, Frye himself looked back at his delineation of Max:

> I established the character through my own shadow.
> It appeared before I did and I made it move slowly
> and with the pauses worked out so that through its
> very contrast with the farce tempo of the piece it
> became very funny.

In *The Love Habit*, Marie the maid (Mary Kennedy) is unsure what to make of Max Duvelleroy (Dwight Frye), a slick Parisian blackmailer and gigolo.

The Love Habit ran 69 performances. The New York press now took note of Dwight Frye as "the busiest actor of the season of 1922-23." Within seven months, he had created roles in four plays—tying the prolific Otto Kruger of Broadway's previous season.

"Mr. Frye has a manner of his own which is inimitable," wrote critic Gordon Whyte after the opening night of *The Love Habit*, "and when he gets just the right sort of a part, he is going to make a whale of a hit, or I miss my guess."

The Love Habit closed as summer neared; by the time it closed, Dwight had succeeded James Rennie in the lead role of the Young Man. Brock Pemberton announced he would star Dwight in a musical version of *Good Gracious, Annabelle*, but it never came to fruition. Instead, Dwight vacationed in Lowville, New York, getting some well-needed rest after a very busy year. It was there that Dwight was contacted about coming back to the Colonial Players of Pittsfield, Mass. for a triumphant "guest return engagement."

The Pittsfield newspapers heralded the return of Dwight Frye to the Colonial, with *The Berkshire Eagle* calling Dwight "...one of the most popular favorites that Pittsfield has known." He acted in "the great sensational melodramatic success," *In Old Kentucky*, which opened at the Colonial July 9, 1923. Publicity heralded Dwight and *In Old Kentucky*'s famed horserace spectacle:

> The most thrilling scene ever offered on any stage—the horse race—will be given in its entirety. The horses have been secured and are being brought from New York. One of the horses is the daughter of the famous "Man-O-War," and Miss (Ruth) Amos will ride this horse in the thrilling race.

Dwight followed at the Colonial with *Rita Coventry* (7/16/23), reprising his Broadway hit as piano tuner Patrick Delaney (Brock Pemberton made an "in-person" appearance at the Colonial during its run) and *The Champion* (7/23/23).

Brock Pemberton had tantalized the Broadway community with news he would begin the 1923/1924 season with Oscar Wilde's *The Picture of Dorian Gray*—starring Dwight Frye. Sadly, it never came to pass; one can only imagine what Dwight might have done with the Gothic role, and what impact it might have had on his career.

Instead, in the fall of 1923, Dwight was touring in the comedy *Underwrite Your Husband*, which boasted Mary Boland and "a new juvenile" named Humphrey Bogart. Dwight played Victor Staunton, described in one review as "the village's prize asininity." By the time the play opened on Broadway in November, under the title *Meet the Wife*, Dwight had left the company for another offer and Clifton Webb had assumed the Victor Staunton role.

Dwight returned to work for Brock Pemberton in a revival of *Six Characters in Search of an Author*, which opened February 6, 1924, at the Forty-Fourth Street Theatre, where it played 17 performances. Dwight again assayed the role of the haughty Son, but only during matinees.

Then came major news: Dwight Frye was definitely set to star on Broadway—in musical comedy!

> We were just a band of brothers,
> Each as good as all the others:
> As the humblest sort of sneak thief you might rank.
> But, when you've been there a week, well

A newspaper cartoon of the stars of *Sitting Pretty* (from Dwight Frye's personal scrapbook). Depicted are Frank McIntyre, Queenie Smith and Dwight Frye.

> You were treated as an equal
> By the swells who killed their wives or robbed a
> bank.
> —Dwight Frye, singing "Dear Old-Fashioned
> Prison of Mine" in *Sitting Pretty* (1924)

Producers F. Ray Comstock and Morris Gest borrowed Dwight from Brock Pemberton to star in *Sitting Pretty*, featuring a book by Guy Bolton, music by Jerome Kern and lyrics by P. G. Wodehouse. The plot: wealthy Mr. Pennington (George E. Mack), disgusted with his own relatives, plans to create a new family by adopting a boy and girl, and then scheming to get them married. Uncle Joe (Frank McIntyre), an old thief, seizes the opportunity to get his young accomplice Horace Peabody (Dwight) adopted, to facilitate robbing Pennington's estate.

"Gee whistikers!" cracks Dwight's Horace as he meets his new family. "What a bunch of prunes!"

Naturally, Horace falls in love with Dixie (Queenie Smith, a soubrette whose dancing verged on the acrobatic), his targeted bride from the orphanage—climactically foiling Uncle Joe's theft and allowing a happy finale.

The pre-Broadway try-out of *Sitting Pretty* faced its first audience at Detroit's Shubert Theatre on March 23, 1924. As the show was fine-tuned, moving on to Buffalo, it won a favorable reception—although Dwight faced the none-too-happy situation of having some of his songs cut. Two of his numbers, "A Romantic Man" and "Ladies are Present," were dropped early on; before the Broadway opening, even the title song, "Sitting Pretty," sung by Dwight and Queenie Smith, got the axe. In Gerald Bordman's biography of Jerome Kern, Queenie Smith offered this recollection of why "Sitting

In *Sitting Pretty*, Dixie Tolliver (Queenie Smith) is placed on a pedestal-of-sorts by Horace Peabody (Dwight Frye).

Pretty" was cut: "Dwight Frye had a slight speech impediment, and his singing of the words 'sit and sit and sit' sounded embarrassingly different."[5]

In any case, *Sitting Pretty* (slightly truncated) opened at the Fulton Theatre in New York on April 8, 1924. The first-night audience beheld Dwight singing the hilarious "Bongo on the Congo" (with Frank McIntyre and Eugene Revere), duetting with Queenie Smith with "Mr. and Mrs. Rorer" and joining the enormously fat Frank McIntyre in "Dear Old-Fashioned Prison of Mine" (aka "Tulip Time in Sing Sing").

The New York Times reported:

The cast of *Sitting Pretty*, at the Fulton Theatre, with the principals front and center.

> A distinct surprise of the evening was Dwight Frye, who, face to face with musical comedy for the first time (sic), showed an astonishing aptitude for it. He revealed a voice that was at least equal to the occasion, and danced in a way that Pirandello never would have thought possible.

Sitting Pretty ran 95 performances — a respectable run, but the only Bolton-Wodehouse-Kern collaboration not to play for at least a season. One contributing factor was that Kern, in response to the musical world's distortion of his previous compositions, decided not to allow the score of *Sitting Pretty* to be played in cabarets or on the fairly new medium of radio. Kern also would not permit phonograph recordings made from any of the show's songs, with the inability of the listening public to hear the music from *Sitting Pretty* probably having an adverse effect on the show's box office.

Dwight was continuing to stun the critics, and Charles A. Collins wrote in his April 26, 1924 review:

> Dwight Frye, the sensation of Broadway last year in four different plays, is seen opposite Queenie. He is having a lark in his initial musical comedy venture. It is a delight to one who hails him as a future (blonde) John Barrymore, to

Dwight Frye's Last Laugh

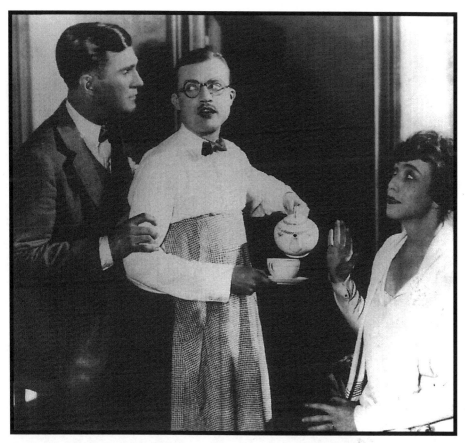

So This is Politics/Strange Bedfellows: **John Buckmaster (Glenn Anders), his brother-in-law Willie Marsden (Dwight Frye) and Nina Buckmaster (Majorie Gateson), the candidate for mayor.**

> witness Dwight Frye in his diversions of dancing
> and singing. What a glorious tragedian—what a
> wonderful satirist he is destined to be.

Dwight departed *Sitting Pretty* in late May of 1924, and was replaced by John Price Jones. He supposedly left to join the company of John V. A. Weaver's play *Love 'Em and Leave 'Em*, but this didn't come to pass.

Instead, Dwight was "loaned-out" by Pemberton again, accepting the comic role of Willie, a bespectacled, mustached, "weakling brother who taught Sunday school" in *So This is Politics*, which opened at Henry Miller's Theatre June 16, 1924. The star was Marjorie Gateson, usually seen in musical comedy; the concept was the then-novel idea of a woman running for Mayor. Two weeks into the run, *So This is Politics* changed its name to *Strange Bedfellows* and became an instant hit. The comedy ran 144 performances (18 weeks), and *The New York Herald-Tribune* praised Dwight's Willie as "one of the memorable funny characters of the season."

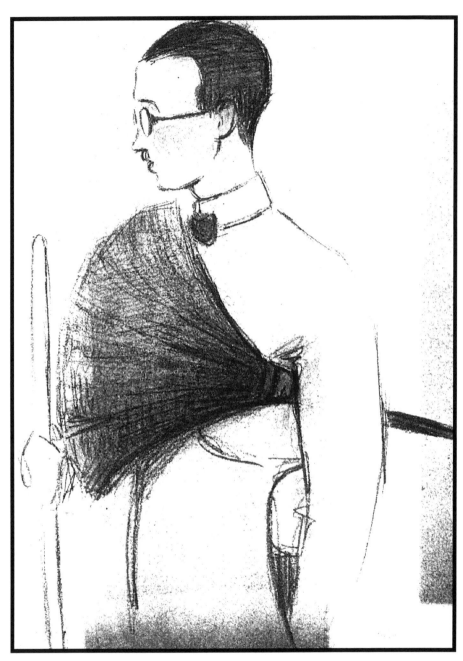

Dwight Frye's personal artistic rendition of his character Willie Marsden from *So This Is Politics*.

A special triumph followed as Dwight prepared for *Puppets*.

Dwight Frye's Last Laugh

...what a villain! He was so real he was disgusting.
Any white slaver is, you know.
—Frank Grace in his review of Dwight
Frye's performance in *Puppets* (1925)

"The new romantic melodrama" was perhaps too subtle a subtitle for *Puppets*, produced by Brock Pemberton, which had its opening night at the Selwyn Theatre March 9, 1925.

The Frances Lightner play[6] concerned a marionette theatre in the "Little Italy" colony of New York City, circa 1915. Nicola Riccoboni (C. Henry Gordon) is the puppet king of Mulberry Street; he is preparing a new marionette play in his Gothic tower theatre when a blonde, runaway-from-Georgia waif named Angela (Miriam Hopkins) sings her way into his life, warbling "Love May Find Me Today." It does; within 15 minutes, she and Nicola are in love. They marry and—on their wedding night—Nicola is called off to war. Three years later, with Nicola long-rumored dead, Angela is about to leave for church to marry Nicola's weakling cousin, Bruno (Fredric March) when—lo!—Nicola returns, deaf from shellshock, but very much alive. He regains his hearing, and learns of Angela's love for Bruno; he responds by challenging Bruno to the Italian game of "Morra"—in which the loser must bare his breast to the winner's knife. Lover Bruno reveals himself a coward; Angela, watching the "Morra" from the stairs, decides she loves her tyrannical (but brave) husband and—in a finale tinged with masochism—snuggles against Nicola's medal-laden chest.

Miriam Hopkins, fated to be Bette Davis's nemesis (on *and* offscreen!) in Warner Bros.' *The Old Maid* (1939) and *Old Acquaintance* (1943), won a flurry of bravos in her first major Broadway role as the singing, sugary sweet heroine. C. Henry Gordon, with his mustache and satanic sneer, would become a noted Hollywood heavy (and act with Dwight in several films). And Fredric March, of course, would become one of the great actors of the American theatre and cinema, whose honors would include Hollywood's Academy Award for *Dr. Jekyll and Mr. Hyde* (Paramount, 1931, in which Hyde's tragic mistress Ivy was played by his *Puppets* co-star, Miriam Hopkins) and *The Best Years of Our Lives* (Goldwyn, 1946), and Broadway's Tony Award for *Years Ago* (1946) and *Long Day's Journey into Night* (1956). *Puppets* also offered a crowd-pleasing marionette show as part of the play.

However, the most wildly melodramatic character of *Puppets* (and the one who most mesmerized the audience) was none of these principals. As *The New York Times* reported:

> ...there is a wicked boy named Frank who plays
> the piano for the show. He betrays girls and sells
> them to white slavers. He loves Angela, the young
> wife, for himself, however. Frank, the villain,
> played by Dwight Frye, wanders rather vaguely on
> the outskirts of the play like a heavy storm in the
> neighborhood of paper dolls. Dwight Frye plays
> the part well, and projects every inch of it over the
> footlights...

The villainous Frank Mohacz (Dwight Frye) glares as Nicki Riccoboni (C. Henry Gordon) removes the knife in the wall, from *Puppets*.

Indeed, as Frank, "the white slaver," Dwight was a sensation. Sporting a derby, smoking a cigarette, playing the piano, Frye's Frank tried to steal away the heroine and actually stole the show. As Alexander Woollcott reported:

A newspaper artist's (Marcus) depiction of Dwight Frye as villainous white slaver Frank Mohacz, from *Puppets*.

Perhaps the fact that so unquenchably dramatic an actor as Dwight Frye embodies the white slaver serves to make his seem the important part of the play... as the white slaver steals in with his sinister confederate to drag the terrified girl across the roofs to thralldom, the onlooker may be pardoned for sitting forward in expectation of the play's coming to a focus...

Indeed, the critics seemed to be trying to outdo each other in describing Dwight's Frank Mohacz: "The serpent-like piano player"; "slug-like in appearance and demeanor"; "particularly despicable"; "that lurid creature"; "an unforgettable figure of refined depravity"; and, "the bold, wicked bad man of Mulberry Street."

As wild and woolly a melodrama as *Puppets* was, Dwight played his role with total sincerity. When critic John Anderson employed a comical canard in describing Dwight's performance, Dwight himself wrote to the newspaper—to thank him for his insight:

> ...The majority of critics are destructive. Their whole tone is bitter. And yet there is a minority who are constructive enough to make me look upon critics as a help... An example: Your critic, writing of *Puppets*, spoke of me as "inclined to mopping up his face with his own features." That one sentence indicated to me that one man thought that not so much facial expression was necessary and that I should rely more upon my voice and on the scene. I have thought of that, therefore, and tried to tone my expression down somewhat...

Puppets ran a decent 57 performances in New York. (After five weeks, the play had changed its name to *The Knife in the Wall* and moved to the Frolic Theatre.) Several critics (and many audience members) had lamented that the mere arrest of Dwight's evil Frank was too mild a fate for so wicked a villain; as a result, during the run, the script was changed to provide him with a more audience-pleasing comeuppance. Following the New York run, Brock Pemberton took *Puppets* immediately to Chicago, where it opened at the La Salle Theatre.

All in all, *Puppets* was a new triumph for Dwight Frye. Charles A. Collins noted Dwight's dominance in the melodrama, and, once again, prophesied a great future:

> ...Dwight Frye, whom we have previously hailed as a future Barrymore, and whom Pemberton introduced to Broadway only two or three seasons ago, takes everything in sight. Some day this young man is going to appear in a play worthy of his talent, and the resulting vibration will be felt west of Denver.

Stark Young was one of the most influential theatre critics of the 1920s. After *The Love Habit,* Young had devoted an entire column to Dwight Frye in *The New Republic.*

Now, after the opening of *Puppets* he wrote again about Dwight in *The New York Times* (March 22, 1925):

Of all the younger men among our players Dwight Frye seems to be the one who can most turn what he does into acting. In "Puppets" it is largely much ado about nothing, but it is all the art of acting, nevertheless something complete in itself and independent of everything outside of it...

With such a sense of the nature of acting as an art and such talent Mr. Frye will always find it hard to play with most of our actors, who are most likely to hit and miss, to be one moment themselves, acting the next moment, and the next sheer accident. His work will be like a bold, clear drawing by a draftsman compared with the mussing and loose form of ordinary sketching where the worker merely fumbles after the likeness without any sense of the nature of his art.

The development and future of such a player as Dwight Frye will not be so much a matter of learning what the art of acting really is — which is something most players never learn at all — it will be a matter of his growth as an artist. Whether he goes on projecting so competently portraits that have little meaning or rises to important creation will depend on the ideas and conceptions which he can acquire with time and labor, and which he will know how to translate into acting terms. But, good or bad, important or unimportant, he will always be an actor.

Dwight Frye and Josephine Hutchinson as they appeared in *A Man's Man* on Broadway.

Dwight Frye's Last Laugh

Chapter Four
Stardom

> If *A Man's Man* is a success, it is because it is
> human. The people in it are humble to the point of
> futility, but they are real, and the audiences seem
> to care about them, almost love them.
>
> —Dwight Frye

Full stardom came to Dwight Frye on the night of October 13, 1925, at Broadway's
52nd Street Theatre. The role was Melville Tuttle; the play was *A Man's Man*, by Patrick
Kearney; and his co-star was Josephine Hutchinson, as his wife Edie.

"...the cruelest little play of the moment" was how critic E. W. Osborn described
A Man's Man. As *The New York Times* wrote of the leading characters:

> Melville Tuttle is a white-collared young man,
> virtually illiterate, physically inconsequent and of
> a social outlook that regards a possible member-
> ship in the Elks as the supreme goal. Edie is an
> ignorant, wistful young wife, clinging pathetically
> to her fancied resemblance to Mary Pickford and
> the possibility that she may thus enter the mov-
> ies and achieve fame and fortune for herself and
> Melville.

According to all reports from the time, Frye was successful in capturing the essence
of Mel's soul—his need to compensate for his inadequate background and his desire
to be considered "a man's man." In an early speech to Edie (Josephine Hutchinson)
about his goal, Mel relates:

> The Elks is big successful men, Edie. Men
> you'd be proud to know. And say, if you're an Elk
> you can get anywhere in business. Think of the
> opportunity, meeting all them big men, fraternal
> like. You see, if a man's a member of your lodge
> he'll do anything for you, anything at all. Why...
> why... I tell you, Edie... it's the greatest thing ever
> happened to me.

Mel pays Charlie Groff (Robert Gleckler) $100 for his Elk application fee, while inviting him to his anniversary celebration. Because of his blind acceptance of Charlie's friendship and subsequent drunkenness at the party, Mel fails to realize that Groff has enticed Edie by playing on her fantasies of movie stardom. In a pathetic revelation, Mel tells Edie how impressed he is by Charlie's philandering, unaware he is talking about his own marital situation:

> Listen, don't I know? Wasn't the boys tellin' me
> about it? Charlie's the boy to get away with that,
> all right. A married woman, too. Takes a real fine
> fellow to get a married woman, you bet. And her
> husband don't know nothin' about it! He sure is a
> great fellow, Charlie is. Gotta hand it to him, all
> right. Can you imagine that dame thinkin' she looks
> like Mary Pickford? Can't you see how funny it
> is? Can't you understand nothin' funny?

After the truth about Edie's loss of marital fidelity and Charlie's deception has been found out, Mel seeks vengeance, but returns in a battered state. Speaking with increasing wildness, Mel tries to preserve the vestiges of his self esteem, glancing at the correspondence school diploma on the wall:

> Sure—whenever I look at that it says to me—
> you're a success—it says to me. You've passed
> with high honors in the course of dominating men
> and women—you can go out in the world and win
> the prizes of life—it makes me feel pretty big to
> have that—and it's true, Edie, I tell you it's true—I
> was a different fellow before I took that course—I
> never could a licked Charlie if I hadn't took that
> course—I would a been scared to touch him—and
> now I just licked hell outa him—just licked hell
> outa him—honest I did, Edie. You don't believe
> me but it's true.

The play ends with Edie holding Mel, she tending to her battered spouse, the two pitiful dreamers talking about the son they might have one day, and Mel imagining:

> You know... that boy won't be just an Elk, he won't.
> Not him—not a chance. He won't be no ordinary
> Elk, no siree. Why I kin see the time when that
> there kid is Grand Master of the Elks.

This was the starring role for which Dwight Frye had waited. Critic E. S. Colling reported:

A Man's Man: Mel (Dwight Frye) and Edie Tuttle (Josephine Hutchinson) are manipulated by S. Barrett Blackstone (Arthur Hughes) into purchasing a book on etiquette.

...Mr. Frye rises to what are commonly known as the heights. In one of the most tense and moving acts which this reviewer has viewed in years, he wrings your heart with the feeling which he puts into the pathetic situation. In this, he was singularly aided and abetted by the work of Miss Josephine Hutchinson, who supported him in a remarkably able manner.

The New York Times gave the top bouquet to the leading lady ("Miss Hutchinson was last night's real sensation, perhaps because she is a newcomer and one has had

A Man's Man: **Edie begs Mel for forgiveness after her affair with Charlie has been re-vealed.**

reason to know that Mr. Frye will always be seen to excellent advantage"). However, the review also lavishly praised the leading man:

> Mr. Frye... gives an exceptionally true performance as the weakling husband. He is required for nearly two acts to play in a hysteria of self-pity and at no time does he approach the exaggerated mood that must lie temptingly near. With a complete avoidance of superfluous histrionics, he makes his character pitifully and pathetically real.

A Man's Man: **The climax of the play during which Edie Tuttle cradles and comforts her bruised and despondent husband, Mel.**

"Dwight Frye, in one of the two principal roles, gives a performance of unerring effect," reported *The Sun*. "Barbed from beginning to end with the morose irony of pity. This puny, hand shaking, unheroic hero of his, battered by fist and failure, grief and ridicule, looms finally as a type of all our dogged, aspiring futilities."

"...my favorite role... Better than anything I ever played," said Dwight Frye of his Melville Tuttle in *A Man's Man*. It would run 120 performances—a solid hit.

St. Patrick's Day, 1995. Almost 70 years after *A Man's Man* opened on Broadway, Josephine Hutchinson, 91 years old, sits in her penthouse atop a very old, very stylish apartment house in New York's East '50s, vividly remembering *A Man's Man*, and Dwight Frye.

Greg Mank had met her there in 1978. She was, at the time, still slender, attractive, distinctive; one would have recognized her almost instantly as the red-haired, ethereal star of the movies *Oil for the Lamps of China* (1935), *The Story of Louis Pasteur* (1936), and *Son of Frankenstein* (1939), in which she co-starred as the lovely Elsa von Frankenstein with Rathbone, Karloff, Lugosi and Atwill. At the time of the 1978 interview, she was married to actor Staats Cotsworth, whom she had met in the early 1930s, when she was a laureled star of Eva Le Gallienne's Civic Repertory Company, and he an apprentice.

Now, all these years later, Mr. Cotsworth is long dead; Miss Hutchinson is white-haired and totally blind. Yet her spirit, her charm and her memory are all amazing; indeed, she can still recite "The Jabberwocky" from *Alice in Wonderland*, her most famous performance in the Civic Repertory back in 1932/1933.

As Mank talks of this biography, she listens and bends forward on the couch.

"Now tell me all about this," she says earnestly. "I want to know everything about it."

She listens with great care about Dwight Frye, about the plans for this book.

"Dwight," she reminisces softly. "A dedicated, frantic actor."

Yet they had not been close during *A Man's Man*; Dwight, as she remembers, was almost unapproachable. Now, she thinks she knows why.

> At the time, I thought Dwight was... odd. Strange. He was so imbued with working on his part that he wasn't very communicative to his fellow players. When he was in the theatre, all he thought about was his performance. Now, all these years later, I realize: Dwight really was the original "Method" actor.

Miss Hutchinson recalls Dwight's total self-absorption in his role of Melville Tuttle—and the consequences.

> I remember, backstage, Dwight kept a sandbox. He was supposed to have gotten into a fight—about me, I think, with the man I thought could make me a star—and he was to be kind of "beat-up" from the fight. Well, he had to dirty himself up, and he was a little "high-handed" with the stagehands that they have the sandbox ready for him, so he could throw the sand on himself.
>
> It was a demand that caused a little problem, because it was eccentric. At the time I thought it was kind of crazy! He should have looked awful; however, most any other actor would have had two suits, wouldn't he? One that was already "dirtied

up," and one that wasn't? Not Dwight; he carried
it to that extent. I can see now why he wanted to get
his costume messy, but at that period in the 1920s,
that was just "crazy."

Miss Hutchinson remembered seeing John Barrymore as Hamlet. At the performance she saw, Barrymore, suffering from a cold, had a handkerchief pinned to his
costume, periodically breaking away from the play to blow his nose, the dirty handkerchief dangling from his costume all the while. Between acts, "mad Jack" ("I'm sure he
was very drunk," says Miss Hutchinson) came before the curtain and entertained the
crowd—telling "Negro jokes" in a black dialect. Barrymore (and virtually all his colleagues) worked via "technique," and he could "put on" the role of Hamlet as easily as
he put on a fedora. Dwight Frye's "Method" approach was considered bizarre, and was
over 20 years ahead of its time and the Actors Studio revolution of the late 1940s.

Over the years, Miss Hutchinson has performed with many "Method" actors; "That's
their way of working," she says, "and they turn in good performances." Dwight stayed
immersed in his role, even as the atmosphere backstage became ugly:

> Dwight, the sandbox... it became a "laughing thing"
> for the stagehands. He became cranky about what
> they did, and they all wanted to kill him; it came to
> "end-of-battle." So, for a dinner scene, the stage-
> hands would intentionally put food there because
> they knew he didn't like it—including tripe! Well,
> I don't like tripe either (ugh!)—and, of course, I
> had to eat it, too!

(Today, Dwight D. Frye remembers his father saying, "There's only one thing I
won't eat—tripe!")

There were other oddities—all stemming from Dwight's passionate involvement
in his work. Although he was playing a very ordinary young man, Dwight used, as
Miss Hutchinson recalls, "this heavy white makeup"—a hangover, she says, from his
success in *Six Characters in Search of an Author*.

"It was kind of 'weirdo,'" says Miss Hutchinson, "and I can see how he got into
horror pictures."

She admits the final product, however, was a great performance.

> Dwight was a wonderful actor in *A Man's Man*.
> For the part he was playing with me, he couldn't
> have been better.

Josephine Hutchinson became a Warner Bros. Hollywood star in 1934. "I never
saw Dwight out there," she recalls. She listens to the details of his early death with
sympathy—"I'm so sorry," she says.

Night was falling in New York. The conversation with this remarkable lady, who
made her first film in 1917, made theatre history with the Civic Repertory in the 1920s

The Goat Song: **Director Jacob Ben-Ami (left) rehearses his cast: (seated) Edward G. Robinson, Albert Bruning, Blanche Yurka, Lynn Fontanne, Helen Westley and Herbert Yost; (standing) George Gaul, Dwight Frye and Alfred Lunt.**

and 1930s, acted in dozens of movies and TV shows (including *Twilight Zone*'s "I Sing the Body Electric" in 1962) ended. Josephine Hutchinson sensitively reviewed what she has said about her unusual co-star of seven decades ago:

> At the time, I really didn't like Dwight—I couldn't.
> He was such a dedicated actor—a "Method" actor.
> I didn't think of him in that term at that time; but
> that sums him up, without being hurtful, and also
> very truthful. A "Method" actor—and a wonder-
> ful actor.

The prestigious Theatre Guild beckoned. On January 25, 1926, Dwight opened at the Guild Theatre as Mirko in *The Goat Song*. The mystical play, set in the Serbian farm land of a century or more ago, was by Austria's Franz Werfel. Alexander Woollcott wrote:

> ...It is a tale spun from the legend of a monster,
> half goat, half man, born in a great house in that
> troubled countryside—a hideous shame hidden

The Goat Song: **Stanja (Lynn Fontanne) is not impressed with her weak-willed husband-to-be, Mirko Milic (Dwight Frye).**

from the eyes of the world but escaping at last...
The Monster is the hovering presence which
makes the play creepy... a thing brooding horribly
over the play, but unseen save for one monstrous
shadow thrown athwart the sun, unheard save for
one dreadful cry out of the shadows, as mighty and
as destroying a sound as ever I heard issue from
human throat.

It was a very prestigious cast: Edward G. Robinson as a Jewish peddler; George Gaul and Blanche Yurka as the monster's shamed parents, who hide the freak in a stone stable; Helen Westley as the beast's nurse and keeper; and Alfred Lunt and Lynn Fontanne (destined to be the "first couple" of the American theatre) in the romantic leads. Also featured in *The Goat Song*: Frank Reicher, who would play Captain Englehorn in *King Kong* and *Son of Kong*; and Zita Johann, who would portray Karloff's long-lost "Anck-es-en-amon" in *The Mummy*.

Finally, there was Dwight Frye as Mirko—the monster's brother. Mirko is in unrequited love with Stanja (Fontanne), losing her to a wandering scholar, Juvan (Lunt). The climax found a riot and revolution, the monster enshrined by the rebels in a temple, Mirko impaled by the sword of a guard while trying to retaliate at Juvan, the monster perishing in a forest fire, Juvan taken off to execution, the hangman carting away the monster's body to exhibit for pennies—and Stanja, having been ravaged by the monster, carrying its child.

All in all, it was a grim, avant-garde affair! Jacob Ben-Ami directed, complete with deafening mob scenes and magnificent sets and costumes by Lee Simonson. Woollcott saluted the Theatre Guild for "blandly biting off more than ever before they tried to chew," and reported "...there is much help brought by such unfailing players as Dwight Frye and Edward G. Robinson." And, as Stark Young wrote in *The Republic*:

> Mr. Dwight Frye, as Mirko, the youth who has grown up in the sordid shadow of his parents' secret shame and who is now tormented with an unrequited love for the girl betrothed to him, gives what is, as acting, the most intact and complete performance in the play.

The Goat Song ran 58 performances.

Dwight immediately followed at the Guild as "A Student" (and a very melancholy one) in the Theatre Guild's *The Chief Thing*, which premiered March 22, 1926. The Russian play, by Nikolai Evreinov, also featured *The Goat Song*'s Edward G. Robinson and Helen Westley, as well as Henry Travers (later cast in James Whale's 1933 *The Invisible Man*, and best remembered as Clarence the Angel in Frank Capra's 1946 *It's a Wonderful Life*); and Estelle Winwood (whose fantasy credits would include 1962's *The Magic Sword*). Future esteemed directors/drama coaches/Group Theatre founders Lee Strasberg and Harold Clurman were also in the play.

The Chief Thing (which, incidentally, according to the play, was "to create the illusion of happiness") found Dwight's Student falling in love with Estelle Winwood's dancer, and saying to her:

> You? Why, you gave me wings. Yes, yes. Don't laugh. You—I can't explain it to you, Aniuta, but you are one of the reasons for my "will to live"... and to live means to fight. It means to stand up and fight for yourself, for your dear ones, and for justice...

The Chief Thing: **Fedya the Student (Dwight Frye) shares his studies with Aniuta (Estelle Winwood), the dancer working as a rooming house servant.**

The Chief Thing ran 40 performances. Stark Young, in his review in *The Republic*, gave a prophetic warning about Dwight Frye's future:

> Mr. Dwight Frye is set to the same purposes as in *Goat Song*, a suppressed, unhappy youth, this time a student who under the strain of keeping his brother's death a secret from his old father, has tried to kill himself. He gives a good performance, well calculated, well projected, with a good sense of theatrical values, the timing, the inner pressure. But it will be a mistake to keep so promising an actor

in the narrow if intense rut of such roles. Mr. Frye can play comedy and farce admirably and has many qualities of pathos already demonstrated.

Dwight Frye on his role of Dr. Pointell Jones in *The Devil in the Cheese* (1926) noted:

> Mr. (Charles) Hopkins was the first person in two years to call me a comedian, and when he said, "I think he's funny," I was overjoyed. I've been having the time of my life playing the role of this eager but inept fellow that never gets anywhere, never quite says anything. No one wants him to marry the girl, though no one dislikes him. They merely find him amusingly ridiculous.

In *The Devil in the Cheese*, Dwight Frye not only romped through comedy; he also met a gorilla, the Egyptian god Min—and Bela Lugosi.

The play was "a fantastic comedy" by Tom Cushing, which premiered December 29, 1926, at the producer's self-named Charles Hopkins Theatre. The mad premise: Mr. Quigley (Robert McWade), American tinned-foods manufacturer/ amateur archaeologist, takes his beautiful daughter, Goldina (Linda Watkins, described by critic Gilbert W. Gabriel as "a pretty composite of six or seven of your favorite ingenues of stage and screen") far off to a 12th century monastery—"high on a precipitous mountain-top" (a wondrous Norman Bel Geddes set). There, Goldina is to make up her mind about the man she will marry: her choice, Jimmie, the dashing steward on the ship (Fredric March); or the father's choice, Dr. Pointell Jones (Dwight)—a bespectacled, goateed nerd (described by critic John Anderson as "a lifeless physician who is by way of becoming a youthful antique"). Pointell has come along on the adventure, to tend to Mr. Quigley's heart (and try to win Goldina's).

After Jimmie amazingly arrives at the monastery by falling from a plane, Mr. Quigley—a cheese fanatic—eats some mummified, 2,000-year old cheese. Presto!—the god Min (Brandon Peters) appears from an Egyptian vase, promising to grant him any wish. Quigley asks to see inside his daughter's head.

He gets his wish—and sees the "virginal imaginations" of his daughter. All present Jimmie as a dashing, swashbuckling hero, vanquishing cannibals in the South Seas, and becoming President of the United States. Pointell, meanwhile, is in her imaginings too—as a fat, bald, totally ridiculous fool! After the dream ends and "real-life" returns, Jimmie truly becomes a hero, saving all from the wicked hands of the Greek bandit chief (who has masqueraded as "Fr. Petros")—Bela Lugosi.

As Dr. Pointell Jones, Dwight was the "butt" of much of the play's humor. He made his entrance in the play in the net/basket, brought to the mountaintop along with Goldina, Quigley and Mrs. Quigley—the last on top of him. ("Don't bother! I can stand it!" the nebbish informs his oppressor.) There are lines like the following:

The Devil in the Cheese: Mr. Quigley (Robert McWade) watches the anxious reaction of Dr. Pointell Jones (Dwight Frye) to the make-shift mountain "bed." Mrs. Quigley (Catherine Calhoun Doucet) questions the doctor's mettle.

> Over here studying strange diseases! Not thir-
> ty—yet he's made his mark! Money—and brains!
> He's got brains!
> Mrs. Quigley: Your father says he's had a terrible
> disease named after him.
> Goldina: I can see why!
> Quigley: The cure—not the disease—was named
> after him...!

Later in the shipwreck episode, Fredric March's Jimmie and Linda Watkins' Goldina name a monkey (who later grows into a gorilla) "Pointell." And Dwight won one of the biggest laughs in the play when he made his entrance in Goldina's fantasy, as her husband's opponent for President of the United States:

> Pointell Jones enters. Goldina rises. He is an
> older and more sinister version of himself. His
> face is pasty white. There are dark lines under

The Devil in the Cheese: **Dwight Frye (far left); Bela Lugosi addresses the captured Fredric March.**

> his eyes. He looks dissolute and unhealthy. He
> is round-shouldered and has a bald head and
> a stomach...

It was Dwight's second Broadway play with Fredric March, his co-star from 1925's *Puppets*, who played the dashing hero, Jimmie. And it was Dwight's first professional meeting with Bela Lugosi. After a great career on the classical stage in Hungary (as well as roles in Hungarian and German films), political refugee Lugosi had made his New York debut as Fernando, the sexy Spanish Apache dancer in *The Red Poppy* (1922), followed by a sheik in *Arabesque* (1925) and an exotic lover in *Open House* (1925-1926) — each play a failure. In *The Devil in the Cheese*, his first Broadway hit, Lugosi played the flamboyant role of Fr. Petros — a bearded monk, who reveals himself in Act III to be the wicked Kardos, the mountain bandit, attired in new costume of kilt, tights and fez.

"Unless you pay the ransom," vowed Lugosi (the Hungarian had learned his English lines phonetically), " — each one of you goes over the precipice!"

Come the end of the play, March's Jimmie heroically subdues Lugosi's Petros with a revolver — and the family descends in the net, along with Dwight's Pointell, and with Lugosi's Kardos, whom they take along to make sure the other bandits don't cut the net.

"I spit at you all!" vowed Lugosi's villain. (Critic Percy Hammond wrote in his review of *The Devil in the Cheese*, "...a foreigner, Bela Lugosi, impersonates a Greek brigand, masked under the habit of a monk, better than I have ever seen a character of the kind portrayed.")

The Devil in the Cheese filled the 299-seat Charles Hopkins Theatre, eventually moving to the Plymouth Theatre to accommodate the crowds. It proved one of the biggest Broadway hits of Dwight Frye's career, running 165 performances. As John Anderson wrote:

> Mr. Frye has a larkish time of turning his slender
> summers into the bald and corpulent forties, and
> did so with shrewd satirical effect.

After its run, Lugosi won the title role in *Dracula*, which opened October 5, 1927 at the Fulton Theatre. Frank Vreeland could not have known that Lugosi and Frye would cross paths again at Universal City, California, four years later for *Dracula*, when he filed his review of *The Devil in the Cheese*:

> All of this might have been more happily borne if,
> with the exception of the deft Dwight Frye and the
> swaggering Bela Lugosi, the play had been more
> appropriately cast...

Dwight Frye acted constantly. On August 11, 1927, he starred at the Stamford Theatre, Stamford, Connecticut in *Dumb Luck*. Advertised with the teaser lines, "One Jump Ahead of the Sheriff" and "The 'Flying Fool' of Comedies," *Dumb Luck* featured, as its leading lady, Laurette Bullivant—actually Dwight's Spokane girl friend, Laura Bullivant, who had adopted "Laurette" as a stage name. *Dumb Luck* never reached Broadway.

Ink played Broadway, but briefly; the satirical newspaper melodrama premiered at the Biltmore Theatre November 1, 1927, with Dwight as Clarence Jerome, a priggish, sanctimonious publisher's son (described by critic E. W. Osborn as an "all-around boob"). *Ink* also featured William Harrigan (later the traitorous Kemp in *The Invisible Man*) and Clara Blandick (later Auntie Em in 1939's *The Wizard of Oz*). It flopped, lasting only 15 performances as it provided Dwight his poorest and worst-reviewed Broadway role. New York audiences that fall were much more interested in such movies as DeMille's *King of Kings*, and Warner Bros.' "talkie," *The Jazz Singer*—as well as such plays as Lugosi's *Dracula*.

Far more successful for Dwight was *The Queen's Husband*, by Robert E. Sherwood (a three-time Pulitzer Prize winner for drama). The comedy (based loosely on the exploits of Queen Marie of Rumania) had its opening night at the Playhouse Theatre January 25, 1928, and ran 125 performances. Roland Young played King Eric, Katherine Alexander was Princess Anne and Dwight played the "unspeakably supercilious" Prince William in wispy mustache and snow-white uniform. Dwight's Prince was supposed to be betrothed to Miss Alexander's Princess—and was as turned off by the idea as she was:

The Queen's Husband: (front): Reginald Barlow, Gladys Hanson, Dwight Frye, Katherine Alexander, Roland Young, (back): Gyles Isham, Helen Cromwell, Marguerite Taylor, William Boren.

> Prince: As I've already hinted—I don't like you. You are almost the opposite of appealing to me. For some reason, your rather glacial charms have failed to stimulate me in the slightest. The prospect of a honeymoon with you leaves me cold and shivering.
>
> Anne: This marriage should be a jolly experience for us both.

"...Mr. Dwight Frye," reported critic Leonard Hall, "who played the lisping princelet for whom the royal marriage had been arranged, positively mowed down the clients."

———

Charles and Ella Frye (they had now adopted the "e," too) had followed their son's success; now they moved to New York City, where Charles took a job as a conductor with the New York Central Railroad. Father, mother and son all shared quarters at 44 West 96th Street. But Dwight wouldn't be with his parents long; he was about to get married.

Dan Cupid announces
the appearance in his own theatre of
Miss Laurette Bullivant
(Courtesy of Dr. and Mrs. James Bullivant)
and
Mr. Dwight Frye
(by arrangement with Mr. and Mrs. Charles Frye)
Co-Starring in
"Engaged"
(written by Eros)
to be followed in the near future by their own version of
"Married"
(Wedding March by Mendelssohn)
Immune from criticism
—Engagement announcement for Dwight Frye and Laurette Bullivant, 1928.

The engagement notice went out during the run of *The Queen's Husband*. The esteem Dwight enjoyed on Broadway can be evidenced by those who honored him with engagement dinners: John Anderson (drama critic for *The New York Evening Journal*) and Mrs. Anderson; Miss Antoinette Perry (theatre producer, for whom Broadway's "Tony" Awards were later named); and Mr. and Mrs. Brock Pemberton.
Honored as well, of course, was "Laurette." As Dwight D. Frye recalls:

> My mother had had a colorful career of her own
> in vaudeville; in fact, she toured the Orient in the
> early 1920s with a vaudeville troupe, run by Julian
> Eltinge, who was the most famous female imper-
> sonator of the time. They toured China, Japan and
> the Philippines, and Hawaii, then came to New
> York. She danced and acted mostly in stock and on
> the road, although she did play Broadway's Palace
> Theatre in vaudeville.

As the couple planned their wedding, Dwight closed in *The Queen's Husband* and began a tour of *A Man's Man*, reprising his Broadway triumph of 1925. Charlotte Wynters (later Mrs. Barton MacLane) took over Josephine Hutchinson's role of Edie, while Pat O'Brien (who had replaced Robert Gleckler as the heavy in the original production) once again played the part. Dwight's reviews, again, were excellent as he played Cleveland, Detroit and Chicago.

Wednesday, August 1, 1928.
The Church of the Transfiguration, located on 29th Street near 5th Avenue, was known as "The Actors' Church." Its more popular nickname was "The Little Church Around the Corner"; the sobriquet had come in 1870, when a man named George Holland had been refused burial from a neighboring church due to his being an actor.

Honeymooning in Bermuda, Dwight and Laura visit the old home of Irish poet Tom Moore. "Very thrilling to us," noted Laura on the back of the snapshot.

The mourners had been told that they had better try for a funeral at "the little church around the corner."

It was at the Little Church Around the Corner that 29-year-old Dwight Iliff Frye wed Laura Mae Bullivant (only two-and-a-half months younger than her husband). They honeymooned in Bermuda, and upon their return, moved into Laura's apartment at 166 West 72nd Street.

> Many years later, my mother showed me that building; she said she used to stand in her window, looking diagonally across to 73rd Street at the Ansonia, the luxurious hotel. I remember her saying

Dwight Frye sports a Roaring '20s bathing suit on his Bermuda honeymoon. "We swam here almost every afternoon," Laura wrote on the back of this photo.

she dreamed of living in the Ansonia at some point;
she never did.

       —Dwight D. Frye

The newlyweds were happy. As Dwight fancifully wrote in an article for *The Spokesman-Review:*

> We knew Cupid was right. We took him at his word. Then fate, with a grin, said: "I knew it would be this way. Forgive me for trying to test you."
> Then we slapped fate's face. And there you are!
> And here we are—insanely happy—I am I know. Wait! I'll ask the young lady! She says yes, she is, too.

It was a happy marriage, and would prove a lasting one, despite many challenges.

> As a personality, my dad was fiery—he had a very hot temper, which he displayed every once

in a while. My mother was very lively, bright and happy; acting was not something she lived and died for, but she understood my father's drive.

—Dwight D. Frye

September 10, 1928: Dwight, back from his Bermuda honeymoon, opened with the Albee Players of Providence, Rhode Island, in George M. Cohan's seven-act epic melodrama, *Yellow*. The title referred to Dwight's role: Val Parker, a villain who betrays and degrades the heroine—who exacts her revenge. One Providence critic likened Dwight's performance to "a cornered rat"; another remarked on how perfectly still the audience was during the powerful melodrama.

Meanwhile, back in New York, Dwight, Laura and his mother Ella joined in a new enterprise: they established their own "Tea Room," at 44 West 69th Street, just off Central Park. The Tea Room attracted a theatrical clientele, as well as many stockbrokers.

Finally, October of the very eventful 1928 saw the release of (possibly) Dwight Frye's first film (not counting those he might have made for O. D. Woodward in Denver). The late movie historian William K. Everson had reported sighting Dwight in a wedding crowd scene in the New York-filmed *The Night Bird*, released by Universal Pictures.

After months of effort and several postponements, Mr. Belasco brought Lenore Ulric to his theatre last night in his own adaptation of Molnar's *Mima*, an enormous and amazing spectacle, representing the interior of Hell, which probably created a vest pocket version of that place in the Belasco pocketbook.

Sheet metal, bolts, boilers, trestles and gadgets are piled up in the clangorous foundry and general office equipment of damnation and the eternal bonfires. Satan and his horned retinue sit in the first row of the orchestra seats and witness with the audience the operations of an elaborate machine guaranteed by its devilish inventor to reduce in one hour the purest man on earth to a creature so infamous that the very rats of hell won't associate with him...

—John Anderson, in his *New York Evening Journal* review of *Mima* (1928).

December 12, 1928: Dwight Frye opened as "Alfons the Spider" in David Belasco's legendary *Mima*—a show prophetic of Dwight's Hollywood career.

Mima: **Janos (Sidney Blackmer) must contend with the Magister's manikins, Mima (Lenore Ulric) and Alfons (Dwight Frye).**

Based on Ferenc Molnar's *The Red Mill*, this mad, $325,000 sex/sin/Christian morality spectacle delivered this diabolic premise: Magister, Hell's great inventor, invites "His Satanic Majesty" and his court to behold his creation, Mima, a synthetic she-devil.

"...beauty embodied, sin incarnate," exults Magister. "What a woman!"

Backing up this manikin temptress and her two hearts ("one madly loving, one cold and cunning") is Hell's monstrous Red Mill, capable of corrupting any human being within an hour (and filling the Belasco Theatre, which was remodeled to accommodate it). The target is Janos, the forester, and the world's most moral man. Mima goes after him, body and soul, and each time he commits a sin, a bell tolls ominously

Mima: **The sardonic Alfons tests the human guinea pig, Janos, who is accompanied by the temptress Mima.**

in the Belasco Theatre. Come the climax, Janos forgives Mima, rather than killing her (which was Magister's plan). Christian virtue triumphs and, as church bells ring, a trumpet sounds and an organ peals, the satanic mill explodes, burns and apocalyptically collapses before the audience. Janos returns to his wife; Mima dies heartbroken and weeping:

> O mortal man! What did he do to my two hearts?
> How they ache... Janos...

And she collapses, "like a toy broken to pieces," into the arms of Magister—who sobs.

"...legendary playwright, producer, actor, director, stage manager, theatre owner, impresario, megalomaniac, lecher, hypocrite and, most lately, ghost," was how *The New York Times* described David Belasco in a 1995 feature, which covered the rumor that his spirit still haunts his theatre. Known as the "Bishop of Broadway" with his tousled white hair, trademark costume of black suit and white clerical collar, and a face Ben Hecht described as "borrowed from a thousand actors, mystic and foolish," the 74-year-old producer spent prodigally on his plays—and in his personal life. When his young daughter Augusta had tragically died, Belasco not only provided a beautiful temple-style mausoleum in Linden Hill Cemetery, Brooklyn: he kept a light burning in the tomb, and even hired a guard to stay at the grave all night—since his little daughter had been afraid of the dark.

Claiming *Mima* to be his 119th New York production, Belasco proved hell-bent on publicity. Playing Mima, and adorned in dazzling costumes and various wigs, was Lenore Ulric, a sexpot dramatic actress and Silent Screen vamp with a passionate following. The raven-haired, dark-eyed Miss Ulric had starred for Belasco in plays with titles like *Tiger Rose*, *The Harem*, *Kiki* and (most notoriously) *Lulu Belle*. (Rumor insisted that Belasco peered at her in her dressing room from a peep hole.) Ulric was a spectacle herself as Mima:

> ...I'll scamper before you in a spring garden of
> Damascus roses—blown and tossed about like
> flowers—dancing, laughing, loving, with noth-
> ing to cover me but my hair and a mantle of
> moonlight.

Much to the delight of Belasco's publicity department, Miss Ulric was delivering this dialogue to Sidney Blackmer—her real-life fiance. (They reportedly married secretly in May of 1929.) Belasco claimed to have spent three years handpicking his *Mima* cast; prominent in it was Dwight Frye as a satanic manikin named "Alfons the Spider," whom Magister (A. E. Anson) describes as "A boudoir pet...loves married women." Elegant in top hat and cape, described by Mima as "my very best friend... evil, clever, sly, cool, unprincipled and good-looking," Dwight served the "Supreme Siren" as partner-in-crime, sometimes lover, and pimp.

"Every time you kiss my hand," says Mima to Alfons, "you bite me."

The part of Alfons the Spider was showy, allowing for menace, comedy and this exchange with Mima:

> Mima: And once I was rid of Janos, you could be
> my lover, Alfons, couldn't you?
> Alfons: As I have always been.
> Mima: That's true... What I liked most about you
> was that I could always kick you out for some other
> man. Kiss me, my true love.

At which time, Dwight got a kiss from Broadway's most alluring vamp.

Few shows ever created such "hype." Belasco featured a scene in which imps stripped Miss Ulric (including her stockings) and dressed her as a bride; there was a big tango number, performed by "The Dancers of the Damned" (featuring "beautiful women of vampire types dancing with dissolute men"). Come opening night, Wednesday, December 12, 1928, *Mima*'s first night audience (including Mayor Jimmy Walker) was in its seats at the Belasco Theatre, on time at 8:20, awaiting a production whose cast, musicians and "stupendous" set had tallied an incredible 1928 cost of over $325,000.

The morning after, Walter Winchell delivered this verdict—titling his column "Deviled Ham":

> ...No more spectacular or pretentious theatrical production has ever been so magnificently and courageously chanced on the local stage by Mr. Belasco nor by any of his contemporaries, but *Mima* for the greater part of the proceedings is an empty and uneventful entertainment.

Burns Mantle, noted New York critic, published this judgment:

> There are batteries of lights and sputtering dynamos in every conceivable corner of the place. Actors make their entrances and exits from both aisles, from the heavens above and the basements below the stage. The devil himself in person, accompanied by all his blackwhiskered and goat-horned court, occupies a throne seat just in front of row A. There are gridirons and hydraulic elevators all over the place, and more actors than can find floor space to act in.
>
> And the pity of it is that Sir David has probably wasted the fortune he has so grandly risked because the Molnar allegory he has staged to go with his scenery is worth no more than the electric power it took to blow it to hell.

Mima was a sensation, despite the generally negative reviews. As John Anderson captured its macabre appeal in his *New York Evening Journal* review:

> ...Dwarfs, hell-rats, monkey imps and gentlemen-devils performed elaborate ballets and rituals... Dwight Frye, reduced to a wraith by arduous rehearsals which are said to have sent nearly everybody except the indomitable Belasco to the very edge of a breakdown, performed an impeccable blackguard impeccably, but the altogether

Andre Dumont, Sidney Blackmer, Lenore Ulric and Dwight Frye in a scene from Belasco's *Mima.*

astonishing and varied performance of the evening was given by Miss Ulric... a performance which I imagine, would make even the Devil sit up and take notice...

In the Armageddon finale, Dwight's Alfons received a juicy comeuppance. As the Red Mill exploded, the devils hissed and the trumpets blared, he begged of the hero (the stage directions included):

Janos, Janos. I didn't want to murder you—I wanted to be your friend; I couldn't because he (meaning Magister) made me with no heart. (In deepest sorrow) Oh dear. I've no heart. Oh, where can I get a heart?
(Looks wildly about for a heart)

Mima lasted 180 performances—the longest-running show of any Dwight Frye play on Broadway. However, its titanic expense impoverished Belasco; he could not recoup its cost. After staging a few more shows, David Belasco died May 14, 1931. His theatre survives.

What about "Mima" and "Janos"? After *Mima*, Lenore Ulric would star in two 1929 "talkies" for Fox, *Frozen Justice* and *South Sea Rose*. She left Belasco's management after the failure of *Mima*, and had a Broadway hit in *Pagan Lady* (1930), but her career strangely nose-dived with a series of flops (including 1931's *The Social Register*, with Blackmer). She was fun as the high-kicking courtesan Olympe, rival to Garbo's *Camille* (MGM, 1937); in 1933, she and Blackmer divorced, and she said:

> I don't think I'm comfortable to live with. I have a temper. I'm difficult. I'm too quick and too impulsive. And men have a right to be comfortable.

She played Broadway in Ernest Hemingway's *The Fifth Column* (1940); acted in a few films, such as *Temptation* (Universal, 1946); made her final Broadway appearance as Charmian in *Antony and Cleopatra* (1947). The once-sensational stage star dropped out of sight and spent the final years of her life at New York's Rockland State Hospital—which had a grim notoriety for its housing of the violently insane. Lenore Ulric died there December 30, 1970.

Her ex-husband and *Mima* co-star fared much better; Sidney Blackmer acted in many films (often as a slick villain, such as "Big Boy" in Warner's 1930 *Little Caesar*), played Teddy Roosevelt several times and scored a special Broadway triumph as "Doc" in William Inge's *Come Back, Little Sheba* (1950), for which he won a Tony Award. In 1942 he married Suzanne Kaaren (leading lady in Lugosi's *The Devil Bat*), and had two sons; among the many honors listed in his *Who's Who in the Theatre* was a 1950 National Father-of-the-Year award. Ironically, the last major role for the hero of *Mima* was as the old warlock in *Rosemary's Baby* (1968). Sidney Blackmer died of cancer in New York City October 5, 1973.

And, as for Belasco's ghost... True Broadway aficionados claim that, when *Oh! Calcutta!* moved into the Belasco in 1971 (from the downtown Eden Theatre), the "nude musical" reportedly scared off the ghost, exorcising the theatre of his presence forever. In July 1995, while Ralph Fiennes was starring as *Hamlet* at the Belasco, several actors in the cast decided to seek the spirit of "the Bishop of Broadway." As Adam Green reported in *The New York Times*, the actors, armed with flashlights, ascended above the theatre, and penetrated Belasco's long boarded-up "Xanadu-like apartment," with its Tiffany skylight, "cathedral-like" living room (with 30 foot ceiling), giant tiled fireplace, Flemish oak balcony...

The only thing they found was a frightened pigeon.

While *Mima* was still playing, Laura Bullivant (who kept the stage name of "Laurette") made her Broadway acting debut in the role of Mary Sutton in *Congratulations*. The play, which starred Henry Hull, opened at the National Theatre April 30, 1929, and lasted 39 performances.

In the week of July 22, 1929, Dwight returned once more to the Colonial Players of Pittsfield, Massachusetts, for a guest engagement in *Rip Van Winkle*. Donald Meek (the bald, diminutive character player, later in such Hollywood classics as 1939's *Stagecoach*) played the title role; Dwight shared star billing with him in the role of Derrick.

It all seemed idyllic—the Broadway work, the critical praise, the tearoom... And then came the stock market crash.

> The 1920s had been a high-flying time for a lot of people, my mother and father included, but the Crash of October, 1929 brought all that to an end. Many of the tearoom customers were stockbrokers, so those customers disappeared, and the tearoom closed.
>
> Fortunately, the Crash happened to coincide with the maturity of talking pictures. People out in Hollywood freaked out, because they had silent film stars like John Gilbert, whose voice turned out to be very high and unmasculine; they had characters like that girl Jean Hagen played in *Singin' in the Rain*. So they came to New York to find actors who could speak the language properly, and transported a whole lot of them to California—and that's how my dad got there.
>
> —Dwight D. Frye

There, Fate was awaiting Dwight Frye—and plotting what would seem to be a cruel, mocking trick on his life and career.

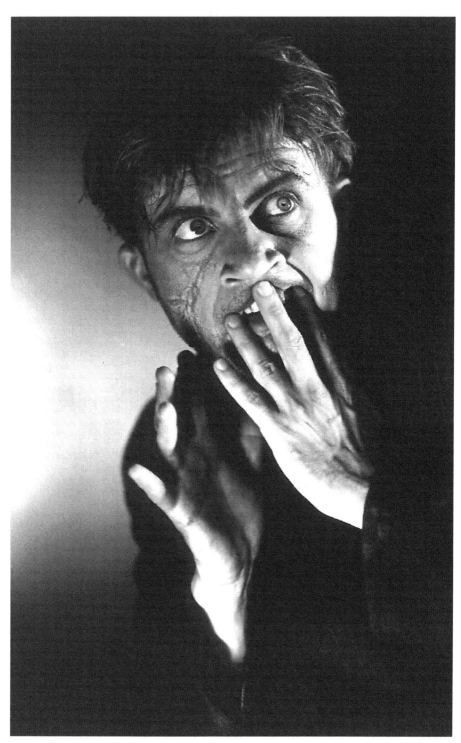

Dwight Frye as Fritz from _Frankenstein_, 1931.

Dwight Frye's Last Laugh

Chapter Five
Dreams to Nightmares
The Horror Classics of 1931

Renfield's face is staring out, his hands flattened against the storm-swept pane—he is moving from side to side, like an animal in a cage—his shirt is open at the throat, his hair disheveled, and he is screaming and laughing and gesticulating, a stark, raving maniac.
> —from the *Dracula* shooting script, September 26, 1930

Raging, yet full of terror, the Monster retreats, snarling. Dwarf rises—a venomous light in his eyes—quickly picks up the whip, again striking at the Monster... The Dwarf seizes the torch, lunges at the Monster...
> —from the *Frankenstein* shooting script, August 12, 1931

1929.

The Hollywoodland sign, atop Mount Lee, was six years old, its 50-foot-high letters aglow at night with 4,000 light bulbs.

It was the tail end of the Babylonian, champagne-out-of-high heel Roaring '20s era in Hollywood; a time of transition to talkies—and a time of much terror. Valentino was dead. Fatty Arbuckle was devastated by scandal. John Gilbert, once the screen's great lover, was bitterly cloistered in his Tower Grove mansion high in Beverly Hills, figuratively castrated by sound; women laughed at his voice in *His Glorious Night*. Greta Garbo and Lon Chaney had yet to make their own talkie debuts—the final two superstar holdouts from the silents.

Full of dreams, Dwight brought Laura to Hollywood, "on spec," gambling for success in the movies. They lived below the stucco castles that loomed in the hills, the palm trees, and what Elsa Lanchester later described as a "navy blue" California sky. They enjoyed driving to the beaches in their 1928 Buick and swimming in the Pacific. Dwight was quick to join the Christian Science Church in Hollywood.

And, at the neighboring Grauman's Chinese Theatre, they beheld that bizarre ritual known as the Hollywood premiere. For example, there would be the May 27,

The Doorway to Hell: **As Morton (Eddie Kane) observes, Monk (Dwight Frye) machine guns a "double-crosser."**

1930, premiere of Howard Hughes' *Hell's Angels*, the searchlights streaking the skies, the film's "platinum blonde" star Jean Harlow speaking at the courtyard microphone, 50,000 fans mobbing the cars of Charlie Chaplin and Gloria Swanson and Buster Keaton as the National Guard rushed in to control the crowds and an actual fighter squadron (hired by Hughes to promote this epic) flying above Hollywood Boulevard.

These bizarre spectacles, part Barnum and Bailey, part Roman Coliseum, could be terrifying, especially for the stars. MGM's Garbo, for example, had a stand-in named Jeraldine Dvorak who, among other duties, eventually pretended to be Garbo at Hollywood premieres. Miss Dvorak would later claim her own tiny piece of movie celebrity: she would play the tall, blonde vampire bride (creeping between the two brunettes) in the Transylvania castle of *Dracula*.

A religious man, Dwight Frye was cautious about Hollywood life. Yet it was very exciting; a number of names who had been totally unknown to movie fans in 1929 would become stars by the end of 1930: Miss Harlow, Clark Gable, James Cagney. And Dwight Frye, with his magnificent Broadway reviews, his proven versatility, his deep love for acting, believed he had as much chance as the next fellow to claim his fame in Hollywood—not as a matinee idol, certainly, but as a novel character actor.

He decided to make his entrance in the movie capital the best way he knew how: via the stage.

Based on the infamous Leopold-Loeb murder case, *Rope's End* was by British author Patrick Hamilton, who would also create the classic thriller *Gaslight*. The premise: two wicked intellectuals kill a school chum, then invite various relatives and friends of the deceased to dinner in their home — serving the meal on a chest in which the body is hidden. One of the guests, an eccentric poet, reveals what the murderers vainly believed was the perfect crime.[7]

In the Fall of 1929, *Rope's End* opened at Hollywood's Vine Street Theatre. Critic Doris Denbo reported:

> This is quite the finest thing the Vine Street has seen in over a year... Dwight Frye as the fear crazed, weaker member of the pair, has a most difficult role to play and rises to great dramatic heights during the unfolding of the weird plot...

Rope's End was a hit and a personal triumph for Dwight; however, even at this early point, he seemed to have a fear of typecasting. As if he could see *Dracula* and *Frankenstein* on the Hollywood horizon, he spoke out to the Los Angeles press the day after the *Rope's End* premiere:

> ...I am a character man. There seems to be an impression I do one type of thing. I don't and I haven't. One of my first successes was in comedy. I played the lead opposite Queenie Smith in *Sitting Pretty*... That was low comedy. I did a season in *The Devil in the Cheese* and in *The Queen's Husband*. Last year I appeared opposite Miss Lenore Ulric in David Belasco's *Mima*.
>
> I don't like specialization. I have no interest in anything but character work, and I have made it a point to vary my roles as much as possible.

Rope's End ran for six weeks in Los Angeles, and also played an engagement in San Francisco.

Dwight followed with a revival of his great Broadway success *A Man's Man*, which opened at Los Angeles' Figueroa Theatre, June 5, 1930.

He hoped — and prayed — that Hollywood would take heed of his notices and award him worthy movie roles.

Movies did beckon, eventually, and Dwight made his Hollywood film debut in *The Doorway to Hell*, which Warner Bros. released October 18, 1930. "The Motion Picture Gangdom Dared Hollywood to Make!" read the advertisements. Lew Ayres was a bootlegger, trying to go straight; playing his chief lieutenant (in his second film) was

Man to Man: **Emily Saunders (Lucille Powers) voices her suspicions about Vint Glade (Dwight Frye) as members of the cast look on. [Donald Maurer collection]**

James Cagney. Dwight Frye's role: "Monk," a gangster, who exits a pool hall carrying a tommy gun in a violin case.

"I'm going out to teach a guy a lesson," he sneers.

After leaving the pool hall, "Monk" enters a car, in which he assembles a tommy gun with ruthless efficiency. Then he guns down a fellow gang member who is believed to be an informer.

Things looked up as Dwight landed a juicy role in *Man to Man*, also for Warners, released December 6, 1930. Dwight played Vint Glade, a Kentucky bank clerk, in unrequited love with Emily (Lucille Powers). Confessing to stealing $2,000, he acts a richly dramatic breakdown scene, complete with tears and a Dixie ("Ah" for "I") accent:

> Yes, Ah stole the money! Ah stole it!... Ah was in
> love with Emily. Ah was afraid Mike would get
> her—she liked him better than she did me. Oh,
> Ah didn't want the money—Ah loved her! Please,
> please don't arrest me! Don't arrest me, please!

There was new reason to hope for Dwight's success in the movies: Laura was expecting a baby.

Universal, meanwhile, was "expecting" *Dracula.*

> "Among the rugged peaks that frown down upon
> the Borgo Pass, are found crumbling castles of a
> bygone age—"
> —the opening line of *Dracula* (Universal,
> 1931), spoken in the coach by the secretary (Carla
> Laemmle)

Carl Laemmle, Jr., the "baby mogul," who had received the job of general manager of Universal Studios, California, as a 21st birthday present from his father in 1929, loved horror movies. Indeed, his life eventually became one: ousted from his job in 1936, suffering from hypochondria, never producing another movie, living out his life a crippled recluse, he became perhaps the most colossal has-been of Hollywood history. He died on September 24, 1979—the 40th anniversary of the death of Carl Laemmle, Sr., his mercilessly domineering father, with whom he's entombed in the Laemmle mausoleum at Home of Peace Cemetery in Los Angeles. His life was a bizarre Hollywood tragedy.

In 1930, however, "Junior" was a power figure. The "crown prince" of Universal reigned (erratically) over his 230-acre "City of Enchantment," with its giant soundstages; the back lot spread into the mountain foothills with such cinema landmarks as the cathedral from *The Hunchback of Notre Dame,* the casino from *Foolish Wives* and the wild west town. Junior had produced *All Quiet on the Western Front* (despite the protests of his dad). It would win Universal glory, prestige and—on November 5, 1930—the Academy Award for Best Picture.

As *All Quiet...* reaped international praise, Junior, proud of the fact that Lon Chaney's Notre Dame Hunchback and Opera Phantom had lurked on Universal's hallowed grounds, sought a horror production. His choice: *Dracula.*

Studio readers had been warning Universal against *Dracula* since the summer of 1927, even before the Broadway play had opened ("Were this story out on the screen, it would be an insult to every one of its audience"... "It is blood—blood—blood..." "Absolutely No!"...). Junior was simpatico, however, with the response of one "Miss Hall," who had filed this June 15, 1927 inter-office communication:

> Beautiful women with voluptuous mouths
> dripping with blood—huge bats with flapping
> wings—wolves with hungry mouths—vaults,
> dark and ominous—dusty chapels hung with cob-
> webs—graves—ships steered by dead men—a man
> with sharp, white teeth and eyes as red as fire—a
> vampire feeding on the blood of innocent girls
> and children in order to perpetuate himself and
> his kind—a lunatic eating flies, spiders, sparrows
> in order to have devoured as many lives as pos-
> sible—all this and much, much more is contained
> in *Dracula...*

> ...It is daring but if done there can be no doubt as
> to its making money.

Junior originally envisioned Lon Chaney as Dracula; the director would be Tod Browning, "the Edgar Allan Poe of the screen," who had directed such Chaney MGM melodramas as *The Unholy Three* (1925), *London After Midnight* (1927) and *The Unknown* (1927). However, as the studio blueprinted production, "The Man of a Thousand Faces" died of throat cancer on August 26, 1930. In the wake of his death, there were plenty contesting for the role of Dracula (and Renfield) in the film Universal would promote as "The Strangest Passion the World Has Ever Known."

For a time, Ian Keith was rumored to have won the part of Dracula, over such candidates as Conrad Veidt, Paul Muni, William Courtenay and Lugosi (who also had toured widely in the role—and whom Laemmle originally had rejected in a March, 1930 telegram to his agent).

Bernard Jukes, who had created the role of Renfield in the London and Broadway productions (as well as touring the country in the part), was actively campaigning for the film role, sending out photographs of himself as the lunatic. For decades those photographs were destined to be mistaken by horror fans as photos of Dwight Frye.

If Dwight hadn't read the novel *Dracula* (which Bram Stoker had published in 1897, two years before Dwight was born), he was certainly familiar with the play. *Dracula* had opened on Broadway at the Fulton Theatre (where Dwight had enjoyed his singing and dancing role in *Sitting Pretty*) on October 5, 1927. A solid hit, the melodrama had run 265 performances (opening several weeks before Dwight had premiered in *Ink* and running a few weeks past Dwight's closing in *The Queen's Husband*). Of course, it had been a triumph for Lugosi, with whom Dwight had acted in the long run of *The Devil in the Cheese* in 1926/1927.

For *Dracula*, the final tests, the agent dealings and the 11th hour front office decisions remain shrouded in six-decades-old mystery. Of course, it was Bela Lugosi who found his bittersweet destiny by signing to recreate his role of Dracula; Dwight Frye won what many considered *Dracula*'s true plum role: Renfield.[8]

On Monday, September 29, 1930, *Dracula* began shooting on a $355,050 budget and a six-week schedule. That day, the coach rolled down the hill of Universal's back lot, delivering Dwight's Renfield to the village, just in time for Walpurgis Night; it was the baptism of the golden age of Hollywood horror.

Dracula would be a strange set: Lugosi, vaingloriously parading before a full-length mirror, roaring at his reflection, "I *am* Dracula!"; Tod Browning, lethargic, burnt-out, non-communicative; Karl Freund, the 300-lb. Bohemian cinematographer, barking directions as Browning lounged in the shadows; Edward Van Sloan, creator of the Van Helsing role on Broadway and on the national tour, wondering why Browning bypassed several of the play's most dramatic moments; and Helen Chandler ("Mina"), a blonde angelic-looking ingenue, familiar to Dwight for her many Broadway successes—sitting with David Manners ("Jonathan Harker") on the set sidelines and laughing at the whole thing. (In Helen Chandler's case, perhaps it was nervous laughter; *Dracula* is a tale of addiction—and she, in 1930, was already a "spectacularly self-destructive" alcoholic.)

Dwight Frye as Renfield meeting Bela Lugosi's Count at Borgo Pass in *Dracula*, released by Universal in 1931.

Yet a legend was born. Lugosi would literally wear his *Dracula* cape to his grave; and Dwight, like his co-star, would bring total passion to his portrayal of the fly-and-spider-gobbling Renfield—a macabre role he would play in the great Jekyll and Hyde tradition.

The Renfield of the opening of *Dracula* is a bit foppish, as he arrives Walpurgis Night in the little mountain village in Transylvania. Yet we can almost see the goose pimples rise on him as the peasants warn of Dracula and his wives—and the old peasant woman places the rosary around his neck, intoning the classic line:

"Wear this—for your mother's sake!"

Thereafter, it's fun to watch Dwight as he meets Lugosi's Count at Borgo Pass at midnight; his timorous reading of the line, "The coach to Castle Dracula?"; his eyes wide as he peers outside the coach—and sees a bat guiding the horses to the castle. Inside the ancient fortress, he becomes the audience; it is through Renfield's eyes and ears that we behold Bela's magnificent entrance on the decaying staircase, hear the howl of the wolves and listen to Bela's classic line:

"Listen to them. The children of the night! What music they make!"

Poking his way through the great spider web, Dwight's Renfield is the recipient of another timeless Lugosi line: "The spider, spinning his web for the unwary fly. The blood is the life, Mr. Renfield!"

"Why, uh... Yes!" replies Dwight.

Count Dracula discusses the lease on Carfax Abbey with Renfield (Dwight Frye).

Upstairs in the castle, by the giant fireplace, Dwight strikes a magic chemistry with Lugosi; the famous cutting of his finger on the paper clip and Bela's advance at the sight of the blood; playing straight man to Bela's famous "I never drink — wine" line. Dwight also spikes the scene with one amusingly comic reading. After Bela says, "I have chartered a ship, to take us to England. We will be leaving — tomorrow evening" — (slowly delivered, with *great* ominousness!), Dwight gives a little "take," slightly rolls his eyes and replies with fine comic timing, "Everything will be ready!"

The bat in the great arched windows... the three vampire women... Lugosi waving them away, to claim Renfield for himself...

We next see Renfield on the ship, the *Vesta* ("bound for England"); wild-eyed, grinning that toothy, savage smile; resplendently insane. And as the ship with its dead crew docks in England, we hear, for the first time, that unforgettable, four-note laugh.

"Why, he's mad!" says Tod Browning (performing the off-screen role of the Harbormaster) as Karl Freund's camera peers down the hatch at Dwight's Renfield. "Look at his eyes! Why, the man's gone crazy!"

Those big eyes were all the better to haunt audiences with; Dwight doesn't act the mad Renfield — he takes Satanic possession of him. His dementia is magnificent in his classic soliloquy as he relates his unholy pact with the Count:

> A red mist spread over the lawn, coming on like a
> flame of fire. And then he parted it. And I could

Dwight with Edward Van Sloan, who became a close personal friend.

> see that there were thousands of rats, with their eyes
> blazing red—like his, only smaller. And then he
> held up his hand, and they all stopped and I thought
> he seemed to be saying—"Rats! Rats! Rats! Thou-
> sands! *Millions* of them! All red blood! All these
> will I give you, if you will obey me...!"

Making the role all the more rich is the pathos with which Dwight imbues the
madman. His pitiful weeping in his sanitarium cell; the agony in his face as he stares

Dwight David—"Buddy"—was born December 26, 1930, prior to the release of *Dracula*.

down from the barred window at the Count who satanically controls him, begging not to have to hurt Mina ("...Master... please don't ask me to do that... not her... Please!"). It all climaxes on the great, Gothic staircase of Carfax Abbey; "I can't die with all those lives on my conscience—all that blood on my hands!" shrieks Dwight unforgettably, as the Count slays him, breaking his neck, the madman tumbling down the stairs below the vampire king and Mina.

Bela Lugosi is *Dracula*'s demon lover; Dwight Frye, the film's lost soul.

Tod Browning completed *Dracula* November 15, 1930, after 42 days of shooting. Meanwhile, by night, George Melford had been directing a Spanish version of *Dracula* on the same sets, with Carlos Villarias as Dracula, Lupita Tovar as Mina and Pablo Alvarez Rubio as Renfield. (Browning would shoot "added scenes" for his version December 13; on January 2, 1931, there were retakes in Dracula's chambers and Seward's office.)

Meanwhile, Dwight and Laura Frye had become parents. On Friday, December 26, 1930, Dwight David Frye was born in Laura's hometown of Spokane, Washington. When the baby was six weeks old, Laura brought the baby home to Hollywood, and Dwight saw and held his newborn son for the first time.

Dracula premiered at New York's Roxy Theatre Thursday, February 12, 1931. The national release date was Valentine's Day, 1931. One theatre in which *Dracula* opened that Saturday was the Alhambra, in Milwaukee. "All Attendance Records Shattered," crowed the Alhambra three days later; as the film completed its first week, the theatre advertised:

> Milwaukee Loves
> Excitement
> Banner Attendance
> Forces Us to Hold
> This Weird,
> Fascinating hit
> one more week

On Friday, March 27, 1931, *Dracula* opened at the Orpheum Theatre in Los Angeles, with the counterpoint "lively stage revue" called *World of Pleasure*. Critic Marquis Busby of the *Los Angeles Examiner* wrote:

> ...The cat has crept, the bat has whispered, and the ghost has walked, but *Dracula* would make the hair rise on a brass monkey. However, I wasn't really scared until some lady in the audience let out a piercing scream...

Busby conjectured the lady was a plant; even if she was, it was "disconcerting" to the crowd. Busby continued:

> Bela Lugosi, who created the role of Count Dracula in the play, assumes his original characterization in the picture. He is excellent as the man who has been dead for 500 years... Dwight Frye is perfect as the madman, Renfield, who has a somewhat upsetting appetite for flies and spiders. Edward Van Sloan is particularly fine... Tod Browning's direction achieves the maximum of horror and spine-tickling thrills...

Dracula proved a phenomenon, Universal's hit of the season. *Billboard* reported that Bela Lugosi was "brilliant"; that Helen Chandler and Dwight Frye were "outstanding." It would be the great role of Dwight's film career, forever transforming, for good and evil, the direction of his life; as his son says:

Count Dracula prepares to kill Renfield, who pleads not to die "with all that blood on my hands."

As far as my father being proud of his film roles, I think his favorite would have to have been *Dracula*. Certainly that film, I think, made him known in the business—he wasn't known to the public much, but he was known in the business. Renfield typecast him, but it also made people in the film industry aware of his name.

Dwight Frye's Last Laugh

The Black Camel: Jessop (Dwight Frye) the butler shows concern for Anna (Violet Dunn) the maid, with Tarneverro (Bela Lugosi) staring at Charlie Chan (Warner Oland). [Donald Maurer collection]

For all the glory Dwight would win as Renfield, it was Bela Lugosi who emerged from *Dracula* a movie star. Coming so early in Dwight's film work (his third movie), film audiences had no image other than Renfield to compare him to; he was, in their minds, the giggling fly-eater of *Dracula*. Sadly, it would be decades before Dwight Frye's Renfield fully won recognition as one of the classic portrayals of the golden age of Hollywood horror.

In the wake of *Dracula*, Dwight Frye got work. For Fox, he acted the role of Jessop, a butler who really *did* do it, in *The Black Camel* (1931), a Charlie Chan mystery. Warner Oland played Chan; Bela Lugosi had an impressive "red herring" role. Bela was paid $1,000 per week, and got to go along on the Hawaii location trip; Dwight got $500 per week (and no trip to Hawaii).

For Warner Bros., Dwight played Wilmer, the psychopathic punk taunted by Sam Spade in the 1931 *The Maltese Falcon*. Ricardo Cortez, Bebe Daniels, Dudley Digges, Otto Matieson and Dwight had the roles played to perfection in John Huston's 1941 remake by Humphrey Bogart, Mary Astor, Sydney Greenstreet, Peter Lorre and Elisha

Dwight Frye as Wilmer Cook from *The Maltese Falcon* (Warner Bros., 1931).

Cook, Jr. In some aspects, the 1931 pre-Code version is more racy than its celebrated descendant. For example, Cortez strip-searches Bebe Daniels (offscreen); and the unwholesome (and gay) relationship between Digges' "Fat Man" and Dwight's Wilmer is accented far more clearly.

Then, in June of 1931, Dwight received a callback to Universal to test for the role of Fritz, the hunchbacked dwarf in the studio's new melodrama, *Frankenstein*.

> We will each write a ghost story.
> —George Gordon, Lord Byron, summer, 1816

A wild and stormy night, June, 1816. In Villa Diodati, Italy, 18-year-old Mary Wollstonecraft Shelley was spending that "haunted summer," flanked by Percy Shelley and Lord Byron. It was there, that wicked night, in a kind of parlor game among the three as to who could tell the best ghost story, that Mary conceived the tale of *Frankenstein*, conjuring up the Monster, the monster maker...

But no Fritz.

Indeed, the hunchbacked dwarf would never enter Mary's novel, published in 1818. However, the character (or his prototype) had quickly made his entrance in an 1823 London dramatization of the tale—and here he was, in the test reel Robert Florey was adapting and directing for *Frankenstein*.

Florey shot his test on June 16 and 17, 1931. Dwight's *Dracula* confrere (and personal friend) Edward Van Sloan joined him in the test (shot on the *Dracula* set) as Dr. Waldman; so did stock players as Frankenstein and Elizabeth; and so, of course, did Bela Lugosi, himself testing for the Monster (in what Van Sloan later described as Golemesque makeup—"like something out of *Babes in Toyland*").

The test, shot over two days, was of the creation sequence. As directed and co-written by Florey (with Garrett Fort), the role of Fritz was mute. Florey, in later years, would insist the test was a triumph; others claimed it was a fiasco; Lugosi had virtually nothing to do but "come alive" in a climactic closeup that reportedly caused Junior Laemmle to explode with laughter. The legendary test (despite rumors over the years of its discovery) apparently perished—amidst Universal politics and Lugosi's temperament. "I was a star in my country" (which he was), "and I will not play a scarecrow over here!"

The project seemingly fell through. Dwight, in these Depression days, mortgaged his 1928 Buick to the Hollywood Loan Company.

Fate, once again, intervened.

Frankenstein attracted a Byronic, red and silver haired, cigar-smoking Englishman named James Whale—Universal's bitter, brilliant, homosexual "ace" director.

> I chose *Frankenstein* out of about 30 available stories because it was the strongest meat and gave me a chance to dabble in the macabre... It offered fine pictorial possibilities, had two grand characterizations, and dealt with a subject which might go anywhere—and that is part of the fun of making pictures.

After directing Tiffany's film version of *Journey's End* (1930), the WWI saga he'd staged so brilliantly in London, New York and Chicago, Whale had joined Universal. The former actor/*London Bystander* cartoonist/tango dancer had a genius for dramatizing tragic misfits—such as the tormented, alcoholic Captain Stanhope (Colin Clive) of *Journey's End*, and the pitiful streetwalker Myra (Mae Clarke) of *Waterloo Bridge*—

Frankenstein's director James Whale delighted in Dwight Frye's gift for quirky humor.

which he'd just completed as his first Universal project. Junior pampered Whale; Whale usurped *Frankenstein* — and Florey got Poe's *Murders in the Rue Morgue*, with Lugosi.

Whale revamped *Frankenstein*. For the "Modern Prometheus," he sent to England for Colin Clive, his Stanhope of *Journey's End* on the London stage and in the Hollywood film, who — like Stanhope — was a high-strung alcoholic. Whale picked Mae Clarke, his heartbreaking Myra of *Waterloo Bridge*, for leading lady Elizabeth. And he retained Van Sloan and Dwight (whose character Fritz, as revamped by Whale, was given dialogue).

Finally, Whale found (in his words) his "damned awful Monster!" — 43-year-old English émigré Boris Karloff — sipping tea in the Universal commissary. The gaunt, doe-eyed stage and screen character player gave a superb test in the Jack P. Pierce makeup, but it was a spiritual insight that made his "dear old Monster" a classic. As Boris said:

> The most heartrending aspect of the creature's life, for us, was his ultimate desertion by his creator. It was as though man, in his blundering, searching attempts to improve himself, was to find himself deserted by his God.

On Monday, August 24, 1931, Hollywood history was made when *Frankenstein* began shooting. The budget was $262,007; the shooting schedule, 30 days. Dwight, in hump, wild hair and makeup by the legendary Pierce, took his place, with Colin Clive, on the old mountain churchyard set.

There seemed to be magic in the air, that summer of 1931, below the giant mountains of Universal. James Whale made *Frankenstein* an askew morality play: Clive (described by Mae Clarke as having "the face of Christ"), a tormented, would-be God of a Frankenstein; Karloff, as his Monster, heartbreakingly revealing a soul that a Creator far greater than Frankenstein has given him. And there was Dwight Frye as Fritz, the little hunchback from Hell, whose sadistic taunting of the Monster with whip and torch unleashed the most infamous (and beloved) of Hollywood fiends.

Having devoured spiders in *Dracula*, Dwight seemed to be playing one in *Frankenstein*, as he scuttled about the graveyard and tower laboratory. Whale delighted in Dwight's gift for quirky humor; indeed, probably the most famous "sight gag" of classic horror is Frye's Fritz, hobbling up the tower steps, tucking his tiny walking stick under his arm — and bending over to pull up his sock.

"I always remember my father being grateful to 'Jimmy' Whale," says Dwight David Frye, "and often praising him."

The *Frankenstein* set was happy — if a bit tense at times. Colin Clive was a spine-chilling Frankenstein as he screamed "It's alive!" over the Monster's moving hand; in real life, he was playing Jekyll and Hyde. Fraught, chain-smoking, Clive was a tragic alcoholic; his "Jekyll" side was a shy, gentle Englishman ("the dearest, kindest man," sighed Mae Clarke, who admitted to being smitten with him), who loved animals and games; his "Hyde" could be frightening. There was worry that "Jekyll" might become "Hyde" one Hollywood night, and *Frankenstein* would never be the same. However, his slips proved minor, as Whale directed him with great sensitivity, and Clive "discovered" American coffee (an antidote for the alcohol).

Then there was Karloff. One of the most bizarre sights at Universal City was the "Monster," between scenes of *Frankenstein*, high on one of the studio hills, smoking a cigarette, playing with the lambs who grazed on the hillside — and seeking a merciful breeze.

"Dear Boris Karloff," reminisced Mae Clarke. "A pussy-cat!"

Meanwhile, between scenes of *Frankenstein*, Dwight Frye remained a spider. As on Broadway, as in *Dracula*, Dwight threw himself into the role of Fritz with a "Method" approach. In the morning, as he reported to Jack Pierce and the makeup bungalow, Dwight (as Mae remembered) was quiet, charming and might even make a joke. How-

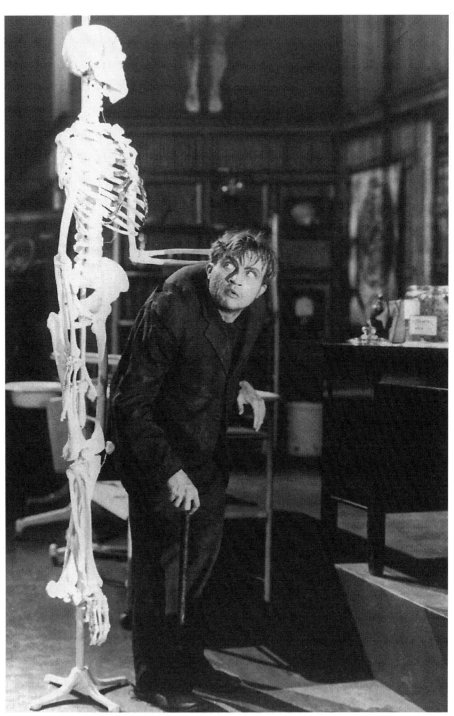

Fritz (Dwight Frye) is alarmed by the medical school skeleton during his quest for a brain for the Monster.

Dwight Frye's Last Laugh

ever, once in makeup (and under hump), he would skulk about the soundstage—and "scare the hell out of everyone!" Indeed, Dwight between takes was (in Mae's words) "sometimes more frightening than the Monster"; this was understandable, since the "Monster," at his leisure, was likely to relax in his beach chair, light up a cigarette, sip his tea and sing a Cockney ditty.

Come the week of September 28, 1931, James Whale began the final week's work on *Frankenstein*. The company visited a mountain lake near Malibu for the Monster's tragic meeting with "little Maria" (Marilyn Harris). Back at Universal, Whale showed his own sadistic side: jealous of the attention Boris was receiving, he made him run up and down the mountain to the windmill all night, Colin Clive on his shoulder. The climactic pageantry of *Frankenstein* and the villagers marching through the back lot Tyrolean village with their torches, the Monster perishing in the fiery windmill, was (as directed by Whale) superb.

Frankenstein "wrapped" Saturday, October 3, 1931. The preview in Santa Barbara was notorious, as people reportedly ran from the theatre out into the streets, terrified by what they saw. Junior Laemmle feared his new horror film possibly *too* horrible. Universal released *Frankenstein* in several key cities prior to its Broadway and Los Angeles openings; one was Milwaukee, where *Frankenstein* premiered at the Alhambra Theatre (*Dracula*'s former home) on Friday, November 20, 1931. "Warning! The Monster is Loose!" proclaimed the Alhambra's newspaper ad on the eve of *Frankenstein*'s opening:

> Note: Karloff is the actor nominated as Lon Chaney's successor... here he is more uncanny than Chaney ever dared to be.

The premiere night was a smash, and the Alhambra filled the newspapers with testimony to the film's box office power:

> Shout it from the housetops! Milwaukee has gone for this picture in a great big way!
> 2nd Week with capacity crowds cheering this thrilling, chilling masterpiece
> Here He Is... the Super-Natural Creature Who Has Aroused Universal Curiosity and Enthusiasm...
> Wide-Spread Enthusiasm Carries This Phenomenal Picture into a 3rd Gala Week

The movie house had become almost reverential about *Frankenstein*'s record-breaking performance. On the eve of Thanksgiving, the Alhambra ran a cartoon of a turkey; across its tail feathers was the proclamation:

> Give Thanks
> For A Really Great Picture
> Carl Laemmle Presents
> *Frankenstein*

Fritz, Victor Moritz (John Boles), Dr. Waldman (Edward Van Sloan), Elizabeth (Mae Clarke), Henry Frankenstein (Colin Clive) and the Monster (Boris Karloff).

"It Holds the Season's Record!" advertised the Alhambra.

Meanwhile, *Frankenstein* had its Broadway premiere at the RKO-Mayfair Theatre Friday, December 4, 1931. Opening night was rainy—but the Mayfair was packed. And what the audience saw that night would become folklore:

The opening in the old churchyard, as Clive's Frankenstein and Dwight's Fritz steal the body in the moonlight... the evil smile on the hunchback's face as he pulls the coffin from the grave leering, "Here he comes!"...

The scene at the gibbet... Fritz wiggling out on the crossbeam, a knife between his teeth, cutting down the corpse in search of a brain... ("The neck's broken!" hisses Clive. "The brain is useless. We must find another brain!")

The famous episode in Dr. Waldman's classroom... Fritz clambering through the window, startled by a gong (of a clock) and dropping the jar containing the "Normal" brain smashing to the floor... his comic fidgeting—then desperately grabbing the "Abnormal" brain. (Fritz probably can't read!)

The spectacle in the Gothic tower laboratory, on that wicked, stormy night, as Frankenstein prepares to create his blasphemous miracle of life... Fritz, scampering on the rainy top of the tower, fixing the electrodes... the arrival of Elizabeth, Victor and Dr. Waldman... Fritz, with his lantern and tiny walking stick, hobbling down the tower staircase, madly mumbling to himself, like the porter in Hell's production of *Macbeth*...

Colin Clive, Edward Van Sloan, Dwight Frye and Boris Karloff in a sadistic scene from *Frankenstein.*

The trio gaining access—to see Frankenstein send his creation to the rooftop, to receive the life-giving lightning... Frankenstein watching with zeal, Fritz grinning insanely... the creation's hand moving...

"It's alive!" rejoices Clive's Frankenstein. "It's alive! It's alive! It's alive!"...

Later, the entrance of Karloff's Monster (backward!) as he slowly turns for those classic closeups... creator slowly, almost tenderly coaching his creation to sit down... the Monster's beautiful discovery of light... and, just as the audience senses its profound pity for the Monster, the arrival of Fritz, with torch, to terrorize this virtual new-born baby and engender our sympathy for him...

The tower dungeon, where Fritz mercilessly, sadistically tortures the hapless Monster with whip and torch, delighting in finding a being more pathetic than himself. There's something deeply disturbing about watching this hunchbacked dwarf gleefully terrorizing this strangely noble Monster, but it doesn't last long—for soon we hear, from the dungeon, the screams of Fritz...

Dwight Frye's Fritz lasts only for the first half of *Frankenstein*, before receiving his richly-deserved comeuppance. Yet his impression is unforgettable, and he survives as the ghoul who launched Hollywood's Frankenstein Monster on his celebrated way to macabre glory.

As *Variety* reported of the Broadway premiere of *Frankenstein*:

> Looks like a *Dracula* plus... a high voltage climax,
> tricked out with spectacle and dramatic crescendo...
> Colin Clive, the cadaverous hero of *Journey's End*,
> is a happy choice for the scientist... He plays it
> with force, but innocent of ranting. Boris Karloff
> enacts the Monster... the bizarre figure with its
> indescribably terrifying face of demoniacal calm,
> a fascinating acting bit of mesmerism.

Karloff was the top sensation of *Frankenstein*; as the film became Universal's yuletide present to Depression America, Boris, by Christmas Eve, had his gift of a Universal star contract. Yet there was glory for all. *Frankenstein* opened at the Orpheum Theatre in Los Angeles on January 1, 1932, supported by a Chic Sale comedy *Many a Sip*, a Tom and Jerry cartoon, a *Screen Snapshot* with Moran and Mack and the Pathé Newsreel. Louella Parsons wrote in her *Los Angeles Examiner* column:

> So grotesque and horrible is the characterization
> of Boris Karloff in *Frankenstein* that all adults
> become little children... James Whale has done
> an unusually deft job of direction... Colin Clive...
> leaves nothing to be desired as young Franken-
> stein... A notable performance is given by Dwight
> Frye as the Dwarf...

Frankenstein proved an international phenomenon. On January 25, 1932, the film premiered in London, where *To-day's Cinema* was soon running headlines like this one:

Pulpit Protests Against
Frankenstein
A Week of Packed Houses the Result

To-day's Cinema hailed the "passion and despair" of Karloff's Monster, the "earnestness" of Clive's Frankenstein, the "Grand Guignol" flourish of Whale's direction and reported,

> ...Dwight Frye's dwarf is an effective study of
> a mind as ill-formed as the body in which it is
> housed.

All in all, *Frankenstein* was show business history. In *Photoplay* magazine (February 1932), "The Answer Man" led off his column with this report:

> Chills and shivers! The latest horror sensation,
> *Frankenstein*, has everyone thrilled and the most
> outstanding question this month has been, "Was

the Monster real or was it mechanical?" Movie-goers say it seems unbelievable that anything so terrifying and ghastly could be human. But it's true. Boris Karloff was the chap who made you and you and you stiffen with fright each time he appeared on the screen...

...Another actor the fans are asking about is Dwight Frye, who played the role of the dwarf in *Frankenstein*. Dwight is a native of Salina, Kan. He is 33 years old... Off the screen he stands very erect and is quite handsome.

Dwight Frye had the distinction of playing juicy roles in two of the biggest moneymakers Universal had ever produced. By June, 1932, *Dracula* had reaped an international gross of $1.2 million; *Frankenstein* already had tallied a world-wide $1.4 million—remarkable money for a Depression-plagued world.

Yet it was an extremely mixed blessing. Within the calendar year of 1931, millions had seen Dwight Frye's Renfield in *Dracula* and Fritz in *Frankenstein*; the passion, color and personality this brilliant young Broadway star had given these Grand Guignol roles would ironically warp his career. As David J. Skal wrote in his book, *Hollywood Gothic*:

> Once prized for his range and versatility, Frye was typecast as the prototypical monster's assistant. Wild-eyed, hunchbacked, or zoophagous, Dwight Frye became a subgenre unto himself.

The black magic of Universal had seemingly thrown a curse on Dwight Frye, a curse cast in the shadows of Dracula's castle and Frankenstein's tower laboratory. The actor who so desperately wanted to act a variety of roles was suddenly typed as a ghoul; more personally and ironically, a Christian Scientist with a deep sense of religion found himself linked with movies blazing with the occult, blasphemy and the supernatural.

Inevitably, the fly-eater Renfield and hunchbacked Fritz would join Lugosi's Count and Karloff's Monster in haunting the nightmares of Depression America moviegoers. Meanwhile, Dwight Frye's nightmare was to find himself trapped as Hollywood's favorite lunatic.

It would become, tragically, a night-mare-come-true.

Dwight Frye as Chick Lewis, from *By Whose Hand?* (Columbia, 1932)

Dwight Frye's Last Laugh

Chapter Six
"...Please, God...!"

If God is good, I will be able to play comedy,
in which I was featured on Broadway for eight
seasons and in which no producer of motion pictures will give me a chance! And please, God,
may it be before I go screwy, playing idiots, half-
wits, and lunatics on the talking screen!
—Dwight Frye, in the pressbook for *The
Vampire Bat* (Majestic, 1933)

How does an actor follow playing the fly-eater of *Dracula* and the hunchback of *Frankenstein*?

At box offices across 1932 America, horror was triumphant. Boris Karloff was Universal's top attraction, scoring as Morgan, the drunken, bearded butler of James Whale's *The Old Dark House*. MGM borrowed Boris to adorn him in dragon lady apparel and those five inch fingernails for the crazy, kinky *The Mask of Fu Manchu*. By the time Universal's *The Mummy* opened on Broadway in January, 1933, Karloff's "Im-Ho-Tep" face filled a giant billboard above Times Square, heralding "Karloff the Uncanny" and glowing at night in yellow, green and purple lights.

Bela Lugosi mesmerized his fans in 1932, too: raving Dr. Mirakle in Universal's *Murders in the Rue Morgue*, Murder Legendre in *White Zombie* and the hirsute "Sayer of the Law" in Paramount's *Island of Lost Souls*. Bela's reckless spending might have plunged him into bankruptcy by late 1932, but there was plenty of consolation—includ-ing passionate fan mail which, Bela proudly insisted, rivaled Gable's.

The genre was thriving. The Motion Picture Academy's Best Actor of 1932 was Fredric March (Dwight's Broadway co-star from *Puppets* and *The Devil in the Cheese*), who won the Oscar[9] for Paramount's *Dr. Jekyll and Mr. Hyde*.

March, Lugosi and Karloff enjoyed glory; Dwight Frye faced a career limbo. He dearly wanted to act a variety of roles. And he had to keep busy, to support not only Laura and baby Dwight, but his mother. His father had died, and now Ella came west—lodging with her son, his wife and the new baby in Hollywood.

Dwight found work at Columbia, in a trio of 1932 films. *Attorney for the Defense* saw Dwight as James Wallace, wrongly sent to his death via a clever D.A. (Edmund Lowe); in desperate, high-strung manner, he proclaims his innocence and voices ac-cusations at the prosecutor before being led off to face his execution. *By Whose Hand?* (believed to no longer exist) cast Dwight as weak, neurotic Chick Lewis, who had in-formed on a notorious killer (Nat Pendleton). While traveling on a train in custody of a detective (William Halligan), Dwight escapes, menaces heroine Barbara Weeks and then is stabbed to death by Pendleton—who had escaped from prison and was hiding

Attorney for the Defense: Dwight Frye (center) as wrongly convicted James Wallace in the grasps of the police while Douglas Haig and Dorothy Peterson look on in dismay.

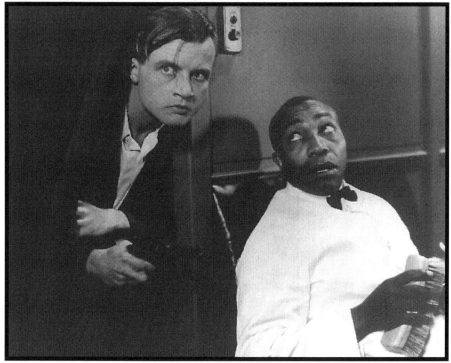

Chick Lewis (Frye) surprises the Pullman porter (Oscar Smith) in *By Whose Hand?*

Dwight Frye's Last Laugh

The Western Code: Dwight Frye is almost provoked into a gunfight but Tim McCoy prevents Wheeler Oakman from drawing his pistol. Between McCoy and Oakman is Cactus Mack.

A Strange Adventure: Nadine Dore, Dwight Frye, Harry Myers, Eddy Chandler and Regis Toomey.

Dwight Frye as Herman, in *The Vampire Bat*, is chased by an angry mob.

on the train inside a coffin. And there was Columbia's *The Western Code*, offering the surprise of Dwight in cowboy hat and attire (and handling a horse quite well!). As Dick Loomis, Dwight actually got to punch classic western heavy Wheeler Oakman and was later almost the victim of a lynch mob—before Tim McCoy saved the day.

Dwight's fourth and final 1932 release was *A Strange Adventure*, his first independent film (produced by one of the founders of Monogram Pictures, I. E. Chadwick). He played Robert Wayne, sulking nephew of the eventually murdered wealthy old miser, William V. Mong. It was a red herring role which gave him little to do but mug for the camera.

The horror/hysteria stigma had stuck. And, having acted with Lugosi and Karloff, Dwight now met a third superstar of horror.

Mad? Is one who has solved the secret of life to
be considered *mad*?
　　　　　—Lionel Atwill, in *The Vampire Bat*
(Majestic, 1933)

"Frankly, I've had my fill of art," said Lionel Atwill, a great matinee idol of the Broadway of the '20s as *Deburau* (1920), in *The Outsider* with Katharine Cornell (1924), in Shaw's *Caesar and Cleopatra* with Helen Hayes (1925). The plump, cat-eyed

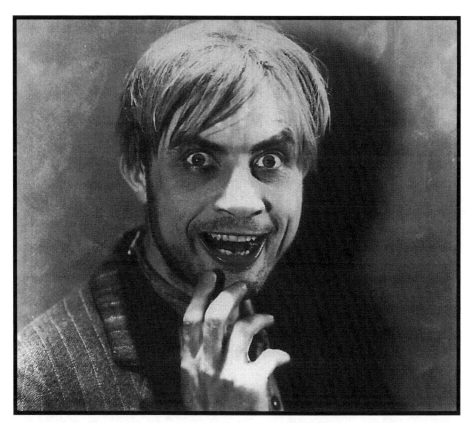

That Frye could pull off a role like Herman in *The Vampire Bat* is a tribute to his skill.

Englishman had come to Hollywood, reminding *Motion Picture* magazine that Shakespeare's most popular characters were, after all, Richard III ("...that deformed man... !") and Hamlet ("...with his pitiful diseased mind"), happily becoming a horror star. He was triumphant in Warner Bros.' *Doctor X* (1932) and *Mystery of the Wax Museum* (1933); now, ever-dapper with his toupee, monocle and that lascivious look in his eye, "Pinky" Atwill (whom *Parade* magazine would remember in 1985 as "a notorious Hollywood sex fiend") was starring in Majestic Studio's *The Vampire Bat* as mad Dr. Otto von Niemann:

> Life! Created in the laboratory... Ha! You shudder in horror... but what are a few lives when weighed in the balance against the achievement of biological science?... I have created life... From the lives of those who have gone before, I have created life!

The lovely recipient of this climactic *The Vampire Bat* mania was Fay Wray, who had left her blonde wig at RKO, where she was filming *King Kong*. During *Kong*, RKO had farmed out Fay for *Doctor X* and *Mystery of the Wax Museum*, both with Atwill.

Herman, in *The Vampire Bat*, offers a bat to nervous Gussie Schnappmann (Maude Eburne).

Melvyn Douglas was the police inspector, who solves the "blood murders" in the little village of Kleinschloss (German for "little castle" — and actually Universal's *Frankenstein* village, leased by *The Vampire Bat* producer Phil Goldstone).[10] Maude Eburne played Atwill's comic housekeeper, and Lionel Belmore was the Burgomaster — just as he had been in *Frankenstein*.

And who is the poor soul whom Atwill blames for the vampire murders? It's Herman, the village idiot, with a Renfield-like laugh and the habit of collecting pet bats — played by Dwight Frye. Dwight offers a fascinating bit of dementia as he baby-talks his way through this Poverty Row gem:

"Bats... They soft... like cat!... They not bite Herman!"

How many actors could pull off a role like Herman? That Frye did (wonderfully) is a tribute to his skill. He's richly entertaining, be he climbing a lamp post to snare a bat or playing a terrific comic episode with Maude Eburne and a Great Dane:

See? Blood! Mmmm!... Herman like you... Me
Herman! You give me apples — Herman give you
nice soft *bat*!

Dwight actually brings pathos to a gut-wrenching death scene, in which, having been chased by torch-bearing villagers through the countryside (actually Hollywood's Bronson Canyon), he cowers in a cave. "No... Herman 'fraid!" cries the halfwit, just before he screams and leaps hysterically 50 feet to his death.

Considering his Broadway fame, and his marriage to an heiress (the former wife of General Douglas MacArthur, and worth $100,000,000), it's curious that Atwill favored fare like *The Vampire Bat*. Of course, he also attended Los Angeles murder trials, kept an exotic macaw named Copulate and allegedly hosted "orgies" that eventually had their wicked way with his life and career.

The Vampire Bat opened at Broadway's Winter Garden Theatre Friday night, January 20, 1933, neighboring such attractions as the three Barrymores in MGM's *Rasputin and the Empress*, Charles Laughton and Bela Lugosi in Paramount's *Island of Lost Souls* and Fox's *Cavalcade*, which would win the Academy Award as Best Picture of 1933. *The New York Times* review gave away the chiller's mystery (which most audiences would no doubt guess anyway):

> Dwight Frye wins a few mild chills with his sinister portrait of a peasant who domesticates bats for his amusement and who is ultimately chased with torches through the night. But they have the wrong man there. Mr. Atwill is the man to be watched by those who expect to be terrorized by *The Vampire Bat*.

Lionel Atwill reported to Paramount for *Murders in the Zoo*, in which he merrily tossed Kathleen Burke ("the panther woman" of *Island of Lost Souls*) into an alligator pool.

Dwight, meanwhile—desperate to escape jobs like Herman in *The Vampire Bat* (even as he played them with his usual passion and creativity)—went back to the stage.

> Dwight Frye, that brilliant young actor whose métier for portraying weird and rather gruesome parts has not yet been fully appreciated, was shudderingly realistic in the part. He has a gift for conveying a naive charm of manner and yet, at the same time, of sending shudders down your back! In the final speech of the play—a speech that is practically a monologue on his life—he gave one of the finest readings of his career.
>
> —Muriel Elwood, in her book *Pauline Frederick: On and Off the Stage* (1940), discussing Frye's portrayal in *Criminal at Large* (1933)

On March 24, 1933, *King Kong* had its gala premiere at Grauman's Chinese Theatre. On March 26, Dwight had a Hollywood premiere of his own: he opened at the El

Capitan Theatre as mad Lord Lebanon in the play *Criminal at Large*, an Edgar Wallace melodrama. The play had begun its tour at the Alcazar Theatre in San Francisco February 22, 1933; the star was Dwight's friend, the venerable Pauline Frederick, silent star of such films as *Madame X* (1920), then acting in Hollywood fare like *The Phantom of Crestwood* (RKO, 1932). *Criminal at Large* toured the country. Then, after appearing with Miss Frederick in May, 1933 in *Her Majesty, the Widow* and *Amber* at the Biltmore Theatre in Los Angeles, Frye barnstormed with the star and her company in a repertory tour of those two plays. As Peter Lawton in *Amber*, Dwight again played Miss Frederick's son, but was said to have struggled "...with a role to which he isn't suited." Laura (who acted in the company) and two-year-old "Buddy" went along, across the country.

"I remember going back and forth from Los Angeles to New York on trains," says "Buddy," "the Pullman sleeping cars, with their curtains at night."

Many of this company became life-long friends of the Frye family. Dwight, Laura and "Buddy" were very close to Pauline Frederick. For "Buddy," she was "Aunt Polly," and the family spent happy nights at Miss Frederick's Beverly Hills house, where they played Mah Jongg. Indeed, when Pauline Frederick died in 1938, she left her elaborate hand-made Mah Jongg chest to the Fryes. Dwight D. Frye still has it.

Meanwhile, movie audiences that May saw Dwight Frye raving mad again in Columbia's *The Circus Queen Murder* (1933). This wild, big top melodrama featured Dwight as the crazy Flandrin, "a murderous aerialist," vengefully slaying unfaithful "circus queen" spouse Josie La Tour (Greta Nissen) on a Friday the 13th. The madman also tried to kill her lover Sebastian (Donald Cook) before "Thatcher Colt" (Adolphe Menjou, playing the suave New York police commissioner of the Anthony Abbot mystery novels) saved the day. *Variety* gave insight to this sadly lost thriller:

> Scene of Sebastian on the high trapeze and the maddened Flandrin peeping down from the tent top as the rope unravels is provided with even more suspense than when the circus queen, Josie, slips from the same perch later with a poisoned arrow in her back.

Roy William Neill (who would direct Dwight a decade later in *Frankenstein Meets the Wolf Man*) made the most of the atmospherics: 13 cannibals (with Dwight disguising himself as #14!), clowns, a menagerie including a lion, elephant, horses and a giant gorilla and a juicy death scene for Dwight. As he had told Katherine Hill of the *San Francisco Chronicle* during his *Criminal at Large* tour:

> In *The Murder of the Circus Queen*, the picture I finished just before coming to San Francisco, I depart hence by throwing myself, in a moment of despondency, off a circus trapeze. It begins to look as if my business in the films is to provide ever fresh and variegated spectacles of sudden death.

Dwight Frye portrays the murderous aerialist Flandrin from the 1933 *The Circus Queen Murder.*

> If there are new ways of coming to a bad end, I'd like to know about them, because sooner or later they'll probably crop up in a script, and someone will say, "send for Frye!"

> Dwight Frye, elaborately made over as an ancient Chinee, is effectively weird.
> — *New York Daily News* review of the Broadway play *Keeper of the Keys* (October, 1933)

Frye's Ah Sing in *Keeper of the Keys* was a flashy role for Dwight.

Dwight had been upbeat about his Hollywood horrors—"They're lots of fun," he'd told the *San Francisco Chronicle*. However, as the big parade of Dwight's "idiots, half-wits and lunatics" threatened to be endless, the actor kept touring with the Pauline Frederick troupe. He was delighted when his work won him an invitation to return to where he wanted to be—on Broadway.

"Charlie Chan's Stage Premiere" was how the press described *Keeper of the Keys*—based on the last Chan novel of Earl Derr Biggers. After a Boston and Philadelphia try-out (under the title *Inspector Charlie Chan*), *Keeper of the Keys* opened at Broadway's

Frye worked with long-time friend William Harrigan who portrayed Charlie Chan in *Keeper of the Keys*.

Fulton Theatre Wednesday night, October 18, 1933. William Harrigan (a very close friend of the Frye family) played Chan, and Dwight acted Ah Sing, a mysterious Oriental. It was a flashy role for Dwight; the 34-year-old affected an elaborate, old age Chinese makeup (balding head, drooping mustache), and acted Ah Sing with a shuffling limp.

Indeed, Halloween of 1933 was a great one on Broadway; besides Dwight Frye, both "Dracula" and "Dr. Frankenstein" were on the "Great White Way," live-and-in person:

While Dwight was performing at the Fulton on 46th Street, Bela Lugosi was on 42nd Street at the New Amsterdam Theatre, in Earl Carroll's musical extravaganza *Murder at the Vanities*, which had opened September 12, 1933. Bela played "Siebenkase," a red-herring mystic; the huge cast also featured Olga Baclanova (the evil "Cleopatra" from *Freaks*) and a chorus heralded by Carroll as "The Most Beautiful Girls in the World."

On October 28, Colin Clive premiered in *Eight Bells*, a sea melodrama, at the Hudson Theatre on 44th Street. Clive's role: Captain Dale, a drunken swine of a ship master, murdered by his mutinous crew. The leading lady: Rose Hobart (who had played Muriel in 1931's *Dr. Jekyll and Mr. Hyde*).

One wonders if Dwight ever crossed paths with Lugosi or Clive as they walked through the theatre district!

Laura, "Buddy" and Dwight pose for a family photo in 1933.

Unfortunately, the time for all these horror celebrities to be working simultaneously quickly evaporated after All Hallow's Eve. Bela dropped out of *Murder at the Vanities* the first week in November, as the show moved to the Majestic Theatre (where it played into the spring of 1934); he opted for an 18-minute version of *Dracula* for vaudeville. Dwight's *Keeper of the Keys* collapsed after only 24 performances, closing election night, November 7. And as for Clive's *Eight Bells*: it folded November 11, sinking after only 17 performances.

Strangely enough, *Keeper of the Keys* closed just in time for the November 17, 1933, premiere of Universal's *The Invisible Man* at Broadway's Roxy Theatre. James Whale's new melodrama, starring Claude Rains as "the invisible one," featured *Keeper of the Keys'* erstwhile "Charlie Chan" William Harrigan as the traitor Kemp; Dwight had a bit as a reporter. Bespectacled and sporting a typical 1930s reporter's garb of slouch hat and raincoat, Dwight asks questions of police inspector Dudley Digges on the topic of capturing the Invisible Man—including, "Why not bloodhounds?" and, "Why not put wet tar on all the roads, then chase the black soles of his feet?"

Dwight surely had been happy to work again with Whale; "Jimmy" no doubt was happy to have him, even in such a tiny role. Yet it's a shock to see Dwight, so prominent in *Dracula* and *Frankenstein*, popping up in this unbilled bit—and so prosaic a part. As Ethan Mordden wrote in his book, *The Hollywood Studios*:

> Dwight Frye, Dracula's slave and Frankenstein's sadistic tormentor, is here demoted to a bit role among a group of reporters. This is sad; Frye doesn't project as a square.

Christmas of 1933 found Dwight opening on stage at Boston's Tremont Theatre as Albert Adam, "romantic young composer" of *The Play's the Thing*. A Boston newspaper heralded Dwight as "The Youngest of the Horror Men":

> A new Dwight Frye is to be found in *The Play's the Thing*. He has the normal use of all his limbs. He talks, smiles and laughs quite amicably. He makes love, he even composes music... And, if there is any truth in the rumors that will leak out of rehearsal rooms, he can he as pleasant, delicate and charming at one end of the line as he can be ugly, unpleasant and horrible at the other.

The press "warned" audiences:

> Boston movie fans will be delighted to learn that the old fly-eating gentleman from *Dracula* is in our midst; that the hunchback from *Frankenstein* is walking Boston's streets and that the husband in *The Circus Queen Murder* is now to be seen at the Tremont.

It was a pleasant change-of-pace engagement.

If Dwight was wishing to avenge himself on Hollywood for his typecasting as the cinema's top lunatic, the chance seemed to come via *Queer People*. The Broadway comedy, based on the popular novel by Carroll and Garrett Graham, aimed to be a sexy, rip-roaring lampoon of Hollywood, backed by the fortunes of no less than Howard Hughes (who also nabbed the screen rights). Elaborately produced ($40,000 Depression dollars for the sets alone), *Queer People* set a hard-drinking reporter named "Whitey" (Hal Skelly) loose in the movie capital, where, as critic Percy Hammond noted,

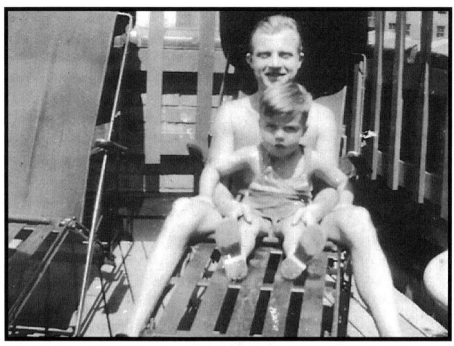

Dwight and "Buddy" on the roof of the Knickerbocker Hotel, New York City.

Dwight and "Buddy" enjoy a carefree moment.

Dwight Frye's Last Laugh

Platinum blondes exert their ambiguous charms on magnates with paunches, and slimy actors and directors seduce, marry, divorce and pose in revolting fashion... There are two self-conscious orgies in it and a careful scene in a Los Angeles bawdy house, none of which is quite competent to inflame you...

Dwight's role in this "comedy in three acts" was Frank Carson, "a tragic husband" whose wife dumps him as she becomes a star.[11] The cast was impressive, including Gladys George and Nita Naldi (the "bad girl" of John Barrymore's 1920 *Dr. Jekyll and Mr. Hyde*).

On Thursday night, February 15, 1934,[12] *Queer People* had its gala opening night at Broadway's National Theatre, a la Hollywood's Grauman's Chinese—complete (as *Variety* noted) with "a mike in the lobby, floodlights, red carpeting and all the trimmings." However, as *Variety* also reported:

> *Queer People* is doubly bad, for it's a libel on Hollywood, as well as an exceedingly bad play... It's all a mess and a hodgepodge of feverishly imaginative Hollywood doin's that never ring true.

Most of the critics liked Skelly and Gladys George; "Dwight Frye is sufficiently distrait as the forsaken husband!" exclaimed *Variety*. However, even Howard Hughes' money couldn't keep *Queer People* running. The play ignominiously folded after only 13 performances. Hughes scrapped the movie rights. The script for *Queer People* was never even published. Significantly, Dwight listed none of his film credits in the "Who's Who" section of the *Queer People* program—even though two of them had made show business history.

It was the biggest flop in Dwight Frye's New York stage career—and his final Broadway appearance.

Horror was still sensational with moviegoers. On May 3, 1934, Universal's *The Black Cat*, the first teaming of "Karloff and Bela Lugosi," premiered at Hollywood's Pantages Theatre. Yet Dwight was determined to escape the Grand Guignol typecasting and stay on the stage. In spring of 1934, he played at Philadelphia's Broad Street Theatre as Austin Lowe in S. N. Behrman's *The Second Man*, with Bert Lytell and Rosalind Russell. *The Philadelphia Public-Ledger* critiqued:

> Dwight Frye, once seen here as the spider-catching neurotic of *Dracula*, does a finely etched job as the other man. He has some marvelous intonations in his voice, which convey comedy through their solemnity.

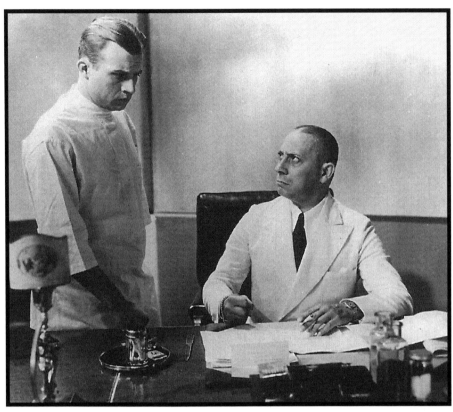

Dwight Frye and Erich von Stroheim appeared together in Republic's *The Crime of Doctor Crespi*.

Laura Frye (still using the stage name Laurette Bullivant) played on the New York stage one more time, joining Pauline Frederick in *Her Majesty, the Widow* (in which she and her husband had toured with Miss Frederick). It opened June 18, 1934, at the Ritz Theatre (now the Walter Kerr) and played 32 performances.

July 16, 1934: Dwight appeared at the John H. Hessel Memorial Hall, Woodmere, Long Island, in *Squaring the Circle*, a Soviet drama by Valentine Kataev. The cast included Frank Shannon (destined to play Dr. Zarkov in Universal's *Flash Gordon* serials) and Ray Miller.

Dwight and Laura toured the summer and fall of 1934 in *The Pursuit of Happiness*, a Revolutionary War comedy. He played a Hessian, Max Christmann; she was Prudence Kirkland. A popular scene in *The Pursuit of Happiness* found Dwight and Laura "bundling"—i.e., sharing a bed, fully-dressed, with a board between them. As always, they took along their three-year-old "Buddy," who remembers:

> I was the one who ran around backstage, knocking on the door, telling everybody when it was time to get ready to do the play. I'm sure the stage manager loved that!

Dwight Frye as Dr. Thomas (left) and Dr. Arnold (Paul Guilfoyle, driving) rush to the hospital with the man whom Dr. Crespi buried alive (John Bohn) from *The Crime of Doctor Crespi.* **[Donald Maurer collection]**

Meanwhile, another horror film—this one offering a "good guy" role—baited Dwight Frye.

The Crime of Doctor Crespi was primarily a vehicle for Erich von Stroheim, Hollywood's cruelly humbled director of such classics as *Foolish Wives* (1922) and *Greed* (1925), and fated to be billed on *The Crime of Doctor Crespi* posters with his old sobriquet of "The Man You Love to Hate." Based loosely (*very* loosely!) on Poe's *The Premature Burial*, the Liberty production was filmed at the Biograph Studios in the Bronx, where D. W. Griffith had shot his last film, *The Struggle* (1931). Von Stroheim was Doctor Crespi, a chainsmoking madman who keeps a dwarf's skeleton on his desk and who buries alive a romantic/professional rival (John Bohn); Dwight was Dr. Thomas, bullied about by "von's" sadistic Crespi. Come the climax, he avenges himself, digging up "the dead man" and setting him loose on von Stroheim.

It was a remarkable shoestring production. Budapest-born John H. Auer (later a top director for Republic) was *The Crime of Doctor Crespi*'s producer/director/writer. On September 19, 1934, Auer began shooting the picture at the tiny Biograph Studios, going on a location exterior to shoot the bizarre funeral episode. "Auer Needs Only Eight Days Work," headlined *The Hollywood Reporter*, September 27, 1934:

New York.—John H. Auer took a shot at the speed record for production by completing *The Crime of Doctor Crespi* at the Biograph Studios in eight days.

Auer, who directed the picture himself, started last Wednesday, and will have everything done except the cutting some time today. Erich von Stroheim, who played the lead, returns to the coast tonight. Release date of the production is October 15.

It was a madcap (but presumably pleasant) eight days. The cast included Dwight's personal friend Paul Guilfoyle (who assists Dwight in rescuing the victim from his grave) and, as that victim, John Bohn (who had written *Dumb Luck*, in which Dwight and Laura had played on the road in 1927). The chiller even offered Dwight a hint of romance, as, in the final closeup, he asks the blonde nurse for a date. Playing the nurse is Jeanne Kelly (aka Jean Brooks)—fated to star as Jacqueline, the Satanist in the black Cleopatra wig in Val Lewton's *The Seventh Victim* (1943). The fade-out offered the spectacle of the erstwhile Renfield of *Dracula* flirting with the future Jacqueline of *The Seventh Victim*:

> Frye: Uh—doing anything tonight?
> Brooks: Oh—"Doc" Thomas!

The October 15, 1934, release date did not come to pass. Liberty Studios was in financial peril, and *The Crime of Doctor Crespi* fell into limbo, sitting on a shelf, forlornly awaiting a release.

Dwight and Laura kept touring in *The Pursuit of Happiness*, and then came a new Hollywood offer. Once again it was for a horror film.

This one, however, was irresistible.

Frye Sticks to Hunches

Dwight Frye, who played the hunchback in the original *Frankenstein* for Universal, plays another hunchback in the sequel which has been retitled *The Bride of Frankenstein*.
—*The Hollywood Reporter*, January 12, 1935

January 2, 1935. James Whale, with a $293,750 budget and a 36-day schedule, had begun shooting *The Return of Frankenstein*—fated to be released and revered as *Bride of Frankenstein*

Back was Karloff (as Universal now above-the-title billed him), at $2,500 per week, as the talking, smoking, drinking, crucified and lovesick Monster; so was Colin Clive (at $1,500 per week) as agonized Henry Frankenstein.

***Bride of Frankenstein*'s director James Whale was so fond of Dwight Frye's talent that he combined for him three roles in the original script.**

A third alumnus of *Frankenstein* joined the cast. Whale was so fond of Dwight Frye's talent that he happily combined for him three roles in the original script: "Karl," the village creep who murders his Uncle and Auntie Glutz and blames it on Karloff's forlorn Monster; "the first ghoul," who aids Ernest Thesiger's merrily mad Dr. Pretorius in robbing graves; and "Fritz," who assists Clive's monster maker and Thesiger's wizard in the creation of Elsa Lanchester's female monster—including securing a "fresh heart."

The horrid hybrid was named "Karl," and Universal's production blueprint set Dwight for three weeks work—at a salary of $500 per week. There was the bonus of new, creepy Jack P. Pierce makeup. And *The Hollywood Reporter* was slightly in error when it referred to Karl as a hunchback: actually, the ghoul had legs of different length—and wore a "skate" on his left shoe to handle the deformity.

Bride of Frankenstein was a mad, crazy masterpiece. The foxy Whale made Karloff's Frankenstein Monster a Christ symbol, heartbreakingly noble as he hangs crucified on a pole, the villagers (including Dwight's Karl) jeering in sadistic glee.

"...I don't think anybody could have presented the Monster more beautifully than Jimmy Whale," said Valerie Hobson (who played "Elizabeth" in Christmas angel hair and gowns, and on a Gothic pitch)—"along with Boris, of course."

Bride of Frankenstein: **Boris Karloff, E. E. Clive, Tempe Pigott, Gunnis Davis and Dwight Frye (note the skate on his left foot).**

> Karloff is so moving—like one of the great clowns
> who make you cry... You really felt that here was
> one whose heart was absolutely bleeding to get out
> of his monstrous self and to find someone to love
> and who would love him. Very
> moving!

Of course, Whale slyly spiked his bitter empathy for the Monster with hilarious black comedy—and a kinky sexuality. He cast Elsa Lanchester as both female monster and Mary Shelley of the prologue ("James' feeling," said Elsa, "was that very pretty, sweet people, both men and women, had very wicked insides... evil thoughts."). Whale gloried in grotesques: Ernest Thesiger, as a brazenly effeminate Pretorius... Una O'Connor, as a raucously screaming Minnie the housekeeper...

And, in *Bride of Frankenstein*, Dwight's flair for horror and comedy would fully bloom. He totally fits the movie's mad audacity; indeed, in his Crazy Guggenheim hat, his mugging face and that Jack O'Lantern smile, Dwight's Karl seems like a baggy-pants comic from a Transylvania burlesque house:

Studying the cadaver of the teenage lady who will provide the anatomy for the Monster's mate: "Pretty little thing in her way, wasn't she?"

Bride of Frankenstein: **Ernest Thesiger, Dwight Frye and Neil Fitzgerald.**

Advising his graverobber cohort after this ghoulish crypt raid: "What d'ya say, pal, if there's much more like this, we give ourselves up and let 'em hang us... This is no life for murderers!"

Exclaiming joyously after Frankenstein extols the new human heart Karl has provided (and, unbeknownst to Frankenstein, murdered to get): "It was a very fresh one!"

Whale even presents a little "homage" to Frye's Fritz of the original *Frankenstein*: dispatched to get a fresh heart, Dwight's Karl scuttles down the tower steps (just as Fritz had done!), madly mumbling to himself in Fritz style. The scene is nowhere to be found in the shooting script, and one gets the impression that Dwight's almost lyrical ravings are his own creation:

> I'll get her heart... I'll go into that room and I'll
> take my knife out—and I'll get her! I'll hold her
> down, and there she'll be! Where, I ask you, where
> will she be?!

It was a happy set. Everyone got into the spirit of the mad, gloriously misanthropic sequel: "the Monster," sipping tea between scenes in robe and ascot; "Pretorius," merrily crocheting; "Jimmy" Whale, having a smoke and striking comic poses with the Monster's dummy stand-in. And there was Elsa Lanchester, the vainglorious "Bride"

In a deleted scene from *Bride of Frankenstein*, Karl gazes gleefully into the room anticipating killing his uncle (Gunnis Davis) for his money and then blaming the Monster.

herself—yanking up her bride wedding shroud between scenes and merrily "flashing" the company with the sight of her entirely naked body.

Tragically, Colin Clive was "Hyde" more and more often; he was drinking very heavily, and actually dangerous—as he had taken to "joyriding" a plane through the Hollywood skies. Yet Whale would use the actor's decay to *Bride*'s advantage; those closeups of Clive's gaunt, agonized face in the creation sequence are spine-chilling, and this would-be God seems almost as freakish and pathetic as his Monster.

Bride of Frankenstein also gives Dwight his most spectacular death scene. Atop the tower laboratory, as the Bride comes to blasphemous life, Frye's Karl, in lab smock and that floppy hat, runs afoul of Karloff's Monster, who chases the torch-waving villain across the windy roof. The Monster grabs Karl, and tosses him off the tower—all punctuated by a caterwauling Frye scream, a streak of lightning and Franz Waxman's classical musical score.

Bride of Frankenstein ran over schedule and budget; there was a hiatus while Whale awaited the availability of O. P. Heggie, who played the saintly blind hermit. Whale finally completed *Bride of Frankenstein* on March 7, 1935, 10 days over schedule and $100,000 over budget. Universal previewed *Bride of Frankenstein* the first week of April, 1935. The trade papers raved at the preview, but Fate was not entirely kind; prior to national release, Universal would cut 15 minutes from *Bride of Frankenstein*—including Dwight's introduction as gallows bird assistant to Dr. Pretorius, and his reign

Dwight Frye's Karl, here menacing Valerie Hobson, remains one of his best-remembered portrayals.

of terror through the village, in which he slays his Uncle Glutz (Gunnis Davis) to get his gold, then goes after his Auntie Glutz (Tempe Pigott), blaming the mania on Boris' forlorn Monster:

> Very convenient to have a Monster around. (He
> looks around the room)
>   This is quite a nice cottage—I shouldn't be
> surprised if he visited Auntie too.

The release version of *Bride of Frankenstein* also virtually eliminated that curious "Karl" characteristic: Dwight's "skate," worn under his left shoe, suggesting that his legs weren't the same length. The final cut of the movie never fully focuses on this bizarre accouterment.

On Saturday, April 20, 1935, *Bride of Frankenstein* premiered at Hollywood's Pantages Theatre—the crazy, baroque climax of Hollywood's golden age of horror. Even with the cuts, Dwight Frye's Karl remains one of his best-remembered showcases—a grand goblin, played with Gothic frills and a vaudevillian's comic timing. Dwight's creepy Karl helped James Whale capture his mad, bitter "vision" of *Bride of Frankenstein* which widely reigns as Universal's most brilliant horror movie.

Frye, with Nancy Carroll, in Columbia's 1935 *Atlantic Adventure*.

Dwight Frye went home from *Bride of Frankenstein* with good pay and a sense of pride; Whale had "let him loose" and made sure Universal paid him properly. However, very few directors would take the trouble to see that Dwight received vivid screen time and a fair salary.

Columbia's *Atlantic Adventure* (1935) saw Dwight as Spike, a jewel thief masquerading as the son of his accomplice Mitts (John Wray, Sr.). Spike harasses leading lady Nancy Carroll during the proceedings.

In Universal's *The Great Impersonation* (1935), starring Edmund Lowe and Dwight's *Bride of Frankenstein* colleague Valerie Hobson, Dwight played Roger Unthank, "the Ghost of the Black Bog."

> The screams of Roger's ghost will drive you off...
> He haunts the Black Bog, where you killed him on
> your wedding night, because he loved her and you
> took her from him. He'll haunt you! He'll haunt
> you out of this house!

Thus does housekeeper Mrs. Unthank (Esther Dale) warn Sir Everard Dominey (Lowe) in *The Great Impersonation* (which had already been filmed by Paramount in

The villagers hover over the dead body of Roger Unthank (Dwight Frye). A police constable (John Powers) holds Mrs. Unthank (Esther Dale), Roger's mother, while Lord Dominey (Edmund Lowe, below Dale) checks the body in *The Great Impersonation*.

1921). While Dwight's appearance as "the Ghost of the Black Bog" is pitifully brief, his folklore is the most colorful aspect of this spy melodrama/Gothic thriller.

The highlight of the film comes when Lowe, desperate to prove there's no ghost to save his wife's sanity, has the villagers set the Black Bog afire at night. Dwight's Roger Unthank appears, a maniac in a long red beard, screaming like a wounded beast. He runs to Dominey Hall, terrifying Nan Gray's maid; then, atop the staircase (borrowed from James Whale's 1932 *The Old Dark House*!), we see the shadows of Dwight and Miss Hobson—the madman attacking the heroine, both screaming. A shot—and the Black Bog Ghost lunges into view, before toppling down the staircase (a la Renfield in *Dracula*). Firing the shot: Mrs. Unthank. "You saved her?" asks Lowe, indicating his wife. The housekeeper soliloquizes:

> I saved my son. I'd rather have him dead, than have
> you get him. Oh, I know it was wrong. Keeping
> him out there, taking him food, upsetting her. But
> he was happier that way—happier than he would
> have been locked up with a lot of crazy people. He
> was my son. I loved him.

Alan Crosland (who directed Warner Bros.' historic *The Jazz Singer*, 1927) only shows Dwight in long shot, probably to heighten a sense of mystery; still, one longs for a closeup. As reported in *Universal Horrors* by Michael Brunas, John Brunas and Tom Weaver, Dwight was set for one day's work on *The Great Impersonation*—and a full salary of $100. It nevertheless was a memorable role—especially for four-year-old Dwight D. Frye:

> At this time, 1935, we were living in a Spanish-style house, with a view, up on Blue Canyon Drive, on the San Fernando Valley side of the Hollywood Hills—a very darkly wooded area, very dark at night. One night, my mother, grandmother and I were just sitting down to dinner when there came a knock on the door. My mother opened it, and there stood my father, in that makeup from *The Great Impersonation*, with the terrible long beard and everything—and he scared the *hell* out of my mother! She never let him forget that—and he never did anything like that again!

Dwight's impromptu trick-or-treat in his Ghost of the Black Bog makeup brings up a curious point: how did Dwight Frye, a deeply devoted Christian Scientist, feel playing in films increasingly denounced by churches, PTAs and various civic groups?

In many ways, Dwight, with his wife and son, his devotion to his mother, his deep religious beliefs, was worlds apart from the complex men he worked with in the horror movies. By 1935, Karloff, Lugosi and Atwill had accumulated a combined total of 11 (possibly 12) wives, each with one more to come. James Whale lived openly (daring, for the era) with a man, producer David Lewis. Colin Clive was rumored to be bisexual; estranged from his London-based wife, actress Jeanne de Casalis, he had taken up in Hollywood with a red-haired showgirl/actress named Iris Lancaster.

Dwight Frye lived simply, and religiously. As his son says:

> My father was a very ardent Christian Scientist. We went to the Fifth Church, on the corner of Hollywood Boulevard and La Brea Avenue, where he observed all the ceremonies. There would be Sunday school in the morning, Sunday service at 11:00 a.m., and a Testimonial service on Wednesday evenings. Part of the Wednesday night meeting was devoted to people standing up and saying how Christian Science had healed them. I remember at those testimonials hearing people say, "My cancer is gone," or "My paralysis is cured," or "My brain tumor has disappeared"—the impossible happened, presumably.

So Dwight Frye was devoted to his Christian Science religion—although, as his son says, "He smoked, and he drank." He made sure that "Buddy" was in Sunday

Dwight Frye, pictured with his mother, son and wife, held deep religious beliefs putting him worlds apart from the complex men he worked with in the horror movies.

school every week; Laura ("an Episcopalian, and not as religious as my father") would go along to the Fifth Church each Sunday. The faith had been passed down to Dwight by his mother—to whom Dwight was as devoted to as he was to his religion. As "Buddy" remembers:

> His mother was a fanatic Christian Scientist; she was an original follower of Mary Baker Eddy, founder of the Christian Science Church. She wouldn't have an aspirin in the house. Neither she nor my father would ever deal with a doctor. As a boy, when I would have headaches, the Christian Science practitioner would be called, and there would be a "laying on of hands," with a reading from the Bible and from Mary Baker Eddy's book, *Key to the Scriptures*.

For Dwight Frye, horror films were a job—just as *Girls Will be Girls* had been in vaudeville, or the Satanic *Mima* had been on Broadway. And after all, these 1930s horrors all ended with Christian morality triumphant; in a very real sense, they were the most moral movies that Hollywood produced.

Then, once again, screen horror loomed—as *The Crime of Doctor Crespi* found a distributor.

Many horror fans hold a special regard for *The Crime of Doctor Crespi* due to Dwight Frye's major billing—and heroic role.

"The Man who has Died a Thousand Deaths" is at last permitted to live! The man is Dwight Frye, famous screen portrayer of half-wits, lunatics and moon-maddened neurotics who has come to a violent end in every film he has made. He gets his chance to be in at the finish, alive and triumphant, in *The Crime of Doctor Crespi...*

—from the pressbook for *The Crime of Doctor Crespi* (Republic/ Liberty, 1935)

The Crime of Doctor Crespi: **The cast poses with their director: Dwight Frye, Harriet Russell, John H. Auer, Erich von Stroheim, Paul Guilfoyle, Geraldine Kay and John Bohn.**

In 1935, Republic Pictures bought the completed works of the defunct Liberty (and Majestic) studios, and released *The Crime of Doctor Crespi* late that year.

One conjectures how much a part von Stroheim played in the direction of *The Crime of Doctor Crespi*; its sick, warped style reminds one of those flamboyantly wicked touches with which von Stroheim had daubed his Silent classics. The dwarf skeleton which adorns Crespi's office is certainly "Stroheim-esque," as is the remarkable funeral sequence. The sight of Crespi in the church, comforting the widow and child as he proceeds to have their husband/father buried alive, certainly must have indulged von Stroheim's taste for the macabre. And those cemetery closeups of the widow (Harriet Russell), her face in grotesque closeup through her black veil, an organ madly playing as she watches her spouse's coffin lowered into the ground, the dirt shoveled right into the face of the camera, make for one of the most grim episodes of "Golden Age" horror.

For all of von Stroheim's dominance, many horror fans hold a special regard for *The Crime of Doctor Crespi* due to Dwight Frye's major billing—and heroic role. As Dr. Thomas, Dwight has a major scene with von Stroheim as he accuses him of vengefully slaying Dr. Ross:

> Dwight: ...Ross was poisoned. And you can't get
> away with it!

von Stroheim: You be careful, Thomas!

Dwight: I know you did it, and I know why you did it. You couldn't explain!

von Stroheim (hitting Dwight—hard!): Explain that...!

Dwight: Go on, hit me! I don't care! I still say you poisoned him!

(As von Stroheim chokes him)

And you murdered him! You can't beat that out of me! You can't shut me up! You murdered him...!

Later, as Dwight tries to persuade Dr. Arnold (his real-life friend Paul Guilfoyle) to help him steal Ross's body from the cemetery to perform an autopsy, he has a memorable line worth quoting:

It won't take long. We can dig him up, cut him open, and if we can't discover any poison, we can have him back in the cemetery within two hours!

The Crime of Doctor Crespi provided Dwight major billing on the film's credits and posters; it also offered Dwight ample publicity in the pressbook—and hailed him as Hollywood's "Man of a Thousand Deaths." When it played New York's Rialto in January of 1936, *The New York Times* reported:

The only redeeming presence in the picture is that of Dwight Frye, as Doctor Crespi's assistant. Mr. Frye, once chosen as one of the ten best legitimate actors on Broadway, makes the best of a bad situation which, of course, is not very good.

Erich von Stroheim's personal critique of *The Crime of Doctor Crespi*: "It was the crime of Republic!"

With no Broadway prospects, and a living to be made, Dwight Frye came back to Hollywood. The roles remained small, the movies unspectacular. He was Mack, a member of a gang of robbers headed by Joseph Calleia in *Tough Guy* (MGM, 1936), starring Rin Tin Tin, Jr.; when Dwight balks at eliminating young Jackie Cooper, he gets a sound thrashing from his boss. In *Florida Special* (Paramount, 1936), he played Jenkins, a secretary guarding the jewels of a wealthy old man (Claude Gillingwater) on a train; the "B" movie also featured Frances Drake (leading lady of *Mad Love* and *The Invisible Ray*), and found Frye murdered.

Tough Guy: Dwight Frye, Edward Norris, Jackie Cooper, Edward Pawley, Wally Maher.

Florida Special: J. Farrell MacDonald, Frances Drake and Dwight Frye.

Frye (left) in *Alibi for Murder* observes William Gargan and Egon Brecher.

Frye (left) in *Beware of Ladies* with Russell Hopton, William Newell and William Crowell.

Dwight Frye's Last Laugh

Dwight had one of his most underrated roles as Alvin McBride, assistant to a murdered scientist in Columbia's *Alibi for Murder* (1936). He confronts a munitions mogul (Egon Brecher) with a fervent, "You wholesale dealer of death!" and speaks with great ardor, in pacifist tones, of the imminent danger of science in the wrong hands: "It was for you he was inventing even greater horrors than the world has yet known!"

Beware of Ladies (Republic, 1936) saw Dwight as Swanson, a gang member who is planted as a volunteer worker in Donald Cook's campaign headquarters. The infiltrator role also gave Dwight a rare chance to display his comic touch on film.

Giving these little roles everything he had, Dwight Frye kept hoping they would all lead to something better.

Ultimately, they would not.

———————————

Many of the people Dwight had worked with in New York were reaping the glories of movie fame: Fredric March, Miriam Hopkins, Edward G. Robinson, Josephine Hutchinson were all stars; Sidney Blackmer, Florence Eldridge, Roland Young, C. Henry Gordon and Henry Travers were top featured players; Bela Lugosi was a horror icon. Dwight had been their peer on the legitimate stage; indeed, he even had eclipsed several of them in applause and critical praise. Yet there they were, and here he was...

In the days before *Dracula* and *Frankenstein*, Hollywood's "Man of a Thousand Deaths" had been a star.

He desperately hoped and prayed that he might be one again.

Dwight Frye as the mysterious horse handler Vindecco from *The Shadow*.

Dwight Frye's Last Laugh

Chapter Seven
The Best of a Bad Situation

"I have a... hunch!"
—Dwight Frye, as Vindecco, the hunchback in *The Shadow* (Columbia, 1937)

"I've seen evil," Vincent Price once remarked. He cryptically added that Hollywood "used to be one of the most evil places on earth" when he arrived there in the late 1930s.

"No, I'm not joking," said Price.

1937 was an especially "evil" year in Hollywood, offering a circus maximus of tragedy. Business was booming. Louis B. Mayer was the USA's highest-paid man ($1,300,000); and there were classics like Warners' *The Life of Emile Zola*, MGM's *Captains Courageous*, Columbia's *Lost Horizon*, Universal's *One Hundred Men and a Girl*, and Disney's *Snow White and the Seven Dwarfs*. Yet in no other year had so many garish tragedies happened...

January 2: Warner star Ross Alexander took a rifle (allegedly the same one his wife had used in 1935 to commit suicide) and, as his friend Henry Fonda remembered, "blew his head off." January 17: director Richard Boleslawski died suddenly — some sources reporting a heart attack, others mysteriously alluding to poisoned water. January 23: former Mack Sennett "bathing beauty"/star/sound casualty Marie Prevost was found dead in her Hollywood apartment, apparently dead from starvation, her body nibbled on by her dachshund...

Meanwhile, amidst so much scandal and heartbreak, there were peaceful times for Dwight Frye and his family. They lived simply, and it was now that "Buddy" began to form more memories of his father:

> We had left Blue Canyon, and had moved to a
> little residential complex called "The French Vil-
> lage," right across the street from the Hollywood
> Bowl — it's gone now. There was a bunch of little,
> "Normandy"-style village houses, with a garden in
> the middle — very nice. It was there that I had a
> pet, a little wire-haired fox terrier. We always had
> a piano, and Dad played for his own enjoyment,
> and ours — and he was very good.
>
> Up the hill, maybe half-a-mile away, Edward
> Van Sloan, who, of course, acted with my Dad in
> *Dracula* and *Frankenstein*, had a house. We used
> to visit a lot, and he and my Dad, and his wife and

The Frye family at the beach with family friend, actress Grayce Hampton.

my mother, were good friends right up until my
father died.

For the time, Dwight took what he could get. With the Depression still waging,
and so much operatic tragedy playing around him in Hollywood, he bided his time,
ever hoping for his luck to change.

> Dad had a hot temper—but didn't lose it very often.
> I'd say he was rather an easy-going man, consider-
> ing the fact that he was frustrated for a good number
> of years over his inability to get roles he wanted,
> and not being able to work as often as he liked.
> —Dwight D. Frye

1937 audiences saw Dwight in small but colorful roles: as a radio operator who
goes crazy reporting a ship's fire on the *S.S. Paradise* in RKO's *Sea Devils* (the Coast
Guard radio operator with whom Dwight frantically communicates, by the way, was
his long-time personal friend Paul Guilfoyle)... As a disturbed medical patient who
tries to leap out of an airplane ("Nurse Subdues Maniac in Flying Hospital," reads the
movie's newspaper headline) in RKO's *The Man Who Found Himself* ("Buddy" Frye,
who acted briefly in movies despite his parents' reluctance, can be glimpsed in this one
being removed from a train wreck)...

One of the true scandals of 1937 would involve Universal and Dwight's loyal director, James Whale. The Laemmles had lost Universal in 1936. The new regime was
showcasing Deanna Durbin, but also gave Whale the green light for *The Road Back*, the
long-awaited sequel to *All Quiet on the Western Front*. Costuming himself in German
officer's waistcoat and a beret, Whale (a former P.O.W.) made a passionately anti-Ger-

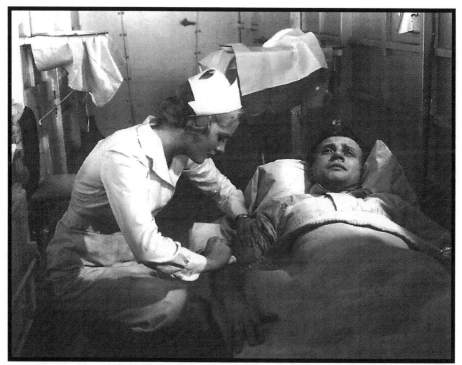

Nurse Doris King (Joan Fontaine) prepares to medicate the disturbed patient (Dwight Frye) on the ambulance plane, from *The Man Who Found Himself*.

The Road Back: Dwight Frye explains the purpose of the town meeting to returning veterans Willy (Andy Devine), Ernst (John King) and Ludwig (Richard Cromwell).

man film; in his original ending, a grotesque dwarf was shown, viciously drilling boys to fight for the Fatherland.

One might imagine that Whale had cast Dwight as the dwarf, a la *Frankenstein*. Instead, he cast him as a comic eccentric in a mob scene, shot at night on the back lot European village set. Dwight waves his umbrella, almost orchestrating the parade of villagers leading the mayor and others to a town assembly; the role was small, but Whale gave Dwight closeups worthy of a Hollywood star. It was yet another of 1937's tragedies that Universal caved in when the Nazi party protested *The Road Back*; Charles R. Rogers (Junior Laemmle's successor) ordered 21 separate cuts, had director Edward Sloman shoot new comedy scenes, and butchered Whale's version. James Whale's protests would seal his doom with the new Universal.

The tragedies kept coming. April 20, 1937: Arthur Edmund Carewe, whose horror roles included Svengali in *Trilby* (1923), the Persian in *The Phantom of the Opera* (1925), the scar-faced doctor with the black monocle in *Doctor X* (1932) and the dope-addicted "Sparrow" of *Mystery of the Wax Museum* (1933), shot himself in the head. June 7, 1937: Jean Harlow, MGM's "platinum blonde bombshell," died at Good Samaritan Hospital. The cause of death was kidney failure. She was 26 years old. The story in Hollywood was that her mother, an ardent Christian Scientist, had refused her medical care until it was too late.

The British ban on horror films, with its censorship of near-vigilante proportion, was catching up with horror and its stars. Boris Karloff would keep prospering; he took star character jobs at Warner Bros., would begin the *Mr. Wong* series at Monogram, perform on radio and even act Poe's "The Tell-Tale Heart" in vaudeville. Lionel Atwill restrained those wicked flourishes he'd revealed in his early 1930s horror films, and stayed busy as a dignified supporting player. Bela Lugosi, however, soon ran out of work. In 1937, he acted in San Francisco and Los Angeles in a stage production of *Tovarich*; on June 11, he signed to play evil "Boroff" (seemingly a contraction of his rival's name!) in the Republic serial *SOS Coast Guard*. It would be his last film role for almost a year-and-a-half. As Lugosi would tell Ed Sullivan:

> They had branded me with the stamp of an animal.
> I was a horror actor, an animal, and they would not
> give me a chance.

Before things would improve, Bela would lose his Outpost Drive mansion—shortly after the birth of Bela, Jr.

Yet Dwight Frye, the most "zoophagous" of the horror "animals," kept working. A refreshing change-of-pace was Grand National's *Something to Sing About* (1937), as a gay hairdresser. "When I look at that hairline," shrieks Dwight as the hairdresser, "I could almost cry!"—as he plans to paste a Robert Taylor-style widow's peak toupee on the forehead of James Cagney.

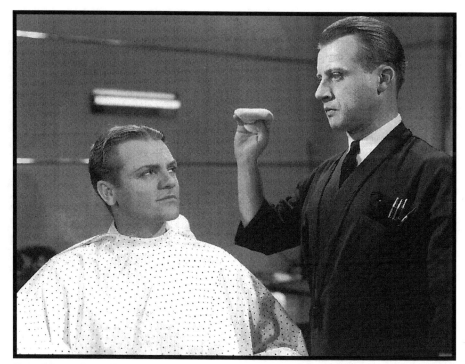

Something to Sing About was a refreshing change of pace for Dwight Frye (seen here working on James Cagney).

Not so picturesque a role came in Grand National's *Renfrew of the Royal Mounted*, starring James Newill as the singing Mountie, Renfrew. Dwight's role: a desk clerk of the Totem Pole Lodge.

———————

Meanwhile, high in the Hollywood Hills, near the Griffith Observatory, Colin Clive had turned into Mr. Hyde. There, in his Spanish-style aerie, Clive drank and wept and feared doctors would have to amputate his leg, injured years before in a horse fall. He had been "Hyde" on his last two films, *History Is Made at Night* (UA, 1937), as Jean Arthur's demonically jealous spouse, and *The Woman I Love* (RKO, 1937), as a LaFayette Escadrille leader; he was drunk, bitter and sometimes hysterical. Clive had been acting at 20th Century-Fox in *Lancer Spy*, with Peter Lorre (who served as one of his pallbearers) at the time of his final breakdown; Lionel Atwill replaced him. On the morning of June 25, 1937, Colin Clive died at Cedars of Lebanon Hospital, a victim of consumption and his real-life "monster"—alcohol.

Colin Clive lay in a funeral bed at Edwards Brothers Colonial Mortuary; his funeral June 29, 1937, attracted 300 curious Hollywoodites. Late that day he was cremated, and there is a sad mystery as to whatever happened to his ashes.

Dr. Frankenstein of *Frankenstein* and *Bride of Frankenstein* was dead. With his death, the British ban on horror films, and the shutdown of melodramas in Hollywood, it appeared the horror genre was dead as well.

The Shadow: **Marc Lawrence, Charles Quigley and Dwight Frye.**

Curiously, in the wake of Colin Clive's death, Dwight landed another hunchback role: Vindecco, the "twistbacked horse-handler," in the "B" circus melodrama *The Shadow* (Columbia, 1937), starring Rita Hayworth. He met his end via a poison dart while trying to warn Miss Hayworth. *The Shadow* offers Dwight a line of dialogue which bears repeating. At one point, Dwight's "Vindecco" makes a prediction, and is asked why he feels that way.

"I have a... hunch!" says the hunchback—and Dwight can barely suppress the twinkle in his eye as he delivers the double entendre.

1937 remained a year of tragedy in Hollywood: George Gershwin died July 11 at age 38 from a brain tumor; serial queen Ruth Roland died September 22 of cancer; and Ted Healy, original leader of The Three Stooges, died mysteriously December 21 — possibly beaten to death while celebrating the birth of his son. Dwight had been working, but primarily in "B" films and small roles. He was restless for creativity—and, that year, he began a Christmas tradition that his son remembers vividly:

> Dad was an artist, and it was in 1937, in fact, during a period when he was "at liberty," as they say, that he began the tradition of his Christmas cards. He would start out in August, saw out 4"

Dwight Frye's 1937 handmade Christmas card.

by 4" squares of plywood, sand them down, stain
them, color them, design the painting, do the actual
painting in many different colors—then address
them on the back to his friends. It was a five-month
process, with some 150 cards, all out in time for
Christmas.

———————————————

1938. Dwight's first feature release of the year was Columbia's *Who Killed Gail
Preston?* The role was flashy, if not substantial. Gail Preston (Rita Hayworth) is murdered during her nightclub act. We see "Mr. Owen" (Dwight) firing a shot and racing
out the door. Chased by the police, Owen climbs a fire escape to a fourth-story roof,
where he admits to the crime—and leaps to his death. It's discovered that he was Gail
Preston's estranged husband, and that his bullet is not the one that killed her. John
Gallaudet did it.

Dwight Frye appears as the estranged husband of Gail Preston in *Who Killed Gail Preston?* Inspector Kellogg (Don Terry) attempts to seize Mr. Owen (Frye).

Dwight (right) joined forces with C. Henry Gordon, his co-star from *Puppets*, in *Invisible Enemy*.

Dwight Frye's Last Laugh

In May 1938 Dwight returned to the stage in *Night Must Fall* at the Mason Opera House pictured here with Adelaide Melnotte.

Dwight joined forces again with C. Henry Gordon, his co-star from Broadway's *Puppets*, in *Invisible Enemy*. Gordon played an unscrupulous international dealer in munitions; Dwight was Alex, his henchman.

His film career, already humble, was declining. Even James Whale, himself *persona non grata* at Universal since *The Road Back*, would give Dwight only an embarrassingly small bit in *Sinners in Paradise* (Universal, 1938). Dwight played Marshall, who makes certain that his attractive, wealthy employer (Charlotte Wynters) safely boards an airplane incognito heading to the Pacific.

The part was doubly embarrassing. Charlotte Wynters had inherited the Josephine Hutchinson role in the 1928 road tour of *A Man's Man*, in which Dwight had recreated his 1925 Broadway triumph. Now, Miss Wynters had a good featured part in *Sinners in Paradise*—while Dwight had a bit.

Once again, he tried the stage. In May 1938, Dwight played Danny, the psycho who carries the head of a female victim in a hatbox, in a WPA/Federal Theatre production of Emlyn Williams' *Night Must Fall* at the Mason Opera House in Los Angeles. The play provided a reunion with a ghost from Dwight's past: *Night Must Fall*'s director, O. D. Woodward, who had given Dwight his first professional job and directed so much of his early stock work in Denver and Spokane.

Dwight Frye (center), posing as a steward, spies on Roland L. Got and Robert Livingston in *The Night Hawk*.

Paul Kelly, Dwight Frye and C. Henry Gordon in *Adventure in Sahara*.

Dwight Frye's Last Laugh

MGM's *Fast Company* featured Dwight as Sidney Z. Wheeler, who fixes up rare stolen books for a fence (Louis Calhern). The flashy role found him shooting Melvyn Douglas in the posterior and sharing a bottle of booze with a floozy; Calhern later shoots Dwight to avoid implication in a murder mystery being investigated by Douglas. *Fast Company* was Dwight's first film with another excellent actor destined for horror movie infamy: George Zucco.

Dwight screamed some more as an arsonist who accidentally blows himself up in *Think It Over* (1938), an entry in MGM's *Crime Does Not Pay* short subject series, directed by Jacques (*Cat People*) Tourneur. In Republic's *The Night Hawk*, Dwight played John Colley, a killer working for Robert (*King Kong*) Armstrong. Also in 1938 Dwight had a juicy role as "the Jackal," informing on his fellow Foreign Legionnaires to a sadistic commandant (C. Henry Gordon, again) in Columbia's *Adventure in Sahara*.

Meanwhile, *Dracula* and *Frankenstein* became a sensation all over again.[13] On August 4, 1938, the Regina Theatre in Los Angeles offered both films (plus *Son of Kong*), and the triple bill played to capacity business for five weeks.[14]

Universal re-released *Dracula* and *Frankenstein* nationally, to record business. As David J. Skal wrote in his book, *The Monster Show*:

> In Cincinnati, the demonic duo broke a six-year house record; in Indianapolis, the same combination was doubling the theatre's normal box office. In Manhattan, the Rialto ran *Dracula* and *Franken-stein* around the clock, filling the house to capacity ten times a day.

The December 20, 1938, issue of *Look* magazine gave a splashy layout to both films (with several stills of Dwight's Renfield and Fritz). Meanwhile, Dwight decided it was time for his son to become familiar with his Dad's most famous screen performances, and proudly took seven-year-old "Buddy" to see *Dracula, Frankenstein* and (as he recalls) *King Kong*:

> ...and I got the feeling the next day that he was disappointed that I hadn't been scared to death! Apparently I took it all in stride—the fact that he was up there in two of those three movies didn't bother me at all, and certainly didn't frighten me. I remember my mother telling me later that he was disappointed.

For Dwight Frye, there would be many disappointments to come—and one immediately awaiting him at Universal City.

I was in *Frankenstein, Bride of Frankenstein* and
Son of Frankenstein... quite the proper order. It was
all very respectable — the *Bride* came first!
—Boris Karloff

The phenomenal success of *Dracula* and *Frankenstein* in national reissue inspired Universal to produce a new sequel, *Son of Frankenstein*, which began shooting November 9, 1938. It was a powerhouse cast: Basil Rathbone (in the title spot) as Dr. Wolf von Frankenstein; Karloff (in his third and final appearance as the Monster); Bela Lugosi (as bearded, broken-necked old Ygor); and Lionel Atwill (as Inspector Krogh, cocking his wooden arm to salute). Josephine Hutchinson, Dwight's Broadway co-star in *A Man's Man*, played the lovely Baroness Elsa von Frankenstein, Wolf's wife.

Portraying council members in *Son of Frankenstein* were Michael Mark (little Maria's father of *Frankenstein*) and Lionel Belmore (the burgomaster of *Frankenstein*) — both slain in the new melodrama by Karloff's Monster.

And — before cuts were made in the film — Dwight Frye was in *Son of Frankenstein* too.

It was a crazy production. James Whale was no longer in favor at Universal, and Rowland V. Lee became producer/director of *Son of Frankenstein*. He tossed out Willis Cooper's original script (featuring a talking Monster) and made up the picture as he went along: merrily defying Universal's hopes for a 27-day shoot and a $300,000 budget; keeping Cooper a virtual hostage at Universal throughout the Thanksgiving, Christmas and New Year's holidays; demanding that the writer put words to the episodes that Lee would whimsically imagine.[15]

None of the stars knew how the picture was going to end. Universal production reports wailed about Lee's prodigal spending and shooting. When Boris Karloff missed a day's work due to the birth of his daughter Sara Jane, Universal desperately contacted Karloff's agent to make sure he worked his last day on the film gratis.

Dwight Frye reportedly was in *Son of Frankenstein*. Due to the mad style in which Lee shot the film (working from a few script pages at a time), no actual shooting script of what ultimately emerged as *Son of Frankenstein* has been found (and possibly never existed) to indicate what role Dwight played in the film; reportedly, he acted "an angry villager." [16] However, as *Son of Frankenstein* "wrapped" at 1:15 a.m. on January 5, 1939, after 46 shooting days (19 days over schedule) and a cost of $420,000 ($120,000 over budget), Universal began a mad, around-the-clock schedule to prepare the film for its Friday, January 13 preview at the Hollywood Pantages.

Dwight Frye's footage was cut entirely.

Son of Frankenstein was a box office smash. One wonders if Dwight Frye went to see the movie, and left in anger — feeling the Curse of Frankenstein more keenly than ever.

Dwight worked once more for James Whale — as a foppish valet in *The Man in the Iron Mask* (UA, 1939), preparing the sinister Fouquet (Joseph Schildkraut) to attend the marriage of King Louis XIV. He had no billing.

The Man in the Iron Mask: **After being dressed by his valet (Dwight Frye), Nicholas Fouquet (Joseph Schildkraut) receives a plate from a herdsman. Edgar Norton is on the right.**

According to rumor, Dwight played the "Cat-man" in Paramount's *The Cat and the Canary* (1939), starring Bob Hope and Paulette Goddard. However, his name appears in no production notes available on the film.

Dwight appeared as Bruno, bank-robbing companion of Bruce Cabot, in *Mickey the Kid* (Republic, 1939).

In *Conspiracy* (RKO, 1939), Dwight played Lt. Keller, working from the inside to help revolutionaries overthrow a totalitarian Central American government. He's viewed at a radio receiver getting a message from a cohort (Henry Brandon). Keller is discovered to be a traitor and is presented with a package containing a pistol—with the implication that he's to commit (offscreen) suicide.

Dwight had scenes as a doctor in a clinic in MGM's disastrous Spencer Tracy/Hedy Lamarr *I Take This Woman* (1940). After many revisions and changes in cast and director, he was entirely cut from the film.

He made his only serial—playing Professor Anderson, a museum curator, in Republic's 15 chapter 1940 cliffhanger *Drums of Fu Manchu*. Henry Brandon played Fu Manchu, whose "Dacoits" ("men of murder") attack the professor in hopes of getting the stone tablet known as the Kardac Segment. Dwight appeared only in Chapter 5 ("The House of Terror"); it's he who realizes that the Dacoits have switched places with some of the museum's wax statues.

Dwight was Pinky the gunman in Republic's *Gangs of Chicago* (1940), serving as gangster/henchman to Barton MacLane, wounding Ray Middleton and being killed

Bankrobber Jim Larch (Bruce Cabot) holds his fallen accomplice Bruno (Dwight Frye) outside the Merchants Trust Company in *Mickey, the Kid*.

Robert Kellard holds a package from Dwight Frye in *Drums of Fu Manchu*.

Dwight Frye's Last Laugh

Dwight Frye (left) portrays a hired assassin in _Phantom Raiders_, seen here with Walter Pidgeon and Donald Meek.

by reformed Lloyd Nolan. He had a nice part in MGM's slick "B" _Phantom Raiders_ (1940), second in Metro's "Nick Carter" series, this one concerning ships disappearing in the Panama Canal zone. Dwight was Eddie Anders—almost killed by his own men as Walter Pidgeon's Nick tricks him into revealing that killers are after the detective.

A curiosity came along via _Sky Bandits_ (Criterion and Monogram, 1940), Dwight's second exploit with the ever-warbling "Renfrew of the Royal Mounted" (James Newill). Dwight played Speavy, a mad inventor with a pet rabbit, a mystery ray that destroys planes—and the Renfield laugh! Also, Dwight's laboratory apparatus in _Sky Bandits_ reportedly came from Kenneth Strickfaden, recycling a few of the old gizmos he'd provided Universal for _Frankenstein_ and its sequels.

Roles were becoming smaller and less frequent. Dwight, Laura and "Buddy" relocated to Culver City (Dwight's mother had moved to Pomona with her brother). As Dwight's son remembers, they resided in Culver City in "a cut-rate rental house" on Van Buren Street that Dwight leased from a friend. It was only a few blocks from the Selznick Studios, where "Buddy" recalls playing on the front lawn of "Tara" from _Gone With the Wind_.

For Dwight Frye there were frustrations and temper tantrums. And there was the sad realization that, after ten years in Hollywood, he apparently had achieved no reputation at all.

Spencer Tracy, Jack Carson, Don Castle and Dwight Frye in *I Take This Woman*.

Dwight Frye (left), Lloyd Nolan and Barton MacLane in *Gangs of Chicago*.

Dwight Frye's Last Laugh

Louise Stanley, Dwight Frye, William Pawley and Joseph Stefani in *Sky Bandits*.

Montagu Love, Louis Hayward, Frye and Clayton Moore in *The Son of Monte Cristo*.

At the Famous Monsters Convention in 1993, I was asked if I was ever teased by children while I was growing up about my father being in horror movies. I replied, "I'd tell my Dad to eat them—like the spiders and flies in *Dracula!*" In fact, however, the other kids never asked, because nobody ever knew who my father was when he was alive. The fact that my name was the same as his didn't ring bells with anybody. My Dad never received any recognition from the public throughout his lifetime. Nor had he achieved any kind of security at all. We went through some tough financial times.

—Dwight D. Frye

Dwight's last release of 1940 was UA's *The Son of Monte Cristo*, with Louis Hayward as hero, Joan Bennett as heroine and George Sanders as villain; Rowland V. Lee directed. Dwight appears in a pitifully brief bit as a secretary to Prince Pavlov, and is coerced by Hayward, Montagu Love and Clayton (*The Lone Ranger*) Moore into opening a safe. Curiously, the actor playing Prince Pavlov was Michael Visaroff, who (unbilled) had played the innkeeper who had warned Dwight against going to Borgo Pass in *Dracula*.

In *The Son of Monte Cristo*, Michael Visaroff had billing. Dwight Frye did not.

One of the most famous rumors about Dwight Frye's career states that the desperate actor wanted work so badly that he played in a stag film.

In *Famous Monsters of Filmland* magazine #126 (July, 1976), Bob Scherl reported in a Dwight Frye tribute, "Dracula's Disciple Renfield," that

> ...it is known for certain that he starred in a nudist colony film... mostly hiding in the bushes watching the camp members play volleyball—but unfortunately the title is unknown.

While this information is no more "certain" today than it was 20 years ago, Scherl (a reputable collector and fan) has reported that friends had attended an evening of stag movies from the 1930s and 1940s. All were film buffs; all "definitely" had recognized Dwight Frye as the voyeur in the bushes.

It's possible—but why would it have happened? A cruel joke played by an agent on a former Broadway star with deep religious beliefs? A job whose true nature wasn't discovered until Dwight reported for work?

If it is true, the genuine tragedy is that Dwight felt financially compelled to take the work.

One wonders if the pornography ended up in the collection of Lionel Atwill.

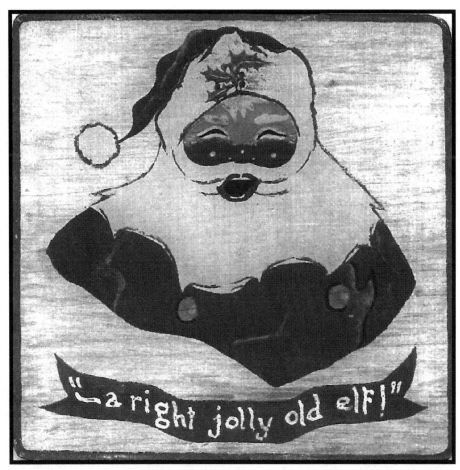

Dwight Frye mailed these handmade Christmas cards to friends and family in 1940.

Christmas Holidays, 1940: the legend goes that Lionel Atwill had dressed up as Santa Claus at his Pacific Palisades house, had shown his guests *The Plumber and the Girl* and *The Daisy Chain*, and led the guests in stripping and reprising the pornography on a tiger skin rug before a roaring fireplace as Viennese waltzes played on the piano.

Atwill would deny all, to no avail (and to an eventual perjury conviction). Yet his Gothic orgy came at an appropriately baroque time for Hollywood melodrama. It took place as Boris Karloff was nervously preparing for his Broadway debut in *Arsenic and Old Lace*, and just after Lon Chaney, Jr. had passed (with flying colors) a Universal trial run for a contract in *Man Made Monster* (shot full of electricity by Atwill). Bela Lugosi had recently completed the first of his Poverty Row horrors of the 1940s, PRC's *The Devil Bat*.

War drums of Germany and Japan were thundering on the horizon. A new chapter in Hollywood and world history was about to begin.

This was the scenario as Dwight Frye began the final act of his career and life.

A portrait of Dwight Frye taken shortly before his death.

Dwight Frye's Last Laugh

Chapter Eight
"All That Blood on My Hands"

> My father was afraid to leave the telephone (in this
> era before answering machines), for fear his agent
> would call with a job—and he'd miss it....
> —Dwight D. Frye

Hollywood horror of the war years.

It was the era of Lon Chaney, Jr., achieving true folklore status as Universal's *The Wolf Man* (1941), baying under Universal's full moon... "The new master character creator" blustering his way through portrayals of Frankenstein's Monster and the Mummy and Dracula with violent alcoholic outbursts that became the stuff of Universal legend and lore... of Evelyn Ankers, Universal's blonde "queen of the horrors," she of the magnificent scream, experiencing true horror as a loose 600-lb. bear chased her up into the catwalks on *The Wolf Man* set... of a 60-year-old Bela Lugosi collapsing in his Frankenstein's Monster makeup and costume on the set of *Frankenstein Meets the Wolf Man*.

It was an era when RKO's Val Lewton was revolutionizing the genre with novel, poetic films like *Cat People*, *I Walked with a Zombie* and *The Seventh Victim*... even while Monogram was purveying *The Ape Man*, in which Louise Currie lashed a hairy Lugosi with a whip.

It was a time when a young, 300-lb. actor named Laird Cregar became one of Hollywood's greatest movie villains, scoring at 20th Century-Fox as the insane detective of *I Wake Up Screaming* (1941) and Jack the Ripper of *The Lodger* (1944), playing with bravura style and peppering the roles with kinky sexual innuendo... only to die in 1944, at age 31, following a crash diet to become a leading man.

There was John Carradine, wearing his slouch hat like a pirate, looking (and sounding) like a wild west Shakespearean actor as he changed a gorilla into Acquanetta in Universal's *Captive Wild Woman*... George Zucco, playing trembling high priests in the Universal *Mummy* series and patronizing Poverty Row horrors to buy more animals for his Mandeville Canyon ranch.

This was the genre in which Dwight Frye still found himself typecast.

Many of his Hollywood colleagues of the early 1930s had left the arena. Colin Clive was dead. Carl Laemmle, Jr., ousted "crown prince" of Universal, had not produced another movie after losing Universal in 1936; nor would he ever produce one. *Dracula* director Tod Browning had retired to Malibu; *Frankenstein* and *Bride of Frankenstein* director James Whale was in exile in Pacific Palisades. Helen Chandler, of *Dracula*, was unemployable due to her alcoholism; Mae Clarke, of *Frankenstein*, was trying to get work as a character actress. Edward Van Sloan's career had disintegrated into bit roles almost as unworthy as those being offered Frye.

Still, Dwight believed he could adjust. If only he had the right role, in the right film...

Ironically, during these turbulent times, the "king of horror" was on Broadway. On January 10, 1941, Karloff had made his Broadway debut at the Fulton Theatre (where Dwight Frye had starred in *Sitting Pretty* and *Keeper of the Keys*; where Bela Lugosi had starred in *Dracula*) in *Arsenic and Old Lace*. As mad Jonathan Brewster, whom a drunken plastic surgeon had facially refashioned to resemble Hollywood's top bogeyman, he explained his murder of one Mr. Spenalzo with the line, "He said I looked like Boris Karloff!"....

And the opening night audience roared with laughter.

His "jolly luck" had come through again; Boris Karloff was in one of the historic hits of the American Theatre. Not only did he have the joy of playing to live, SRO audiences; not only did he reap a $2,000 per week salary plus a percentage; he avoided a stormy, colorful, revolutionary period for horror in Hollywood. The prestige he'd win in this hit play would exceed any glory won in horror films by his competitors of this time. After a year-and-a-half in New York, Karloff came home to Hollywood, starred in Columbia's *The Boogie Man Will Get You* (1942) and began a national tour of the play, commencing in the summer of '42 at the Biltmore Theatre in Los Angeles. Dwight D. Frye attended:

> I went downtown in Los Angeles by myself
> to see a matinee of *Arsenic and Old Lace*, and
> went backstage to introduce myself to Karloff.
> He couldn't have been nicer—very English, very
> polite, very nice, and not at all like the Monster!
> Obviously, he knew my father, and was very
> pleasant to me.

Karloff spent another year-and-a-half on tour with *Arsenic and Old Lace*. He returned to Hollywood again in January of 1944, just in time for both Universal delirium (*House of Frankenstein*) and Val Lewton poetry (including *The Body Snatcher*, starring Boris in his magnificent title role performance).

By the time of Karloff's Hollywood homecoming in 1944, Dwight Frye was dead.

———————————

In 1941, Dwight reprised Renfield in a revival of the play *Dracula* at the Beaux Arts Theatre in Los Angeles; Frederick Pymm played the Count. Dwight D. Frye remembers there being very little ballyhoo regarding his father's Renfield encore.

> I remember two things primarily about that stage
> production of *Dracula* in 1941. First, I remember
> feeling, as a 10 year old, that Frederick Pymm, as
> Dracula, wasn't very scary. And I recall going back
> stage, and my father showing me a trick in which he
> held a "blood"-soaked sponge in his hand, to pro-

In 1941 Dwight returned to the stage in a revival of *Dracula*, starring Frederick Pymm.

duce the "blood." He also showed me how the
bat worked, on a wire. At 10 years old, I should
have figured that out myself!
— Dwight D. Frye

Desperately trying to support himself, Laura and "Buddy," Dwight acted in 1941
in usually unbilled movie bits: Rader, one of a group of spies and saboteurs deported
on Columbia's *Mystery Ship*... a jury foreman in MGM's *The People vs. Dr. Kildare*...
Leo Qualen, a spy tossed into a roaring motor in Paramount's *Flying Blind*... a barber
in Columbia's *The Blonde from Singapore*... a radio operator in Republic's *The Devil
Pays Off*.

Cy Kendall, John Tyrrell, Dwight Frye, Eddie Laughton and Larry Parks in *Mystery*

Dwight Frye as a radio operator watches J. Edward Bromberg, Osa Massen, Margaret Tallichet and William Wright in *The Devil Pays Off*.

Dwight Frye (center) seen with Brandon Hurst and Otto Hoffman in *The Ghost of Frankenstein.*

December 7, 1941 was Pearl Harbor. Days later, Universal began shooting its fourth *Frankenstein* saga.

> You Can't Keep a Good Monster Down!
> Here's Universal's Midas Again!...
> Out For More Gold!
> With every chill a thrill...
> with every chill he fills your till!
> —Universal trade ad for *The Ghost of Frankenstein* (1942)

"Destroy the castle!" raved Dwight in the opening of *The Ghost of Frankenstein,* which premiered at New York City's Rialto Theatre April 3, 1942. "Strike the last traces of these accursed Frankensteins from our land!" Lawrence Grant, the Burgomaster from *Son of Frankenstein*, gives consent as do Michael Mark and Lionel Belmore (both slain by Karloff's Monster in the previous film).

"We'll blow it up!" rants Dwight apocalyptically.

Off go the torch-bearing villagers to dynamite Castle Frankenstein. We see Dwight, scampering about with the mob, as old Ygor (Lugosi again, in a terrific performance) shoves giant stones crashing down from atop the tower. Explosions... the Monster (Lon Chaney, Jr.) freed from the sulfur... Ygor joyful as he frees his "friend"...

And Dwight's anonymous villager is never seen again.

The new Universal *Frankenstein* opus billed Chaney, fresh from *The Wolf Man*, as "The new master character creator." As Karloff's first successor, the hard-drinking actor was a formidable monster but gave the role none of the Pagliacci-style emotion of Karloff. Erle C. Kenton (who had stylishly directed Paramount's 1932 *Island of Lost Souls*) staged the film with slick, atmospheric efficiency, and the starring cast was excellent: Sir Cedric Hardwicke as Dr. Ludwig Frankenstein, the "second son" of the original monster maker; Ralph Bellamy as Erik, the heroic town constable; Lionel Atwill as Dr. Bohmer, who wickedly transplants Ygor's brain into the Monster's skull in a mad power plan that explodes in the fiery climax; and Evelyn Ankers, a beautiful Elsa Frankenstein, sounding her classic scream.

The cinematography by Milton Krasner and Elwood Bredell was top-notch; the Hans J. Salter musical score thrilling. But... the fairy tale ambiance of the first three films, the style of James Whale (and even of Rowland V. Lee), and, of course, the Karloff Monster were all profoundly missing, just as they would be in the ensuing films in the series.

Strangely, *The Ghost of Frankenstein* reminds us of these legendary predecessors. As Evelyn Ankers shivers one stormy night over the records of her infamous grandfather, *The Ghost...* shows flashbacks from *Frankenstein*, and we see Colin Clive's Monster Maker and Dwight's hunchback; there's even a closeup of Clive from *Bride of Frankenstein* They remind us of the glory days of Universal horror, and of just how far Dwight Frye—who has two lines in the opening of *The Ghost of Frankenstein*, and no billing—had fallen in a decade.

A second "Mug" in Republic's *Sleepytime Gal* (1942)... a hotel desk clerk, who greets Louise (*Son of Dracula*) Allbritton in Universal's *Danger in the Pacific* (1942)...

Dwight landed a juicy role in yet another MGM short—this one entitled *Don't Talk*, which was Oscar-nominated for best short subject of 1942. He played a saboteur named Ziggy, in the employ of Axis spies. Playing his boss, ironically, was Gloria Holden—who had starred in the title role of Universal's 1936 *Dracula's Daughter*.

By now, the Frye family had moved to 2590 N. Beachwood Drive, in the Hollywood hills, a little colony of Spanish-style houses, under the Hollywoodland sign. The upstairs bedroom of Dwight and Laura had a balcony, facing south, from which one could see all the way to Long Beach on a clear day. Dwight D. Frye recalls standing on this balcony one night, air raid sirens wailing, searchlights sweeping the skies and anti-aircraft firing at airplanes erroneously believed, in the post-Pearl Harbor panic, to have been Japanese bombers.

The United States was at war; it was an era of air raids, blackout curtains and a new job for Dwight Frye—as a tool designer at Douglas Aircraft in Santa Monica. As his son remembers:

> My Dad had been too young for World War I, and he was too old for World War II, which made him feel a little guilty. So he worked the graveyard shift at Douglas, which was in Santa Monica, a long drive from where we lived on Beachwood Drive. It was from midnight to eight in the morning, I think, a shift which he took so that he could work on films during the day.

Dwight Frye's Last Laugh

2590 N. Beachwood Drive, Hollywood; Dwight's former home has the striped awning.

Dwight approached his work at Douglas (he'd acquired a draftsman's skill in his high school years) just as he did his work as an actor—with total dedication. And, as he settled into this new day and night routine, a dream-come-true presented itself—a chance to return to Broadway.

The play was *The Patriots*, the playwright was the celebrated, Pulitzer Prize-winning Sidney Kingsley, and the role was Alexander Hamilton. It presented every chance of success: a new play by one of America's top playwrights, and a rich historic role. Dwight hadn't enjoyed the thrill of a Broadway hit in over a decade, and the plum role of Hamilton gave promise of winning him the critical praise he had so deeply missed.

He rejected it.

Why did Dwight Frye forsake such an opportunity? There were several reasons. He didn't want to leave his family in Hollywood during wartime. Nor would his conscience allow him to give up his war effort job at Douglas (where reportedly he was working on a special bombsight). Believing a true "patriot" would do what he ought to do (and not what he wanted to do), Dwight gave up *The Patriots*. It nearly broke his heart.

The Patriots opened at New York's National Theatre January 29, 1943, with House Jameson as Hamilton. It was a very respected hit, running 172 performances and winning the Critics Circle Prize for Best Play.

Meanwhile, audiences saw Dwight Frye in his final films.

> When they started making George do horror
> pictures, it was a big mistake. A *big* mistake.
> —Mrs. George Zucco, 1991

Stately, bald, dynamic George Zucco was a superb British actor. He'd won London stage stardom (along with Colin Clive) in *Journey's End* (1929), directed by James Whale; he'd come to New York as Disraeli in *Victoria Regina* (1935), co-starring with Helen Hayes and Vincent Price. At MGM, he supported Garbo, Harlow, Crawford, Norma Shearer and Jeanette MacDonald; but his flair for villainy soon led to horror films. Zucco was still welcome at MGM, Paramount and Warners as a character player, but he was becoming notorious as the evil high priest of Universal's *The Mummy's Hand* (1940) and *The Mummy's Tomb* (1942)—and had dropped by PRC, lowliest of the Poverty Row lots, to unleash Glenn Strange's wolfman monster in *The Mad Monster* (1942).

On Valentine's Day, 1943, PRC Studios released *Dead Men Walk*, offering two George Zuccos for the price of one (and one Dwight Frye). Zucco played the dual roles of twin brothers, Dr. Lloyd Clayton and his vampire sibling Elwyn. Dwight's role: Zolarr—the vampire's hunchbacked, grave-robbing acolyte. "You'll pray for death long before you die!" Dwight promises the "good" Zucco. Dwight plays Zolarr with his usual passion. However, spoiling this "homage" to Renfield and Fritz are not only the shoddy production values of this 63-minute, Sam Newfield-directed potboiler (shot in six days, starting September 11, 1942), but seeing how sadly aged Dwight Frye looks. In his book *Poverty Row Horrors!*, Tom Weaver notes Frye's "tired and bloated" appearance, but writes:

> Frye gives his all to the demeaning hunchback
> role... Dressed like a cat burglar, his hair combed
> into an unflattering widow's peak, he spews his vit-
> riolic dialogue with aplomb and trundles Elwyn's
> coffin around like the professional grave-robber
> that (in movies) he was...

Dead Men Walk must have been a painful misadventure for Dwight Frye. Looking haggard in some closeups, puffy in others, Dwight's hunchbacked, vampire-tending Zolarr might have verged on self-parody—but for the incredible, dynamic intensity he gallantly gives the performance. PRC featured Dwight prominently in the poster art,

Dwight Frye was featured prominently in PRC's poster art for *Dead Men Walk*.

Dead Men Walk **must have been a painful misadventure for Dwight Frye.**

George Zucco as Elwyn Clayton teamed with Dwight Frye as his servant Zolarr in *Dead Men Walk.*

and took a stab at providing him well-deserved publicity in the *Dead Men Walk* press-book, with appropriately headlined stories:

> Horror Epics are Frye's Dish
> Always to Die is Fate of Frye

However, being PRC, there was a backfire. In the "Horror Epics..." story, the publicist ran down Dwight's credits in *Dracula, Frankenstein* and *Bride of Frankenstein*, then ventured to describe *The Great Impersonation*, in which Dwight played the Ghost of the Black Bog. There was an unfortunate typo:

> In *The Great Impersonation*, he played the mad
> son who was hidden away in the **bag**.

Much of *Dead Men Walk* is so bad, so atrociously staged, so sordid that (despite the impeccable trouping of Zucco and Dwight), it's almost unwatchable. Yet, come the climax, Zolarr attacks the "good" Zucco with a poker, and the camera gives Dwight subjective closeups. Dwight's ferocity is almost startling. Eyes wild, teeth bared, his face fills the screen with a hatred that is haunting. Fire erupts, Dwight's hunchback is pinned beneath furniture, and as the flames destroy the vampire and Zolarr, he screams, "Master!"

Dr. Frank Mannering (Patric Knowles), under the scrutiny of Rudi (Dwight Frye), questions Maleva (Maria Ouspenskaya) in *Frankenstein Meets the Wolf Man*.

"The Man of a Thousand Deaths" has died once more.

"*Dead Men Walk* Bad Even For Horror Film," headlined *The Hollywood Reporter*.

And then...

Could it be the Monster again? Frankenstein's Monster?
—Dwight Frye, in *Frankenstein Meets the Wolf Man* (1943)

"The Monster! The Monster!"

A fall night, 1942. It's the old Frankenstein village of Universal City; the camera aims down from the Tyrolean rooftops to the cobbled streets below.

The movie is *Frankenstein Meets the Wolf Man*, and we've watched the "Festival of the New Wine," where Gypsy singer Adia Kuznetzoff sings the famous "Faro-La, Faro-Li" song:

> Come one and all and sing a song,
> Faro-La, Faro-Li!
> For life is short, but death is long,
> Faro-La, Faro-Li!

Roy William Neill is directing the episode. Now, at the cry of "action," a couple runs through the cobbled streets, the woman screaming, the man crying out "the Monster!"

The man is Dwight Frye, five for five in Universal's *Frankenstein* series, playing Rudi, a nervous villager.

The atmosphere of *Frankenstein Meets the Wolf Man* is pure Oktoberfest, yet with a sinister undercurrent. It almost seems a Hollywood purgatory for actors whose pasts were catching up with them.

There's blonde, Hungarian diva Ilona Massey, as Baroness Elsa Frankenstein; once MGM's "Singing Garbo," blackballed by a Metro sex scandal, going through a nasty divorce from actor Alan Curtis and sentenced now to movies like *Frankenstein Meets the Wolf Man*. There's Lon Chaney, in his first encore as Larry Talbot, "the Wolf Man"; trying to go clean from his alcohol and food binges in a doomed hope of joining the Marines as a cook. And there's Lionel Atwill, as the mayor, facing a conviction for perjury committed during the infamous "orgy" trial.

And, as hundreds of villager "extras" go crazy, there waddles into the village square Bela Lugosi—60 years old, cruelly humbled into playing the Monster he'd scorned in 1931. Whatever sins of arrogance Bela had committed at Universal in his palmy 1930s, he was burning for them now.

"A quiet and lonely man... seemed unhappy," said the late Patric Knowles (who played romantic lead "Dr. Mannering" in the film) about Bela Lugosi.

Sara Schwartz, bit player and longtime Universal "Screamer," lets out a scream so wild that Lugosi jumps out of character; director Neill must do a retake.

Stuntman Eddie Parker, also in Monster makeup, takes over as Bela retreats, silently puffing his cigar on the set sidelines as Parker climbs onto a carriage, kicking wine barrels at the pursuing villagers.

It's all in a night's work on *Frankenstein Meets the Wolf Man*, Dwight Frye's final horror film. There seemed to be a curse on *Frankenstein Meets the Wolf Man*—fated to be a troubled shoot from start to finish:

October 12, 1942: shooting of *Frankenstein Meets the Wolf Man* begins at Universal; producer George Waggner plans for Chaney to play both Wolf Man and Monster.

October 13, 1942: "One Monster Is Enough, So Lugosi Does The Other," headlines *The Hollywood Reporter*. Worried how the erratic, hard-drinking Chaney might cope with both roles, Universal desperately offers the part to Bela—who, everyone remembers, had refused it in 1931. Bela accepts with some salvaged pride: in Curt Siodmak's script, the Monster is blind, and *speaks*.

October 15, 1942: Lionel Atwill is convicted of perjury. His rationale: "I lied like a gentleman to protect friends." Rumor claims Universal will toss him out of *Frankenstein Meets the Wolf Man*, but he remains (and gives a surprisingly high-spirited performance).

Come the climactic battle, and Gil Perkins doubled the Monster, while Eddie Parker shifted to the Wolf Man. Yet somehow, it all came together; *Frankenstein Meets the Wolf Man* would become one of Universal's most popular horror movies of the 1940s. And one of the reasons for the film's great status with horror genre disciples is Dwight's ample screen time as Rudi. He looks well in his Tyrolean garb (indeed, far more healthy than he had in *Dead Men Walk)*, nicely plays some fine moments and delivers some rich dialogue:

Frankenstein Meets the Wolf Man: Adia Kuznetzoff (with lantern), Don Barclay, Rex Evans, Harry Stubbs (police hat), Martha Vickers, Beatrice Roberts and Dwight Frye.

"What animals are around here that can kill people?" asks Dwight, under the full moon of Vasaria, after a village girl (Martha MacVicar, later starlet Martha Vickers) is killed. As if in response to his question, we hear the howl of Chaney's Wolf Man! "Yes a wolf, that's his cry!" says Dwight, and the chase is on to the Frankenstein ruins.

"Come on, speak up, old witch!" orders Dwight to venerable Maria Ouspenskaya (reprising her wonderful Maleva the Gypsy from *The Wolf Man*), as the mob apprehends her at the ruins. "Where's that strange man that was with you?"

At the Festival of the New Wine, as Adia Kuznetzoff belts out the "Faro-La, Faro-Li" song, we see the curious spectacle of Dwight actually smiling, singing with the chorus and dancing! (Playing the woman who fans have surmised is Rudi's wife is Beatrice Roberts, memorable as the evil "Queen Azura" in Universal's 1938 serial *Flash Gordon's Trip to Mars*. She was allegedly the off-screen mistress of Louis B. Mayer.) [17] Actually, the original script called for Rudi and his wife to be newlyweds. It also called for Dwight to dance with the bounteous Ilona Massey at the Festival—a privilege usurped by Lionel Atwill in the film.

After the Monster crashes the Festival, Dwight offers this line, back at the tavern: "Much as I'd like to kill the Monster, I'd hate to crawl around through those dark catacombs of Frankenstein's castle in the black of the night!"

Later in the tavern, Dwight voices this suggestive line (rather funny, considering Ilona Massey's flamboyant sex appeal) about the Monster, the Wolf Man, the Gypsy,

George Irving, Dwight Frye, Emmett Vogan and Walter Brennan in *Hangman Also Die!*

Elsa and Mannering hiding out in the Frankenstein ruins: "But doesn't it strike you as strange that Mannering and that Frankenstein girl never tell us what they're doing up there?"

All the cast plays with superb style. Yet *Frankenstein Meets the Wolf Man* never escaped its "curse." On November 5, 1942, Lugosi collapsed in his Monster guise; a doctor blamed his Monster makeup and costume, and sent him home to recover. The same day, a cart carrying Chaney and "Madame" Ouspenskaya overturned, and the venerable Russian actress had to enter the hospital.

Happily, Dwight gets the last line of the movie. Atwill inquires as to the whereabouts of raving villager Vazec (Rex Evans)—and Dwight intones ominously: "He said he'd blow up the dam!" We see "the beast battle of the century," Monster vs. Wolf Man, the dam indeed blowing up, the waters spectacularly rampaging down the mountain to the castle, Atwill and Frye and villagers gazing at the spectacle as Hans J. Salter's score swells for the end.

Frankenstein Meets the Wolf Man's dark cloud hovered even after the actors went home. Producer George Waggner and staff found Lugosi's dialogue "so Hungarian funny" (as Curt Siodmak put it) that Universal cut all his lines; also pruned were all references to his blindness. Bela's Monster proved a debacle. Yet despite these troubles (and perhaps partially because of them!), fans love *Frankenstein Meets the Wolf Man*, which opened at the Rialto Theatre in New York City on March 5, 1943. And it's moving for many Universal aficionados to see, one last time, the name "Dwight Frye" in the closing credits.

Dwight Frye, Niles Asther, Richard Arlen and Marc Lawrence in *Submarine Alert.*

Dwight's follow-up roles were far less impressive. *Hangmen Also Die!* (UA, 1943), based on the assassination of Nazi Reinhard Heydrich, was produced and directed by Fritz Lang (who also collaborated on the story with famed German writer Bertolt Brecht). The solid cast included Brian Donlevy as the assassin, Anna Lee (Karloff's leading lady in 1936's *The Man Who Changed His Mind* and 1946's *Bedlam*) as the heroine and Walter Brennan as Lee's professor father—a change-of-pace role that Brennan acted with goatee (and teeth). Dwight played an imprisoned Czech patriot; also in the scene with him was Emmett Vogan, with whom he had acted in stock in Denver and Spokane. Dwight had no billing.

Audiences saw Dwight as one of a gaggle of spies in *Submarine Alert* (Paramount, 1943). He played the "1st Hoodlum," harassing Evelyn Keyes in *Dangerous Blondes* (Columbia, 1943), a *Thin Man* clone starring Allyn Joslyn and Miss Keyes as Nick and Nora Charles imitators. Completed June 19, 1943, *Dangerous Blondes* not only afforded Dwight no billing; it also gave him no dialogue.

He broke off with his agent. It was a frightening time for Dwight Frye, and his son recalls:

> I think, from what I heard from my mother, that my
> Dad was obviously very worried about finances,
> frustrated, and maybe even a bit bitter about the

Horace MacMahon, Evelyn Keyes and Dwight Frye in Frye's last film, *Dangerous*

fact that nobody would give him work except in
films like *Dead Men Walk*.

Dwight persevered. As Laura worked part-time as a sales clerk at the Broadway/ Hollywood Department Store at Hollywood & Vine, Dwight, with no agent, had to seek acting jobs himself. After a long night's work at Douglas, he would visit casting offices, waiting with beauty contest winners and 4-F Adonises who had decided to give Hollywood a break. Often he came home angry, exhausted, humiliated, desperate to vent his frustrations however he could:

> My Dad played the piano, right up to the very end.
> And he painted a lot—he would do paintings of
> flowers on glass, and frame them, and paint stand-
> ing screens and so forth in the house...

He threw himself into his work at Douglas. Inevitably, the harrowing schedule took its toll:

> We learned after my Dad's death that he'd had a
> couple of heart attacks—not serious ones, I guess,
> but still heart attacks—at work. But, because
> he was an ardent Christian Scientist, who would

not go for medical help, he had made those who
worked with him promise never to tell his family
about the attacks.

—Dwight D. Frye

He desperately made himself believe he was well; made himself believe he might
still have a chance of steady work as an actor. The dream of "big-name" success in
Hollywood had burned out long ago. Yet was it too much to believe that he might make
a good living as a character player? Still he hoped and prayed for that one role, and
that one movie.

In the last 10 days of his life, he believed he had found both.

————————

Well, I talked to the casting director Tues. & as
the test was in Technicolor there was a delay and
he hadn't seen it. I called him yesterday & he
had. He said it was grand & I looked just like I'd
walked out of the book. He was very happy about
it. Said he thought Darryl Zanuck would see it by
Tues. or Wed...

—Dwight Frye, letter to his Mother, October
24, 1943

Fall, 1943. Boris Karloff was wrapping up his national tour in *Arsenic and Old
Lace*. Lugosi was at Monogram, starring as the *Voodoo Man*, backed up by John
Carradine as a bongo-paying geek named Toby and George Zucco as a high priest of
"Ramboona." There was method in Carradine's madness; he took his *Voodoo Man*
check, poured it into his Shakespearean repertory company and opened a few nights
later in San Francisco as *Hamlet*.

Lionel Atwill, free from his perjury conviction on a legal appeal, was playing the
"Scarab," super villain of Republic's serial *Captain America*. Laird Cregar was completing his bravura performance as Jack the Ripper in 20th Century-Fox's *The Lodger*.

And Dwight Frye believed he had found the movie job that might end his
typecasting curse.

The movie was *Wilson*—a biography of President Woodrow Wilson and the most
epic production Darryl F. Zanuck and his 20th Century-Fox Studios had ever mounted.
Alexander Knox had won the role of Wilson; Geraldine Fitzgerald would play Wilson's
wife Edith; Henry King would direct the Technicolor production and Fox would lavish over $4,000,000 on this historic biography. The top supporting cast would include
Thomas Mitchell (as Joseph Tumulty), Sir Cedric Hardwicke (as Senator Henry Cabot
Lodge) and Vincent Price (as William G. McAdoo). Zanuck vowed that *Wilson* would
be one of the great movies of all time, confidently joking that if it failed, "I'll never
make another movie without Betty Grable in the cast!"

Through a friend, Dwight managed to get on the 20th Century-Fox lot (where he
had never made a picture before) and underwent Technicolor tests for the epic production. His role: Secretary of War Newton D. Baker. "I remember him telling us that the

studio made him up," says Dwight D. Frye, "and that he looked exactly like Newton Baker—which is part of the reason he got the part." On Halloween, 1943, Frye triumphantly wrote to "Muzzie":

> Well, now, I *got* the picture... Zanuck O.K.'d me
> but they wanted to do something about my hair.
> So I went out and they are making me a hair piece
> and will darken my own hair to match. I may get
> 4 wks. if it stays as it is now scheduled but if they
> change it I may not get more than one or two but
> I'm grateful for it. I'll get $400 a week...

While never blueprinted as a starring role (or even a major supporting one), the part of Newton Baker presented Dwight the chance to play a normal, non-maniacal, historical person in a film everyone hoped would become one of the greatest movies ever made. *Wilson* was a project that promised to be a very impressive credit in any actor's resume; it would also be Dwight's first color film. His son remembers how much the job meant to his father:

> There used to be a very nice restaurant on Vine
> Street, just north of Hollywood Boulevard, and we
> used to go there all the time. I remember our all
> going there one night, after Dad had received word
> he'd gotten this part in *Wilson*—and it was a very
> jubilant evening for him. This was to have been
> a prominent, straight role at a time when he was
> approaching 45, and could have launched him, con-
> ceivably, into a whole other area of film work.

Friday, November 5, 1943. Dwight and Laura had given each other early Christmas gifts: she gave him a black mahogany spinet desk ("Laura and I like it so much," he wrote to his mother); he was giving her a chair to go with it; and they were giving each other a joint gift of new drapes. The desk had arrived, the drapes were hung and now Dwight was waiting for the delivery of the chair as Laura prepared to leave for work. He wrote to his mother:

> ...We are so happy about the desk, we hope we
> feel the same way about the chair... I have already
> ordered our turkey and we'll have our Thanksgiv-
> ing the Sunday after... Haven't been out to have my
> wig tried on yet but expect a call any day now... Am
> working hard at the plant... Buddy is re-painting
> some of the things in his room. It will be very nice.
> I don't think I have any more news right now but
> will probably write again on Sunday. I know you
> must be busy with the yard but you'll be thru with

canning and certainly that was a hard job well done
and we'll be grateful all winter.
Love from us all
—Dwight

Sunday, November 7, 1943. It had been, as "Buddy" recalls, "a very high week" for his family. Meanwhile, the Hollywood Pantages Theatre was offering a double feature: RKO's *A Lady Takes a Chance*, starring John Wayne and Jean Arthur, and Universal's *Sherlock Holmes Faces Death*. That night, Dwight Frye took Laura and "Buddy" to the movies.

> My Dad took us to the Pantages Theatre... There
> was a long line, and a long wait to get into the
> theatre; I have a recollection that it was hot in the
> theatre, although this was November...
> —Dwight D. Frye

As *Sherlock Holmes Faces Death* filled the Pantages screen, and Basil Rathbone and Nigel Bruce took to solving the "Musgrave Ritual," the film presented Dwight a surprise: the Universal production employed the old crypt from *Dracula* and the European village from *Frankenstein*. What did he feel when he saw those sets that night? Pride? Bitterness?

They were, ironically, among the final images Dwight Frye would ever see. His son remembers:

> ...After the movie, we came out, walked half-a-
> block to the corner of Hollywood & Vine, where
> we'd pick up the bus to take us up Beachwood
> Drive. We got on the bus—and I think the bus had
> not even pulled away from the curb when my Dad
> fell right in the middle of the aisle.
> He was not dead then. Obviously, somebody
> called an ambulance and we went to Hollywood
> Receiving Hospital nearby. I remember my mother
> and I waiting... I guess it was an hour later, that the
> doctor came out and said that he had died.
> My Dad was 44 years old. I was 12.

Dwight Frye had died at 11:15 p.m. of coronary thrombosis. Whether earlier medical care (which he had rejected as a Christian Scientist) might have prolonged his life can only be conjecture.

"Tool designer," reads the death certificate.

Wednesday, November 10, 1943: the funeral took place at the Utter-McKinley Mortuary, 8814 Sunset Boulevard, in West Hollywood—the funeral parlor incongruously neighboring such Sunset Strip night clubs as Ciro's, the Trocadero and the Mocambo.

I think it was my first funeral. It was an open casket. I remember that my mother had asked that he be dressed in a suit he had bought just recently, which was a kind of gray and white herring-bone tweed... And I remember leaning over the casket, touching his face and kissing him.

—Dwight D. Frye

Dwight Frye's Last Laugh

The hearse drove to Forest Lawn Memorial Park, Glendale. It passed "the great mausoleum," with the tombs of Jean Harlow, Irving Thalberg, Carole Lombard and Lon Chaney, and headed to a section called "Graceland." There, at the top of a very steep hill, the family buried Dwight Frye. The gravestone reads:

Dwight Iliff Frye
Loved Husband, Father, Son
1899   1943

Since Pearl Harbor, there had been a "blackout" of Hollywood searchlight premieres; it was feared the lights might attract the enemy, or be mistaken for an air raid. However, at 8:30 p.m. on November 10, 1943, Grauman's Chinese Theatre proudly hosted "Hollywood's first 'light-up' premiere since Pearl Harbor" as 20th Century-Fox's *Guadalcanal Diary* opened, the proceeds to go to war charities. "Hollywood's most glamorous stars in person!" promised *The Los Angeles Times*.

As Dwight Frye's family mourned on Beachwood Drive that night, searchlights festively swept the Hollywood skies.

Chapter Nine
Milestones

After Dwight's death, Laura realized she was the sole bread-winner in the family. She gave up her low-paying job at the Broadway/Hollywood department store and went to work in the Hollywood offices of Western Airlines, processing tickets and reservations. Her son entered Hollywood High School.

Meanwhile:

November 27, 1943: twenty days after Dwight's death, Republic released a 68-minute feature version of the 1940 15-chapter serial, *Drums of Fu Manchu*. The movie included Dwight's performance as Professor Anderson.

December 8, 1943: four weeks after Dwight's funeral, a *Daily Variety* critic attended the opening of Frye's last film, Columbia's *Dangerous Blondes*. (The 12/9/43 critique called it "the smartest murder-mystery-with-comedy turned out in many months.") The site of the screening was ironic: the Hollywood Pantages theatre. Ironic, too, was the title of the Kelley Roos novel on which Dwight Frye's posthumously released film was based: *If the Shroud Fits*.

August 1, 1944: *Wilson* had its world premiere at New York City's Roxy Theatre. Reginald Sheffield, father of Johnny Sheffield ("Boy" in the Tarzan films), had replaced Dwight Frye in the Technicolor, two-hour and thirty-four-minute, $4,000,000-plus production. The Newton Baker role ultimately emerged as little more than a bit; Dwight's son believes the part was cut down severely after his father's death: "I saw *Wilson* not long ago on television," he says, "and the part almost didn't exist." *Wilson* proved to be one of the legendary bombs in Hollywood history, losing a record $2.2 million for 20th Century-Fox.

December 15, 1944: *House of Frankenstein*, Universal's sixth film in the Monster saga, opened at New York's Rialto Theatre. "All Together...!" proclaimed the posters. "Frankenstein's Monster! Wolf Man! Dracula! Hunchback! Mad Doctor!" Boris Karloff, back in the fold after his *Arsenic and Old Lace* triumph, was the Mad Doctor; Lon Chaney, of course, the Wolf Man; John Carradine, in cape and stylishly cocked top hat, a slick Dracula; and former cowboy heavy Glenn Strange a hulking Monster. The 70-minute, Erle C. Kenton-directed "monster rally" provided work for Lionel Atwill (as an Inspector) and George Zucco (as "Prof. Bruno Lampini," whose Chamber of Horrors is pirated by Karloff).

And, as for the Hunchback... those honors (with special billing) went to J. Carrol Naish, as Karloff's homicidal familiar, "Daniel." While the part owed its inspiration mostly to Lon Chaney, Sr.'s 1923 *The Hunchback of Notre Dame* (especially in his love for Gypsy Elena Verdugo), the role inevitably evokes memories of Dwight Frye's Fritz of the 1931 original *Frankenstein*.

December 21, 1945: Universal's new "monster rally," *House of Dracula*, premiered at New York's Rialto Theatre. Chaney's Wolf Man, Carradine's Dracula and Glenn Strange's Monster were all back, in the seaside castle of "mad doctor" Onslow Stevens; even Lionel Atwill was back, once more in Inspector's uniform. This time, the "Hunchback" emblazoned on the posters was a female! Pretty brunette Jane Adams, a former Conover model, played Nina, the hunchbacked nurse to Stevens' Dr. Edelmann. Her deformity unfairly told against her in the finale; despite her sweet nature, Miss Adams' Nina is strangled by the Jekyll/Hyde mad doctor and tossed into a hole.

August 15, 1946: Laura Frye remarried. Her second husband was Alexis Luce, a former actor about 15 years her senior. As was noted earlier, Luce had been the leading man that the Seattle press had so extolled during Dwight's stock company days there in 1922. Both Luce and his late wife had acted with Dwight and Laura; "My Dad died about the same time his wife had died," says Dwight David Frye. "My mother and stepfather kept corresponding, and it grew into the marriage." They wed in Boston; after the wedding, Luce returned to his retirement in his childhood home in Bucksport, Maine, while Laura spent a year apart from her new husband, back in Hollywood on Beachwood Drive, so her son could graduate from Hollywood High School in the summer of 1947. The family then united in Maine, where Dwight David went to the University of Maine, earning Bachelor's and Master's degrees in Chemical Engineering.

Meanwhile:

April 22, 1946: Lionel Atwill, 61, died at his Pacific Palisades house, a victim of bronchial cancer. He'd acted as long as he could, playing the villain in Universal's serial *Lost City of the Jungle*; a double had completed the dying actor's scenes. He reportedly died deeply bitter, raging to the last about his sex scandal, and left a $250,000 estate to his 29-year-old widow and their six-month-old baby Lionel.

June 25, 1948: Universal-International (as it was known now, following its merger) premiered *Abbott and Costello Meet Frankenstein* at the Forum Theatre in Los Angeles. Bud and Lou capered with Chaney's Wolf Man, Strange's Monster and Bela Lugosi, back as a resplendent Count Dracula. It was an affectionate and official finale to a grand era of Universal horror.

August 16, 1956: Bela Lugosi, 73, died of a heart attack in his Hollywood apartment. He had spent final years in classic degradation, including Ed Wood films and his self-commitment to a state hospital as a drug addict (an illness he heroically conquered). Buried in his *Dracula* cape at Holy Cross Cemetery in Los Angeles, Lugosi left behind a $2,900 estate, his fifth wife Hope, his son, Bela Lugosi, Jr., (today a very successful Los Angeles lawyer who looks after his father's now-legendary legacy), and an Oscar-winning role for Martin Landau in *Ed Wood* (1994).

May 29, 1957: James Whale, 67, long-retired, drowned himself in the pool behind his Pacific Palisades house. His long-concealed suicide note expressed his fear of illness and old age. Dwight Frye's favorite director left an estate of $600,000.

October 6, 1962: Tod Browning, 82, director of *Dracula*, died at the Los Angeles home of friends who had been caring for him. He had left MGM in 1942, spending his final decades in Malibu Colony, never discussing his career (recently excellently documented in David J. Skal and Elias Savada's book *Dark Carnival*).

November 22, 1965: the musical *Man of La Mancha* opened at New York's ANTA Theatre in Washington Square, starring Richard Kiley as Cervantes/Don Quixote and Joan Diener as Aldonza. Dwight David Frye, who had begun his acting career on the stage in California in 1956, was part of the company of this legendary production, both as assistant to director Albert Marre and on-stage briefly as a member of the Inquisition. About this time, he took, by chance, a top-floor-front apartment at 44 West 69th Street—not realizing at the time that it was the same building in which his father, mother and grandmother had operated the Tea Room back in the 1920s.

Since that time, Dwight Frye has aided Mr. Marre in productions of *Man of La Mancha* in London, Brussels and Paris, as well as being very active in the production end of New York musicals and plays (*Dance a Little Closer, So Long 174th Street, Knickerbocker Holiday, The Sorrows of Frederick* and *Odyssey*, aka *Home Sweet Homer*), and has produced several original cast record albums (*Do Black Patent Leather Shoes Really Reflect Up?, Rags,* a live concert recording of Cole Porter's *Nymph Errant* and a studio cast recording of an early musical version of *The Secret Garden*, starring Barbara Cook, John Cullum and George Rose).

Mrs. Ella Frye remained an ardent Christian Scientist all of her life. She would outlive her beloved son by 25 years, dying in the late 1960s. After her death, it was discovered that Dwight Frye's Hollywood scrapbook, which had gone to her, had been stolen.

February 2, 1969: Boris Karloff, 81, the "king" of Hollywood horror, died in his beloved England—wealthy, celebrated, cared for by his loyal fifth wife Evelyn, and working almost to the end, as he had wished—"with my boots, and my greasepaint on." Today, Karloff's daughter Sara supervises "Karloff Enterprises" in Rancho Mirage, California. The passing of this beloved star was the end of an era.

Yet for Karloff, Lugosi, Atwill, Whale, Browning—and Dwight Frye—the legend was just beginning.

Dwight Frye's Last Laugh

Chapter Ten
Immortality

The first fan letter had come way back in 1945. It was from Donald Maurer, a Dwight Frye fan from Perkasie, Pennsylvania. Laura Frye had asked 15-year-old "Buddy" to answer it.

In 1948, *Abbott and Costello Meet Frankenstein* had officially dropped the curtain on the golden age of horror. It was then the "atomic age," with a new repertoire of horrors, like giant bugs (*Them!, Tarantula*). Yet the old horror classics, like the richly theatrical goblins who populated them, just kept coming back. Realart Pictures licensed the Universal horror films in the late 1940s, re-releasing them into the early 1950s.

In the fall of 1957, *Shock Theatre* was a TV sensation. *Dracula* and *Frankenstein* led the big parade of Universal horrors out over the airwaves, heralded by such TV horror hosts as New York's Zacherley (John Zacherle, still getting mileage out of the "Cool Ghoul") and Baltimore's Dr. Lucifer (Richard Dix, today a noted Shakespearean actor). Fans took note of the name of Dwight Frye. He subsequently won attention through the 1960s in such magazines as Forrest J Ackerman's *Famous Monsters of Filmland* and the late Calvin Beck's *Castle of Frankenstein*.

By the early 1970s, Alice Cooper had recorded "The Ballad of Dwight Fry(e)" — "A form of flattery, you might say," says Dwight's son, "although I don't remember being able to decipher the lyrics!" Richard Bojarski and Gary Dorst wrote tributes to Frye in horror magazines; in April, 1974, he received his first in-depth coverage in James T. Coughlin's feature in *Film Fan Monthly*. Editor Leonard Maltin treated Frye to the cover (a portrait from *Frankenstein*).

More and more fans began contacting Dwight D. Frye. Strangers recognized his name on credit cards, and insisted on performing their rendition of the Renfield laugh. In the mid '70s, Dwight was on the production staff of the musical *Odyssey* (based on Homer's epic), starring Yul Brynner and Joan Diener:

> I remember that we rehearsed at the Belasco The-
> atre for a week or ten days. It seemed very tiny to
> me; I'd seen stills from *Mima*, that enormous set,
> and I wondered, "How did they get all that into
> this tiny theatre?" But the stage manager (unbe-
> knownst to me) was a huge fan of my Dad's. He
> never mentioned it until we got into the Belasco
> Theatre. Well, he knew that *Mima* had been done
> at the Belasco, and he knew that my father had
> been in *Mima*, and he obviously was a *Dracula*

Dwight David Frye at the Famous Monsters Convention, May 1993.

fan. And he started doing the Renfield laugh—all
through rehearsals!

As more and more attention came, Dwight shared the phenomenon with his mother
(his stepfather, Alexis Luce, had died in 1968):

> Of course, I told my mother about this "cult status"
> that Dad was enjoying, and she said the obvious
> thing—"Too bad he wasn't aware of it before he
> died." My mother was not one to dwell on the
> past; even after a stroke in 1974, from which she
> never fully recovered, she was still bright, happy
> and cheery. She died in 1979, and her ashes are

Dwight Frye's Last Laugh

buried in Maine beside my stepfather; it's really been since she died that I've gotten this rather enormous amount of attention from the fans. So I was never able to tell her about that.

Come the 1980s and the dawning of the video age, and *Dracula* and *Frankenstein* were among the earliest video releases of MCA/Universal. By 1986, MCA had restored *Frankenstein*, adding long-censored scenes — including closeups of Dwight Frye's leering Fritz and Karloff's crying Monster in the dungeon torture episode. *Dracula* also received a restoration, with long-lost sound cues added — such as the sound of Lugosi's Dracula breaking the neck (back?) of Renfield on the great staircase of Carfax Abbey.

Meanwhile, the son kept becoming acquainted with fans of his father — some very famous:

> Back in 1989, I did a benefit at the New York State Theatre, called *An Evening with Alan Jay Lerner* — a memorial to Alan, whom I'd known from working on his ill-fated *Dance a Little Closer*. His widow was there, and a whole bunch of stars, including Van Johnson — whom I'd never met. When I introduced myself to Van, he said, "Dwight Frye? Oh my God!" And he carried on all evening! He'd known my father and me back in 1933, when we were living at the Knickerbocker Hotel on 45th Street in New York, and he was a kid, living there too, looking for a job. He remembered that we'd constantly gone up and down in the Knickerbocker elevator together, and used the "roof garden" to sun in, and so forth. Van couldn't get over it. During the day of the rehearsal for the benefit, he'd go up to people like Douglas Fairbanks, Jr., and say, pointing to me, "Do you know who this is?!" I finally said, "Van, they don't care." And he'd say, "Well, I do!"

1991: it was the 60th anniversary of the release of *Dracula* and *Frankenstein*, and MCA celebrated by releasing a special boxed set of the "restored" *Dracula* and *Frankenstein*. The video packaging of *Frankenstein* now featured Dwight's Fritz on the cover, along with Karloff's Monster and Colin Clive's monster maker.

Then, come Memorial Day Weekend, 1993, the Famous Monsters Convention took place in Crystal City, Virginia. The "con" was primarily in honor of Forrest J Ackerman and his *Famous Monsters* magazine, with a dazzling guest list: Ray Bradbury, Ray Harryhausen, Robert Bloch, Gloria Stuart, Carroll Borland, Curt Siodmak, Ann Robinson, Zacherley. And also a guest of honor, along with Boris Karloff's daughter Sara Jane, Bela Lugosi, Jr., and Lon Chaney, Jr.'s grandson Ron, was Dwight D. Frye.

At the Famous Monsters Convention: (seated left to right) Dwight David Frye, Sara Karloff, Bela Lugosi, Jr. and Ron Chaney; (back) Sara's husband Bill Sparkman.

"That was the eye-opener for me," he says. "It boggled my mind."

There he came face-to-face with the incredible folklore status that his Dad has attained. On Saturday afternoon, Forry Ackerman hosted a program in which Sara, Bela, Ron and Dwight all took to the ballroom stage; thousands of fans filled the ballroom, flashbulbs popping like they did in the theatre climax of *King Kong*. There was a terrific ovation.

Afterwards, people stood in line for hours to get the autographs of Sara, Bela, Jr., Ron and Dwight. After the first event, Dwight found he couldn't walk through the lobby without fans surrounding him to express their admiration for his father. He met Joe Dante, director of such recent horror hits as *The Howling* and *Gremlins* — and who had named his company "Renfield Productions," and who displays a portrait of Frye in his Hollywood office. Indeed, in that one weekend, Dwight David Frye experienced the phenomenon of fandom more than his father had ever witnessed it in his entire career.

"Astounding," he says.

Then, on Sunday, November 7, 1993, the 50th anniversary of his father's death, son Dwight was guest of honor at the Montclair, New Jersey Film Society's tribute to his father. The tribute had its own share of drama. Spearheading the tribute was Randye Cohen, a librarian and life-long Frye fan. Randye confided to Greg Mank early that day that she'd learned only the day before that she was seriously ill with cancer.

Dwight Frye's Last Laugh

Yet she bravely kept her illness a secret from all but a few there (including Dwight), insisting on hosting the event which, she tearfully told the audience, was for her "a dream come true." (Randye Cohen died of cancer in 1995.)

The Vampire Bat was shown, and Dr. Jim Coughlin presented a collage of clips from many of Dwight Frye's films. Afterwards, Dwight spoke about his father.

"Thank you all for coming," said a very sincere Dwight D. Frye. "This has never happened before. It's been a great treat for me."

The legacy keeps going. A 1995 Christmas movie release was Mel Brooks' *Dracula: Dead and Loving It*; Leslie Nielsen played the Count, Brooks acted Prof. Van Helsing and Peter MacNicol portrayed Renfield—providing a remarkable "homage" to Dwight Frye. MacNicol (known for such films as *Sophie's Choice* and TV's *Chicago Hope*) resembled Frye as the madman, had his body language down pat and (of course) giggled the laugh to perfection: he even got a daub of the lost soul quality into the affectionate spoof. Bill Warren, interviewing MacNicol for *Fangoria* #150 (March, 1996), reported that the actor grew up in Texas, forbidden by his parents to watch the old horror films on *Nightmare Theatre*. Nevertheless, as MacNicol said:

> I could snake my way from the bedroom along the wall, like one of Renfield's vermin, secrete myself between the sofa and the wall and watch *Nightmare Theatre*. That's where I saw *Frankenstein, Son of, Bride of,* all the *Dracula* pictures, all the *Mummy* pictures. My lullabies were the music of Hans J. Salter and Frank Skinner and Franz Waxman. That's what I heard before I went to bed on Saturday night. I loved, loved, loved horror films. I made my own spiderwebs. I created a kind of Necropolis in my bedroom.

Bill Warren reported that MacNicol

> ...hopes that audiences realize how much he respects Dwight Frye's take on the role in the Tod Browning version. "There is something so pungent about that portrayal," he says. "It's one of the most distinctive performances in the history of the horror film."

As MacNicol continued:

> In my performance, I feel like I'm cooing a love song to my betters, to those movies that came before and those actors who were there. Not just Dwight Frye, but Colin Clive and Ernest Thesiger,

the music they had in their performances. These people didn't just act scenes, they sang them, they declaimed them to the heavens, and I just love that. I was smitten with it as a kid, and I still am.

Indeed, clearly, many others are too.

The legend grows. On June 11, 1996, Alice Cooper played Dallas' Coca-Cola Starplex (as an opening act for the Scorpions). Teresa Gubbins filed this report on "Mr. Cooper's Technicolor song-and-dance act" to the *Dallas Morning-News* (6/13/96):

> (Cooper) fulfilled the audience's wishes by doing plenty of big hits... but it was "Ballad of Dwight Fry" that provided the corniest-grandest scene of all, when three "hospital interns" in whites bound Mr. Cooper in a straitjacket. In a moment of mock poignancy, he hunched over, his head flailing, straining to sing into a microphone that was lodged in the jacket. And then the denouement, when he finally freed himself from the confines of the straitjacket, sneaked up behind the oh-so-oblivious remaining "intern" and strangled him from behind. Awright!

Then there was the August, 1996 edition of *Autograph Collector* magazine, which ran a report of the R & R Enterprises March, 1996 memorabilia auction:

> A rare last-name signature of legendary horror character actor Dwight Frye on the return address portion of an envelope went for $1,885.

The price paid for this autograph (last name only!) surpassed dollars spent for such memorabilia as a James Cagney sports coat ($520), a Lon Chaney, Jr. signed photo ($795), a portrait signed by both Laurel and Hardy ($1,065) and "a complete collection of a dozen signed 8 x 10 NASA photos of all the men who have walked on the moon" ($1,560).

An actor is a package of his own energy, imagination and physical characteristics. When fate is kind, the actor finds a role that perfectly accommodates and showcases those attributes. Had Dwight Frye been an actor 30 years later, he might have excelled as the M.C. of *Cabaret*, a role which won a Tony Award, an Oscar and lasting stardom for Joel Grey. Dwight could easily have captured the M.C.'s demonic quality; he also had the song and dance skills necessary for the part.

However, the roles that came his way in the defining hour of his career were Renfield of *Dracula* and Fritz of *Frankenstein*. Dwight gave them everything he had; they, in turn, cast him into a career limbo. But it would prove an ultimate blessing as well as a curse. Just as Poe would find his fame posthumously, so did Dwight Frye, decades after his death, realize his status as a legendary figure of the horror film.

In the lore of horror film stars, Dwight Frye always has evoked one of the many "tragedies" suffered by a strange number of major figures of the genre. Yet, the big picture of Frye's character and his colleagues shows his life—despite his early death—in rather a different light.

Colin Clive, a major screen and stage star—yet drinking himself to death before age 40. Lionel Atwill, after a grand career as a stage matinee idol and a major Hollywood villain, raving on his death bed about the sex scandal that had crippled his career and the cancer that was ending his life. Bela Lugosi, heroically triumphing over his dope addiction at age 72, yet spending a final year of almost unrelieved misery and despair. James Whale, drowning himself in his Pacific Palisades pool. The sad list goes on and on...

Yet Dwight Frye had his family. He had his faith. He had the idealism to work all night at Douglas Aircraft. He'd faced a career nose dive that would have made the most Pollyanna-ish of actors bitter, yet he still hunted film jobs and, at the time of his death, had what every actor wants—a promising, new kind of role to which he could look forward.

And today, Dwight Frye has his status as one of Hollywood horror's most beloved stars—which is a deep satisfaction to his son:

> My Dad would be totally stunned by this recogni-
> tion! I'm sure it's the last thing he ever could have
> imagined. If he had any fans at the time of his
> death, he was never aware of it—unlike Karloff
> and Lugosi, who were stars, and knew it at the
> time. And I think this recognition would just knock
> him over. He would be astounded and very happy
> about it.

Dwight D. Frye died on emphysema on March 27, 2003 at the Veterans Hospital in the Bronx. He was 72 years old. He was cremated, and the ashes will be interred in the family plot at Silver Lake Cemetery, Bucksport, Maine, with his stepfather and beloved mother.

The co-authors of this book will always treasure Dwight's trust, memories and especially his friendship. He is missed.

Dwight Frye, photographed while he was working on *The Maltese Falcon.*

Dwight Frye's Last Laugh

Notes

Chapter 1

1. Emmett Vogan also appeared in his share of horror movies, including *The Mummy's Tomb* (1942), *The Mummy's Ghost* (1944), and *The Vampire's Ghost* (1945).
2. He was also one of the founders of the U.S.O. When he died in 1950, Brock Pemberton's death would receive Sunday front page coverage in *The New York Times*.

Chapter 2

3. *The Cat and the Canary* received such cinema incarnations as Universal's 1927 release, starring Laura La Plante, and Paramount's 1939 version, starring Bob Hope and Paulette Goddard. In fact, rumors insisted (falsely) for years that Dwight Frye played the "Cat-man" in this film. *The Monster* became a 1925 vehicle for Lon Chaney. Vincent Price and Agnes Moorehead were the stars of Allied Artists' *The Bat* (1959).
4. Presumably Miss Eldridge *did* wear lingerie in *The Cat and the Canary*; as *The New York Times'* Alexander Woollcott described one of her scenes as the imperiled heroine: "...the little silly sort of half undresses, peeks prettily under the bed and climbs into bed without thinking to lock the door. Not a bright girl, Annabelle."

Chapter 3

5. No one else, however, ever complained about this "impediment," least of all Stark Young, who would surely have mentioned it in his March 1923 critical essay.
6. Dwight had tried out in an early version of *Puppets* entitled *The Marionette Man*, in the role of Bruno; Claudette Colbert had played Angela in that production, which tried out in Washington, D.C. and Stamford, Connecticut in January 1924. Largely re-written, the play tried out again under the title *The Knife in the Wall*, with the New York cast, prior to Broadway, in Providence, Rhode Island and New Haven, Connecticut.

Chapter 5

7. Alfred Hitchcock filmed the play as *Rope* (1948), with James Stewart as the hero and John Dall and Farley Granger as the murderers. It was Hitchcock's first color film.
8. It's been reported that Dwight won the role after Browning saw his performance in *Man to Man*; however, this film was released in December 1930—after principal photography of *Dracula* was finished. Browning probably saw Dwight in his West Coast revival of the play *A Man's Man*. As for Dwight's major competition for Renfield, Bernard Jukes, he was killed during the London blitz.

Chapter 6

9. Although the Best Actor race that year was announced as a "tie," March actually had defeated the "other" Best Actor of 1932, Wallace Beery (of MGM's *The Champ*) by one vote.
10. Goldstone also used Universal's set from *The Old Dark House* for Atwill's house; the *Frankenstein* wine cellar became *The Vampire Bat*'s morgue.

11. In the novel *Queer People*, Dwight's character commits suicide. No copy of the play is presently available to check if he met the same fate on stage.

12. This time, Dwight just missed Colin Clive, who had closed in *The Lake*, with Katharine Hepburn, the Saturday night before *Queer People* opened.

Chapter 7

13. By now the Motion Picture Producers and Distributors Association had censored *Dracula* and *Frankenstein*, officially cutting scenes some local censors had cut during the original releases. *Dracula* lost its sound effects of Lugosi breaking Dwight's back/neck (as well as Lugosi's own cries of anguish as he was staked). *Frankenstein* lost closeups of Dwight's Fritz torturing Karloff's Monster with a torch—as well as Colin Clive's "In the name of God! Now I know what it feels like to *be* God!" line in the creation sequence, some scuffling in the Clive/Frye/Van Sloan/Karloff fight in the laboratory, the closeup of Van Sloan sticking the hypodermic needle into the Monster, and, of course, the actual footage of Karloff tossing "little Maria" into the lake.

14. Ed Sullivan related that the manager of the Regina, who should have had "a gold medal struck off in his honor" by Universal, instead had to surrender his prints because Universal "jacked up the film rental on him to such an exorbitant extent that he had to give up the pictures after the fifth week." (*New York Post*, 1/9/39).

15. Cooper would later dramatize the situation in the "Rain on New Year's Eve" episode (12/29/47) of his radio show *Quiet, Please*, although he was careful to claim in the script that the film he was writing about was **not** *Son of Frankenstein*!

16. Another report claims that Dwight acted in color test footage with Karloff's Monster, which was reportedly discovered in the late 1980s, promised for video release—then mysteriously lost again.

Chapter 8

17. As Charles Higham wrote of Beatrice Roberts in *Merchant of Dreams*: "Mayer had noticed her when she appeared as a guest in a party scene in *San Francisco* (1936); soon afterward, he began dating her. He fell in love with her; for years she was the love of his life. She shared with him a passion for operettas and Viennese waltzes; she was an accomplished pianist, which, of course, appealed to him..." Higham reported that, while Mayer's executive staff refused to allow him to make her a star, "Mayer insisted on keeping her under contract, loaning her out for picture after picture... He had an under-the-table arrangement with Universal to have her placed on semipermanent loan-out, and for years she appeared in Universal films as maids, nurses or secretaries, glimpsed for an instant; an attractive, fascinating dark presence, living out a ghostly career on the sidelines."

Appendix A
Filmography

The Night Bird
Universal, 1928; Director: Fred Newmeyer; Scenarist: Earle Snell; Titles: Albert De Mond; Adapters: Nick Barrows and Earle Snell; Original Story: Frederick Hatton and Fanny Hatton; Cameraman: Arthur Todd; Film Editor: Maurice Pivar; Running Time: 68 minutes; Release Date: September 16, 1928

CAST: Reginald Denny (Kid Davis); Betsy Lee (Madelena); Sam Hardy (Gleason); Harvey Clark (Silsburg); Corliss Palmer (blonde); Jocelyn Lee (redhead); Alphonse Martel (Pete); George Bookasta (Joe); Michael Visaroff (Mario); **Dwight Frye (wedding guest)**

NOTES: The late film historian William K. Everson was the first to notice Dwight Frye in the crowd at the wedding scene in *The Night Bird*, during a film society screening. Frye probably worked on *The Night Bird* in July 1928, after the midwestern tour of *A Man's Man* and just prior to his own August 1, 1928 wedding to Laura Bullivant.

The Night Bird represents Frye's only silent film, unless he did appear in some of O. D. Woodward's two-reelers shot in Colorado in 1918. Castmember Michael Visaroff (Mario) would again work with Frye in *Dracula* (1931), as the innkeeper who cautions Renfield about Castle Dracula, and *The Son of Monte Cristo* (1940), as Prince Pavlov (Frye played his secretary).

The Doorway to Hell
Warner Brothers, 1930; Director: Archie Mayo; Screenplay: George Rosener; Original Story: Rowland Brown; Cameraman: Barney McGill; Music Director: Erno Rapee; Running Time: 79 minutes; Release Date: October 18, 1930

CAST: Lew Ayres (Louis Ricarno); Dorothy Mathews (Doris); Robert Elliott (Pat O'Grady); James Cagney (Steve Mileaway); Charles Judels (Sam Marconi, florist); Leon Janney (Jackie Lamarr); Kenneth Thomson (Captain, military academy); Jerry Mandy (Joe); Noel Madison (Rocco); **Dwight Frye (Monk)**; Eddie Kane (Dr. Morton); Edwin Argus ("Midget"); Tom Wilson, Al Hill, Richard Purcell (gangsters); Ruth Hall (girl); Bernard "Bunny" Granville (bit)

NOTES: *The Doorway to Hell* was based on *A Handful of Clouds*, an unpublished play by Rowland Brown. Brown's original story won an Academy Award nomination. *A Handful of Clouds*, which was also the film's release title in England, is explained by Mileaway (James Cagney) as "...the kind that come out of a 38-automatic."

In *The Doorway to Hell*, Frye's first sound film, Dwight was listed in the credits as "gangster," but his character's name was Monk. At the beginning of the film, Mileaway approaches Monk, who is shooting pool, and whispers something in his ear. Monk responds, "Oh yeah, where is he?" Told the man in question is down in the car, Monk has Mileaway take his place at the pool table and fetches his violin case. When asked where he is going, Monk offers, "I'm going out to teach a guy a lesson."

The car pulls up before a tenement building, with Monk asking a woman to tell Whitey that he needs to see him. Monk carefully assembles the Tommy gun in the car and machine guns Whitey, who had double-crossed the gang.

From then on in *The Doorway to Hell*, Frye only has brief scenes. When Ricarno (Lew Ayres) announces he is taking over as leader of all the gangs, he opens a window to reveal Monk and another gangster pointing machine guns, assuring everyone Louis means business. With peace prevailing among the gangs for awhile, Monk sits with friends in a nightclub, commenting, "It just goes to show you what organization will do!" Monk is last seen, glaring icily at Midget (Edwin Argus), who questions Ricarno leaving the rackets.

Noel Madison, who was very effective as Ricarno's chief rival Rocco, had some months earlier appeared with Frye in the play *Rope's End*, with Warners noticing them both. In later years, it was revealed that *The Doorway to Hell* star Lew Ayres had coveted the role of Renfield, won by Frye, in *Dracula* (1931).

Man to Man
Warner Brothers, 1930; Director: Allan Dwan; Screenplay: Joseph Jackson; Original Story: Ben Ames Williams; Cameraman: Ira Morgan; Music: Louis Silvers and Erno Rapee; Running Time: 68 minutes; Release Date: December 6, 1930

CAST: Phillips Holmes (Michael Bolton); Grant Mitchell (Barber John Bolton); Lucille Powers (Emily Saunders); Barbara Weeks (Alice, Michael's college girlfriend); George Marion, Sr. (Jim McCord); **Dwight Frye (Vint Glade)**; Russell Simpson (Uncle Cal Bolton); Charles Sellon (judge); Paul Nicholson (Ryan); Robert Emmett O'Connor (sheriff); Otis Harlan (Rip Hendry); Bill Banker (Tom); Johnny Larkins (Bildad); James Neill (B. B. Beecham); James Hall

NOTES: *Man to Man* was based on Ben Ames Williams' original story *Barber John's Boy*, which was also the working title for the film. When the Museum of Modern Art hosted a retrospective of director Allan Dwan's work in the early 1970s, both Dwan and Peter Bogdanovich decided to eliminate *Man to Man* from the program, in that they intensely disliked the film. *Man to Man* may be slow-moving, but it seems to capture the essence of small town America in the late twenties.

Frye, as bankteller Vint Glade, is interested in fellow employee Emily Saunders (Lucille Powers), becoming jealous when she favors Michael Bolton (Phillips Holmes). When Michael's father Barber John (Grant Mitchell) returns from prison, Vint sarcastically notes to his son:

> Nice little shop your father's got. We won't have far to
> go for a shave now.

On the first day Barber John comes into the bank, he drops his cigar in Michael's teller cage, after his son had stepped away. Vint later tells Michael:

> It was funny when your dad dropped his stogie. I heard
> him curse and looked around. I thought he was coming
> right through the wicket after it. His arm was through
> to the shoulder.

That same day Michael comes up $2,000 short and asks Vint to check his figures. "Mike, is this a three or a five?" Vint knowingly inquires, providing Michael with a temporary out for the missing money.

After Michael and Barber John both confess to the theft to shield one another, Jim McCord (George Marion, Sr.) receives evidence that Glade is behind the crime. After being summoned and accused of taking the money, Vint responds, "That's a rotten lie." Three witnesses, including Emily, implicate Vint, who maintains his innocence, but eventually breaks down.

Vint, in tears, still tries to bargain, vowing to return the money, as they take him away.

Frye affected a decent Kentucky drawl in the role of Glade. The part had depth, allowing Dwight to display jealousy, be sarcastic, and, finally, break down into total self pity. Whether or not this role had anything to do with Tod Browning choosing Frye to play Renfield in *Dracula*, Frye was able to evoke the same pathetic pathos in *Man to Man* that he would so aptly utilize in his next, most famous part as the vampire's spider-eating slave.

Dracula

Universal, 1931; Producer: Carl Laemmle, Jr.; Director: Tod Browning; Associate Producer: E. M. Asher; Screenplay: Garrett Fort (based on the 1897 novel by Bram Stoker and the play by Hamilton Deane and John L. Balderston; Additional dialogue by Dudley Murphy); Cinematography: Karl Freund; Art Director: Charles D. Hall; Film Editor: Milton Carruth; Supervising Film Editor: Maurice Pivar; Recording Supervisor: C. Roy Hunter; Makeup: Jack P. Pierce; Set Designers: Herman Rosse, John Hoffman; Scenario Supervisor: Charles A. Logue; Musical Director: Heinz Roemheld; Set Decorations: Russell A. Gausman; Costumes: Ed Ware and Vera West; Casting: Phil M. Friedman; Photographic Effects: Frank J. Booth; Miniatures: William Davidson; Research: Nan Grant; Art Titles: Max Cohen; Assistant Director: Scotty R. Beal; Second Assistant Director: Herman Schlom; Script Girl: Aileen Webster; Still Photographer: Roman Freulich; Running time: 75 minutes; Filmed September 29—November 15, 1930; additional scenes completed December 13; Retakes completed January 2, 1931; Mountain location work, Vasquez Rocks, Chatsworth, California; Opened at the Roxy Theatre, New York City, February 12, 1931

Renfield (Dwight Frye) begs Martin (Charles Gerrard), the sanitarium guard, to return his "juicy" spider in *Dracula*.

CAST: Bela Lugosi (Count Dracula); Helen Chandler (Mina); David Manners (John Harker); **Dwight Frye (Renfield)**; Edward Van Sloan (Prof. Van Helsing); Herbert Bunston (Dr. Seward); Frances Dade (Lucy); Joan Standing (Briggs); Charles Gerrard (Martin); Moon Carroll (Maid); Josephine Velez (English nurse); Michael Visaroff (Innkeeper); Daisy Belmore (English passenger); Nicholas Bela (Transylvanian passenger); Carla Laemmle (passenger in glasses); Donald Murphy (passenger); Dorothy Tree; Jeraldine Dvorak; Cornelia Thaw (Dracula's vampire wives); Tod Browning (Voice of the Harbor Master)

NOTES: Renfield was the key role in the life of Dwight Frye—the performance that cruelly typecast him for the rest of his days, while assuring him a posthumous fame he surely never imagined.

Some facts and figures on the production:

Bram Stoker's novel *Dracula* was published in the spring of 1897. Pre-Hollywood dramatic versions include F. W. Murnau's German *Nosferatu* (1922); Hamilton Deane's play *Dracula*, which opened in London February 14, 1927, with Deane as Van Helsing and Raymond Huntley as Dracula; and the Broadway version of Deane's *Dracula* ("Anglicized" by John L. Balderston), which opened at the Fulton Theatre October 5, 1927, with Edward Van Sloan as Van Helsing—and Bela Lugosi as Dracula.

Dracula's original budget was $355,050, on a six-week shooting schedule. The film ran one week over schedule, yet (according to Universal figures) came in under budget at a cost of $341,191.20.

Lugosi signed a $500 per week contract to play Dracula; total salary: $3,500. "If I had one percent of the millions *Dracula* has made," said Lugosi while reviving the play in London in 1951, "I wouldn't be sitting here now."

The film *Dracula* had two other players from the original Broadway cast: Edward Van Sloan as Van Helsing, and Herbert Bunston as Dr. Seward. Members of the Van Sloan family recently told Doug Norwine that, on the day of *Dracula*'s Broadway opening, Van Sloan took his son for a walk in Central Park; the boy became lost, and Van Sloan shouted so much finding him that he had almost lost his voice come the first night curtain. Producer Horace Liveright rushed a prominent New York throat specialist to his aid, and the show went on.

Tod Browning, director of *Dracula*, had risen from carnival performer to assistant to D. W. Griffith to the director of such MGM Lon Chaney classics as *The Unholy Three* (1925), *The Unknown* (1927) and *London After Midnight* (1927). "The Edgar Allan Poe of the screen" was, by all reports, remarkably listless directing *Dracula*; his follow-up horror films (all for MGM) included the notorious *Freaks* (1932), *Mark of the Vampire* (a virtual remake of *Dracula*, complete with Lugosi as a vampire, 1935), *The Devil-Doll* (1936) and—his last film—*Miracles for Sale* (1939).

Karl Freund (1890-1969), the Bohemian cinematographer, had been cameraman of such European classics as *The Last Laugh* (1924) and *Metropolis* (1926). He went on to be cinematographer of Robert Florey's *Murders in the Rue Morgue* (Universal, 1932) with Lugosi; became a director with *The Mummy* (Universal, 1932), starring Karloff; directed MGM's horror classic *Mad Love* (with Peter Lorre and Colin Clive, 1935) and then returned to cinematography, winning an Oscar for *The Good Earth* (MGM, 1937). He later became the pioneering TV cameraman of the *I Love Lucy* show.

David Manners, the only surviving star of *Dracula* since the 1965 death of Helen Chandler, has confessed that he never saw *Dracula*. As of his 96th birthday in April, 1996, he still had no plans to do so.

The Spanish *Dracula* shot at night on the same Universal sets that the original company used by day. Here are the credits.

Spanish version:

Supervisor: Paul Kohner; Director: George Melford; Screenplay: Garrett Fort; Dialogue Director: Enrique Tovar Avalos; Spanish Dialogue: Baltasar Fernandez Cue; Cinematography: George Robinson; Art Director: Charles D. Hall; Film Editor: Arturo Tavares; Sound Supervisor: C. Roy Hunter; Makeup: Jack P. Pierce; Running time: 102 minutes; Filmed October 23-November, 1930; Opened in Havana, Cuba, March 11, 1931; in New York, April 24, 1931

CAST: Carlos Villarias (Count Dracula); Lupita Tovar (Eva); Barry Norton (Juan Harker); Pablo Alvarez Rubio (Renfield); Eduardo Arozamena (Prof. Van Helsing); Carmen Guerrero (Lucia); Jose Soriano Viosca (Dr. Seward); Manuel Arbo (Martin); Amelia Senisterra (Marta)

The opera scene at "Albert Hall" was shot on Universal's soundstage 28—the stage built for the Paris Opera House of Lon Chaney's 1925 *The Phantom of the Opera*.

Universal perpetuated its vampire lore with *Dracula's Daughter* (1936, starring Gloria Holden); *Son of Dracula* (1943, with Lon Chaney as Count "Alucard"—spell it backward); *House of Frankenstein* (1944, with John Carradine's Dracula joining Karloff's Mad Doctor, J. Carrol Naish's Hunchback, Lon Chaney, Jr.'s Wolf Man and Glenn Strange's Frankenstein Monster); *House of Dracula* (1945, once more with Carradine's Count, mixing it up with Chaney's Wolf Man, Strange's Monster, Onslow Stevens' Mad Doctor and Jane Adams' Hunchback). And there was Universal-International's *Abbott and Costello Meet Frankenstein* (1948), with the comics meeting Chaney's Wolf Man, Strange's Monster—and Lugosi's Dracula.

Bela Lugosi, Jr., today a prominent Los Angeles lawyer, waged a lengthy court battle for a share of the royalties Universal had earned marketing Lugosi's likeness in *Dracula* merchandise. The fight (which began in the mid-1960s) lasted into the early 1980s. Today, Bela, Jr. controls the marketing of the "likeness" of his famous father (who is buried at Los Angeles' Holy Cross Cemetery in his *Dracula* cape).

Other actors to have scored as Dracula: Christopher Lee (in the Hammer film series); Jack Palance (the 1973 TV special); Louis Jourdan (the 1978 British TV film *Count Dracula*); George Hamilton (in the 1979 farce *Love at First Bite*, with Arte Johnson as Renfield); Frank Langella (the 1977 Broadway revival and the Universal 1979 film *Dracula*); and Leslie Nielsen (in Mel Brooks' 1995 *Dracula: Dead and Loving It*, which featured Peter MacNicol's great Dwight Frye take-off as Renfield).

Universal "restored" *Dracula* in the late 1980s, returning the film to its original frame ratio, and providing two sound cues (found at the British Film Institute) cut before the film's late 1930s re-release: the sound of Renfield's neck being broken by Dracula, and Dracula's cries as Van Helsing drives the stake through his heart. In original release, *Dracula* also featured a curtain speech (as had the play) by Edward Van Sloan—a speech also cut before the film's re-release, and sadly too fragmentary to be restored:

> Please! One moment!
> Just a word before you go. We hope the memories of *Dracula* won't give you bad dreams—so just a word of remembrance! When you get home tonight and lights have been turned out and you're afraid to look behind the curtains—and you dread to see a face appear at the window—why, just pull yourselves together and remember—that, after all, there are such things!

Dracula survives today as the professional moment in time not only for Bela Lugosi, but for Dwight Frye; the mad Renfield laugh is itself a classic, and his passion, dramatic fireworks and moving mania make this lost soul a legend in the golden age of horror.

REVIEWS

—*The Billboard*, February 21, 1931: "Popular *Dracula* is now seen on the screen... It has been done splendidly... Cast has been excellently chosen, with quite a few members giving rare performances. Bela Lugosi is Count Dracula and gives a brilliant portrayal, with his original stage work in that role meaning much. Other outstanding performances are given by Helen Chandler and Dwight Frye. Latter, who is known in legit, gives a characterization of a maniac that is most convincing."

—*A Pictorial History of Horror Movies*, by Denis Gifford, 1973: "Dwight Frye's definitive performance."

The Black Camel

Fox, 1931; Director: Hamilton McFadden; Screenplay: Barry Conners and Philip Klein; Adaptation: Hugh Stange; Cameramen: Joseph August and Daniel Clark; Running Time: 67 minutes; Production Dates: Mid-April-early May 1931; Release Date: June 7, 1931

CAST: Warner Oland (Charlie Chan); Sally Eilers (Julie O'Neill); Bela Lugosi (Tarneverro aka Arthur Mayo); Dorothy Revier (Shelah Fane); Victor Varconi (Robert Fyfe); Robert Young (Jimmy

Bradshaw); Marjorie White (Rita Ballou); Richard Tucker (Wilkie Ballou); C. Henry Gordon (Van Horn); **Dwight Frye (Jessop)**; Violet Dunn (Anna); Murray Kinnell (Smith); William Post, Jr. (Alan Jaynes); J. M. Kerrigan (Thomas MacMaster); Mary Gordon (Mrs. MacMaster); Otto Yamaoka (Kashimo); Rita Roselle (Luana); Robert Homans (Chief of Police); Louise Mackintosh (housekeeper)

NOTES: The film was based on the novel *The Black Camel* by Earl Derr Biggers. Some of the filming was done on location in Hawaii, although it is believed that Frye was not among the cast to make that trip.

As Jessop the butler, Frye expresses concern for Anna (Violet Dunn), establishing his unrequited love early on:

> You look as if you'd seen a ghost. You're not happy
> here, Anna. Let's leave, go somewhere else.

When Anna tries to distance herself from Jessop, he persists:

> But I love you. And you're in trouble. There isn't
> anything in the world I wouldn't do to help you.

When Chan assembles the suspects at the hotel, Jessop takes both Tarneverro's (Bela Lugosi) and Chan's hats, before relating an important piece of information about Shelah (Dorothy Revier) to Charlie (Warner Oland):

> This morning I found her crying in her room over a
> man's photograph.

Jessop inquires, "Do you have to do all this?," as Kashimo (Otto Yamaoka) tears Shelah's room apart, looking for the photo.

After Chan has all the guests assume their same seats at the hotel table as on the night of the murder, Jessop reveals that he and Anna sat down for some coffee ("We needed it badly!") after the others had departed. This helps Chan pinpoint Anna as Shelah's killer. Before Chan and the Police Chief (Robert Homans) can take Anna away, Jessop draws a gun, tells them to stand back and tries to exit with Anna. Tarneverro and the chief subdue Jessop, with Chan noting the butler's gun had been used to shoot Smith. Jessop, with the usual Frye intensity, declares:

> Yes, I killed him because he knew too much. And you
> know too much. Nobody would have known anything
> about us if it hadn't been for you. I'm sorry I didn't get
> you with that knife!

Chan then puts together the entire puzzle: Jessop slew Smith (Murray Kinnell) to protect Anna, who had murdered Shelah, and Jessop had thrown a knife at Chan as the detective was searching for tell-tale scratches and other evidence.

The Black Camel was the fifth Charlie Chan film and the second (of 16) starring Warner Oland as the Oriental sleuth. Frye and Bela Lugosi had just completed *Dracula* together a few months earlier. *The Black Camel* also reunited Frye with C. Henry Gordon, with whom he had appeared on Broadway in 1925 in *Puppets*. Barry Conners, who co-wrote the screenplay for *The Black Camel*, wrote the play *So This is Politics* in which Frye was seen on Broadway in 1924.

As Joel Cairo (Otto Matieson) watches, Sam Spade (Ricardo Cortez) disarms gunsel Wilmer Cook (Dwight Frye). Caspar Gutman (Dudley Digges) looks on in *The Maltese Falcon*.

The Maltese Falcon

Warner Bros., 1931; Director: Roy Del Ruth; Screenplay and Dialogue: Maude Fulton, Lucien Hubbard and Brown Holmes (based on the 1930 novel *The Maltese Falcon*, by Dashiell Hammett); Cinematography: William Rees; Vitaphone Orchestra Conductor: Leo F. Forbstein; Running Time: 78 minutes; Release date: May, 1931

CAST: Bebe Daniels (Ruth Wonderly); Ricardo Cortez (Sam Spade); Dudley Digges (Caspar Gutman); Una Merkel (Effie); Robert Elliott (Dundy); Thelma Todd (Iva Archer); Otto Matieson (Dr. Cairo); Walter Long (Miles Archer); **Dwight Frye (Wilmer)**; J. Farrell MacDonald (Polhaus); Oscar Apfel (District Attorney); Agostino Borgato (Captain Jacobi); Morgan Wallace...(Bit)

NOTES: Many are the fans who venerate Warner Bros.' 1941 *The Maltese Falcon*—and well they should. But those who rave about John Huston's adaptation and direction of the classic version should take a look at the 1931 *The Maltese Falcon* (which plays the Turner Classic Movies cable channel under the name *Dangerous Female*). Not only are many of the scenes virtually identical to Huston's take on the Dashiell Hammett novel—but there's actually a lot more spice in this pre-Code picture.

Leading lady Bebe Daniels (1901-1971) has a cheesecake scene in which she keeps a wad of cash stashed in her garter (a bit of business Mary Astor couldn't try when she made the role her own in 1941). Ricardo Cortez (1899-1977), as Sam Spade, strip-searches Bebe (off-camera—an

Dwight Frye's Last Laugh

inference censors wouldn't allow Bogart to share with Astor in the Huston movie). And the hint of homosexuality between "the fat man" and his "gunsel," "Wilmer" (barely suggested between Sydney Greenstreet and Elisha Cook, Jr. in 1941), is surprisingly obvious as the 1931 Fat Man (Dudley Digges, 1879-1947) wickedly chortles about the 1931 Wilmer (Dwight):

> Why, I feel toward Wilmer exactly as if he were my own son!

Digges' little chuckle and habit of patting Dwight on the cheek add to the impression — as does Cortez's line to Digges after Dwight takes a powder, "Your little boyfriend checked out!"

Dwight makes Wilmer a fine, baby-faced creep, in his cap, long overcoat and perpetual sneer; "...make him lay off me or I'll fog him!" he vows as Cortez's taunting Spade mocks him. He also takes a shot at the detective (who punches him out). And, while the villains are reported to have been arrested in the Huston film, we hear via the police that Wilmer (betrayed by Gutman) got his revenge by gunning down Gutman and Cairo (offscreen) in this original film adaptation.

Warners had remade *The Maltese Falcon* as *Satan Met a Lady* (1936), starring Bette Davis and Warren William, and directed by William Dieterle. Columbia later released a comic version, *The Black Bird* (1975); Neil Simon satirized *The Maltese Falcon* (as well as *Casablanca* and *The Big Sleep*) in 1978's *The Cheap Detective*. The 1931 version can proudly stand on its own.

REVIEW
— *Motion Picture Catalogue*: "Frye, who played the part of the nutty Renfield in *Dracula*, released the same year, essays the role of the gunsel, Wilmer, like a man with permanent St. Vitus Dance."

Frankenstein

Universal, 1931; Producer: Carl Laemmle, Jr.; Director: James Whale; Associate Producer: E. M. Asher; Screenplay: Garrett Fort, Francis Edwards Faragoh, John Russell and Robert Florey (based upon the composition by John L. Balderston, adapted from the play by Peggy Webling, from the 1818 novel by Mary Wollstonecraft Shelley); Cinematography: Arthur Edeson; Scenario Editor: Richard Schayer; Special Electrical Properties: Kenneth Strickfaden; Electrical Effects: Raymond Lindsay; Electrician: Frank Graves; Special Effects: John P. Fulton; Technical Advisors: Dr. Cecil Reynolds, Gerald L. G. Sampson; Makeup: Jack P. Pierce; Art Director: Charles D. Hall; Set Designer: Herman Rosse; Recording Supervisor: C. Roy Hunter; Sound Recorder: William Hedgcock; Supervising Film Editor: Maurice Pivar; Film Editor: Clarence Kolster; Musical Director: David Broekman (music by Bernhard Kaun and Giuseppe Becce); Dance Arranger: C. Baier; Assistant Directors: Joseph A. McDonough, Harry Mancke; Costumes: Ed Ware, Vera West; Second Cameraman: Allen Jones; Assistant Cameramen: Jack Eagan, George Trafton; Assistant Makeup Man: Tony Mattaracci; Casting: Phil M. Friedman; Art Titles: Max Cohen; Script Clerk: Helen McCaffrey; Still Photographers: Sherman Clark, Ray Jones, Roman Freulich; Running time: 68 minutes; Filmed August 24-October 3, 1931; Mountain lake location shooting, Malibou Lake, California; Premiere: RKO-Mayfair Theatre, New York City, December 4, 1931

CAST: Colin Clive (Henry Frankenstein); Mae Clarke (Elizabeth); John Boles (Victor Moritz); Boris Karloff (the Monster); Edward Van Sloan (Dr. Waldman); **Dwight Frye (Fritz)**; Frederick Kerr (Baron Frankenstein); Lionel Belmore (The Burgomaster); Marilyn Harris (Little Maria); Michael Mark (Ludwig); Arletta Duncan, Pauline Moore (Bridesmaids); Francis Ford (Extra at Lecture/Wounded Villager on Hill); Cecilia Parker (Maid); Joseph North (Butler); Ted Billings, Inez Palange, Harry Tenbrook (Villagers); Paul Panzer (Mourner); William Yetter (Gendarme); Cecil Reynolds (Waldman's Secretary)

Fritz (Dwight Frye) cuts the body of the hanged man down from the gallows in *Franken-stein*.

NOTES: *Frankenstein* was, remains and most likely will forever be the most celebrated horror movie of all time.

A few facts and figures:

Dramatic versions of Mary Shelley's 1818 novel *Frankenstein* date all the way back to 1823, and the London play *Presumption, or The Fate of Frankenstein*. T. P. Cooke played the Monster, and Mary Shelley herself attended a performance.

The first film of *Frankenstein* was Edison's 1910 version, directed by J. Searle Dawley, with Charles Ogle as the Monster.

James Whale (1889-1957) had been a London cartoonist, stage manager and actor, whose credits included playing Charles Laughton's mad son in *Man with Red Hair*. His brilliant direction of R. C. Sherriff's WWI saga *Journey's End* in London won him the chance to direct the

Broadway version, and the Tiffany film of *Journey's End* (1930). He had made his Universal directorial bow with *Waterloo Bridge* (1931).

Colin Clive (1900-1937), who played so agonized a Henry Frankenstein, had acted the alcoholic Captain Stanhope in Whale's *Journey's End*, both in London and in the Hollywood film. "It is a grand part," Whale wrote to Clive about *Frankenstein*, "and I think will fit you as well as Stanhope."

Mae Clarke (1906-1992) had portrayed Myra, the tragic prostitute of Whale's *Waterloo Bridge*. Also in 1931, she played Mollie, the hooker of UA's *The Front Page*—and got the famous grapefruit in the face from James Cagney in Warner Bros.' *The Public Enemy*.

John Boles (1895-1969) was an all-purpose Universal leading man, and a singing baritone in such studio fare as 1930's *Captain of the Guards*. He'd been a spy in WWI in Germany, Bulgaria and Turkey.

Boris Karloff (1887-1969), nee William Henry Pratt of Dulwich, England, played in at least 13 Hollywood releases of 1931, including Columbia's *The Criminal Code*, in which he reprised his Los Angeles stage role of Galloway. From the beginning, Karloff's approach to the Monster was one of deep compassion: "That Monster is one of the most sympathetic characters ever created in the world of English letters."

Frankenstein began shooting August 24, 1931, with a budget of $262,007 and a 30-day shooting schedule. It ran five days over schedule, "wrapping" October 3, 1931; the final cost was $291,129.13.

The laboratory electricity came via Kenneth Strickfaden, a Montana-born ex-Marine/Army pilot/speed boat racer/Ford Model "T" assembly line worker/photographer whose wizardry on Hollywood back lots won him the nickname "Mr. Electric." Strickfaden also contributed to *Bride of Frankenstein* and *Son of Frankenstein*, as well as Universal's *Flash Gordon* serial (1936), MGM's *The Wizard of Oz* (1939) and Disney's *Fantasia* (1940). (On MGM's 1932 *The Mask of Fu Manchu*, Strickfaden not only provided the electrical apparatus, but stood in for Karloff—receiving a shock that sent him flying through the air.) He toured his *Kenstrick Space Age Science Show* coast to coast and came out of semi-retirement for Mel Brooks' 1974 satire, *Young Frankenstein*. Kenneth Strickfaden died in 1984.

Jack P. Pierce, Universal's legendary makeup genius, created the makeups of all of Universal's monsters during his years (1927-1947) at the studio. He never forgave Universal for dropping him (they felt his methods were too slow and archaic) and resented the royalties Universal collected on monster masks and models—none of which he shared. Jack Pierce died in 1968, at the age of 79.

Universal added the "happy ending" denouement, in which old Baron Frankenstein (Frederick Kerr) toasts his son's recovery with the maids, at the last possible minute; Clive had left for England and Mae Clarke was no longer available. Robert Livingston, who became a noted "B" western star, doubled Clive in the long shot; an anonymous would-be starlet doubled Miss Clarke.

Northern Ireland, Sweden and Italy all banned *Frankenstein* in 1932; Czechoslovakia followed in 1935.

In 1986, Universal, working with materials from the Library of Congress and the British Film Institute, released a restored *Frankenstein* on laser disc. Scenes cut by some local censors upon the film's original release (and officially cut by the censors when the film was re-released in the late 1930s) now came back. They included most of Clive's "In the name of God! Now I know what it feels like to *be* God!" line in the creation scene (thunder still drowns out the tag of the line); a longer battle in the laboratory involving Clive, Edward Van Sloan, Frye and Karloff; a closeup of Van Sloan injecting a hypodermic needle into the Monster; a closeup of Frye torturing the Monster with a torch, and closeups of the terrified Monster; and most of the lake episode, including the shot of Karloff tossing little Maria (Marilyn Harris) into the lake. The original exit music was also added. The restored *Frankenstein* became available on video cassette in 1987.

The *Frankenstein* Monster became one of the most profitable personalities in the history of Universal City; the character currently sings and dances in punk rocker fashion in Universal City's California and Florida."Beetlejuice Graveyard Revue," along with Dracula, the Bride, the Wolf Man, the Phantom of the Opera (and, of course, Beetlejuice himself).

Coming in the wake of *Dracula*, *Frankenstein* and the role of Fritz made Dwight Frye both a horror legend and a victim of typecasting. For all his bizarre appetites for spiders and flies, Renfield of *Dracula* had pathos; Fritz of *Frankenstein* has none. There's something truly chilling as we watch this hunchbacked dwarf leeringly torturing the pitiful Monster; the sadism is haunting. Fritz's one moment of charm: stopping on the tower laboratory staircase to adjust his sock.

Frye's Fritz was ancestor to a long line of mad doctor assistants, including Bela Lugosi's Ygor in *Son of Frankenstein* and *The Ghost of Frankenstein*, J. Carrol Naish's Daniel in *House of Frankenstein* and Marty Feldman's "Igor" in *Young Frankenstein*. For all the spin-offs and satires, the character still packs a wallop; Dwight Frye's Fritz is the true villain of *Frankenstein*, and the characterization is a classic.

REVIEWS

—*A Pictorial History of Horror Movies*, by Denis Gifford, 1973: "Boris Karloff, a long-standing small-part player, stomped to stardom as the synthetic yet soulful creation of Colin Clive, unnatural victim of nature's freak, Dwight Frye."

—*Classics of the Horror Film*, by William K. Everson, 1974: "In key supporting roles, Edward Van Sloan and Dwight Frye were towers of strength in the kind of roles they were to specialize in throughout their careers."

—*Cult Movie Stars*, by Danny Peary, 1991: "Dwight Frye (1899-1943)... Small, squirmy, crazed-eyed character actor who brought a welcome touch of hysteria and morbid lunacy to a number of classic Universal horror films. He was ideal as the doctor's grubby heart-procuring assistant in *Frankenstein*, a fiendish hunchback who, to show his superiority over at least one creature on earth, brutally beats the Monster—but the Monster will get revenge."

Attorney for the Defense

Columbia, 1932; Director: Irving Cummings; Screenplay: Jo Swerling; Original Story: J. K. McGuinness; Cameraman: Ted Tetzlaff; Running Time: 70 minutes; Production Dates: March 17-April 9, 1932; Release Date: May 21, 1932

CAST: Edmund Lowe (William J. Burton); Evelyn Brent (Val Lorraine); Constance Cummings (Ruth Barry); Donald Dilloway (Paul Wallace); Douglas Haig (Paul Wallace, as a boy); Dorothy Peterson (Mrs. Wallace); **Dwight Frye (James Wallace)**; Bradley Page (Nick Quinn); Nat Pendleton (Mugg Malone); Wallis Clark (James A. Crowell); Clarence Muse (Jefferson Q. Leffingwell)

NOTES: As *The New York Times* review of *Attorney for the Defense* describes, "In the initial sequence this William J. Burton (Edmund Lowe) is attacked vociferously by a man named Wallace (Frye), who has been convicted of murder." James Wallace loudly swears that he is innocent, while making accusations at Burton and his methods. Wallace is then led off, before the tearful eyes of his wife (Dorothy Peterson) and young son (Douglas Haig), to face death in the electric chair.

Although killed off at the film's beginning, Frye's character establishes the motive for prosecutor Burton rethinking his values and making a dramatic career shift to handling defense cases. *Attorney for the Defense* was the first of twelve films Frye would make for Columbia Pictures Corp., the most Dwight would be involved in for any one studio.

By Whose Hand?

Columbia, 1932; Director: Ben Stoloff; Screenplay: Isadore Bernstein and Stephen Roe; Original Story: Harry Adler; Cameramen: Teddy Tetzlaff and Joseph Walker; Running Time: 64 minutes; Production Dates: May 16-June 1, 1932; Release Date: July 6, 1932

CAST: Ben Lyon (Jimmy Hawley); Barbara Weeks (Alice Murray); William V. Mong (Graham); Ethel Kenyon (Mazie Wilson aka Eileen Ayensworth); Kenneth Thomson (Chambers); Nat Pendleton ("Killer" Delmar); Tom Dugan (Drunk); William Halligan (Detective); Helene Millard (Mrs. Delmar aka Mrs. Leonard); **Dwight Frye (Chick Lewis)**; Lorin Baker (Bridegroom); Dolores Rey (Bride); Oscar Smith (Pullman porter); Tom McGuire (Conductor)

NOTES: *Murder Express* was the working title for *By Whose Hand?* Frye had a fairly substantial role as Chick Lewis, the crook who squealed on his pal Delmar (Nat Pendleton) on the way to prison. Although a print of *By Whose Hand?* was not available for viewing (it may be one of two lost Frye films, along with *The Circus Queen Murder*), existing stills witness some of Frye's scenes: Being handcuffed and in the custody of the detective (William Halligan); escaping, securing a gun and menacing Alice (Barbara Weeks); and finally meeting his demise via a knife thrust on the platform of the train as Chick is attempting to disembark.

William V. Mong, the veteran silent screen actor, writer and director, would later appear with Frye in *A Strange Adventure* and *The Vampire Bat*. Mong, who wound up his career in the early sound era playing mean, sniveling, miserly types, had a number of intriguing fantasy-related roles in *A Connecticut Yankee in King Arthur's Court* (1920), *Code of the Air* (1928), *Ransom* (1928), *The Haunted House* (1928), *The House of Horror* (1929) and *Seven Footprints to Satan* (1929).

The Western Code

Columbia, 1932; Director: J. P. McCarthy; Screenplay: Milton Krims; Original Story: William Colt MacDonald; Cameraman: Benjamin Kline; Running Time: 61 minutes; Production Dates: August 1-August 6, 1932; Release Date: September 16, 1932

CAST: Tim McCoy (Tim Barrett); Mischa Auer (Chaplin); Nora Lane (Polly Loomis); **Dwight Frye (Dick Loomis)**; Wheeler Oakman (Nick Grindall); Gordon DeMaine (Sheriff Purdy); Matthew Betz (Warden); Emilio Fernandez (Joe, the half-breed); Bud Osborne (Hutch Miller); Chuck Baldra (Chuck); Cactus Mack

NOTES: *The Western Code* was Dwight Frye's only pure western genre film, although he would eventually be seen in two entries from the *Renfrew of the Royal Mounted* series. For those used to viewing Frye strictly in horror films, it is somewhat of a surprise to see him dressed in cowboy attire, handling a horse quite well.

As Dick Loomis, Frye wants to seek vengeance on Nick Grindall (Wheeler Oakman), who has duped him out of his inheritance, for insulting his sister Polly (Nora Lane):

> Do you think I could walk through the street with
> my head up, Polly, and the whole town knowin' he'd
> proposed marriage to my sister. I'm going!

Dick is halted by Tim Barrett (Tim McCoy), who cautions Loomis, offering alternatives to violence. Barrett helps Dick devise a trap, confronting Grindall about the phony will. When Grindall refers to Dick's mother as "crazy," Frye has one of his rare screen moments, getting to punch out a classic western heavy in Oakman. Before Barrett can escort Loomis away, Dick threatens:

I'm not leavin' and you might get me, Grindall, but if
you do, you can be sure of one thing. Before I go down,
I'll get you.

Grindall feigns his own death, with Dick claiming to have killed him in the mistaken belief he is protecting Polly. Warden (Matthew Betz) leads a lynch mob to hang Dick on "the old oak," with Barrett intervening just in time.

Barrett interrogates Dick in jail, attempting to invalidate his story. Not only does Dick have the time-frame wrong, but makes the preposterous claim:

I walked right into him with my shotgun, and when he
started something, I let him have it right in the face.

Still trying to protect his sister, Dick holds to his confession, while Barrett, knowing both Loomis siblings are innocent, seeks another solution.

Frye plays the role of Dick Loomis in a sincere, convincing manner, without indulging in the self pity of some of his other characters, like Vint Glade in *Man to Man*. *The Western Code* provides some evidence of Frye's versatility, which he was rarely able to exhibit once he became typecast.

Some sources wrongly list McCoy's character as "Carroll" rather than "Barrett," and Auer's as "Chapman" instead of "Chaplin."

A Strange Adventure

Monogram, 1932; Director: Phil Whitman and Hampton Del Ruth; Screenplay: Lee Chadwick; Original Story: Arthur Hoerl; Cameraman: Leon Shamroy; Running Time: 62 minutes; Release Date: November 20, 1932

CAST: Regis Toomey (Detective Mitchell); June Clyde ("Nosey" Toodles); Lucille LaVerne (Mrs. Sheen, housekeeper); William V. Mong (Silas Wayne); Jason Robards, Sr. (Dr. Bailey); Eddie Phillips (Claude Wayne); **Dwight Frye (Robert Wayne)**; Nadine Dore (Gloria Dryden); Alan Roscoe (Stephen Boulter); Isabelle Vecki (Sarah Boulter); Snowflake/Fred Toomes (Jeff); William J. Humphrey (coroner); Eddy Chandler (Sergeant Kelly); Harry Myers (Officer Ryan)

NOTES: *A Strange Adventure*, also known as *The Wayne Murder Case*, Frye's first independent film, was produced by I. E. Chadwick, one of the founders of Monogram Pictures.

In *A Strange Adventure*, Frye portrays Robert Wayne, the sulking nephew of Silas Wayne (William V. Mong), a miserly old rich man. Robert refers to his uncle as "that old buzzard," as the summoned relatives wait to learn about Silas' will. Before the old man is able to read the will, Silas is murdered, with Robert looking on in a suspicious manner. When Detective Mitchell (Regis Toomey) arrives, Robert demands to leave and is almost imprisoned. Mitchell then reads the will, revealing that Robert is to receive one dollar. Robert's fiancee, Gloria Dryden (Nadine Dore), was to get the entire estate, provided she not marry Robert. "He thought he was going to take you away from me," states the despised nephew. "I knew he wouldn't be able to" (in that the will wasn't signed). Despite having reasons for wanting Silas dead, Robert turns out to be nothing more than a red herring in the midst of suspects like Lucille LaVerne, Eddie Phillips and Alan Roscoe.

A Strange Adventure made use of melodramatic plot devices, like a mysterious hooded figure, a wisecracking reporter (June Clyde) and a frightened black servant (Fred "Snowflake" Toomes), while being short on any real horror or suspenseful moments. As Robert Wayne, Frye is bland and prone to exaggerated takes during the course of the film. In fact, Regis Toomey provides the most natural acting in *A Strange Adventure*, with usually solid character people like Mong, LaVerne and Robards tending to overact.

The Vampire Bat

Majestic, 1933; Producer: Phil Goldstone; Director: Frank Strayer; Screenplay: Edward T. Lowe; Cinematography: Ira Morgan; Art Director: Daniel Hall; Editor: Otis Garrett; Sound: Richard Tyler; Sound System: RCA Photophone; Musical Score: Meyer Synchronizing Service; Running time: 67 minutes; Completed November 19, 1932. Opened at the Winter Garden Theatre, New York City, January 20, 1933

CAST: Lionel Atwill (Dr. Otto von Niemann); Fay Wray (Ruth Bertin); Melvyn Douglas (Karl Brettschneider); Maude Eburne (Gussie Schnappman); George E. Stone (Kringen); **Dwight Frye (Herman Gleib)**; Robert Frazer (Emil Borst); Rita Carlisle (Martha Mueller); Lionel Belmore (Burgomaster Gustav Schoen); William V. Mong (Sauer); Stella Adams (Georgiana); Harrison Greene (Weingarten); Paul Weigel (Holdstadt); William Humphrey (Haupt); Fern Emmett (Gertrude); Carl Stockdale (Schmidt)

NOTES: Possibly the most perennially popular "poverty row" horror movie of the 1930s, *The Vampire Bat* was the product of Majestic Studios, which sprouted in Hollywood in 1932, withering on the vine before the end of 1935. Its ingredients are irresistible:

Lionel Atwill (1885-1946), as Dr. Otto von Niemann, had already completed *Doctor X* and *Mystery of the Wax Museum* for Warner Bros. by the time he polished his monocle for *The Vampire Bat*. The British-born Atwill had come to Hollywood from Broadway, where he had triumphed as *Deburau* (for David Belasco, 1920) and become one of the top matinee idols of the day; he'd also acted in silents, such as the "man-siren" in *Eve's Daughter* (1918). Atwill and Frye must have been well aware of each other from the New York theatre of the 1920s; they would both appear in *The Road Back, Son of Frankenstein, The Ghost of Frankenstein* and *Frankenstein Meets the Wolf Man*. "I am one of those few stage actors who really like the films," Atwill had told *The New York Times* in 1932, "and admit it!"

Fay Wray was completing the legendary role of Ann Darrow in *King Kong* (RKO, 1933); during the lengthy shooting, *Kong*'s producers had farmed her out for *Doctor X, Mystery of the Wax Museum* and *The Vampire Bat*—all with Atwill. In recent years, Miss Wray (one of the last of the great golden age survivors) confessed that, as of that interview, she had never seen *The Vampire Bat*.

Melvyn Douglas (1901-1981) had played the stylish hero Roger Penderel in James Whale's *The Old Dark House* (Universal, 1932); the New York stage actor had also just served as Garbo's leading man in *As You Desire Me* (MGM, 1932). Douglas later proved himself a powerhouse Broadway star and won Oscars for *Hud* (1963) and *Being There* (1979).

Indeed, horror veterans abound. The producer, Phil Goldstone, had just produced Lugosi's *White Zombie*. The screenplay is by Edward T. Lowe, whose credits included Universal's 1923 Lon Chaney *The Hunchback of Notre Dame* (and would later include 1944's *House of Frankenstein* and 1945's *House of Dracula*). Robert Frazer (who played the mesmerized killer Emil in *The Vampire Bat*) had just played the doomed plantation owner in *White Zombie*, while Lionel Belmore (*The Vampire Bat*'s Burgomaster) had also been the Burgomaster in *Frankenstein* (and would later appear in *Son of Frankenstein* and *The Ghost of Frankenstein*).

Even the sets look familiar, and with good reason: Majestic leased space at Universal Studios to shoot the film.

Director Frank Strayer (1891-1964) began his career with Columbia in the mid-1920s; he also directed such poverty row horrors as *The Monster Walks* (Mayfair, 1932), *The Ghost Walks* (Chesterfield, 1935) and *Condemned to Live* (Chesterfield, 1935). He later moved up to direct Columbia's 1938 *Blondie* (plus ten of its sequels), ending his career with Astor's 1951 *The Sickle and the Cross*.

It's a great little horror show, with its top cast and deluxe atmospherics, and Dwight has a field day as Herman. He nicely mixes comedy into his performance, particularly in his scene with Maude Eburne (who believes he's a vampire):

"You give me apples," baby-talks Herman. "Herman give you nice, soft bat!"

And he removes a bat from his jacket, bestowing it upon the hilariously hysteric Maude Eburne!

Come his death scene, however, and Dwight is heartrending as he screams in terror, the villagers scaring him so he jumps to his death. (The scene was shot in Bronson Canyon, in Hollywood, where 1953's *Robot Monster* later lurked.)

For many years, an old abandoned movie studio stood at 5823 Santa Monica Boulevard in Hollywood; it had once been the home of Majestic Studios. Guidebooks claimed that scenes were shot there for *The Vampire Bat*. While Universal was certainly the primary locale for the film's shooting, it's possible that some scenes were shot at this studio; at any rate, it no longer exists. Damaged by the 1994 earthquake, the old studio was torn down and an empty lot now awaits historians who want a look at the historic site.

The Vampire Bat was the feature shown at the Montclair, New Jersey Film Society's Tribute to Dwight Frye on the 50th anniversary of his death, November 7, 1993.

REVIEWS

—*Forgotten Horrors: Early Talkie Chillers from Poverty Row*, by George E. Turner and Michael H. Price: "Dwight Frye, who gained a following as a portrayer of nervous lunatics at Universal, has a meaty role here as the village idiot."

—*The Encyclopedia of Horror Movies*, edited by Phil Hardy: "One of the best of the independent films churned out to meet the new vogue of horror... backed by clever camerawork, the admirable quartet of Atwill, Wray, Frye and Douglas keep the film afloat."

The Circus Queen Murder

Columbia, 1933; Director: Roy William Neill; Associate Producer: Robert North; Screenplay: Jo Swerling (based on Anthony Abbott's novel *About the Murder of the Circus Queen*); Photography: Joe August; Editor: Richard Cahoon; Recording Engineer: Edward Bernds; Filmed February 6-February 24, 1933; Opened at the Rialto Theatre, New York City, the week of May 5, 1933

CAST: Adolphe Menjou (Thatcher Colt); Greta Nissen (Josie La Tour); Ruthelma Stevens (Kelly); Donald Cook (Sebastian); Harry Holman (Dugan); George Rosener (Rainey); **Dwight Frye (Flandrin)**; Esther Escalente (Aerialist)

NOTES: This circus melodrama, a sadly "missing" film (if not altogether "lost"), gave Dwight Frye one of his most juicy roles: Flandrin, the crazed big top trapeze star. Audiences reportedly were thrilled as Frye had a field day, doing everything from disguising himself as a cannibal, to climbing atop the tent to slay his "circus queen" adulteress wife, to shooting a blow gun, to—climactically—playing a flamboyant suicide scene.

Director of *The Circus Queen Murder* was Roy William Neill (1890-1946), Dublin-born artist who excelled at atmosphere in such beloved horror films as Columbia's *The Black Room* (1935, featuring Karloff's virtuoso "twin" portrayals) and Universal's *Frankenstein Meets the Wolf Man* (1943, one of Frye's final films). Based on production stills, Greta Nissen was an eyeful in her circus tights as the blonde "circus queen" Josie La Tour. Miss Nissen (1906-1988) had a rather sad footnote in film history: she was the original star of *Hell's Angels* (1930) before Howard Hughes decided to convert his epic to sound (with James Whale as "ghost director"). Greta's accent proved too thick, so she was fired—and replaced by Jean Harlow.

Apparently, the film was an exceptional "B" thriller. Critics praised the star turn of Adolphe Menjou (1890-1963) as Thatcher Colt (he had played the role in Columbia's 1932 *The Night Club Lady*; a third projected Thatcher Colt movie was never made). And Neill reportedly captured a terrific big top ambiance. Hopefully, *The Circus Queen Murder* will soon surface so film addicts can enjoy this vintage melodrama—and a major Dwight Frye performance.

REVIEW
— *The Hollywood Reporter*: "...one of the best murder stories in many a moon... a top-notch cast... The circus grounds, the huge tent, the ornate wagons, the snarls, yelps, howls and screams of the animals which accompany the murders and the unravellings all seem to carry with them the authentic smell of the circus and add more definite drama to the picture than might be imagined. You can't go wrong on this one."

The Invisible Man
Universal, 1933; Producer: Carl Laemmle, Jr.; Director: James Whale; Screenplay: R. C. Sherriff (based on the novel by H. G. Wells); Cinematography: Arthur Edeson; Special Effects: John P. Fulton; Art Director: Charles D. Hall; Editor: Ted Kent; Makeup: Jack P. Pierce; Sound Supervisor: Gilbert Kurland: Recording Engineer: William Hedgecock; Assistant Recording Engineer: John Kemp; Retake Photography and Miniatures: John J. Mescall; Music: W. Franke Harling; Chief Grip: Pete Abriss; Chief Prop Man: Wally Kirkpatrick; Camera Operator: King Gray; Assistant Cameraman: Jack Eagan; Editing Supervisor: Maurice Pivar; Still Photographer: Roman Freulich; Running Time: 71 minutes; Filmed Summer, 1933; opened at the Roxy Theatre, New York City, November 17, 1933

CAST: Claude Rains (The Invisible One, aka Jack Griffin); Gloria Stuart (Flora Cranley); William Harrigan (Dr. Kemp); Henry Travers (Dr. Cranley); Una O'Connor (Jenny Hall); Forrester Harvey (Mr. Hall); Holmes Herbert (Chief of Police); E. E. Clive (Police Constable Jaffers); Dudley Digges (Chief of Detectives); Harry Stubbs (Police Inspector Bird); Donald Stuart (Inspector Lane); Merle Tottenham (Milly); **Dwight Frye (Reporter)**; John Carradine (Informer); John Merivale (Boy); Walter Brennan (Man with Bicycle); Jameson Thomas, Crauford Kent (Doctors); Violet Kemble Cooper (Woman); Robert Brower (Farmer); Bob Reeves, Jack Richardson, Robert Adair (Officials); Monte Montague (Policeman); Ted Billings, D'Arcy Corrigan (Villagers)

NOTES: The third in James Whale's classic quartet of horror movies, *The Invisible Man* is superbly funny and frightening, filled with the director's sense of mad comedy and macabre tragedy. Claude Rains (1889-1967) won stardom in his first Hollywood role (for which Karloff and Colin Clive had been considered), thrillingly delivering the film's juicy dialogue:

> Even the moon's frightened of me—frightened to death!
> The whole world's frightened to death!

Una O'Connor (1880-1959) was comically horrific (or vice-versa!) as screaming Jenny Hall, a wonderfully eccentric performance, and John P. Fulton's special effects still amaze. *The Invisible Man* was a box office smash and eventually spawned the Universal sequels *The Invisible Man Returns* (1940, with Vincent Price in the title spot), *The Invisible Woman* (1941, starring Virginia Bruce in the title role, with a failing-fast John Barrymore), *Invisible Agent* (1942, with Jon Hall disappearing), *The Invisible Man's Revenge* (1944, with Hall again in the lead) and *Abbott and Costello Meet the Invisible Man* (1951, with Arthur Franz as the Invisible Man).

It's a shock to see Dwight Frye pop up in *The Invisible Man* in so small a role, after such juicy jobs in *Dracula* and *Frankenstein*. He suddenly appears amidst a crowd of reporters, in Clark Kent-style reporter apparel of hat, overcoat and glasses, firing these few queries at the Chief of Detectives (Dudley Digges, Dwight's "fat man" from *The Maltese Falcon*):

> Dwight: Can you tell us what plans you've got for capturing him?
>
> Digges: A hundred thousand men are searching and watching.
>
> Dwight: Yes, I know, but have you any special secret means of getting him?
>
> Digges: The police have offered 2,000 crowns for the first effective means.
>
> Dwight: Why not bloodhounds?
>
> Digges: The bloodhounds have lost the scent.
>
> Dwight: Why not put wet tar on all the roads, then chase the black soles of his feet?
>
> Digges: Because he's not a fool...!

John Carradine and Walter Brennan also play bits in *The Invisible Man*, and spotting them (along with Dwight) adds to the film's great popularity today. James Whale would provide a far richer role for Dwight come *Bride of Frankenstein*.

Bride of Frankenstein

Universal, 1935; Producer: Carl Laemmle, Jr.; Director: James Whale; Screenplay: William Hurlbut (based on an adaptation by Hurlbut and John L. Balderston, based on the characters created by Mary Wollstonecraft Shelley in her 1818 novel *Frankenstein*); Cinematography: John J. Mescall; Special Effects: John P. Fulton; Musical Score: Franz Waxman; Musical Director: Bakaleinikoff; Art Director: Charles D. Hall; Editor: Ted Kent; Makeup: Jack P. Pierce and Otto Lederer; Sound: Gilbert Kurland; Special Electrical Properties: Kenneth Strickfaden; Assistant Directors: Harry Mancke, Fred Frank and Joseph McDonough; 2nd Cameraman: Alan Jones; Assistant Cameraman; William Dodds: Script Clerk: Flo Brummel; Producer's Secretary: Buddy Dagget; Running Time: 75 minutes; Original Title: *The Return of Frankenstein*; Filmed January 2-March 7, 1935; Premiered at the Hollywood Pantages Theatre, April 20, 1935

CAST: Boris Karloff (The Monster); Colin Clive (Dr. Henry Frankenstein); Valerie Hobson (Elizabeth); Ernest Thesiger (Dr. Septimus Pretorius); Elsa Lanchester (Mary Wollstonecraft Shelley/The Monster's Mate); Gavin Gordon (Lord Byron); Douglas Walton (Percy Bysshe Shelley); Una O'Connor (Minnie); E. E. Clive (The Burgomaster); Lucien Prival (Albert, Chief Servitor); O. P. Heggie (The Hermit); **Dwight Frye (Karl)**; Reginald Barlow (Hans); Mary Gordon (Hans' Wife); Ann Darling (Shepherdess); Ted Billings (Ludwig); Gunnis Davis (Uncle Glutz); Tempe Pigott (Auntie Glutz); Neil Fitzgerald (Rudy); John Carradine (A Hunter); Walter Brennan (A Neighbor); Helen Parrish (Communion Girl); Rollo Lloyd (A Neighbor); Edwin Mordant (The Coroner); Lucio Villegas (Priest); Brenda Fowler (A Mother); Robert A'dair (A Hunter); Sara Schwartz (Marta); Mary Stewart (A Neighbor); John Curtis (A Hunter); Arthur S. Byron (Little King); Joan Woodbury (Little Queen); Norman Ainsley (Little Bishop); Peter Shaw (Little Devil); Kansas DeForrest (Little Ballerina); Josephine McKim (Little Mermaid); Billy Barty (Little Baby); Frank Terry (A Hunter); Frank Benson, Ed Piel, Sr., Anders Van Haden, John George, Grace Cunard, Maurice Black, Peter Shaw (Villagers); Helen Gibson (woman); Murdock MacQuarrie

(Sympathetic Villager); Elspeth Dudgeon (Old Gypsy Woman); Monte Montague, Peter Shaw (Double for Ernest Thesiger); George De Normand (Double for Reginald Barlow)

NOTES: Golden age Hollywood's most magnificent, bitter fairy tale, *Bride of Frankenstein* reigns as classic horror's masterpiece. A few tidbits on its production:

Karloff dislocated a hip while filming the scene in the millpond; he simply reported to the studio infirmary, had the hip bandaged and promptly returned to work.

James Whale scorned his original $293,750 budget and 36-day schedule; the final cost was $397,023.79, and the shooting days tallied 46.

Elsa Lanchester told Greg Mank in 1979 that she based the Bride's climactic hiss on an angry swan she'd observed at London's Regent's Park.

Universal reportedly considered both Claude Rains and Bela Lugosi for the role of Pretorius, which Ernest Thesiger played to such marvelously macabre effect.

Universal supposedly composed the Monster's "44-word vocabulary" based on the test papers of the studio's child actors.

Valerie Hobson, Irish-born starlet, was only 17 when she played Elizabeth. She remembers the *Bride* company with great affection, telling Greg Mank in 1989: "...my memories of that particular film—because they were all so good to me, and I was so newly arrived from England—are as warm as possible. They really are."

Franz Waxman, whom Whale personally engaged to write the score for *Bride of Frankenstein*, won a Universal contract for his efforts. The studio later scavenged the score for many other films, including the 1936 *Flash Gordon* serial.

Although popular at the box office, *Bride of Frankenstein* was a scandal with the domestic and international censors. E.g., Ohio cut Dwight Frye's line, "It was a very fresh one!," regarding the heart he murderously provided for the Female Monster; Palestine and Hungary had rejected the film outright.

For Dwight Frye, *Bride of Frankenstein* provided a terrific comic/terror role: Karl, murderer, grave-robber, lab assistant, capering about in his floppy hat, hobgoblin smile and (although barely glimpsed in the release print), that "skate" on his deformed left foot. The role flamboyantly displayed his talents for Gothic villainy and wicked comedy. Whale had combined the roles of "the first ghoul" (assistant to Pretorius), Karl (the murdering, robbing village idiot) and "Fritz" (an assistant in the lab sequence), all for Dwight—surely proof of the director's great appreciation of the actor's skills. One can only imagine the impact "Karl" might have made had all his scenes remained in the release print! Based on the shooting script and surviving production stills, one can reconstruct those unkind cuts:

Originally, Karl made his entrance right after Thesiger's Pretorius showed Clive's Frankenstein the miniature people. Karl opened the door, gave "a startled and frightened cry":

> Pretorius: You hangman's fodder! How dare you? How
> many times have I told you never to come into
> this room.
> Karl (stammering): I only wanted to ask...
> Pretorius (slamming door in his face—shouting): GET
> OUT!

According to the shooting script, Dwight was to run to a cellar room, shake another man from his "drunken sleep," and say:

> He is the Devil I tell you—and now he's got a lot of little
> devils all in bottles, no higher than that! It's witchcraft!
> He ought to be burned at the stake!

To which the drunken man replied, "Oh, go and bury your grandmother."

Cut was a sequence in which the Burgomaster (E. E. Clive) presided over a hearing re: the Monster's rampage through the village; Dwight was in the scene, as Una O'Connor's Minnie raved about "the most horrible murders" and the Burgomaster dismissed the crowd as "superstitious infidels!" The Monster then appeared outside, and dragged the Burgomaster through the window—creating a new riot.

Uncle Glutz (Gunnis Davis) and Auntie Glutz (Tempe Pigott) are among the fleeing villagers; they are exasperated as their nephew Karl keeps turning to watch the Monster beating the Burgomaster ("the incident has great attraction for him" noted the script):

> Aunt: Where is that good-for-nothing, Karl?
> Uncle: Let him get murdered—a good riddance.

Uncle and Auntie enter their "homestead," where Uncle went to the bedroom, pulled back the mattress, and revealed his money bag. Meanwhile Dwight's Karl is peeking in the window. According to the shooting script:

> A sly look is darkening his face... The nephew steps—
> without making any noise over the window sill and in
> one step he is behind his uncle. With a quick movement
> he throttles the old miser, lowers him to the floor, helps
> himself to what he wants of the money—listens to see
> that he is not detected—slips the bag back into the hiding
> place and is out the window again. He has been an adept
> pupil of the Monster's.

"It's only me, Auntie," cried Karl as he came to call at the front door. He pushed his way in, and as Auntie backed away:

> Auntie: Not one penny do you get. (To husband) Jo-
> seph, that good-for-nothing nephew is here again. Don't
> you give him any more money.

Finding her husband dead, she shrieked, "The Monster! The Monster has been here!" The script then gave Dwight a closeup, and the pre-murder speech:

> Very convenient to have a Monster around. (he looks
> around the room) This is quite a nice cottage—I shouldn't
> be surprised if he visited Auntie too.

While these scenes were still in the movie when Universal previewed it early in April, 1935, they were cut by the time *Bride of Frankenstein* opened at the Hollywood Pantages Theatre April 20, 1935. Occasionally there are rumors that a full print has been found, but so far, an uncut *Bride of Frankenstein* remains a movie lover's daydream.

A new version of the tale, *The Bride*, visited theatres in 1985, with Sting as the Monster Maker and Jennifer Beals as the Bride.

Bride of Frankenstein survives as Universal's greatest horror film, a lasting tribute to Karloff's magnificent acting and Whale's directorial genius. Perhaps more than any of his horror roles, Dwight Frye's Karl allows the actor to display his remarkable range, and the film is all the more brilliant for his unique, delightfully eccentric performance.

REVIEWS

—*The Hollywood Studios*, by Ethan Mordden: "Whale apparently decided to make *Bride of Frankenstein* Universal's most ghoulish horror film, also its funniest and psychologically most endearing. It's something of an old-home-week of the stock company, with Colin Clive, Ernest Thesiger, and Dwight Frye... It's touching and disturbing, the Monster made human—the ghoul and mortal worlds harmonized."

—*Classics of the Horror Film*, by William K. Everson: "Dwight Frye, too, gets some of the best and juiciest lines of his career in this film."

Atlantic Adventure

Columbia, 1935; Director: Albert Rogell; Screenplay: John T. Neville and Nat N. Dorfman; Original Story: Diana Bourbon; Cameraman: John Stumar; Running Time: 68 minutes; Production Dates: June 12-June 27, 1935; Release Date: August 25, 1935

CAST: Nancy Carroll (Helen Murdock); Lloyd Nolan (Dan Miller); Harry Langdon (Snapper McGillicuddy); Arthur Hohl (Frank Julian); Robert Middlemass (Van Dieman); John Wray (Mitts Coster); E. E. Clive (McIntosh); **Dwight Frye (Spike Jones)**; Nana Bryant (Mrs. Julia Van Dieman); Thurston Hall (Rutherford); Edwin Maxwell (DuPont); Maidel Turner (Mrs. Murdock); George McKay (Louie); Victor Kilian (Brannigan); David Clyde (Fisher); Eddie Kane (Johnson); Sam Flint (Barnett); Will Stanton (steward); Gunnis Davis (locksmith); Guy Usher (Lt. Kelly); Cornelius Keefe (Douglas); Ernest Wood (Smith); Montague Shaw (Captain); Gerald Rogers (Billings)

NOTES: *Atlantic Adventure* was based on Dorothy Bourbon's short story, "Atlantic Adventurer." In addition to this film, Albert Rogell would later direct Frye in *Sleepytime Gal* (1942).

Reminiscent of Frye's Broadway roles in *The Plot Thickens* and *Sitting Pretty*, Dwight played the younger accomplice to a seasoned criminal in *Atlantic Adventure*. Billed eighth as Spike Jones, Frye pretended to be the son of alleged murderer Mitts Coster (John Wray). Spike himself has an "itchy trigger finger," as he frequently brandishes a pistol on board the *Gigantic*. It is Jones who comes upon the intrusive Helen Murdock (Nancy Carroll), accosting her at gunpoint and imprisoning her in the closet in Coster's cabin.

Silent film comedian Harry Langdon received good reviews ("splendid foil") as Lloyd Nolan's photographer buddy. Other interesting members of the cast of *Atlantic Adventure* include E. E. Clive, who was seen with Frye in *The Invisible Man* and *Bride of Frankenstein*, and Gunnis Davis, who played the uncle whom twisted Karl (Frye) kills while the monster runs amok in the cut sequence from *Bride of Frankenstein*.

The Great Impersonation

Universal, 1935; Producer: Edmund Grainger; Director: Alan Crosland; Executive Producer: Fred S. Meyer; Screenplay: Lt. Comm. Frank Wead and Eve Greene (based on the 1920 novel *The Great Impersonation*, by E. Phillips Oppenheim); Cinematography: Milton Krasner; Art Director: Charles D. Hall; Editor: Philip Cahn; Musical Score: Franz Waxman; Sound: Gilbert Kurland; Special Cinematography: John P. Fulton; Gowns: Brymer and Vera West; Running time, 67 minutes; Shot September 12-October 12, 1935; New York opening: Roxy Theatre, December 13, 1935

CAST: Edmund Lowe (Sir Everard Dominey/Baron Leopold von Ragastein); Valerie Hobson (Eleanor); Wera Engels (Princess Stephanie Eiderstrom); Murray Kinnell (Seaman); Henry

Mollison (Eddie Pelham); Esther Dale (Mrs. Unthank); Brandon Hurst (Middleton); Ivan Simpson (Dr. Harrison); Spring Byington (Duchess Caroline); Lumsden Hare (Duke Henry); Charles Waldron (Sir Ivan Brunn); Leonard Mudie (Mangan); Claude King (Sir Gerald Hume); Frank Reicher (Dr. Trenk); Harry Allen (Perkins); Nan Grey (Middleton's daughter); Willy Castello (Duval); Priscilla Lawson (Maid); Pat O'Hara (Chauffeur); Virginia Hammond (Lady Hume); Thomas R. Mills (Bartender); Tom Ricketts, Frank Terry, Robert Bilder (Villagers); Lowden Adams (Waiter); Violet Seaton (Nurse); **Dwight Frye (Roger Unthank, "the Ghost from the Black Bog")**; David Dunbar, Frank Benson (English farmers); John Powers (English police man); Leonid Snegoff (Wolff); Harry Worth (Hugo); Adolph Milar (German); Henry Kolker (Dr. Schmidt); Douglas Wood (Lord Allison)

NOTES: Previously filmed by Paramount in 1921, *The Great Impersonation* offers much for a classic horror fan to enjoy. Edmund Lowe (1890-1971, who had played the title role in Fox's 1932's *Chandu the Magician*, sparring with Lugosi's evil "Roxor"), got star billing, a $16,500 salary and the double role, which he plays in smooth, 1930s matinee idol fashion. Valerie Hobson, Elizabeth of Universal's *Bride of Frankenstein* earlier in 1935, is nicely cast as the hysterical Lady Eleanor; she lurks through Dominey Hall, flashing a knife and later a gun, threatening Lowe as she speaks of Dwight's "ghostly" Roger:

> His spirit cries and cries... Why did you kill him?..
> His blood all over you... I can see it!

The supporting cast has faces familiar to genre fans. Frank Reicher (1875-1965), whose most famous horror credit was Capt. Englehorn in *King Kong* and *Son of Kong*, plays Leopold's spy compatriot Dr. Treak. Universal starlet Nan Grey (1918-1993), victim of *Dracula's Daughter* (1936) and leading lady of *Tower of London* (1939) and *The Invisible Man Returns* (1940), appears as a maid (whom Roger scares into a faint when he crashes the manor house). And Brandon Hurst (1866-1947), whose horror credits include the lascivious aristocrat of Barrymore's *Dr. Jekyll and Mr. Hyde* (1920), the villain of Chaney's *The Hunchback of Notre Dame* (1923) and the butler of Lugosi's *White Zombie* (1932), has a sizable role as Middleton, the old family servant, who says of Roger's ghost:

> Every week it howls around the place at night — like
> an animal that's hurt!

The Great Impersonation had a Friday, December 13, 1935 opening at New York City's Roxy Theatre, complete with a lavish musical revue stage show, *Everything Goes*, starring Olsen and Johnson. Although technically not a horror show, *The Great Impersonation* was part of the original *Shock!* TV package in 1957. Besides the staircase from *The Old Dark House,* it offers a glimpse of the old *Frankenstein* tower laboratory stairs come the final climax. And the Gothic bed in which Valerie Hobson rests is the same bed in which she and Colin Clive had snuggled in *Bride of Frankenstein.*

Universal remade *The Great Impersonation* (1942), with Ralph Bellamy in the dual role and Evelyn Ankers as leading lady. It bore little relation to the 1935 film — and featured no Ghost of the Black Bog.

REVIEW
—*The Encyclopedia of Horror Movies*, Edited by Phil Hardy: "...sets from *Frankenstein* (1931) and *The Old Dark House* (1932) are put to good use, and there is some conventional creepy fun to be had from Dale as the inevitable sinister housekeeper and Frye as a maniac who haunts the Black Bog with blood-curdling screams."

The Crime of Doctor Crespi

Republic/Liberty, 1935; Producer and Director: John H. Auer; Associate Producer: Herb Hayman; Screenplay: Lewis Graham and Edward Olmstead (based on a story by John H. Auer, from Edgar Allan Poe's tale *The Premature Burial*); Cinematography: Larry Williams; Editor: Leonard Wheeler; Art Director: William Saulter; Recorder: Clarence Wall; Musical Director: Milton Schwartzwald; Makeup: Fred Ryle; Production Supervisor: W. J. O'Sullivan; Sound System: RCA Victor; Running Time: 63 minutes; Filmed at the Biograph Studios, New York City, September, 1934; Release date, October 21, 1935

CAST: Erich von Stroheim (Dr. Andre Crespi); **Dwight Frye (Dr. Thomas)**; Paul Guilfoyle (Dr. Arnold); Harriet Russell (Mrs. Estelle Ross); John Bohn (Dr. Stephen Ross; "the Dead Man"); Geraldine Kay (Miss Rexford); Jeanne Kelly (Miss Gordon); Patsy Berlin (Jeanne); Joe Verdi (Di Angelo); Dean Raymond (Minister)

NOTES:

> When Dwight Frye doesn't die in a picture, the fans will agree that that's news! In the new Erich von Stroheim thriller, *The Crime of Doctor Crespi*, Dwight Frye, the player who has gasped his last in such famous films as *Dracula*, *The Vampire Bat*, *Frankenstein*, *Doorway to Hell* and *The Maltese Falcon*, actually is up and on his feet as the last reel comes to a final fade-out.
> —from the pressbook of *The Crime of Doctor Crespi* (1935)

By 1934, life had reached a low point of almost classical tragedy proportion for Erich von Stroheim (1885-1957). His wife, Valerie, had been terribly disfigured in a beauty parlor fire. Their son was seriously ill. And his days as auteur-terror of such artful extravaganzas as *Foolish Wives* (1922) and *Greed* (1924) were long behind him, in a legendary wake of profligate spending and Teutonic temperament.

"Von" was surviving as an actor, and hence accepted *The Crime of Doctor Crespi*. The chiller, based on Poe's *The Premature Burial* ("Edgar Allan Poe's Super Shocker!" hawked the publicity), not only gave a rich starring part to von Stroheim (billed on posters once again by his old nickname, "the man you love to hate"), but gave major billing (second lead on posters, third billing on the film's credits) to Dwight Frye for the first (and last) time in his movie career.

It was a curious production, to say the least. Shot in New York's Bronx at D. W. Griffith's old Biograph Studios, *The Crime of Doctor Crespi* was the brainchild of John H. Auer—later a fixture of Republic (which bought *The Crime of Doctor Crespi* from Liberty Studio). Auer produced and wrote the story—in addition to directing the film in only eight days. Budapest-born Auer had begun his career directing Mexican films such as *Life for Another* and *The Pervert* (both 1934); he would go on as a Republic director and producer for almost 20 years. (He later directed Dwight there in 1938's *Invisible Enemy*.)

The Crime of Doctor Crespi afforded considerable pressbook PR for Dwight. In bestowing upon him the cinema sobriquet of "The Man Who Has Died a Thousand Deaths," Republic was not above employing a bit of hyperbole:

> Hitherto, Frye has met with violent death in every feature in which he has been seen. He has been stabbed, poisoned, hung, thrown from speeding trains, tossed over cliffs, drowned and torn to bits by wild animals... all for the sake of film art.

The publicity played up that Dwight survived in this one, with the pressbook headline heralding, "Dwight Frye Lives At Last in Horror Epic, *Doctor Crespi*."

Not everyone regarded *The Crime of Doctor Crespi* as a "horror epic." *Variety* was aghast and opined that "Dwight Frye is hopelessly sunk by his part." But *The New York Times*, while dismissing the movie as "an almost humorously overstrained attempt at grimness," praised Dwight, alluding to his great Broadway career and finding him the film's "only redeeming presence."

The film has a limited but interesting musical score; the opening credits use Rubinstein's "Kammenoi Ostrow," which also figured prominently as Karloff's favorite musical piece in *The Walking Dead* (Warner Bros., 1936). Other versions of Poe's *The Premature Burial* include the 1927 British short *Prelude*; an episode on NBC's Karloff-hosted *Thriller* (in which Karloff himself acted, October 2, 1961); and American-International's 1962 *The Premature Burial*, with Ray Milland and Hazel Court.

An offbeat, bizarre and quite fascinating horror show in its own right, *The Crime of Doctor Crespi* has special significance for Dwight Frye fans, as it gave him "The Man Who Has Died a Thousand Deaths" nickname, a "good guy" role, major billing, a hint of romance—and what must have been a very refreshing dash of respect.

REVIEW
—*Forgotten Horrors: Early Talkie Chillers from Poverty Row*, by George E. Tuner and Michael H. Price, 1979: "...a delightful Poe-inspired chiller... Stroheim... comes across as the most utterly despicable bad man since Bela Lugosi's sorcerer in *White Zombie*. Paul Guilfoyle, Dwight Frye and John Bohn provide excellent support, with Frye displaying the nervous mannerisms which so perfectly served the moods of *Dracula*, *Frankenstein* and *Bride of Frankenstein*..."

Tough Guy

MGM, 1936; Director: Chester M. Franklin; Original Story and Screenplay: Florence Ryerson and Edgar Allan Woolf; Cameraman: Leonard Woolf; Art Director: Cedric Gibbons; Musical Director: Dr. William Axt; Running Time: 76 minutes; Production Dates: November 6, 1935-January 3, 1936; Release Date: January 24, 1936

CAST: Jackie Cooper (Freddie); Joseph Calleia (Joe Calerno); Rin Tin Tin, Jr. (Duke); Harvey Stephens (Chief Davison); Jean Hersholt (pet doctor); Edward Pawley (Tony); Mischa Auer (Chi); Robert Warwick (Frederick Vincent); **Dwight Frye (Mack)**; Wally Maher (Shorty); Edward Norris (Bud); William Tannen (Heming); Arthur Housman (Waring); Sue Moore (Mrs. Waring); Ivan Miller (Wilson); Russell Hicks, Phillip Morris (G-Men); Sidney Bracey (Briggs); Sherry Hall (Jones); Jack Daley (Finley); John Kelly (Rooney); Hal Craig (Murphy); Frank LaRue (Clark); Edward McWade (elderly man); Max Hoffman, Jr. (Jensen); Victor Adams (gangster)

NOTES: The working title for *Tough Guy* was *The Getaway*. Some exteriors were shot in Big Tujunga Canyon, California. Essentially, *Tough Guy* is the story of a boy and his dog, with Rin Tin Tin, Jr. cleverly handled throughout the film. Joseph Calleia, as the mobster, does a nice job evolving into a sympathetic character through his relationship with Freddie and Duke.

Frye has a number of scenes in *Tough Guy*. He is first viewed with a menacing closeup during the armored car robbery. At the old house where the gang meets after the caper, Mack (Frye) is ordered by Calerno (Joseph Calleia) to kill Freddie (Jackie Cooper). Mack balks:

> No, I ain't gonna do it. I ain't gonna have murder han-
> gin' over me. I won't. You hand me all the dirty jobs
> to do. I'm through.

As Mack attempts to leave, Calerno first suggests that he be killed instead of the boy, then knocks Mack to the ground.

Later, when the gang learns of the reward being offered for Freddie's return, Mack questions Tony (Edward Pawley) about their revised plans:

> Hey, wait a minute. If this thing goes through, what's gonna happen if you return that kid and he squeals on us to the coppers?

Tony assures Mack that won't happen. Mack is viewed helping the gang capture Freddie by a cave, escorting the boy through the woods and forcing him into their car. When Calerno surprises the gang on the abandoned boat, Mack is the only one to draw his gun, getting shot in the hand for his effort. (Frye has some good close-ups while the gang is held at bay by Duke, the dog, as Calerno flees with Freddie.) Finally, Mack is cornered by the police when they descend upon the boat.

Despite the fact *Tough Guy* was made by a major studio (MGM) and Frye had ample screen time, most references missed this film credit for Dwight. Frye's expressions of fear and displays of neurotic traits in *Tough Guy* were by now becoming Dwight's signature piece for a film.

Florida Special

Paramount, 1936; Director: Ralph Murphy; Screenplay: David Boehm, Marguerite Roberts, Laura Perelman and S. J. Perelman; Original Story: Clarence Budington Kelland; Cameraman: Leo Tover; Special Effects: Farciot Edouart and Loyal Griggs; Running Time: 68 minutes; Production completed: March 16, 1936; Release Date: May 1, 1936

CAST: Jack Oakie (Bangs Tucker); Sally Eilers (Jerry Quinn); Kent Taylor (Wally Nelson); Frances Drake (Marina Stafford); Claude Gillingwater (Simeon Stafford); J. Farrell MacDonald (Captain Timothy Harrigan); Sam Hearn (Schlepperman); Sidney Blackmer (Jack Macklyn); **Dwight Frye (Jenkins)**; Clyde Dilson (Dominic); Matthew Betz (Herman Weil); Dewey Robinson (Skeets); Harry G. Bradley (Conductor); Jean Barry (Violet); Mack Gray (Louie); Garry Owen (Joe); Stanley Andrews (Armstrong); Norman Willis (nurse); Sam Flint (doctor); Jackie Heller (singer)

NOTES: As the bespectacled secretary Jenkins, Dwight Frye had a number of scenes in the early going of *Florida Special*. Jenkins is first viewed with his employer, extremely eccentric Simeon Stafford (Claude Gillingwater), and Stafford's niece Marina (Frances Drake), preparing to board the train. Talkative newshound Bangs (Jack Oakie) tries to obtain a story from Simeon and Jenkins, but the secretary is then found unconscious in Stafford's stateroom. Harrigan (J. Farrell MacDonald) discovers that the briefcase, formerly handcuffed to Jenkins' right wrist, has been removed and is missing. Despite the circumstances under which he has been found, Jenkins becomes a suspect in the disappearance of Simeon Stafford. In league with the jewel thieves, Jenkins is confronted by Weil (Matthew Betz), who, upon discovering the valise had been stuffed with old paper, accuses the secretary of trying to double-cross him. Jenkins informs Weil of his suspicion that Marina must have the jewels. After Marina reports the jewels as missing, Harrigan returns to the Stafford stateroom. Jenkins is found dead from a gunshot fired through the window.

The consensus among the reviewers of *Florida Special* was that the film was a "pleasant," "fairly amusing" comedy with a fast-moving pace that "...gives one little time to ponder on the improbabilities of the plot." Although Frye had a fairly substantial role as the duplicitous secretary Jenkins, he was mentioned by only one review (*New York American*) as "mingling with the other characters." Frances Drake, who played Marina in *Florida Special*, was seen to better advantage in two fantasy genre roles: Yvonne Orlac in *Mad Love* (1935) and Diane Rukh in *The Invisible Ray* (1935).

Jack Oakie's character, Bangs Tucker, is incorrectly listed in the pressbook and reviews as Bangs Carter.

Alibi for Murder

Columbia, 1936; Director: D. Ross Lederman; Original Screenplay: Tom Van Dycke; Cameramen: George Meehan and Irving Lippman; Running Time: 61 minutes; Production Dates: July 18-July 31, 1936; Release Date: September 23, 1936

CAST: William Gargan (Perry Travis); Marguerite Churchill (Lois Allen); Gene Morgan (Brainy Barker); John Gallaudet (Billy Howard); Romaine Callender (E. J. Easton); Egon Brecher (Sir Conrad Stava); Drue Leyton (Mrs. Norma Foster); Wade Boteler (Conroy); **Dwight Frye (Alvin McBride)**; Raymond Lawrence (Harkness); Norman Willis (Joel Balerino); Edward McWade (Walter Emerson); Stanley Andrews (Earl Quillan); Robert Riske (Aviator); Marda Deering (Gloria Dawn); Eddie Kane (Venuti); Harry Harvey (Bennett); William Worthington (John J. Foster)

NOTES: The working title of *Alibi for Murder* was *Two Minute Alibi*. Dwight Frye would later work with director D. Ross Lederman on *Adventure in Sahara*.

Frye's role of Alvin McBride is one of his more interesting screen characterizations. McBride, the murdered Foster's assistant, is deemed a suspect early on as he was the first to come upon the scientist's body. While being questioned, McBride exposes Foster as not a great scientist, but a "butcher," adding:

> You spoke of him working for humanity, contributing to mankind. He never cured, he killed. Do you know why he got the Nobel Prize? For his work in steel, but what sort of steel? Steel to be used for construction? Not at all. Not even the Nobel Prize committee knew it, but his invention, Fosterite Steel the world calls it, is intended only for the making of big guns, for war, for slaughtering people. He was civilization's Public Enemy number two. He deserved to be killed.

When Sir Conrad Stava (Egon Brecher) condescendingly berates McBride's "undigested pacifism," Frye's character becomes even more intense, lashing out at the munitions mogul as "a wholesale dealer of death." McBride continues his tirade at Stava:

> Foster's work was child's play compared to yours. You took his steel and turned it into instruments of destruction. It was for you he was inventing even greater horror than the world has yet known. He was merely a puppet, but you, you're the real enemy of society.

As the exchange of threats escalates, McBride lunges at Stava, forcing Perry (William Gargan) to knock Alvin to the ground. Perry later refers to McBride as the "pacifist who's a little too odd."

Given that *Alibi for Murder* was made in 1936, Frye, as Alvin McBride, almost represents the social conscience against the mounting threat of war and destruction that was all too near at hand. *Alibi for Murder* is a rarely televised or screened film, but it allows audiences to view Frye acting with a passion for an ideal—rather than a fervent desire for spiders.

Beware of Ladies
Republic, 1936; Director: Irving Pichel; Original Screenplay: L.C. Dublin; Cameraman: William Nobles; Music: Harry Grey; Running Time: 62 minutes; Production Dates: October 26-early November 1936; Release Date: December 21, 1936

CAST: Donald Cook (George Martin); Judith Allen (Betty White); George Meeker (Freddie White); Goodee Montgomery (Gertie); Russell Hopton (Randy Randall); William Newell (Sniff); **Dwight Frye (Swanson)**; Thomas Jackson (Albert Simmons); Josephine Whittell (Alice McDonald); William Crowell (Tony Baxter); Robert Strange (John Williams); Robert Emmett Keane (Charles Collins); Eric Wilton (Henry); Phil Dunham (J. Robert Slank)

NOTES: The working title for *Beware of Ladies* was *Between Two Loves*. Director Irving Pichel was also a talented character actor, rendering a memorable performance as Sandor in *Dracula's Daughter* (1936).

Billed seventh as Swanson, Frye is initially referred to as "eagle eye" by gang leader Randall (Russell Hopton), establishing Swanson's propensity for finding "dirt" on individuals. Randall arranges for Swanson to work at the campaign headquarters of George Martin (Donald Cook), with the henchman playing up his role. When Martin tells Swanson he is "right on the job," Frye's character offers:

> That's me boss. Hope you hand it out to those Williams'
> heels in your spiel tonight.

Later at the headquarters, Frye has a very good exchange with Josephine Whittell, as Alice McDonald. In this scene, Dwight had the rare opportunity to display his sense of humor and comic delivery on screen. Some of Swanson's lines from this sequence are:

> Ain't you blowing the whistle, "Mackey?" Knocking off.
> It's time for little boys and girls to go home.
>
> Aw, come on. Tell you what, I'll set you up to a
> real feed.

Swanson feigns concern for McDonald, working her for information about Betty White (Judith Allen):

> Say, you sure hit it. You'd think that White dame
> was running, wouldn't you? Hey, that's a good one.
> (laughs) Running for D. A. Get it? Running after
> the D. A.

After McDonald leaves the office, Swanson telephones Randall:

> Then she spills it that the White dame is married.

Although Swanson is a sneaky, nosy character, eavesdropping on phone conversations and searching through garbage for bits of information, Frye was able to imbue this role with more humor and dimension than most of the "two-bit" hood types he was often reduced to playing.

Frye and star Donald Cook had previously appeared together in *The Circus Queen Murder* (1933).

Sea Devils

RKO Radio, 1937; Director: Ben Stoloff; Original Story and Screenplay: Frank Wead, John Twist and P. J. Wolfson; Cameramen: J. Roy Hunt and Joseph August; Art Director: Van Nest Polglase; Music Director: Roy Webb; Special Effects: Vernon Walker; Technical Advisor: Lieutenant H. C. Moore; Running Time: 85 minutes; Production Dates: mid-October-early December 1936; Release Date: February 19, 1937

CAST: Victor McLaglen (William "Medals" Malone); Preston Foster (Mike O'Shay); Ida Lupino (Doris Malone); Donald Woods (Steve Webb); Helen Flint (Sadie); Gordon Jones (Puggy); Pierre Watkin (Commander); Murray Alper (Brownie); Billy Gilbert (Billy the cop); Barbara Pepper (17-year old girl); **Dwight Frye (radio operator, *S.S. Paradise*)**; Paul Guilfoyle (Charlie, radio operator); Fern Emmett (McGonigle, librarian); Frank Moran (bartender); Otto Hoffman (Monty, pawnbroker); George Irving (doctor); Frank Mills, Ralph Dunn, Harry Cording, Harry Strang (sailors); Charles Lane (judge); Vinton Haworth (prosecutor); Alan Curtis (records clerk); Eddy Chandler (shore patrolman); Sam Flint (yacht captain)

NOTES: *Sea Devils*, an Edward Small production, had a number of working titles, including *Coast Guard*, *Coast Patrol* and *Rough, Ready and Handsome*. Some of the action was actually filmed aboard the Coast Guard cutter *Taroe*.

Dwight Frye appears at the opening of *Sea Devils* as the radio operator aboard steamship *Paradise* attempting to contact the Coast Guard at New London, Connecticut. "The fire is spread-
ing aft. Send all help available," the operator implores. The Coast Guard, aboard the *Taroe*, rushes to the scene, while the radio man, covered with sweat and surrounded by flames, yells, "Hello Coast Guard, send help at once." Charlie (Paul Guilfoyle), the Coast Guard radio operator, assures him that help is already on board the *Paradise*. Obviously under stress, Frye's character continues, "The passengers—I hear them screaming!" He keeps verbalizing his distress about the passengers until Malone (Victor McLaglen) bursts into the radio room and sees the man is hysterical. Malone throws the operator over the shoulder of Steve Webb (Donald Woods) to be carried to safety.

Besides *Sea Devils*, Ben Stoloff had earlier directed Frye in *By Whose Hand?* (1932). It is interesting to note that the two radio operators exchanging messages in the film's opening sequence, Frye and Paul Guilfoyle, were personal friends off the screen.

The Man Who Found Himself

RKO Radio, 1937; Director: Lew Landers; Screenplay: J Robert Bren, Edmund L. Hart-mann, G. V. Atwater and Thomas Lennon; Original Story: Alice P. Curtis; Cameraman: J. Roy Hunt; Special Effects: Vernon L. Walker; Art Director: Van Nest Polglase; Running Time: 67 minutes; Production Dates: January 12-early February 1937; Release Date: April 2, 1937

CAST: John Beal (Dr. James Stanton, Jr. aka Jim Jones); Joan Fontaine (Doris King); Philip Huston (Dick Miller); Jane Walsh (Barbara Reed); George Irving (Dr. James Stanton, Sr.); James Conlin ("Nosey" Watson); Frank M. Thomas (Roberts); Diana Gibson (Helen Richards); **Dwight Frye (hysterical patient)**; Billy Gilbert (fat hobo); Alec Craig (thin hobo); Stanley Andrews

(Inspector Grey); Jonathan Hale (Dr. Tom Smythe); George Meeker (Howard Dennis); Edward Van Sloan, Douglas Wood (doctors); Edward Gargan (cop); Dwight David Frye (boy pulled through train window)

NOTES: *The Man Who Found Himself* was based on Alice Curtis' unpublished story *Wings Of Mercy*, which also was the working title of the film. When *The Man Who Found Himself* opened at the Palace in New York City in early April 1937, it played on the same bill as *Sea Devils*, another RKO Radio film featuring a bit by Dwight Frye.

Billed ninth as "patient" in *The Man Who Found Himself*, Frye is involved in the sequence of the first emergency call for the ambulance plane. A patient (Frye), described as "a very sick man," is taken from an ambulance to the ambulance plane, piloted by Jim (John Beal). With the plane now airborne, the patient, in bed, appears very distressed. Doris (Joan Fontaine), the nurse, fixes his blanket and, noting the escalating level of agitation, prepares a needle. The patient screams:

> I can't stand it. No! Let me go! I want to get out that
> door. Let me go. No. Let me go! No!

Doris and the patient struggle. Jim puts the plane on automatic pilot, comes back and administers a sedative to the patient by needle. After landing, the sedated patient is transferred to an ambulance, while Jim tells reporters of Doris' heroics. Newspaper headlines flash, "Nurse Subdues Maniac in Flying Hospital."

Dwight David Frye, six years old at the time of the making of *The Man Who Found Himself*, had been pestering his parents for some time about getting the chance to be in a movie. He got his wish with this particular film. "Buddy" Frye, as he was referred to in those days, can be observed after the train wreck in *The Man Who Found Himself* as the young boy being lifted out through the broken train window. Injured during the crash, the boy is taken to where the elder Dr. Stanton is performing surgery.

Although *The Man Who Found Himself* is not an important film, it is significant in that it is the only picture to include both Dwight Iliff Frye and his son, Dwight David Frye.

The Road Back

Universal, 1937; Director: James Whale; Screenplay: R. C. Sheriff and Charles Kenyon; Cameraman: John J. Mescall and George Robinson; Special Effects: John P. Fulton; Music Director: Charles Previn; Musical Score: Dimitri Tiomkin; Running Time: 105 minutes; Production Dates: January 27-April 21, 1937; Release Date: August 1, 1937

CAST: John King (Ernst); Richard Cromwell (Ludwig); Slim Summervilie (Tjaden); Andy Devine (Willy); Barbara Read (Lucy); Louise Fazenda (Angelina); Noah Beery, Jr. (Wessling); Maurice Murphy (Albert); John Emery (Von Hagen); Larry Blake (Weil); Etienne Girardot (Mayor); Lionel Atwill (Prosecutor); Henry Hunter (Bethke); Gene Garrick (Geisicke); Spring Byington (Ernst's mother); Frank Reicher (Ernst's father); Marilyn Harris (Ernst's sister); Laura Hope Crews (Ernst's aunt); Charles Halton (Uncle Rudolph); Arthur Hohl (Heinrich); Al Shean (Mr. Markham); Edwin Maxwell (Principal); Robert Warwick (Judge); **Dwight Frye (small man at rally)**; Edward Van Sloan (president at rally); E. E. Clive (General); Samuel S. Hinds (Defense Attorney); William B. Davidson (Bartscher); Jean Rouverol (Elsa); Clara Blandick (Willy's mother)

NOTES: *The Road Back* was based on the novel of the same name by Erich Maria Remarque, who had authored what was adapted into one of the most famous of all antiwar films, *All Quiet on the Western Front* (1930). Universal had owned the rights to the sequel for a number of years, with the studio entrusting the project to top-flight director James Whale, in the hope he could replicate the success of *The Road Back*'s predecessor. Actor Slim Summerville was the only performer to be featured in both films.

The Road Back was beset with problems from the beginning. Powder man George Daly was injured the morning of February 24 by an exploding bomb and died en route to the Cedars of Lebanon hospital. (Andy Devine was much nearer the bomb than Daly, but was uninjured.) Heavy rains and other delays resulted in Whale bringing the film in well over its $770,000 budget and beyond the shooting schedule. Even worse, in response to pressure from the German government, Universal ordered 21 separate cuts and had writer Charles Kenyon fill gaps by adding comedy scenes with Summerville and Andy Devine. Whale, balking at the increased comedy, as well as the reediting, left the project, with director Edward Sloman and new editor Charles Maynard finishing the patch up job on *The Road Back*. Many film historians consider this experience the beginning of the end of James Whale's cinematic career.

Some critics feel that Whale handled his old standbys better than the leads. Although a war-related movie, *The Road Back* is loaded with horror film veterans: Frye, Lionel Atwill, Edward Van Sloan, E. E. Clive, Frank Reicher, Marilyn Harris ("Little Maria" from *Frankenstein*), Harry Cording, Arthur Hohl and others.

Frye is involved in a lengthy sequence of *The Road Back*, wherein villagers demand the mayor (Etienne Girardot) leave his home and accompany them to their meeting. When Willy (Andy Devine) questions why they want to do this, Frye's character responds, "Must have the mayor. Makes it official." Frye uses his umbrella to unofficially lead the band, while directing the mayor and throng to the rally, regrouping, at one point, to avoid a horsedrawn wagon.

After the group assembles, Willy wonders what it is all about. Frye tells him they do it every day, gathering the workers and soldiers "...to keep them awake." Willy probes for more specifics, like what they are supposed to do. "Do? Why, justice, freedom and all that sort of thing!," responds Frye.

The president of the rally (Van Sloan) reads a proclamation, which is hard to hear. Frye tells Willy, "He's telling us to be calm, prudent, patient and to go home." The returning soldiers query why they came all the way for this. Frye becomes indignant, offering. "What else did you expect?" and "What sort of thing would you do?" Willy tells the smallish, mustachioed townsperson (Frye) to "Shut up," as the veterans walk away in disgust.

Something to Sing About

Grand National, 1937; Producer: Zion Myers; Director: Victor Schertzinger; Story and Music: Victor Schertzinger; Cinematography: John Stumar; Musical Director: C. Bakaleinikoff; Choreographer: Harland Dixon; Art Directors: Robert Lee and Paul Murphy; Alternate Title: *Battling Hoofer*; Running Time: 90 minutes; Filmed late June-late July, 1937; Previewed at Grauman's Chinese Theatre, August 26, 1937

CAST: James Cagney (Terry Rooney); Evelyn Daw (Rita Wyatt); William Frawley (Hank Meyers); Mona Barrie (Stephanie Hajos); Gene Lockhart (Bennett O. Regan); James Newill (Orchestra Soloist); Harry Barris (Pinky); Candy Candido (Candy); Cully Richards (Soloist); William B. Davidson (Cafe Manager); Richard Tucker (Blaine); Mark Windheim (Farney); **Dwight Frye (Easton)**; John Arthur (Daviani); Philip Ahn (Ito); Kathleen Lockhart (Miss Robbins); Kenneth Harlan (Transportation Manager); Herbert Rawlinson (Studio Attorney); Ernest Wood (Edward Burns); Chick Collins (man Terry fights); Duke Green (Other Man); Bill Carey (Singer); Frank Mills (Cabby); Duke Green (Stuntman); Larry Steers (Studio Official); Edward Hearn (Studio Guard); Harland Dixon, Johnny Boyle, Pat Moran, Johnny (Skins) Miller, Joe Bennett, Buck Mack, Eddie Allen (Dancers); "The Vagabonds" (Specialty); Elinore Welz, Eleanor Prentiss (Girls); Eddie Kane (San Francisco Theatre Manager); Dottie Messmer, Virginia Lee Irwin,

Dolly Waldorf ("Three Shades of Blue"); Robert McKenzie (Ship's Captain); Alphonse Martel (Head Waiter); Pinkie and Pal (Arthur Nelson's Fighting Cats); Percy Launders, Paul McLarnad (Band Members); Bo Peep Karlin, Paul McLarand, William Ruhl, Buck Mack, Jim Toney, Joe Bennett, Joe Niemeyer, Eddie Allen (Bits)

NOTES: After feisty James Cagney (1899-1986) had sued for release from his Warner Bros. contract (his technicality: the studio had starred him in five 1935 releases, and his contract had called for only four), he shocked Hollywood by signing with new and very humble Grand National Studios. His first film there: *Great Guy* (1936), in which he co-starred with Mae Clarke (who had received Cagney's grapefruit in her face in Warners' 1931 *The Public Enemy*). His second (and last) with Grand National: *Something to Sing About*, which allowed Cagney to showcase his song-and-dance talents (which had originally won him celebrity on Broadway), and to satirize the cutthroat Hollywood establishment of the 1930s.

Victor Schertzinger (1889-1941) not only directed, but also wrote the story and songs, which included "Any Old Love" (sung by Cagney and the "Three Shades of Blue"), and "Right or Wrong," "Loving You," "Out of the Blue" and "Something to Sing About"—all delivered by leading lady Evelyn Daw. Indeed, Schertzinger even laid claim to having discovered Miss Daw (formerly of Geddes, South Dakota), who was singing at the Philharmonic in Los Angeles and who landed the lead after "a single audition" with the film's director/writer/composer. Frank S. Nugent's *The New York Times* review of *Something to Sing About* would report:

> Miss Daw has a pleasant voice for the Schertzinger tunes,
> but whenever she started to act we wished Mr. Cagney
> had another grapefruit handy.

Evelyn Daw's movie career would be short-lived.

The $450,000 production has much to recommend it. Cagney's hoofing is impressive (he engaged Harland Dixon, his old dancing instructor from New York, to choreograph and dance in the film); Cagney also reportedly practiced his *Something to Sing About* routines with Fred Astaire. The Hollywood satire is slick, featuring a delightful lampoon of a femme fatale star ("Stephanie Hajos") by Mona Barrie, performed in accent and blonde wig.

And there's Dwight Frye—in a surprise change-of-pace comedy role as Mr. Easton, prissy makeup man of Galore Pictures, Hollywood. Dwight camps it up as he meets Cagney, and prepare to make him up:

> The hairline—gracious! It belongs on an entirely dif-
> ferent face...!

> Mr. Rooney, if you don't mind—you distract me!

> When I look at that hairline, I could almost cry!

Cagney refuses Dwight's plan to glue a tiny toupee, Robert Taylor widow-peak style, to his forehead. Dwight flits his way through other scenes ("I just ache to take a poke at that chin!" he says at one point, observing Cagney). When Cagney's Terry is supposedly engaged at one point to Galore Picture's siren supreme Stephanie Hajos, Dwight gushes, "My dear Terry, I want to be the first to congratulate you!"—at which point William Frawley (as press agent Hank Meyers) tosses Dwight off the set.

It was one of Dwight's two appearances in film musicals (*Sleepytime Gal* being the other), and the film earned an Oscar nomination for musical score (losing to Universal's Deanna Durbin vehicle, *One Hundred Men and a Girl*). The film was re-released in 1947 as *Battling Hoofer*.

Something to Sing About was Cagney's last film for Grand National; Warner Bros. lured Cagney back, and little Grand National soon toppled in his absence. James Cagney's song-and-dance talents climaxed, of course, with his Oscar-winning performance as George M. Cohan in Warner Bros.' *Yankee Doodle Dandy* (1942).

Renfrew of the Royal Mounted

Grand National, 1937; Director: Al Herman; Screenplay: Charles Logue; Cameraman: Francis Corby; Musical Director: Arthur Kay; Running Time: 57 minutes; Production completed: July 27, 1937; Release Date: October 8, 1937

CAST: James Newill (Sergeant Renfrew); Carol Hughes (Virginia Bronson); William Royle (George Poulis); Herbert Corthell (Mr. James Bronson); Kenneth Harlan ("Angel" Carroll); Chief Thundercloud (Pierre); Dickie Jones (Tommy MacDonald); Donald Reed (Sergeant MacDonald); David Barclay ("Dreamy" Charles Nolan); Robert Terry (Duke); William Gould (Inspector Newcomb); William Austin (Constable Holly); **Dwight Frye (Totem Pole Lodge desk clerk)**; Lightning (the dog)

NOTES: *Renfrew of the Royal Mounted* was the first of eight films based on the *Renfrew* books by Laurie York Erskine. Betty Laidlaw and Robert Lively wrote three songs for the film: "Little Son," "Mounted Men" and "Barbecue Bill." James Newill, formerly a singer on the Burns and Allen radio program, made a decent transition to films in the role of Sergeant Renfrew.

Dwight Frye appeared, unbilled, as the desk clerk at the Totem Pole Lodge in *Renfrew of the Royal Mounted*. He is first seen welcoming James Bronson (Herbert Corthell) to the lodge, informing him that his daughter hasn't arrived yet, "but there is somebody waiting to see you, right there in the office." The somebody turns out to be "Angel" Carroll (Kenneth Harlan), a former criminal associate of the recently paroled Bronson.

After Renfrew's plane crashes, with the sergeant parachuting to safety (but feigning injury), Renfrew is carried inside the Totem Pole Lodge. The desk clerk battles his way through the onlookers, toward Renfrew, bantering:

> Just a minute. One side, please. One side, please. I'll
> take charge of this, if you don't mind. Excuse me!

Frye's character examines Renfrew, determining him to be "dazed," then searches for identification. "Why, he isn't an aviator," the desk clerk declares. "He's a mounted policeman."

Frye apparently shot his scenes for *Renfrew of the Royal Mounted* just prior to working on *Something to Sing About*. Grand National chose to release the two films in the reverse order of when they were shot, with the studio's priority being an attempt to capitalize on James Cagney's box office drawing power.

David Barclay, who played "Dreamy" Nolan in *Renfrew of the Royal Mounted*, is better known as Dave O'Brien. O'Brien would be featured in later entries in the *Renfrew* series, including *Danger Ahead* (1940) and *Sky Bandits* (1940), playing Renfrew's sidekick, Corporal Kelly. He is best remembered, perhaps, for his role of Johnny Layton in *The Devil Bat* (1940) and his appearance in the cult film *Tell Your Children* (aka *Reefer Madness*, 1938).

The Shadow

Columbia, 1937; Director: C.C. Coleman, Jr.; Screenplay: Arthur T. Horman; Original Story: Milton Raison; Cameraman: Lucien Ballard; Art Directors: Stephen Goosson and Lionel Banks; Musical Director: Morris W. Stoloff; Running Time: 59 minutes; Production Dates: August 31–September 16, 1937; Release Date: December 9, 1937

CAST: Rita Hayworth (Mary Gillespie); Charles Quigley (Jim Quinn); Marc Lawrence (Kid Crow); Arthur Loft (Sheriff Jackson); Dick Curtis (Carlos); Vernon Dent (Dutch Schultz); Marjorie Main (Hannah Gillespie); Donald Kirke (Senor Martinet); **Dwight Frye (Vindecco)**; Bess Flowers (Marianne); Bill Irving (Mac); Eddie Fetherston (Woody); Sally St. Clair (Dolores); Sue St. Clair (Rosa); John Tyrell (Mr. Moreno); Beatrice Curtis (Mrs. Moreno); Francis Sayles (Mr. Shaw); Ann Doran (Miss Shaw); Beatrice Blinn (Miss Shaw); Bud Jamison, Harry Strang (ticket sellers); Edward Hearn (circus doctor); Edward LeSaint (Bascomb); Mr. and Mrs. Clemens (knife throwing act); Harry Bernard (watchman); Ernie Adams (roustabout); Ted Mangean (masked figure); George Hickman (messenger boy)

NOTES: The working title for *The Shadow* was *Carnival Lady*. It is peculiar that Columbia would alter the title to that of a popular radio and serial character, *The Shadow*, to which the film bore no connection.

Billed ninth as Vindecco, the "twistbacked horse handler," Frye, affecting some sort of Mediterranean accent, enjoyed one of the more colorful parts of the latter portion of his film career. Vindecco is first viewed being berated, then slapped, by Senor Martinet (Donald Kirke) for leaving the horses unattended while the handler went to the harness shop. "One more blow to remember, eh, Thor?" Vindecco broodingly reflects while stroking Martinet's prize horse. As Vindecco sneaks outside to smoke his pipe ("The odor of tobacco bothers the horses," he explains), he is spotted by Mary Gillespie (Rita Hayworth), Jim Quinn (Charles Quigley) and Kid Crow (Marc Lawrence). They witness the wound on his face, the result of Martinet's cruelty, but Vindecco claims, "It was just an accident."

The night that Martinet threatens to take control of the circus, Quinn and Crow again confront a suspicious looking Vindecco, who assures them Martinet is all right. "I looked at my master to make certain he was [long pause] unharmed," states Vindecco. Quinn further questions Vindecco the next morning. Vindecco begins to respond in his native tongue, then catches himself, relating, "Like in American, you say, I have a hunch." Resisting further interrogation, the handler comments, "My people have a saying: 'He who speaks before he knows all, says nothing.'"

Vindecco unknowingly affixes the rosette, with the poison dart attached, to Thor, resulting in Martinet's death. After the police leave, he discovers this piece of evidence and sneaks over to Mary's wagon. Vindecco climbs in her window, asking for "a look at the weapons on the trophy board." They realize that three poison darts are missing, but Vindecco has the one that killed Martinet in his possession. Vindecco refuses Mary's request that he tell the police what he knows of the possible murderer. "Not until morning," balks Vindecco. "By that time I would have made sure of everything." She wonders how he can withhold evidence. Vindecco responds:

> I have the best of rights. Senor Martinet was... my
> brother. Yes. Once we rode together on Thor's broad
> back. My brother, myself and... and a third Martinet.
> One night in Buenos Aires, I fell. I never rode again.

Before Vindecco can reveal the identity of the third Martinet, Quinn and the police arrive. Vindecco implores Mary not to discuss what he has told her, adding, "My life may depend on your silence." Exiting and returning to his tent, Vindecco is confronted by a hooded figure. "I thought it would be you," Vindecco asserts. "It had to be. Fortunately, I was expecting you." Vindecco pulls a knife, but is slain by a poison dart fired from a blow gun.

Marc Lawrence, as Kid Crow in *The Shadow*, acted with Frye in their first of four films together (also *Who Killed Gail Preston?*, *Adventure in Sahara* and *Submarine Alert*). In an October 8, 1993 note to Jim Coughlin, Lawrence provided some impressions of Dwight Frye:

Memories of D. Frye, a remarkably intense actor, whose performances have always had that quality of unnatural naturalness. Frightening as a figure and penetrating as a face that mirrored nightmares. I admired him much in my memory.

Who Killed Gail Preston?

Columbia, 1938; Director: Leon Barsha; Screenplay: Robert E. Kent and Henry Taylor; Cameraman: Henry Freulich; Art Director: Stephen Goosson; Musical Director: Morris Stoloff; Running Time: 60 minutes; Production Dates: October 15-October 29, 1937; Release Date: February 25, 1938

CAST: Don Terry (Inspector Kellogg); Rita Hayworth (Gail Preston); Robert Paige (Swing Traynor); Wyn Cahoon (Ann Bishop); Gene Morgan (Cliff Connolly); Marc Lawrence (Frank Daniels); Arthur Loft (Jules Stevens); John Gallaudet (Charles Waverly); John Spacey (Patsy Fallon); Eddie Fetherston (Mike); James Millican (Hank); Mildred Gover (maid); **Dwight Frye (Mr. Owen)**; John Dilson (Curran); Vernon Dent (watchman); Bill Irving (Arnold); Ruth Hilliard (cigarette girl); Jane Hamilton (hat check girl); Dick Curtis (Jake); Nell Craig (society woman); Bruce Sidney (society man); Ralph McCullough (Marshall); James Burtis (head waiter); Nick Copeland (Louis)

NOTES: The working title for *Who Killed Gail Preston?* was *Murder in Swingtime*. Rita Hayworth, who only survives the first twenty minutes of the film, had two musical numbers: "It's Twelve O'Clock and All is Not Well" and "The Greatest Attraction in the World," with Gloria Franklin dubbing most of the singing. *Who Killed Gail Preston?* was the second (and final) film in which Dwight Frye appeared with Hayworth, having completed *The Shadow* with her a month earlier.

Frye was unbilled as Mr. Owen, the former husband of Gail Preston (Hayworth), about whom it is later revealed that he couldn't hold a job because he was always drunk. Owen is shown at the Swing Swing Club watching one of Gail's numbers with a look of anticipation. As the camera cuts to him for the fourth time, Owen fires his gun at Gail, then attempts to flee. He yells, "Get away from that door!," while two policemen give chase. The police are joined by Inspector Kellogg (Don Terry), as Owen begins to ascend a fire escape. As he climbs, Owen claims:

Wait. I did it. Sure I did it. I killed Gail Preston and
I'm not sorry—do you hear? I'm not sorry!

Owen gets to the top of the ladder and exclaims, "You'll never get me alive!," before plunging off the roof to his death. It is later determined that his shots did not kill Gail Preston after all.

Invisible Enemy

Republic, 1938; Director: John H. Auer; Screenplay: Albert J. Cohen, Alex Gottlieb and Norman Burnstine; Original Story: Albert J. Cohen and Robert T. Shannon; Cameraman: Jack Marta; Musical Director: Alberto Colombo; Running Time: 65 minutes; Production Dates: February 11-February 24, 1938. Release Date: April 4, 1938

CAST: Alan Marshal (Jeffrey Clavering); Tala Birell (Sandra Kamarov); Mady Correll (Princess Stephanie); C. Henry Gordon (Nikolai Kamarov); Herbert Mundin (Sergeant Alfred M. Higgs); Gerald Oliver Smith (Bassett); Ivan Simpson (Michael); Elsa Buchanan (Sophia); **Dwight Frye**

(**Alex**); Leonard Willey (Sir Herbert Donbridge); Ian MacLaren (Sir Joshua Longstreet); Egon Brecher (Kirman); Frank Puglia (Signor Bramucci)

NOTES: Working titles for *Invisible Enemy* included *Gentleman From London* and *Capital Punishment*. Leonard Willey, who played Sir Herbert Donbridge, was the real-life father of star Alan Marshal. John H. Auer, the director, was also responsible for *The Crime of Doctor Crespi* (1935), featuring Erich von Stroheim and Frye.

As Alex, an agent for Kamarov (C. Henry Gordon), Frye was onscreen for a number of sequences in *Invisible Enemy*. Armed, Alex breaks into a meeting of British oil executives, furthering the Great Eastern Oil Corporation's concerns about Kamarov's intentions. In an attempt to secure information and dispose of Jeffrey Clavering (Alan Marshal), Alex ransacks Clavering's rooms. Interrupted by Bassett (Gerald Oliver Smith), he coldly murders the valet and vacates the premises. Alex is also viewed with his boss, Kamarov (C. Henry Gordon).

The pressbook for *Invisible Enemy* suggests Frye and Gordon spent time on the set reminiscing about appearing together on Broadway in *Puppets* in 1924. The two actors were also both featured in two more films, *The Black Camel* (1931) and *Adventure in Sahara* (1938).

A review of *Invisible Enemy* stated, "...the real dirty work is done with considerable relish by Dwight Frye and Ivan Simpson."

Sinners in Paradise

Universal, 1938; Director: James Whale; Screenplay: Lester Cole, Harold Buckley and Louis Stevens; Original Story: Harold Buckley; Cameraman: George Robinson; Music Director: Charles Previn; Running Time: 65 minutes; Production Dates: March 1938; Release Date: May 6, 1938

CAST: Madge Evans (Anne Wesson); John Boles (Jim Taylor); Bruce Cabot (Robert Malone); Marion Martin (Iris Compton); Gene Lockhart (Senator John P. Corey); Charlotte Wynters (Thelma Chase aka Doris Bailey); Nana Bryant (Mrs. Franklin Sydney); Milburn Stone (T. L. Honeyman); Donald Barry (Jessup); Morgan Conway (Harrison Brand); Willie Fung (Ping); **Dwight Frye (Marshall)**; Jason Robards (Captain); William Lundigan (Radio announcer); Alan Edwards (Wesson); Eric Hansen (first pilot); Gaylord Pendleton (second pilot); Billy Wayne (navigator); Franklin Parker (operator); John Hiestand (land operator); James Eagles (radio announcer); William H. Royle (pilot); Harry Harvey, Robert Spencer (photographers); Lynton Brent, Jack Gardner, Donald Kerr (reporters)

NOTES: *Sinners in Paradise* was based on Harold Buckley's story *Half Way to Shanghai*, which was a working title for the film, as was *Eye of the Needle*. In November 1950, *Sinners in Paradise* was reissued as *Secrets of a Sinner*.

James Whale directed *Sinners in Paradise* in order to complete his contractual obligations to Universal and considered the film one of his "punishment pictures." *Sinners in Paradise* represented the fifth time (out of six) that Dwight Frye would work with Whale, but Frye's role almost seemed a handout when compared to some of their earlier ventures.

As Marshall, Frye is viewed solely at the start of *Sinners in Paradise*, as the passengers prepare to board their Transpacific Express flight. Marshall gazes around outside the terminal, then summons a porter to carry some luggage. His employer, Thelma Chase (Charlotte Wynters), an industrial heiress who has abandoned a strike of 6,000 employees in her Detroit factories, inquires if everything is in order. Marshall responds:

> Yes, Miss Chase. Here are your passports and health
> certificate. I made the reservations in the name of Doris
> Bailey.

Chase thanks Marshall, adding that she'll cable him from Hong Kong. He bids her "a pleasant journey," and then is surrounded by reporters and photographers, who attempt to extract the mysterious woman's identity from Marshall. "Why," Marshall pauses, "Miss Doris Bailey."

Besides Whale and Frye, another 1931 *Frankenstein* alumnus was on hand for *Sinners in Paradise*—John Boles, who played the hero of the melodrama. Boles and Frye did not share any screen time, however.

Fast Company

MGM, 1938; Director: Edward Buzzell; Screenplay: Marco Page and Harold Tarshis; Cameraman: Clyde DeVinna; Art Director: Cedric Gibbons; Music: Dr. William Axt; Running Time: 75 minutes; Production Dates: Late May-June 5, 1938; Release Date: July 8, 1938

CAST: Melvyn Douglas (Joel Sloane); Florence Rice (Garda Sloane); Claire Dodd (Julia Thorne); Shepperd Strudwick (Ned Morgan); Louis Calhern (Elias Z. Bannerman); Nat Pendleton (Paul Terison); Douglass Dumbrille (Arnold Stamper); Mary Howard (Leah Brockler); George Zucco (Otto Brockler); Minor Watson (Steve Langner): Donald Douglas (Lieutenant James Flanner); **Dwight Frye (Sidney Z. Wheeler)**; Thurston Hall (D. A. MacMillen); Horace MacMahon (Danny Scolado); Roger Converse (Asst. D. A. Byers); Natalie Garson (Mildred); Henry Sylvester (auctioneer); Edward Hearn (policeman); James B. Carson (safe expert); Ronnie Rondell (taxi driver); Jack Foss (attendant); Barbara Bedford (secretary)

NOTES: *Fast Company* was based on a novel of the same name by Marco Page (Harry Kurnitz). Some television prints of the film use the title *The Rare Book Murders*. MGM made two more films using the husband and wife characters of Joel and Garda Sloane: *Fast and Loose* (1939), starring Robert Montgomery and Rosalind Russell, and *Fast and Furious* (1939), with Franchot Tone and Ann Sothern in the leads.

Sidney Z. Wheeler in *Fast Company* represents yet another henchman role for Dwight Frye. Wheeler, the tool who fixes up stolen rare volumes for book fence Eli Bannerman (Louis Calhern), is first seen completing his counterfeiting labors as his boss enters. Prideful of his efforts, Wheeler notes:

> This is the first edition of *Leaves of Grass* I got from the
> Wilson collection yesterday. And this is the copy you
> got from Brockler. I've switched parts of the binding,
> moved a lot of pages from one book to the other, so now
> you've got two first editions to sell!

Wheeler is indignant that Brockler (George Zucco) will only pay $2,000 for books that are worth much more. As Bannerman and Wheeler drive to Brockler's residence, Sidney complains, "Just get the dough. That's all I care about."

After Brockler is murdered, Wheeler confronts Bannerman about his possible involvement in the crime. Bannerman hits Wheeler in the jaw, knocking him to the floor. Wheeler rises with a drawn pistol, telling his boss:

> Sit down. Rest yourself. Why don't you hit me now?
> You're going to pay plenty for that wallop, Eli.

Wheeler takes Bannerman's wallet containing Brockler's money and is next viewed having drinks at a nightclub with Mildred (Natalie Garson). He downs shots of whiskey and playfully points the bottle at Mildred, until Bannerman's entrance causes a rapid change of mood. Bannerman tells Wheeler that the police are pinning Brockler's murder on him, so Sidney agrees to call Joel Sloane (Melvyn Douglas), pretending to be from the D. A.'s office. As Joel exits the Reardon Arms, Wheeler, from a car, fires twice, shooting Sloane in the posterior. Wheeler then inquires, "Eli, do you really think I'm safe now?," as Bannerman takes him for a ride in the woods of Long Island. Bannerman murders Wheeler while checking a supposedly soft tire.

Wheeler's clandestine meeting with Brockler is only alluded to and not seen, so Frye and Zucco do not appear together on screen.

Think It Over

MGM, 1938; *Crime Does Not Pay* short #19; Director: Jacques Tourneur; Original Story and Screenplay: Winston Miller; Cameraman: Paul Vogel; Running Time: 19 minutes; Release Date: July 24, 1938

CAST: Lester Matthews (arson gang leader); Charles D. Brown (Inspector Wilson); Donald Barry (Harold Woods); **Dwight Frye (arsonist)**; Robert Emmett Keane (Mr. Johnson); Frank Orth (Croft); Robert Homans; Eddy Waller; John Dilson; Eddie Parker

NOTES: MGM's *Crime Does Not Pay* short subject series encompassed 48 films between the years 1935 to 1947. The shorts were of high quality, initially dealing with various rackets, like loan sharking, phony charities and counterfeiting. Later entries involved espionage and more war-related topics. Veteran MGM directors like Edward Cahn and Leslie Fenton worked on the series, as did newcomers like Fred Zinnemann and Joseph Losey. Casts also mixed old reliable character players, such as Egon Brecher and Arthur Hohl, with up-and-coming talent, like Cameron Mitchell and Barry Nelson.

Dwight Frye was one of the four listed names in the opening credits of *Think It Over*, but his character, the arsonist, is unnamed. He is part of a gang (with Lester Matthews and Donald Barry) that utilizes arson to "help" businessmen collect on fire insurance. After torching a store and returning to a hotel, Frye asks Matthews, "Anything else lined up?" Before leaving town, the gang attempts to do one more job, with the arsonist taking three large bags of celluloid into a building, then making a trail of gunpowder. The arsonist, after lighting a small candle as a fuse, finds both exits blocked by the police and fire department, who have just arrived. Trapped, he attempts to exit from the roof, but is unable to force open the skylight. Flames ignite and spread, as Frye lets out a piercing scream and perishes in the blaze.

Think It Over is but one of two shorts (*Don't Talk* being the other) in which Frye is known to have appeared and both were for MGM. Of particular significance is that *Think It Over* was directed by Jacques Tourneur, who would go on to direct important horror films (mostly for Val Lewton at RKO) such as *Cat People* (1942), *I Walked with a Zombie* (1943), *The Leopard Man* (1943) and *Curse of the Demon* (1958). Tourneur also directed Frye in *Phantom Raiders* (1940).

The Night Hawk

Republic, 1938; Director: Sidney Salkow; Original Screenplay: Earl Felton; Cameraman: Jack Marta; Music Director: Cy Feuer; Running Time: 63 minutes; Production Dates: August 19-August 31, 1938; Release Date: October 1, 1938

CAST: Robert Livingston (Slim Torrence); June Travis (Della Parrish); Robert Armstrong (Charlie McCormick); Ben Welden (Otto Miller); Lucien Littlefield (Parrish); Joseph Downing (Lefty); Paul Fix (Spider); **Dwight Frye (John Colley)**; Roland L. Got (Willie Sing); Cy Kendall (Captain Teague); Billy Burrud (Bobby McCormick); Charles Wilson (Lonigan); Paul McVey (Larsen); Robert Homans (Mulruney); Michael Kent; Clem Willenchick

NOTES: The working title for *The Night Hawk* was *Hell Bent for Headlines*. The song "Never a Dream Goes By," words and music by Walter Kent, Manny Kurtz and Al Sherman, was featured in the film.

Dwight Frye's character, John Colley, is an operative for smuggler Charlie McCormick (Robert Armstrong) aboard the *Pacific Queen*, where he masquerades as a ship's steward. Colley had earlier killed the customs agent who was getting wise to the smuggling ring. When Slim (Robert Livingston) sneaks into a stateroom on the ocean liner, looking for evidence, Colley spots the reporter and knocks him unconscious.

Back on shore, Slim trails Colley to McCormick's nightclub. After Colley checks in with his boss, McCormick devises a plan to kill Colley, frame rival gangster Miller (Ben Welden) for the death, and divert suspicion from himself for all the crimes.

The Night Hawk was a fast-paced film with rather a far-fetched plot. Livingston was not the most believable lead, but Armstrong and the supporting cast were more than adequate. Once again, Frye, as he had in *Florida Special* and *Fast Company*, found himself getting killed off by his villainous employer after Frye's character had outlived his usefulness.

Robert Livingston, best known for starring in numerous "B" Westerns, reportedly doubled for Colin Clive in *Frankenstein* (1931).

Adventure in Sahara

Columbia, 1938; Director: D. Ross Lederman; Screenplay: Maxwell Shane (from a story by Sam Fuller); Cameraman: Franz Planer; Musical Director: M. W. Stoloff; Running Time: 57 minutes; Filmed September 16 to October 6, 1938; Release Date: November 15, 1938

CAST: Paul Kelly (Jim Wilson); C. Henry Gordon (Captain Savatt); Lorna Gray (Carla Preston); Robert Fiske (Lieutenant Dumond); Marc Lawrence (Poule); Dick Curtis (Karnoldi); Stanley Brown (Rene Malreaux); Alan Bridge (Corporal Dronox); Raphael Bennett (Ladoux); Charles Moore (Gungadin); **Dwight Frye (Gravet, "the Jackal")**; Stanley Andrews (Colonel Rancreux); Ed Stanley (Dr. Renault); Sherry Hall (Sick Legionnaire); Boyd Irwin, Sr. (Beauchamp); Joseph De Stefani (Edis); Louis Mercier (Pierre); Rolfe Sedan (Airline Officer); Jean DeBriac (Recruit Officer); Al Herman (Landreau); Blackie Whiteford (Landring); Oscar G. Hendrian (Sergeant); Harry Strang (Jolatar); George Chesebro (Velich); Albert Pollet (Sembland); John Northpole (Fuestral); George Ducont (Gerguson); Jack Lowe (Kranzt); Joe Dominguez (Pascal); Lou Davis (Steward); Homer Dickinson, Joe Palma, Earl Bunn, Ed Randolph, Charles Brinley, Ron Wilson (Soldiers); Eddie Fetherston, Maurice Brierre (Sergeants)

NOTES: This Foreign Legion melodrama was a pint-sized rip-off of both *Mutiny on the Bounty*, MGM's Best Picture Academy Award winner of 1935, and *Beau Geste*, which Paramount had filmed in 1926. *Mutiny on the Bounty* had offered Charles Laughton's classic Captain Bligh, surviving Clark Gable's mutiny to return for revenge; *Beau Geste* had provided the evil sergeant (Noah Beery, Sr.) and his informant (William Powell, long before *The Thin Man*). *Adventure in Sahara* tapped both sources, serving up sadistic, mutiny-inspiring Captain Savatt (C. Henry Gordon) and Frye as Gravet, known as "the Jackal," as he informs on his hapless fellow legionnaires. It was a rather desperate "B" attraction, relying on library stock footage and duplicate running shots to pad out its hour-length.

Leading man Paul Kelly (1899-1956) had achieved a comeback after serving two years in jail for manslaughter; he would win Broadway's Tony Award for his performance in *Command Decision* (1947). Lorna Gray starred with Karloff in Columbia's *The Man They Could Not Hang* (1939), and later changed her name to Adrian Booth; she's best-remembered as the evil Vultura in the Republic serial, *Perils of Nyoka* (1942). Columbia workhorse D. Ross Lederman had previously directed Dwight in the studio's *Alibi for Murder* (1936).

For Dwight Frye, perhaps the most interesting aspect of *Adventure in Sahara* was acting again with C. Henry Gordon—with whom he had played on Broadway in *Puppets* in 1925. The Satanic-looking Gordon had become a top Hollywood heavy in such films as *Rasputin and the Empress* (MGM, 1932) and *The Charge of the Light Brigade* (Warner Bros., 1936); he and Frye had also acted together in the films *The Black Camel* (Fox, 1931) and *Invisible Enemy* (Republic, 1938).

On December 3, 1940, Gordon died unexpectedly at Hollywood Hospital; suffering from a blood clot, he'd had a leg amputated and the complications killed him. He was 57. *The New York Times* eulogized Gordon: "Mild mannered, almost self-effacing, he once said he didn't have the heart to go fishing because 'fish have feelings,' and he also communicated regularly with a fan in Worcester, Mass., who shared a mutual interest in puppet shows."

Ironically, as *Adventure in Sahara* played New York City's Globe Theatre during yuletide of 1938, Paramount was casting its classic 1939 remake of *Beau Geste*—with Gary Cooper as Beau, and Brian Donlevy as the villainous sergeant. J. Carrol Naish played the informant, similar to Frye's "Jackal" of *Adventure in Sahara*; in fact, at one point, Donlevy refers to Naish as "you human jackal!"

Mickey, the Kid

Republic, 1939; Director: Arthur Lubin; Screenplay: Doris Malloy and Gordon Kahn; Original Story: Alice Altschuler; Cameraman: Jack Marta; Musical Director: Cy Feuer; Running Time: 68 minutes; Production Dates: May 2-May 20, 1939; Release Date: July 3, 1939

CAST: Bruce Cabot (Jim Larch); Ralph Byrd (Dr. Ben Cameron); Zasu Pitts (Lillian); Tommy Ryan (Mickey Larch); Jessie Ralph (Veronica M. Hudson); June Storey (Sheila Roberts); J. Farrell MacDonald (Sheriff Willoughby); John Qualen (Mailman); Robert Elliot (Farrow); Scotty Beckett (Bobby); James Flavin (Sanders); Archie Twitchell (Shelley); **Dwight Frye (Bruno)**

NOTES: The working title for *Mickey, the Kid* was *Stand Up and Sing*. Dwight Frye's role was quite brief. As Bruno, he assisted bankrobber Jim Larch (Bruce Cabot) in their heist of the Merchants Trust Company.

The Man in the Iron Mask

United Artists, 1939; Director: James Whale; Second Unit Director: Cullen Tate; Screenplay: George Bruce; Cameraman: Robert Planck; Art Director: John DuCasse Schulze; Special Effects: Howard Anderson; Musical Score: Lucien Moraweck; Music Director: Lud Gluskin; Fencing Director: Fred Cavens; Running Time: 110 minutes; Production Dates: February 26-April 25, 1939; Release Date: August 11, 1939

CAST: Louis Hayward (Louis XIV/Phillipe); Joan Bennett (Maria Theresa); Warren William (D'Artagnan); Joseph Schildkraut (Fouquet); Alan Hale (Porthos); Miles Mander (Aramis); Bert Roach (Athos); Walter Kingsford (Colbert); Marian Martin (Mlle. de la Valliere); Montagu Love (Spanish ambassador); Doris Kenyon (Queen Anne); Albert Dekker (Louis XIII); William Royle (commandant of Bastille); Fred Cavens (Francois); Boyd Irwin (Royal High Constable); Howard Brooks (Cardinal); Reginald Barlow (Jean Paul); Ian MacLaren (Valet de Chambre) D'Arcy Corrigan (tortured prisoner); Robert Milasch (torturer); Harry Woods (first officer); Peter Cushing (second officer); Lane Chandler (Captain of Fouquet's guards); **Dwight Frye (Fouquet's valet)**; Edgar Norton (Fouquet's servant); Nigel de Brulier (Richelieu); Emmett King (King's Chamberlain); Wyndham Standing (doctor); Dorothy Vaughan (midwife); Sheila Darcy (Maria Theresa's maid); the St. Brenden Choir

NOTES: The film was based on *The Man in the Iron Masque*, part three of *The Vicomte de Bragelonne* by Alexandre Dumas. Producer Edward Small entrusted his largest budget to date, one million dollars, to fading director James Whale to bring Dumas' often told tale to the screen. The result was a decent adaptation, with splendid photography and a musical score that earned Academy Award nominations for Lucien Moraweck and Lud Gluskin.

Unbilled, Dwight Frye appeared in only one scene working with director James Whale for the sixth and final time. Frye, as Nicholas Fouquet's valet, helps prepare his master (Joseph Schildkraut) for Louis XIV's wedding to Maria Theresa (Joan Bennett), unaware that the evil twin (Louis Hayward in the dual role) is now imprisoned in the "iron mask." The valet perfumes Fouquet, holding up a mirror for his lord. Frye's character observes:

> It may be his majesty who is getting married, but you,
> your excellency, will be the most handsome man at the
> ceremony—certainly the best dressed!

Commenting further on the preparations, the valet states:

> The carriage of the Princess has just passed over the
> bridge on the way to Fontainebleau. Your own guard is
> waiting with your carriage.

Fouquet's dressing routine is interrupted by another servant (Edgar Norton), who brings in a herdsman with evidence (a plate) about the true identity of "the man in the iron mask" (and it is not the good twin, Phillipe, who is now waiting to be married and rule France).

In addition to containing character roles and bits for actors often seen in the horror genre, like Walter Kingsford, Montagu Love, Edgar Norton, Albert Dekker and Nigel de Brulier, *The Man in the Iron Mask* represented the film debut of Peter Cushing.

Conspiracy

RKO, 1939; Director: Lew Landers; Screenplay: Jerome Chodorov; Original Story: John McCarthy and Faith Thomas; Cameraman: Frank Redman; Special Effects: Vernon L. Walker; Art Director: Van Nest Polglase; Music: Frank Tours; Running Time: 58 minutes; Production Dates: June 20-July 8, 1939; Release Date: September 1, 1939

CAST: Allan Lane (Steve Kendall); Linda Hayes (Nedra); Robert Barrat (Tio); Charley Foy (Studs); J. Farrell MacDonald (Captain); Lester Matthews (Gair); Lionel Royce (Lieutenant); Henry Brandon (Carlson); William Von Brincken (Wilson); Solly Ward (Dr. Fromm); John Laing (Inspector Orderly); **Dwight Frye (Lieutenant Keller)**; John Laird (Radio operator); Al Herman (bartender); Fred Rapport (waiter)

NOTES: *Conspiracy* was based on the story *Salute to Hate* by John McCarthy and Faith Thomas. In the film, Nedra (Linda Hayes) sings "Take the World Off Your Shoulders," by Lew Brown and Samuel Fain.

As was often the case, Frye, billed twelfth as Lieutenant Keller, is seen solely near the film's beginning. Steve Kendall (Allan Lane) enters the radio room of the ship *Paradise* and catches Carlson (Henry Brandon) about to transmit a message. Carlson pulls a gun on Steve, ordering him to broadcast. Lt. Keller (Frye) is viewed at an unknown location, manning a radio receiver. Despite being in the military, Keller is working for the revolutionaries, as is Carlson.

In the military headquarters of the fictitious country in *Conspiracy*, the officers (including Lionel Royce) determine Carlson's message was sent to a "shore station," where it was received by one of their own men. A messenger is dispatched with a parcel for Lt. Keller. The messenger informs the officer that an answer is expected, so Keller says, "All right, outside!," motioning for the man to wait in the hall. Keller unravels the package, which contains a pistol. Found out by his superiors, the implication is that Keller is to commit suicide, but this act is not seen or heard onscreen.

Frye had earlier worked with director Lew Landers in *The Man Who Found Himself* (1937) and would do so again in *Mystery Ship* (1941). A number of the actors in *Conspiracy* had appeared with Frye in other films, like J. Farrell MacDonald, Lionel Royce and Lester Matthews. Of note was Henry Brandon, who would star in *Drums of Fu Manchu* (1940), Frye's only serial. As in *Sea Devils* and *The Devil Pays Off*, Frye's brief role in *Conspiracy* was basically to function as a radio operator.

Drums of Fu Manchu

Republic 15-chapter serial, 1940; Associate Producer: Hiram S. Brown, Jr.; Directors: William Witney and John English; Screenplay: Franklyn Adreon, Morgan B. Cox, Ronald Davidson, Norman S. Hall, Barney A. Sarecky, Sol Shor (suggested by the stories by Sax Rohmer); Cinematography: William Nobles; Music: Cy Feuer; Editors: Ed Todd, William Thompson; Budget, $164, 052; Negative Cost, $166, 312; Filmed December 22, 1939-February 7, 1940; Released March 15, 1940

CAST: Henry Brandon (Fu Manchu); William Royle (Sir Dennis Nayland Smith); Robert Kellard (Allan Parker); Gloria Franklin (Fah Lo Suee); Olaf Hytten (Dr. Petrie); Tom Chatterton (Prof. Edward Randolph); Luana Walters (Mary Randolph); Lal Chand Mehra (Sirdar Prahni); George Cleveland (Dr. James Parker); John Dilson (Ezra Howard); John Merton (Loki); **Dwight Frye (Prof. Anderson)**; Wheaton Chambers (Dr. Humphrey); George Pembroke (C. W. Crawford); Guy D'Ennery (Ranah Sang); Jamiel Hasson (Si Fan Chieftain); James B. Leong (Si Fan Chinese); Tofik Mickey (Si Fan Hindu); Robert Srevenson (Tartar Russian); Norman Nesbitt (Wally Winchester); Harry Strang (Lt. Wade); Robert Blair (Sergeant); Lowden Adams (Blake); Philip Ahn (Dr. Chang); Lee Shumway (Lt. Corrigan); Ken Terrell (Museum Heavy); John Lester Johnson (Cardo); John Picorri (Prof. Krantz); Jenifer Gray (Airline Stewardess); Kam Tong (Oriental Houseboy); John Ward (Wilson); Paul Marion (Native Messenger); Evan Thomas (Major Carlton); John Bagni (Dangra); Eric Lansdale (Richards); Akim Dobrynin (Temple Priest); Michael Vallon (Temple Guard 1); Tony Paton (Temple Guard 2); Carl Sepulveda (Tribesman 1); Jack Montgomery (Tribesman 2); Bob Woodward (Tribesman 3); John Meredith (Sentry 1); Paul Renay (Khandar); Joe De Stefani (High Lhama); Budd Buster, Eddie Kaye, James Flatley (aka Pegai), Alan Gregg, Duke Green, Art Dillard, Al Taylor, Ernest Sarracino (aka Dowlah Rao), Jack Roper, Vinegar Roan, Bill Wilkus, Tommy Coats, Frank Wayne, Ted Wells, Burt Dillard, Johnny Judd (Dacoits); with Dave Sharpe, and Hector Sarno

NOTES: Sax Rohmer (aka Arthur Henry Sarsfield Ward) wrote novels about Dr. Fu Manchu, the redoubtable "Yellow Peril," for over 40 years. The movies soon got into the act: there were the British serials *The Mystery of Dr. Fu Manchu* 1923) and *The Further Mysteries of Dr. Fu Manchu* (1925), with Harry Agar Lyons as Fu; and Paramount starred Warner Oland as Fu in a trio of thrillers: *The Mysterious Dr. Fu Manchu* (1929), *The Return of Dr. Fu Manchu* (1930) and *Daughter of the Dragon* (1931).

Of course, Fu Manchu reached his sinister apex in MGM's *The Mask of Fu Manchu* (1932), starring Boris Karloff as the Yellow Peril, Myrna Loy as his sex fiend daughter and a bevy of spectacular torture devices in this wild, kinky, comic book of a horror movie. Republic's *Drums of Fu Manchu* was Fu's first screen incarnation since the Karloff version.

It was Republic's longest-in-production serial (48 days) and boasted a slick star performance by Henry Brandon, whose credits include evil old Barnaby in Laurel and Hardy's *Babes in Toyland*

(1934) and Chief Scar in John Ford's *The Searchers* (1956). In bald wig and inscrutable gaze, Brandon was a properly diabolic Fu. A dynamic touch in the serial was the "Dacoits"—bald henchmen of Fu, each sporting a forehead scar, souvenir of Fu's lobotomy to rob each of his will power.

Dwight only appeared in Chapter 5, "The House of Terror." As Prof. Anderson, a museum curator, he worked with hero Allan Parker (Robert Kellard) to keep the Kardac Segment out of the nefarious clutches of Fu Manchu. When Republic released *Drums of Fu Manchu* as a feature film (edited from its 15-chapter length of 269 minutes to 63 minutes!), Dwight's performance remained in the feature version (released days after his death).

Drums of Fu Manchu proved popular, and Republic planned a follow-up serial, *Fu Manchu Strikes Again*, but dropped the idea after a 1942 appeal from the Chinese government.

Some of Fu Manchu's other appearances over the years: a 1950 NBC pilot for a *Fu Manchu* teleseries, starring John Carradine as Fu Manchu and Sir Cedric Hardwicke as Sir Nayland; the syndicated 1955 Republic TV series *The Adventures of Fu Manchu*, with Glen Gordon as Fu; a five-film Christopher Lee Fu Manchu film series, commencing with 1965's *The Face of Fu Manchu* and wrapping up with *Castle of Fu Manchu* (aka *Assignment Istanbul*, 1972); and *The Fiendish Plot of Dr. Fu Manchu* (1980), with Peter Sellers (in his last film) playing both Fu and Sir Nayland.

In 1986, the late Henry Brandon spoke with Greg Mank about his career, and *Drums of Fu Manchu*:

> When I played Fu Manchu... I'd go to a theatre nearby here in Hollywood, where they showed it, and sit among the kids (they never recognized me)—and I loved their reactions. Within two or three episodes, they were on my side! It was because I was brighter than the others, and the kids went for intelligence, whether it was bad or good.
>
> But the PTAs—they didn't like it at all, because the kids would wet their beds after seeing it. And the Chinese government raised plenty of hell! And that's childish, because I consider Fu Manchu a fairy tale character—it's not to be taken seriously, for God's sake!

Gangs of Chicago

Republic, 1940; Director: Arthur Lubin; Screenplay: Karl Brown; Cameraman: Elwood Bredell; Musical Director: Cy Feuer; Running Time: 66 minutes; Production Dates: March 25-April 6, 1940; Release Date: May 19, 1940

CAST: Lloyd Nolan (Matty Burns); Barton MacLane (Jim Ramsey); Lola Lane (June Whitaker); Ray Middleton (Bill Whitaker); Astrid Allwyn (Virginia Brandt); Horace MacMahon ("Cry-Baby"); Howard Hickman (Judge Whitaker); Leona Roberts (Mrs. Whitaker); Charles Halton (Bromo); Addison Richards (Evans); John Harmon (Rabbit); **Dwight Frye (Pinky)**; Alan Ladd; Frederick Burton

NOTES: Unlike some of his gangster roles wherein Dwight played the "soft" member of the mob who didn't like to be involved with killing (e.g., Mack in *Tough Guy*), Frye portrayed Pinky in *Gangs of Chicago* as a cold, sadistic, psychopathic gunman. Pinky is dispatched by Virginia Brandt (Astrid Allwyn) to kill Bill Whitaker (Ray Middleton), whom the gang suspects may be spying on them. Pinky has no qualms about eliminating Bill, although Whitaker survives the murder attempt. Later Pinky, with his boss Ramsey (Barton MacLane), invades the Whitaker home, but is killed by Matty (Lloyd Nolan) in the ensuing melee.

In Chicago, due to political outcry, the film played as *Gangs of the City*. Alan Ladd, early in his career, had a bit role.

Sky Bandits

Criterion/Monogram, 1940; Director: Ralph Staub; Screenplay: Edward Halperin; Original Story: Laurie York Erskine; Cameraman: Mack Stengler; Running Time: 62 minutes; Release Date: April 15, 1940

CAST: James Newill (Sergeant Renfrew); Louise Stanley (Madeline Lewis); Dave O'Brien (Constable Kelly); William Pawley (Morgan); **Dwight Frye (Speavy)**; Joseph Stefani (Professor Burton Lewis); Dewey Robinson (Dinwiddie); Jim Farley (Inspector Warner); Ted Adams (Greaseball); Bob Terry (Wolf Hutchins); Jack Clifford (Whispering Smith); Karl Hackett (Hawthorne); Eddie Fetherston (Buzz Murphy); Kenne Duncan

NOTES: *Sky Bandits* was based on the novel *Renfrew Rides the Sky* by Laurie York Erskine. It contained three original songs: "Mounted Men" by Betty Laidlaw and Robert Lively, and "Lady in the Clouds" and "Alley Oop" by Johnny Lange and Lew Porter. *Sky Bandits* was the final entry in Monogram's "*Renfrew of the Royal Mounted*" series, with Frye appearing in both the first (*Renfrew of the Royal Mounted*) and last of these films.

As Speavy, Frye had appreciable screen time in *Sky Bandits*. He is first viewed with the gang, stroking his large white rabbit in the background. When Morgan (William Pawley) brings in Lewis (Joseph Stefani) to increase the power of the beam Speavy invented, Speavy voices his displeasure:

> All I needed was a little more time, but you had to get this university windbag in to develop my invention.

Speavy continues to show contempt for Lewis' efforts, even though he is assured he will still get credit for inventing the ray, plus receive a share of the gold. When Lewis tells his daughter (Louise Stanley), just arrived, that his work is defense-related, Speavy cackles (the closest approximation to the Renfield laugh Frye would perform in any film) and states:

> You fool! You're not working for the government. You're the triggerman for a gang of hijackers. There was a pilot and guard in that plane flying a load of gold. You bumped them off.

Morgan grabs Speavy by the neck to silence him, but it is too late. The gang leader realizes Lewis, his daughter and Speavy all must be eliminated once the beam is perfected. As Speavy grudgingly works with the professor, Lewis accidentally kills the pet rabbit with the ray. After Speavy is again assaulted by Morgan, he decides to betray the gang and alert Renfrew:

> Calling Sergeant Renfrew, calling Sergeant Renfrew (on radio). Listen carefully. Buzz Smith's (movie error—should have been Murphy) plane was crashed by a radio beam perfected by Professor Burton Lewis of Norwood University. Lewis was working for a man who goes under the alias of Morgan and you can capture them at...

Morgan shoots and kills Speavy, adding, "This little squealer has gone to join his rabbit."

Sky Bandits was a low budget production, but it did give Frye the opportunity to play a mad scientist of sorts himself for a change, rather than his usual role of being a henchman to one.

Phantom Raiders

MGM, 1940; Director: Jacques Tourneur; Screenplay: William R. Lipman; Original Story: Jonathan Latimer; Cameraman: Clyde De Vinna; Art Director: Cedric Gibbons; Musical Score: David Snell; Sound: Douglas Shearer; Running Time: 70 minutes; Production began early April 1940; Release Date: June 7, 1940

CAST: Walter Pidgeon (Nick Carter); Donald Meek (Bartholomew); Joseph Schildkraut (Al Taurez); Florence Rice (Cora Barnes); Nat Pendleton ("Gunboat" Jacklin); John Carroll (John Ramsell, Jr.); Steffi Duna (Dolores); Cecil Kellaway (Franklin Morris); Matthew Boulton (John Ramsell, Sr.); Alec Craig (Andy MacMillan); Thomas Ross (Dr. Grisson); **Dwight Frye (Eddie Anders)**; John Burton (Steve Donnigan); Holmes Herbert (Sir Edward); Charles Coleman (Hilton); Guy Bellis (Pierson); Nestor Paiva (inspector); Hugh Beaumont (seaman); Stanley Mann (first mate); Franco Corsaro (Ysidro)

NOTES: *Phantom Raiders* was the second of three entries in the MGM "Nick Carter" series (*Nick Carter, Master Detective*— 1939, being the first; *Sky Murder*— 1940, the third). The working title for *Phantom Raiders* was *Nick Carter in Panama*. Jacques Tourneur, whose outstanding directorial work for Val Lewton at RKO was yet to come, had previously directed Frye in the MGM *Crime Does Not Pay* short *Think It Over* (1938).

As Eddie Anders, Frye is involved in only one fairly lengthy sequence in *Phantom Raiders*. Sneaking into the detective's room at night, Anders attempts to bludgeon Nick Carter (Walter Pidgeon) with a blackjack. Nick is not in bed, however, and captures the would-be assassin. "A little rough stuff, huh?" Eddie queries Nick, but the detective instead tells Bartholomew (Donald Meek) to fetch a bottle of scotch and three glasses. "Poison booze, huh?," states the distrustful Anders. Nick and Bartholomew try to establish who the intruder is, so Eddie offers, "Julius Caesar." They learn his name is Eddie Anders. Nick, in an attempt to discover who sent Anders to kill him, moves Eddie's chair in front of an open window, while the hitman sweats profusely. Anders pleads:

> Listen Nick, cut it out. Cut it out. I ain't got nothin'
> against you. I ain't got nothin' against nobody.

Nick pretends Eddie is an old friend and wants to know if what he supposedly told him about Al Taurez is true. Anders, now desperate, states:

> Close them windows. Give me a chance. You'll get me
> killed. I'll do anything!

Nick kicks Anders' chair out of the way, just as a knife is hurled, breaking a mirror. The thrown knife, a specialty of Al Taurez, implicates the gangster in the murder plot. Anders thanks Nick for saving his life, while requesting to be "thrown in the clink" for his own protection. Nick is not sympathetic, but lets the hitman escape. Anders concludes:

> All right. Maybe I can make a run for it.

Eddie Anders represented a fairly good role for Frye at this point of his career. The above described sequence, in which Frye makes the transition from smug hitman to squirming potential victim, was quite well-played, particularly opposite the enjoyable acting of Walter Pidgeon and Donald Meek. Meek, in the title role, and Frye had appeared together in *Rip Van Winkle* at Pittsfield's Colonial Theatre in 1929.

The Son of Monte Cristo

United Artists, 1940; Director: Rowland V. Lee; Screenplay: George Bruce; Cameraman: George Robinson; Film Editor: Arthur E. Roberts; Music: Edward Ward; Art Director: John DuCasse Schulze; Running Time: 102 minutes; Production began: June 1940; Release Date: January 10, 1941 (New York opening: December 5, 1940)

CAST: Louis Hayward (Count of Monte Cristo); Joan Bennett (Grand Duchess Zona); George Sanders (General Gurko Lanen); Florence Bates (Mathilde); Lionel Royce (Colonel Zimmerman); Montagu Love (Baron Von Neuhoff); Ian Wolfe (Conrad Stadt); Clayton Moore (Fritz Dorner); Ralph Byrd (Gluck); Georges Renavent (French ambassador); Michael Visaroff (Prince Pavlov); Rand Brooks (Hans Mirbach); Theodore von Eltz (Captain); James Seay (Lieutenant); Henry Brandon (Schultz); Jack Mulhall (Schmidt); Lawrence Grant (the Baron); **Dwight Frye (Pavlov's secretary)**; Lionel Belmore (innkeeper); Ernie Adams (informer); Michael Mark (Bishop); Charles Trowbridge (priest); Leyland Hodgson (officer); Charles Waldron (Kurt Mirbach); Wyndham Standing (Chamberlain); Margaret Fealy (innkeeper's wife); Maurice Cass (tailor); Edward Keane, Ted Oliver, Stanley Andrews (turnkeys)

NOTES: *The Son of Monte Cristo* was produced by Edward Small, who also produced *The Man in the Iron Mask* (1939). Director Rowland V. Lee had directed *Son of Frankenstein* (1939) the year before.

Dwight Frye only had one scene in *The Son of Monte Cristo*, but it was critical to the plot line. Seeking proof that Lanen (George Sanders) is a traitor, the Count (Louis Hayward), Dorner (Clayton Moore) and Von Neuhoff (Montagu Love) burst into the Russian Embassy. The alarmed secretary (Frye) to the absent Prince Pavlov (Michael Visaroff) declares:

> An outrage, an outrage! I am the secretary to his high-
> ness Prince Pavlov, the ambassador of His Imperial
> Majesty!

The intruders order the secretary to open the safe containing incriminating evidence against the villainous Lanen. "I refuse!," states the secretary, until he views the weaponry of the three men. "Very well, but I warn you—only under protest!" The Count and his cohorts secure the needed document.

Many of the lesser players in *The Son of Monte Cristo* had appeared with Frye in other films: Michael Visaroff (*The Night Bird, Dracula*), Michael Mark (*Frankenstein*), Henry Brandon (*Drums of Fu Manchu*), Lionel Royce (*Conspiracy*), to list but a few. Of particular interest, however, are the innkeeper and his wife. The innkeeper was played by veteran British character actor Lionel Belmore, who had been the burgomaster in both *Frankenstein* and *The Vampire Bat*. Margaret Fealy, the innkeeper's wife, had been Dwight Frye's acting teacher more than twenty years before, when Frye was living in Denver regularly attending performances of O. D. Woodward's stock company.

Mystery Ship

Columbia, 1941; Director: Lew Landers; Screenplay: David Silverstein and Houston Branch; Original Story, Alex Gottlieb; Cameraman: L. W. O'Connell; Running Time: 65 minutes; Release Date: July 28, 1941

CAST: Paul Kelly (Allan Harper); Lola Lane (Patricia Marshall); Larry Parks (Tommy Baker); Trevor Bardette (Ernst Madek); Cy Kendall (Condor); Roger Imhoff (Captain Randall); Eddie Laughton (Turillo); John Tyrell (Sam); Byron Foulger (Wasserman); Dick Curtis (Van Brock); **Dwight Frye (Rader)**; Kenneth MacDonald (Gorman)

NOTES: Dwight Frye affected a German accent for his portrayal of the deported saboteur Rader. *Mystery Ship* was one of the films that took advantage of Frye's Aryan appearance to cast him as a villain during the war years. Frye had previously worked with director Lew Landers on *The Man Who Found Himself* (1937) and *Conspiracy* (1939).

The People vs. Dr. Kildare
MGM, 1941; Director: Harold S. Bucquet; Screenplay: Willis Goldbeck and Harry Ruskin; Original story: Lawrence P. Bachmann and Max Brand; Cameraman: Clyde De Vinna; Running Time: 78 minutes; Release Date: May 7, 1941

CAST: Lew Ayres (Dr. James Kildare); Lionel Barrymore (Dr. Leonard Gillespie); Laraine Day (Mary Lamont); Bonita Granville (Frances Marlowe); Red Skelton (Vernon Briggs); Tom Conway (Mr. Channing); Walter Kingsford (Dr. Walter Carew); Alma Kruger (Molly Byrd); Diana Lewis (Fay Lennox); Nell Craig (Nurse Parker); Paul Stanton (Mr. Reynolds); Marie Blake (Sally); Chick Chandler (Dan Morton); Eddie Acuff (Clifford Genet, janitor); Frank Orth (Mike Ryan); Gladys B. Lake (Maisie); George H. Reed (Conover); **Dwight Frye (jury foreman)**; Anna Q. Nilsson (juror); Grant Withers (policeman)

NOTES: *The People vs. Dr. Kildare* was released in England as *My Life is Yours*, as people were starting to get confused by all the "Dr. Kildare" titles. This was the eighth of sixteen "Dr. Kildare/ Dr. Gillespie" films, with Lew Ayres playing James Kildare in entries two-through-ten. *The People vs. Dr. Kildare* was the first film in which Ayres and Frye had worked together since *The Doorway to Hell* (1930).
As the jury foreman in *The People vs. Dr. Kildare*, Dwight Frye can be spotted at various times during the courtroom sequences, listening intently to the hypothetical case of Dr. Gillespie (Lionel Barrymore) during one. After deliberating a verdict, the judge is informed that the jury is experiencing a dilemma with their decision. The foreman (Frye) explains:

> We've made up our minds, but we don't know whether
> it's legal until we ask you. Can we bring in a verdict
> that Miss Marlowe should either have her leg cured, or
> get the money?

The judge is taken aback, as the foreman continues:

> Can we decide that she gets the $100,000 only if she's
> still crippled after they try to fix her up?

At first, the judge states he should declare a mistrial, but tells the foreman that the jury's idea contains "good sense." Frances Marlowe (Bonita Granville) elects to take the jury's suggestion, eventually resulting in a cure for her paralysis and return to her skating career.

Flying Blind
Paramount, 1941; Director: Frank McDonald; Screenplay: Maxwell Shane and Richard Murphy; Cameraman: Fred Jackman, Jr.; Music: Dimitri Tiomkin; Running Time: 69 minutes; Release Date: August 23, 1941

CAST: Richard Arlen (Jim Clark); Jean Parker (Shirley Brooks); Nils Asther (Eric Karolek); Marie Wilson (Veronica); Roger Pryor (Rocky Drake); Eddie Quillan (Riley); Dick Purcell (Bob Fuller); Grady Sutton (Chester Gimble); Kay Sutton (Miss Danila); Charlotte Henry (Lorenson's secretary); Joseph Crehan (Nunnally); William Hall (Lew West); **Dwight Frye (Leo Qualen)**; James Seay (Dispatcher)

NOTES: *Flying Blind* was a venture of the William H. Pine/William C. Thomas production team at Paramount. They also produced *Submarine Alert*, which featured Richard Arlen, Nils Asther and Roger Pryor, in addition to Frye, from *Flying Blind*.

Frye was included in two scenes in *Flying Blind*. As the military walk past a bomber, raving about it passing inspection, the pilot (William Hall) greets mechanic Leo Qualen (Frye), who replies, "How are ya?" Leo suspiciously watches Clark's (Richard Arlen) plane land.

Later, as Qualen works on an elevated platform in the airplane factory, Drake (Roger Pryor) climbs stairs to meet him. Qualen states, "I'm watching a 50-hour motor test," as Drake asks him for the stolen blueprints. After mentioning the difficulty of securing the plans, Qualen insists on his money. Drake reneges, so Leo challenges, "Give that back, or give me the dough. I'm taking an awful chance." Feeling double-crossed, Qualen pulls out a pistol and struggles with Drake. The gun goes off, Leo screams and plummets from the platform down into the motor. News quickly circulates around the airport that a mechanic has been killed at the Perry Plant.

Unlike most other films in the latter stages of Frye's career, he was listed in the credits, albeit thirteenth, as Leo Qualen. Another espionage/saboteur role, Qualen made use of Frye's ability to display nervous mannerisms and scream with authority.

The Blonde from Singapore

Columbia, 1941; Producer: Jack Fier; Director: Edward Dmytryk; Screenplay: George Bricker (based on a story by Houston Branch); Cinematography: L. W. O'Connell; Running time, 67 minutes; British title: *Hot Pearls*; Previewed in Columbia projection room, August 26, 1941

CAST: Florence Rice (Mary Brooks); Leif Erikson (Terry Prescott); Gordon Jones ("Waffles" Billings); Don Beddoe (Sergeant Burns); Alexander D'Arcy (Prince Sali); Adele Rowland (Sultana); Lumsden Hare (Sir Reginald Bevin); Richard Terry (Tada); Emory Parnell (Captain Nelson); **Dwight Frye (Barber)**; Charles Irwin (Casino character)

NOTES: It was another unbilled bit for Dwight in a slapdash "B" programmer—and as a barber, no less. Perhaps the film's principal interest is that it's an early credit for Edward Dmytryk, then under contract to Columbia, where he'd just directed the Karloff "mad doctor" movie *The Devil Commands* (1941). Dmytryk went on to direct such RKO hits as *Hitler's Children* (1943) and *Murder, My Sweet* (1944), as well as Universal's *Captive Wild Woman* (1943). After serving a jail sentence as one of "the Hollywood Ten," Dmytryk came back with such major films as *The Sniper* (Columbia, 1952), *The Caine Mutiny* (Columbia, 1954), *Raintree County* (MGM, 1957), and *The Young Lions* (20th Century-Fox, 1958). He's written eight books on Hollywood, including the recently-published *Odd Man Out*, about his experiences as one of the Hollywood Ten.

In a 1996 interview with Tom Weaver, Edward Dmytryk remembered life as a director at Columbia during the era of *The Blonde from Singapore*:

> Actually, I made a couple of fairly good "B" movies there, including the Karloff one... But it was the rat's nest of all the studios—it was the cheapest and the least well-

paid and all that kind of thing. The stages were cramped together because they were right there in the middle of Hollywood and they didn't have much space. And yet I did all right there, I had a pleasant enough time — if you can call making pictures pleasant.

The Devil Pays Off

Republic, 1941; Producer: Albert J. Cohen; Director: John H. Auer; Screenplay: Lawrence Kimble and Malcolm Stuart Boylan (based on a story by George Worthing Yates and Julian Zimet); Cinematography: John Alton; Musical Director: Cy Feuer; Running time: 70 minutes; Release date: November 10, 1941

CAST: J. Edward Bromberg (Arnold DeBrock); Osa Massen (Valerie DeBrock); William Wright (Chris Waring); Margaret Tallichet (Joan Millard); Abner Biberman (Carlos); Martin Kosleck (Greb); Charles D. Brown (Captain Hunt); Ivan Miller (Captain Brigham); Roland Varno (Ship Doctor); **Dwight Frye (Radio Operator)**

NOTES: This Republic "B" was directed by John H. Auer, who had directed Dwight in *The Crime of Doctor Crespi* (1935). The film was a rare lead for J. Edward Bromberg, a character player who won notice as a member of Eva Le Gallienne's Civic Repertory Company in the early 1930s, and as a 20th Century-Fox contract player in such films as *Four Men and a Prayer* (1938), *Jesse James* (1939) and *The Mark of Zorro* (1940). He also acted in several Universal horror films, notably the Technicolor *Phantom of the Opera* (1943) and as the Van Helsing-type Professor Lazlo in *Son of Dracula* (1943).

Bromberg later ran afoul of the Hollywood "witch hunt," refusing to cooperate with the House Un-American Activities and becoming blacklisted. He took a role in the play *The Biggest Thief in Town* in London, where he was found dead in his hotel room on December 6, 1951, at age 47, apparently from a heart attack. His role in the play: an undertaker.

Margaret Tallichet, the heroine, was the real-life wife of director William Wyler. Martin Kosleck, as Greb, won notice for his performances as Nazi Goebbels in a number of WWII films, as well as for his smoothly evil acting in such Universal melodramas as *The Mummy's Curse* (1944), *The Frozen Ghost* (1945) and *House of Horrors* (1946).

In the bit role of a radio operator, Dwight had no billing.

Sleepytime Gal

Republic, 1942; Producer: Albert J. Cohen; Director: Albert S. Rogell; Screenplay: Art Arthur, Albert Duffy, and Max Lief (based on the story by Mauri Grashin and Robert T. Shannon); Cinematography: Jack Marta; Musical Director: Cy Feuer; Running Time: 84 minutes; Release date: March 5, 1942

CAST: Judy Canova (Bessie Cobb); Tom Brown (Chuck Patterson); Ruth Terry (Sugar Caston); Mildred Coles (Connie Thompson); Billy Gilbert (Chef Acropolis); Harold Huber (Honest Joe); Fritz Feld (Chef Petrovich); Jay Novello (Chef Gonzales); Skinnay Ennis (Danny Marlowe); Jerry Lester (Downbeat); Jimmy Ames (Gus); Elisha Cook, Jr. (Ernie); Frank Sully (Dimples); Thurston Hall (Mr. Adams); Paul Fix (Johnny Gatto); Vicki Lester (Blonde); Lester Dorr, Walter Merrill, Pat Gleason, Fred Santley, Mady Laurence (Reporters); Edward Earle (Dr. Bell); Hillary Brooke (Railroad Station Blonde); Ric Vallin, Cyril Ring (Clerks); William Forrest (Hotel Manager); Carl Leviness (Husband); Gertrude Astor (Wife); Marguerite Whitten (Maid); Eddie Acuff (1st Mug); **Dwight Frye (2nd Mug)**; Eugene Borden (Maitre D'Hotel); and Skinnay Ennis' Orchestra

NOTES: This musical comedy was a vehicle for Judy Canova, Republic's hillbilly singer attraction, who also had been successful on Broadway and radio. In *Sleepytime Gal*, Ms. Canova performed such comedy as falling off a fire escape and eating soap-filled cream-puffs; she also sang "I Don't Want Nobody at All," "Barrelhouse Bessie" and "When the Cat's Away" (by Jule Styne and Herb Magidson) and "Sleepytime Gal" (by Richard A. Whiting, Ange Lorenzo, Joseph R. Alden and Ray Egan).

Director Albert S. Rogell directed many "B" melodramas and comedies for Republic, Columbia and Universal (where he helmed the 1941 *The Black Cat*).

Dwight had the ignominious role of the "2nd Mug"; the role was so small that he wasn't listed in the *Sleepytime Gal*'s cast list in the *Film Daily Yearbook*.

The Ghost of Frankenstein

Universal, 1942; Producer: George Waggner; Director: Erle C. Kenton; Original Story: Eric Taylor; Screenplay: W. Scott Darling; Cinematography: Milton Krasner and Woody Bredell; Art Director: Jack Otterson (Associate, Harold H. MacArthur); Editor: Ted Kent; Sound Director: Bernard B. Brown (Technician: Charles Carroll); Musical Score: Hans J. Salter; Gowns: Vera West; Makeup: Jack P. Pierce; Set Decorations: Russell A. Gausman; Assistant Director: Charles B. Gould; Running Time: 67 minutes; Filmed December 15, 1941-January 15, 1942; Opened at the Rialto Theatre, New York City, April 3, 1942

CAST: Lon Chaney (the Frankenstein Monster); Sir Cedric Hardwicke (Dr. Ludwig Frankenstein); Ralph Bellamy (Erik Ernst); Lionel Atwill (Dr. Bohmer); Bela Lugosi (Ygor); Evelyn Ankers (Elsa Frankenstein); Janet Ann Gallow (Cloestine); Barton Yarborough (Dr. Kettering); Olaf Hytten (Hussman); Doris Lloyd (Martha); Leyland Hodgson (Chief Constable); Holmes Herbert (Magistrate of Vasaria); Lawrence Grant (Burgomaster of Frankenstein); Brandon Hurst (Hans); Julius Tannen (Sektal); Harry Cording (Frone); Lionel Belmore (First Councilor); Michael Mark (Second Councilor); Otto Hoffman (Villager No. 1); **Dwight Frye (Villager No. 2)**; Ernie Stanton, George Eldredge (Constables); Elaine Morley (Goose Girl); Eddie Parker (Double for Chaney)

NOTES: Fourth in Universal's *Frankenstein* series, *The Ghost of Frankenstein* (which had the bizarre original title of *There Is Always Tomorrow*) was the first without Karloff as the legendary Monster. The role went to Lon Chaney (1906-1973), who had just triumphed as *The Wolf Man*, and would go on to star in *Son of Dracula*, the *Mummy* series and the *Inner Sanctum* series. The hard-drinking Chaney would play the role amidst a head cold, temper tantrums and snorts from his hip flask; the performance (which has its formidable moments) fell far short of Karloff's classic conception.

Fortunately, the cast surrounding Chaney was superb. Sir Cedric Hardwicke (1893-1964) was a worthy addition to the *Frankenstein* Hollywood family (Colin Clive in *Frankenstein* and *Bride of Frankenstein*, Basil Rathbone as the "first son" in *Son of Frankenstein*), scoring dramatic points both as Ludwig and the apparition of the original *Frankenstein*. Lionel Atwill provided some memorable leers as the crazy, bitter Dr. Bohmer, and Bela Lugosi, of course, was magnificent as old Ygor, gleefully reprising his *Son of Frankenstein* character. Ever-reliable Ralph Bellamy (1904-1991) gave substance to his romantic lead role, and Evelyn Ankers (1918-1985, Universal's blonde "queen of the horrors") is a beautiful Elsa, sounding her classic scream, and making the late Colin Clive (wherever he was) proud to be "grandfather" to so lovely a lady.

Erle C. Kenton (1896-1980), who directed, had Paramount's *Island of Lost Souls* (1932) to his credit. Roy William Neill would direct Universal's next entry, *Frankenstein Meets the Wolf Man* (1943), but the slick and resourceful Kenton would return to direct both *House of Frankenstein* (1944) and *House of Dracula* (1945).

Dwight Frye appears only in the opening of *The Ghost of Frankenstein*, as an angry (and unnamed) villager. "Destroy the castle!" he rages. "Wipe the last trace of these accursed Frankensteins from our land!" For devout fans of the Universal series, the opening is virtually "old home week": also in the scene are Lionel Belmore (the Burgomaster of the original *Frankenstein*, and victim of Karloff's Monster in *Son of Frankenstein*); and Michael Mark (little Maria's father in *Frankenstein*, and also Monster's victim in *Son of...*). Both had been councilors in *Son of Frankenstein*, and here they are in *The Ghost...* as councilors again.

> "The people are right, your honor," says Belmore, as
> Dwight exhorts the villagers to destroy the castle.

> "I agree, your honor," says Mark.

Burgomaster Lawrence Grant (reprising his role from *Son of Frankenstein*!) concurs — "Do what you will with the castle — it's yours."

"We'll blow it up!" raves Dwight, and they're off to the castle, where Dwight can be seen in long shots, as the mob dynamites Castle Frankenstein. Universal publicity noted these familiar faces in *The Ghost*: "Policy enters the scene through the custom of the studio of endeavoring to spot the same faces in each succeeding feature of the *Frankenstein* series."

(Lionel Belmore died in 1953, in his 86th year; Michael Mark, who also appeared in *House of Frankenstein*, died in 1975, at the age of 85.)

Dwight had no billing in *The Ghost of Frankenstein*, and his two-line bit has a tinge of tragedy to it. Later in the film, as Evelyn Ankers reads the Frankenstein records on a stormy night, *The Ghost...* features flashbacks of Colin Clive and Dwight Frye from the original *Frankenstein* (as well as a Clive closeup from *Bride of Frankenstein*). It's poignant to see Dwight in his classic characterization of Fritz — and to realize what "the curse of *Frankenstein*" had done to Dwight Frye in a decade.

Don't Talk

MGM, 1942; "MGM Special" short/*A Crime Does Not Pay* subject; Director: Joe Newman; Original Story and Screenplay: Alan Friedman; Cameraman: Jackson Rose; Running Time: 22 minutes; Copyright Date: March 12, 1942

CAST: Donald Douglas (Jack Sampson); Gloria Holden (Beulah Anderson aka Beulah Binvicko); Barry Nelson (Mark Freed); Harry Worth (Anatol); **Dwight Frye (Ziggy)**; Arthur Space (Otto); Anthony Caruso (FBI agent)

NOTES: Despite the opening credits stating *Don't Talk* is "A Crime Does Not Pay subject," Leonard Maltin, in *The Great Movie Shorts*, asserts the film was not part of the *Crime Does Not Pay* series of shorts. *Don't Talk* was an "MGM Special" short, released in the *Crime Does Not Pay* package for MGM's convenience. A well-made film, *Don't Talk* received an Academy Award nomination in 1942 in the category: Best Short Subject (Two-Reel). It did not win an Oscar, however. Warners' *Beyond the Line of Duty* was 1942's best "two-reeler."

Gloria Holden, who had rendered an intriguing performance in *Dracula's Daughter* (1936), was a convincing fifth columnist in *Don't Talk*. Among the cast were Barry Nelson, an actor with a long and varied career, including roles in *A Guy Named Joe* (1943) and *The Shining* (1980), and Arthur Space, who was in *20 Million Miles to Earth* and numerous television shows, notably *Lassie*.

Although not among the four names listed with the opening credits of *Don't Talk*, Frye had a large, important part as Ziggy. Ziggy is first viewed in the back room of the beauty shop, being questioned by Anatol (Harry Worth) about the Harmon Plant bombing. Ziggy defensively claims:

> Something went wrong. I just got through planting the charge in the first storage bin when the alarm system went off.

At the Paul Green Trucking Company, Ziggy drills holes on the underside of trucks in order to insert explosives. His efforts are interrupted by the return of the owner, so Ziggy takes out a pistol, firing two shots. After killing Green, the saboteur takes his tools and explosives, exiting before completing his task.

Anatol phones Ziggy, providing a cryptic message about the shipment of gear grinders. Ziggy comments on the delivery of "cosmetic supplies," "I'll be expecting it." After Anatol alludes to the great demand for the product, Ziggy assures him, "We'll dispose of it."

Finally, when Anatol learns that the gear grinders are en route by truck rather than train, he helps Ziggy prepare to blow up a bridge. "Just a plunger hook-up and we're ready," states Ziggy. Before they can detonate the explosives, the FBI and Gatestown police arrive, capturing Anatol and Ziggy. As the saboteurs are escorted away, Agent Freed tells them, "Sorry to bust up your show!"

Danger in the Pacific

Universal, 1942; Director: Lewis D. Collins; Screenplay: Walter Doniger and Maurice Tombragel, based on an original story by Doniger and Neil P. Varnick; Cinematography: William Sickner; Musical Director: Hans J. Salter; Art Director: Jack Otterson; Running time: 60 minutes; Released August, 1942

CAST: Leo Carrillo (Leo Marzell); Andy Devine (Andy Parker); Don Terry (David Lynd); Louise Allbritton (Jane Claymore); Edgar Barrier (Zambesi); Turhan Bey (Tagani); Holmes Herbert (Commissioner); David Hoffman (Storekeeper); Paul Dubov (Manola); Neyle Marx (Lobo); **Dwight Frye (Hotel Clerk)**

NOTES: "Minor 'B' actioner, distinguished chiefly by Leo Carrillo tossing around a heavier-than-usual Andy Devine while teaching him Judo," was how *Variety* judged this Universal jungle hokum. Playing the unbilled bit role of a South Seas hotel clerk in this potboiler was a new indignity in Dwight Frye's film career. That he had to play it at Universal, where he'd created his most famous film performances, makes the indignity all the more painful.

Star billing went to Leo Carrillo (1880-1961), usually a sidekick in movies (and TV—e.g., his "Pancho" to Duncan Renaldo's *The Cisco Kid*). Edgar Barrier (1907-1964), as the evil Zambesi, would play the Inspector in Universal's Technicolor *Phantom of the Opera* (1943); Turhan Bey, surprisingly scruffy as wicked Tagani, would clean up for Universal's *The Mummy's Tomb* (1942, as the hot-blooded high priest, tending to Chaney's Mummy) and MGM's *Dragon Seed* (1944). The film has its curiosities; there are rather pitiful headhunters (described by *Variety* as "bales of feathers" which made the extras look like "Sioux Indians"). Musical director Hans J. Salter uses the same lumbering motif to underscore a python that he used to characterize Chaney, Jr.'s Monster in *The Ghost of Frankenstein*.

Danger in the Pacific was the Universal debut of Louise Allbritton (1920-1979), who certainly is the most classy item in the movie. The tall, blonde actress was an excellent Carole

Lombard-style comedienne; nevertheless, she's best remembered as the Southern belle (in black wig) who vamps Lon Chaney's "Count Alucard" in Universal's *Son of Dracula* (1943). She would semi-retire after marrying famed reporter Charles Collingwood in 1946, although the vivacious lady continued to play in films, TV and on Broadway.

Dwight's one scene is with Louise Allbritton; as the servile hotel clerk, somewhere in the Pacific, he waves off a crowd of onlookers and greets Louise with a vague accent:

> Dwight: You will please to excuse the ignorance of those people. They have never seen a woman pilot before.
>
> Louise: Oh, I understand perfectly. Is there a Dr. Lynd stopping here?
>
> Dwight: Dr. Lynd? Ah, I'm sure. Room 22. He is out, but his friends are in his room. Shall I tell them you are here?
>
> Louise: Oh, don't bother. I'll just go on up!
>
> Dwight: Oh. To the left!

And that's the last we see of Dwight Frye in *Danger in the Pacific*.

Dead Men Walk

PRC, 1943; Producer: Sigmund Neufeld; Director: Sam Newfield; Screenplay: Fred Myton; Cinematography: Jack Greenhalgh; Musical Director: Leo Erdody; Musical Supervision: David Chudnow; Makeup: Harry Ross; Production Manager: Bert Sternbach; Running time, 63 minutes; Release date: February 14, 1943

CAST: George Zucco (Dr. Lloyd Clayton/ Dr. Elwyn Clayton); Mary Carlisle (Gayle); **Dwight Frye (Zolarr)**; Nedrick Young (Dr. Bentley); Fern Emmett (Kate); Robert Strange (Harper); Hal Price (Sheriff); Sam Flint (Minister); Al "Fuzzy" St. John (Villager); Forrest Taylor (The Devil)

NOTES: PRC was the most infamous of Hollywood's "poverty row" lots of the 1940s. So cut-throat was its cheap efficiency, so merciless were its week-long shooting schedules, that PRC achieved a grim distinction: it was the only studio to stay open on the day that President Franklin Roosevelt died.

PRC was the perfectly tawdry backdrop, therefore, for *Dead Men Walk*. The sight of Dwight Frye, ill, bloated, yet full of fiery dramatics, giving his all to the role of Zolarr (one part *Dracula*'s Renfield, one part *Frankenstein*'s Fritz) is an emotional experience, to say the least, for any fan of the actor.

Star of *Dead Men Walk* was George Zucco. By the time of *Dead Men Walk*, Zucco was winning distinction in horror films (to his displeasure); he'd already played the high priest in Universal's *The Mummy's Hand* (1940) and *The Mummy's Tomb* (1942), and would follow *Dead Men Walk* in such melodramas as Monogram's *Voodoo Man* (1944), Universal's *House of Frankenstein* (1944) and PRC's *The Flying Serpent* (1946).

Kenneth Anger's *Hollywood Babylon II* provided a tale of Zucco going mad from playing in so many horror films, dying in a "madhouse," and his wife and daughter killing themselves thereafter. The saga upset many—especially Mrs. George Zucco, who gave Greg Mank the true story of George's final years (incapacitated by a stroke, he died in a California sanitarium in 1960) and her daughter's death (due to cancer, in 1962) in a *Filmfax* interview (February/March, 1992). Mrs. Zucco is, as of this writing (fall, 1996), a very hale, hearty and spirited 96-year-old who cherishes the memories of her gentle husband and their beloved daughter.

Mary Carlisle, as blonde heroine Gayle, ended her film career with *Dead Men Walk*; in a *Filmfax* interview with Don Leifert, she fondly remembered Zucco, and compared major studios to PRC as "the difference between a Rolls-Royce and a Ford." Ned Young, as dreary hero Dr. David Bentley, went on to play Vincent Price's alcoholic assistant Leon in *House of Wax* (Warners, 1953); he ran afoul of the Hollywood Communist "witch hunt" and won an Oscar (along with collaborator Harold Jacob Smith) for his script for Stanley Kramer's *The Defiant Ones* (1958 — with Young writing under the nom de plume of Nathan E. Douglas). Fern Emmett, as "Old Kate," murdered by Dwight in *Dead Men Walk*, had appeared with him in Majestic's *The Vampire Bat* (1933). *Dead Men Walk* featured a pre-credit "prologue," with the Devil himself (Forrest Taylor) proclaiming:

> You creatures of the light — how can you say with ab-
> solute certainty what does or does not dwell within the
> limitless ocean of the night? Are the dark-enshrouded
> legions of evil naught but figments of the imagination be-
> cause you in your puny conceit say they cannot exist?

Director Sam Newfield (1899-1964) directed nearly 200 films, sometimes under the names of Sherman Scott or Peter Stewart; his credits include the all-midget western *Terror of Tiny Town* (1938 — scripted by *Dead Men Walk*'s Fred Myton), as well as such PRC horrors as *The Mad Monster*, *The Monster Maker* (1944) and *The Flying Serpent*. *Dead Men Walk* was just one of the 21 PRC films that Newfield cranked out for 1943 release alone!

Variety caught a showing of *Dead Men Walk* at the Vogue Theatre in Hollywood on December 30, 1942. The review was hardly a "rave":

> Horror hounds will take this with gusto. Those who
> think while attending theatres will take it with more than
> a grain of salt and possibly a few grimaces...

PRC nationally released *Dead Men Walk* on Valentine's Day, 1943 — the 12th anniversary of Universal's national release of *Dracula*. It played primarily on double bills, and survives today on scratchy public domain copies. George Zucco, as always, plays with his impeccable professionalism.

And Dwight Frye — his shockingly ill appearance grimly forecasting the premature death that awaited him one year later — movingly gives his all in a part which almost seems a mockery of the very roles which had so mercilessly typecast him.

REVIEW
 — *Leonard Maltin's Movie and Video Guide*: "...it's hard to dismiss any horror film with Dwight Frye as a maniacal assistant."

Frankenstein Meets the Wolf Man
Universal, 1943; Producer: George Waggner; Director: Roy William Neill; Original Screenplay: Curt Siodmak; Cinematography: George Robinson; Art Director: John B. Goodman (Associate: Martin Obzina); Director of Sound: Bernard B. Brown (Technician: William Fox); Set Decorations: Russell A. Gausman (Associate: E. R. Robinson); Musical Director: Hans J. Salter; Editor: Edward Curtiss; Gowns: Vera West; Makeup Artist: Jack P. Pierce; Special Photographic Effects: John P. Fulton; Assistant Director: Melville Shyer; Song: "Faro-La, Faro-Li" — music by Hans J. Salter, Lyrics by Curt Siodmak; Filmed at Universal City, October 12 to November 11, 1942; Running time: 74 minutes; Opened at the Rialto Theatre, New York City, March 5, 1943

CAST: Lon Chaney (Lawrence Talbot, the Wolf Man); Ilona Massey (Baroness Elsa Frankenstein); Patric Knowles (Dr. Frank Mannering); Lionel Atwill (the Mayor); Bela Lugosi (The Frankenstein Monster); Maria Ouspenskaya (Maleva); Dennis Hoey (Inspector Owen); Don Barclay (Franzec); Rex Evans (Vazec); **Dwight Frye (Rudi)**; Harry Stubbs (Guno); Adia Kuznetzoff (the Festival Singer); Torben Meyer (Erno the Gypsy); Charles Irwin (the Constable); Doris Lloyd (the Nurse); Tom Stevenson (tall grave robber); Cyril Delevanti (short grave robber); David Clyde (the Sergeant); Jeff Corey (Cemetery keeper); Beatrice Roberts (Varja, Rudi's Wife); Martha MacVicar [Vickers] (Margareta, Village Girl); Eddie Parker, Gil Perkins (Doubles for Lugosi)

NOTES: *Wolfman Meets Frankenstein* was the original title of Curt Siodmak's revised March 31, 1942 script—a sequel to the million-dollar hit *The Wolf Man* (1941). The German refugee writer had also penned that hit for Universal, including this legendary ditty:

> Even a man who is pure in heart,
> and says his prayers by night,
> can become a wolf, when the wolfbane blooms,
> and the Autumn moon is bright.

Of course, *Frankenstein Meets the Wolf Man* (as it was retitled) became a great hit on its own, with many twists and turns: the original double-casting of Chaney as Wolf Man and Monster; Lugosi's last-minute casting in the Monster role; Atwill's court sentence for perjury (regarding his "orgy" trial) during production; and, of course, the post-production cutting of the Lugosi Monster's dialogue and blindness. An example of what was cut:

> Monster (sadly): If Dr. Frankenstein were still alive—he would restore my sight...He would give me back the strength I once possessed—the strength of a hundred men... so that I could live forever!
> Larry: Don't you ever want to die?
> Monster: Die? Never! Dr. Frankenstein created this body to be immortal! His son gave me a new brain, a clever brain... I will rule the world! I will live to witness the fruits of my wisdom for all eternity!

Lugosi's emoting—with Hungarian accent, of course—reportedly sounded so funny that it was entirely cut throughout the film—and along with it, the references to his blindness. Stuntmen Eddie Parker and Gil Perkins extensively doubled the 60-year-old Lugosi as the Monster.

In Siodmak's script, Dwight's character of Rudi is identified as the village tailor; he's also a newlywed. Indeed, the Festival Singer (Adia Kuznetzoff), in the rousing "Faro-La, Faro-Li" song (lyrics by Siodmak, music by Hans J. Salter), was to interrupt Rudi and wife kissing and serenade them with:

> Now here's a pair of newly-weds,
> Faro-la-faro-li,
> With love and kisses in their heads,
> Faro-faro-li.
> Tonight there's only he and she,
> Just one and two, as you can see—
> But very soon they may be three!
> Faro-faro-li!

The verse, of course, didn't appear in the release print. The script also had Rudi dancing with Elsa Frankenstein at the Festival, but it's Atwill's Mayor who dances with Ilona Massey (and he's beaming all the while!) in the finished film.

The cast is superb. Ilona Massey (1910-1974), MGM's former "singing Garbo" of *Rosalie* (1937) and *Balalaika* (1939), played Broadway in *The Ziegfeld Follies* (1943), made a screen comeback in 1946's *Holiday in Mexico* for MGM (the studio that had blackballed her after her 1940 romantic scandal) and carried on a career in films, radio, TV, theatre and concerts. Patric Knowles enjoyed decades as leading man and later character actor, passing away on Christmas Eve of 1995 at the age of 84. Maria Ouspenskaya had created the role of Maleva in *The Wolf Man*; the venerable Russian émigré/actress/drama coach (who won Academy nominations for Goldwyn's 1936 *Dodsworth* and RKO's 1939 *Love Affair*) died in 1949—a victim of smoking in bed. Adia Kuznetzoff, "The Festival Singer," played in such Hollywood films as Laurel and Hardy's *Swiss Miss* (1938), Karloff's *Devil's Island* (1940), Val Lewton's *The Seventh Victim* (1943) and *Abbott and Costello's Lost in a Harem* (1944); known as "the last of the real Gypsy singers," he also recorded for Decca and was a club emcee. He died in 1954.

Roy William Neill, who had directed Dwight in *The Circus Queen Murder* (1933), as well as Karloff's tour de force as the good and evil twin of *The Black Room* (1935), gave terrific atmospherics to *Frankenstein Meets the Wolf Man*. At this time Neill was mastermind of the Universal Sherlock Holmes series, directing 11 of the 12 films, as well as producing the last nine. As Basil Rathbone wrote in his 1962 memoir, *In and Out of Character*:

> ...there were so many who contributed to our little niche in the hall of fame. There was first our director-producer-writer, the late Roy Neill, endearingly known to his company as "Mousie." There was a nominal producer and some writers also, but Roy Neill was the master and final hand in all these departments.

Neill, who also directed such Universal fare as Acquanetta's *Rhythm of the Islands* (1943) and Maria Montez's *Gypsy Wildcat* (1944), died in London in 1946.

Finally, *Frankenstein Meets the Wolf Man* owes much to the superb work of musical director Hans J. Salter, who had joined Universal in 1938 and would score about 150 movies. The Vienna-born, Oscar-nominated Salter died in July of 1994, at the age of 98.

Frankenstein Meets the Wolf Man would be the final horror film of Dwight Frye. Happily, he looks well, has some juicy dialogue and it's poetic that he gets the final (and unscripted) line in the film. As Atwill demands of the villagers, "Where's Vazec?," Dwight ominously replies, "He said he'd blow up the dam!"

For a Dwight Frye fan, the line sends chills up the spine—and not just due to his delivery.

Hangmen Also Die!

United Artists/Arnold Pressburger, 1943; Producer and Director: Fritz Lang; Adaptation and Original Story by Bertolt Brecht and Fritz Lang; Screenplay: John Wexley; Cameraman: James Wong Howe; Musical Score: Hanns Eisler; Musical Director: Arthur Gutmann; Art Director: William Darling; Editor: Gene Fowler, Jr.; Original running time: 131 minutes; New York City opening: Capitol Theatre, April 15, 1943

CAST: Brian Donlevy (Dr. Franz Svoboda); Walter Brennan (Professor Novotny); Anna Lee (Mascha Novotny); Gene Lockhart (Emil Czaka); Dennis O'Keefe (Jan Horek); Alexander Granach (Alois Gruber); Margaret Wycherly (Aunt Ludmilla); Nana Bryant (Mrs. Novotny); Billy Roy (Beda Novotny); Hans V. Twardowski (Reinhard Heydrich); Tonio Selwart (Haas); Jonathan Hale (Dedic); Lionel Stander (Gabby); Byron Foulger (Bartos); Virginia Farmer (Landlady); Ludwig Donath (Schirmer); Sarah Padden (Mme. Dvorak); Edmund MacDonald (Dr. Pilar);

George Irving (Necval); James Bush (Worker); Arno Frey (Camp Officer); Arthur Loft (Votruba); William Farnum (Viktorin); Reinhold Schuenzel (Ritter); Lester Sharpe, **Dwight Frye**, Emmett Vogan, Billy Benedict, Emmett Lynn (Hostages); Rita La Roy (Prostitute); Otto Reichow (Gestapo Agent); Eddy Waller (Cab Driver); Erville Alderson (Liberal Official); Ralph Dunn (Policeman); Charles Middleton, William Haade, Philip Merivale (Patriots)

NOTES:

> From Hitler's Secret Archives! This script was smuggled out of Europe at risk of death! No wonder it is hailed as one of the most exciting pictures to come out of this war!
> —Publicity for *Hangmen Also Die!*, *The New York Times*, April 15, 1943

In the spring of 1942, an assassin fatally wounded Reinhard Heydrich, the Nazi "Protector" of Bohemia, infamously known as "The Hangman." After his death, Heinrich Himmler unleashed one of Nazi Germany's most barbaric acts against the village of Lidice (near the site of the assassination): all men were shot, all women and children sent to concentration camps and the village totally destroyed.

In the last week of October, 1942, two films began independent production in Hollywood, based on the Heydrich assassination. Seymour Nebenzal began shooting *The Hangman*—starring John Carradine as Heydrich, Patricia Morison as the heroine and Alan Curtis as the assassin. Douglas Sirk directed; MGM released the movie in the summer of 1943 as *Hitler's Madman*. Concurrently, Arnold Pressburger began *Never Surrender*—starring Brian Donlevy as the assassin, and Anna Lee as the heroine. Fritz Lang produced and directed; United Artists released the film as *Hangmen Also Die!*—beating *Hitler's Madman* into theatres in the spring of 1943.

Hangmen Also Die! definitely had the "prestige" advantage, being a property of the celebrated Lang (1890-1976, director of *Metropolis, M, Fury, Man Hunt*); it also boasted a scenario by the German author Bertolt Brecht (who would wage a bitter fight with John Wexley over the screenplay credit), and cinematography by James Wong Howe. The cast was top-notch. Brian Donlevy (1901-1972), who starred as the assassin, was at his personal peak in Hollywood, following such Paramount hits as *Beau Geste* (Oscar-nominated as evil *Sgt. Markoff*, 1939), *The Great McGinty* (1940) and *Wake Island* (1942). Anna Lee was excellent as the heroine; horror fans will remember Miss Lee as Karloff's leading lady in both *The Man Who Changed His Mind* (1936), and (especially) Val Lewton's *Bedlam* (1946). She's still active today as the indomitable Lila Quartermaine on the ABC daytime soap opera, *General Hospital*. Walter Brennan (1894-1974), who was already a three-time Oscar winner by 1942, had a change-of-pace role as Miss Lee's professor father. (Brennan had played bit roles in *The Invisible Man* and *Bride of Frankenstein*.)

Frye appeared as a Czech hostage. "It's clear as daylight!" he says in the prison; "They're trying to use us as a 'cat's paw' to get the assassin for them!" His role may have been larger; the edited version seen today (which completely eliminates Hans V. Twardowski as Heydrich!) runs 89 minutes, as opposed to the original 131 minutes.

Hangmen Also Die! also featured two players-from-the-past for Dwight. Margaret Wycherly, who had played Frye's mother in Broadway's *Six Characters in Search of an Author* (1922), appeared in the movie as Aunt Ludmilla. And Emmett Vogan, leading man of the 1918 Denham Stock Company (Frye's first professional engagement), and later Frye's co-player in the Woodward Stock Company of Spokane, 1921/1922, also enacted a hostage.

When *Hangmen Also Die!* premiered on Broadway, the grim film was incongruously supported by a stage show starring Ozzie and Harriet Nelson. Many felt the movie was strangely lacking in drama and passion. Conversely, *Hitler's Madman*, which opened on Broadway in

August of 1943 (four months after its competitor), was considered *too* passionate, playing like a horror movie; MGM soon withdrew it.

In retrospect, *Hangmen Also Die!* was a "legitimate" credit in Dwight Frye's film resume, coming right on the heels of *Dead Men Walk* and *Frankenstein Meets the Wolf Man*. It sadly proved to be his final "A" film.

Submarine Alert

Paramount, 1943; Producers: William Pine and William Thomas; Director: Frank McDonald.; Original Screenplay: Maxwell Shane; Cinematography: Fred Jackman, Jr.; Editor: William Zeigler; Running Time, 66 minutes; Completion date, June 10, 1942; Tradeshow Date, June 21, 1943

CAST: Richard Arlen (Lew Deerhold); Wendy Barrie (Ann Patterson); Nils Asther (Dr. Arthur Huneker); Roger Pryor (G. B. Fleming); Abner Biberman (Comdr. Toyo); Marc Lawrence (Vincent Bela); John Miljan (Mr. Bambridge/Captain Hargas); Patsy Nash (Tina); Ralph Sanford (Freddie Grayson); **Dwight Frye (Haldine)**; Edward Earle (Dr. Barclay); William Bakewell (Engineer); Stanley Smith (Clerk); Edward Van Sloan (Johann Bergstrom)

NOTES: The producing team of William Pine and William Thomas (known in Hollywood as "the Two-Dollar Bills") made slick, low-budget action films independently, releasing them through a deal with Paramount. (They eventually made a horror/comedy, 1944's *One Body Too Many*, with Lugosi). By the 1950s, they had moved up several pegs, making color outdoor actioners with stars like Ronald Reagan.

In the 1940s, however, their resources were limited. According to *The Hollywood Reporter*, *Submarine Alert* began shooting June 1, 1942, with a 14-day schedule; according to Academy records, Frank McDonald finished directing the film June 10—nine days total!

The film was entertaining. Richard Arlen (1899-1976) was (as ever) a convincing, granite-jaw hero, Wendy Barrie (1912-1978) an appealing and classy leading lady and Nils Asther (1897-1981, making a comeback as a Hollywood heavy after having been a Garbo leading man in MGM silents) was effective as the top villain. Character players like Abner Biberman, John Miljan and the ubiquitous Marc Lawrence (his fourth film with Dwight) give the film pep and style. Unfortunately, the movie was released over a year after its completion—a delay which made it obsolete as a WW II espionage yarn.

As Haldine, Dwight was a radio expert in the employ of a gang of Axis spies. His role runs throughout the film; at one point, he helps his gang escape by tripping up a lawman with a wire. Although billed as "Albert Haldine" in the end credits, Frye's character is listed as "Henry Haldine" in all reviews and publicity material. Haldine is only referred to by his last name in *Submarine Alert*.

Not billed in the film, by the way, was Dwight's good friend (and *Dracula* co-star) Edward Van Sloan. As Johann Bergstrom, inventor of the transmitter, Van Sloan appears in the opening of the film: Asther and Lawrence chase him from his shack, Lawrence guns him down in a field—and then a tractor runs over the wounded inventor. Edward Van Sloan stayed active in movies until the late 1940s, made a final visit to Broadway in the play *The Vigil* in 1948 and died in his native San Francisco, March 6, 1964 at the age of 82.

Dangerous Blondes

Columbia, 1943; Producer: Samuel Bischoff; Director: Leigh Jason; Author: Kelley Roos (from his book *If the Shroud Fits*); Screenplay: Richard Flournoy; Musical Director: M. W. Stoloff; Cameraman: Philip Tannura, A.S.C.; Completion Date: June 19, 1943; Running Time: 80 minutes; Former Titles: *Restless Lady; The Case of the Dangerous Blondes*; Reviewed at the Hollywood Pantages Theatre, December 8, 1943

CAST: Allyn Joslyn (Barry Craig); Evelyn Keyes (Jane Craig); Edmund Lowe (Ralph McCormick); John Hubbard (Kirk Fenley); Anita Louise (Julie Taylor); Frank Craven (Inspector Clinton); Michael Duane (Harry Duerr); Ann Savage (Erika McCormick); William Demarest (Detective Gatling); Hobart Cavanaugh (Pop); Frank Sully (Detective Henderson); Robert Stanford (Jim Snyder); Lynn Merrick (May Ralston); Stanley Brown (Lee Kenyon); Bess Flowers (Madge Lawrence); Mary Forbes (Mrs. Fleming); John Abbott (Roland Smith); Emory Parnell (Policeman McGuire); Shirley Patterson [Shawn Smith] (Bride); Minerva Urecal (Mrs. Swanson); Frank O'Connor (Mailman); **Dwight Frye (1st Hoodlum)**; Horace McMahon (2nd Hoodlum); Grace Lenard (Middle-aged Woman); William Haade (Pugnacious Guy); Max Willenz (headwaiter); Craig Woods (Bridegroom); Broderick O'Farrell (Elderly Man); Harry Strang (Detective Matthews); Ray Neal (Detective Temple); Syd Saylor (Attendant #1); Emmett Vogan (Medical Officer); Joe Garcio (Police Photographer); Raoul Freeman (Police Photographer); Jack Green (Citizen); Jack Ryan (Cop #2); Paul Palmer (Fingerprint Expert); Charles Peery (Interne #2); Tommy Kingston (Interne #1); William Newell (Attendant #1); Gordon Clark (Reporter Haley); Donald Kerr (Reporter Lewis); Constance Worth (Reporter); Jack Kenney (Policeman); Don Wilson (Houston); Jack Rice (Scott); Billy Wayne (Night Clerk)

NOTES: Dwight Frye's final film, *Dangerous Blondes*, opened the week of October 7, 1943 at the Fox Theatre in Brooklyn, New York. In Hollywood, *Daily Variety* reviewed it December 8, 1943—one month and one day after Frye's death.

Frye's role: the "1st Hoodlum," who harasses Evelyn Keyes in a night club. He had no dialogue. The "2nd Hoodlum," incidentally, was played by Horace McMahon (1907-1971), who acted many gangsters before "going straight" in the Broadway and film versions of *Detective Story* and the TV series, *Naked City*. (McMahon had also played in 1938's *Fast Company*, in which Dwight had enjoyed a flashy role.)

This Columbia comedy/mystery took its cue from MGM's William Powell/Myrna Loy *Thin Man* series: Allan Joslyn and Evelyn Keyes played detective story writer Barry Craig and his "thrill-sharing" wife Jane, together solving murders revolving about the a model agency. Joslyn (1905-1981) had come back to Hollywood with fresh prestige after playing Mortimer in the original Broadway cast of *Arsenic and Old Lace* with Boris Karloff. Evelyn Keyes, blonde Columbia starlet ("the kind to excite appreciative whistles among the more susceptible audiences," noted *Daily Variety* in its *Dangerous Blondes* review), had begun her career as a protégé of Cecil B. DeMille at Paramount. She acted Suellen O'Hara in Selznick's *Gone With the Wind,* then joined Columbia, playing in "B"s like *Before I Hang* (1940, with Karloff); she soon progressed to "A" films such as Columbia's mega-hit, *The Jolson Story*. In later years, she wrote a best-selling biography, *Scarlett O'Hara's Younger Sister*, detailing (among many life experiences) her ill-fated marriage to John Huston. (A second volume of memoirs, *I'll Think About That Tomorrow*, followed.)

The film offers a curious cast. Edmund Lowe, leading man of *The Great Impersonation* (Universal, 1935, with Dwight's "Ghost of the Black Bog"), here took third billing as the model agency owner. Anita Louise (1915-1970), once a Warner Bros. leading lady, had a brief "comeback" here as the lady-in-distress who involves the Craigs in the whodunit. Also in *Dangerous Blondes*, as Lowe's "disloyal wife" Erika (who is strangled in the proceedings), is Ann Savage, destined to win acclaim as the psycho femme fatale of Edgar G. Ulmer's *Detour* (PRC, 1945). Emmett Vogan, Frye's old stock company colleague from Denver and Spokane, appeared in a bit as a Medical Officer. It's another irony that Vogan would be involved in both the first and final acting work of Dwight Frye.

Dwight Frye's Unrealized Film Projects

A. Films in which all of Frye's scenes were deleted from the release print:

Son of Frankenstein

Universal, 1939; Producer and Director: Rowland V. Lee; Cast: Basil Rathbone, Boris Karloff, Bela Lugosi, Lionel Atwill, Josephine Hutchinson, Donnie Dunagan, Emma Dunn, Edgar Norton, Michael Mark, Lionel Belmore, Lawrence Grant

Film history has long recorded that Dwight Frye played an "angry villager" in *Son of Frankenstein*, third and most spectacular entry in Universal's Monster series—and that his footage was entirely deleted. Unfortunately, ascertaining that he ever was in the film—and, if he was, just what he did in it—has remained unresolved.

Apparently, in the frantic post-production period between the film's completion and the preview date (Saturday night, January 7, 1939, less than three days after Lee finished the film!)—or in the week preceding the film's official premiere at the Hollywood Pantages Theatre on Friday, January 13, 1939—all of Dwight's footage was cut.

Is there proof that Dwight Frye was truly in the film? Dwight David Frye has a vague memory that his father had acted in it. There is a still of a mob scene, the villagers gathered in the street around Burgomaster Lawrence Grant; an actor on the right end of the crowd looks like it might be Dwight Frye, but the long shot makes absolute identification difficult.

In the late 1980s, rumors abounded that Universal/MCA had discovered an "uncut" *Son of Frankenstein*, along with Technicolor tests of Karloff in Monster makeup, and would release both for the home video market. Fans wondered if Dwight Frye might appear in the uncut version. However, the *Son of Frankenstein* that Universal/MCA released in April, 1989 was the usual 99 minute version—and without the Technicolor tests, which, after their discovery, had again mysteriously disappeared.

Son of Frankenstein gave such vivid dramatic moments to Basil Rathbone as Wolf von Frankenstein, Boris Karloff as the Monster, Bela Lugosi as old Ygor and Lionel Atwill as one-armed Inspector Krogh—as well as providing such beautiful costumes and flattering cinematography for Josephine Hutchinson (Dwight's co-star in Broadway's 1925 *A Man's Man*)—that it's a shame the film couldn't spare a mere moment or two for Dwight Frye.

Jim Hanvey, Detective

Republic, 1937; Director: Phil Rosen; Cast: Guy Kibbee, Tom Brown, Lucie Kaye, Catherine Doucet

The *American Film Institute Catalog: Feature Films*, 1931-1940 cites a news item stating Catherine Doucet had replaced Marjorie Gateson in the role of Adelaide Frost in *Jim Hanvey, Detective*, and that Dwight Frye was also cast in the film. The AFI cataloguers do not believe Frye actually appeared in the final version of *Jim Hanvey, Detective*, although he may have shot scenes that were later cut. It is interesting that Frye worked on Broadway in the 1920s with both actresses mentioned in the news item: Gateson in *So This is Politics* and Doucet in *The Devil in the Cheese*.

I Take This Woman

MGM, 1940; Director: W. S. Van Dyke II; Cast: Spencer Tracy, Hedy Lamarr, Veree Teasdale, Kent Taylor

Production on *I Take This Woman* began in October 1938, with Josef von Sternberg as director, but Frank Borzage assumed directorial charge of the film a few weeks later. Borzage shot extensive footage, stopping in January 1939, when *I Take This Woman* was temporarily shelved. MGM decided to resume production on December 4, 1939, this time with Van Dyke directing. Numerous scenes were cut, with many additions to and subtractions from the original cast. The film was almost re-done in its entirety, leading one writer to quip that it should have been called *I Re-Take This Woman.*

Dwight Frye definitely shot scenes on *I Take This Woman* during the period in which Borzage was directing (as evidenced by still #1070-45, which has Borzage's name on the back description). The extant still depicts Spencer Tracy as Dr. Karl Decker announcing to the interns of the Hester Street Clinic, "I'm in charge here." The interns, Joe (Jack Carson), Ted (Don Castle) and Gus (Frye), are shown playing cards at a clinic table.

B. Disputed Frye film credits:

King Solomon of Broadway

Universal, 1935; Director: Alan Crosland; Cast: Edmund Lowe, Dorothy Page, Louise Henry, Edward Pawley

Some reference books, including David Quinlan's *The Illustrated Encyclopedia of Movie Character Actors,* list *King Solomon of Broadway* as a Frye credit. People who have viewed the film, including the AFI cataloguers, have not spotted Frye in it. Frye did, of course, work with director Crosland and star Lowe later in 1935 on *The Great Impersonation* for Universal. It is possible Frye was in scenes in *King Solomon of Broadway* that wound up on the cutting room floor.

The Cat and the Canary

Paramount, 1939; Director: Elliott Nugent; Cast: Bob Hope, Paulette Goddard, John Beal, Douglass Montgomery, Gale Sondergaard

Film collector/historian Robert Scherl reported that Frye worked on *The Cat and the Canary* as one of the "cat men." "The Cat" in the film turns out to be Douglass Montgomery in disguise. It has been confirmed that another actor, William Abbey, wore "the Cat" makeup for many of the shots during the production of *The Cat and the Canary.* Whether Frye did as well remains uncertain.

C. Erroneously reported Frye film credits:

The Death Kiss

World Wide, 1932; Director: Edwin L. Marin; Cast: David Manners, Adrienne Ames, Bela Lugosi, Edward Van Sloan

Gary D. Dorst, in his seminal *Gore Creatures* Frye piece, listed *The Death Kiss* as a Frye credit, but this assumption could have been due to the fact that three of his *Dracula* fellow players (Lugosi, Van Sloan, Manners) were in it. Frye was not in this film.

Death Flies East

Columbia, 1935; Director: Phil Rosen; Cast: Conrad Nagel, Florence Rice, Raymond Walburn

Although there is an actor in the film who bears some resemblance to Frye (as evidenced by a still), Dwight definitely was not in *Death Flies East.*

Great Guy

Grand National, 1937; Director: John C. Blystone; Cast: James Cagney, Mae Clarke, James Burke

A number of articles and references claim Frye played a barber in *Great Guy.* Frye was Easton, the makeup man, in Cagney's other Grand National venture, *Something to Sing About,* and had scenes in which he worked on Cagney's hair. There is a possibility that researchers confused scenes or stills of one film with the other. Dwight Frye was not in *Great Guy.*

Prisoner of Japan

PRC, 1942; Director: Arthur Ripley; Cast: Alan Baxter, Gertrude Michael, Ernest Dorian, Corinna Mura

There was an actor named Gilbert Frye credited with playing in the U.S. radio operator in *Prisoner of Japan*. Researchers have suggested that Dwight Frye also appeared in the film, wearing heavy makeup as a Japanese spy. Having screened *Prisoner of Japan*, there is no actor in the film, makeup or not, that could be Dwight Frye.

Dwight Frye's final unrealized film:

Wilson

20th Century-Fox, 1944; Director: Henry King; Cast: Alexander Knox, Charles Coburn, Geraldine Fitzgerald, Thomas Mitchell, Sir Cedric Hardwicke, Vincent Price, Sidney Blackmer

In late October 1943, Frye auditioned for and won the role of Secretary of War Newton D. Baker for Darryl F. Zanuck's upcoming spectacular *Wilson* (1944). Frye was said to have borne a remarkable resemblance to Baker, a member of Woodrow Wilson's cabinet. It was after treating his wife Laura and son Buddy to an evening at the movies to celebrate signing for the part that Dwight Frye suffered his fatal heart attack. On November 9, 1943, two days after Frye's death, production on *Wilson* began. Reginald Sheffield assumed the role of Baker and, apparently, the part was shortened from that which Frye had anticipated playing.

A late 1924 White Studio portrait of Dwight Frye.

Dwight Frye's Last Laugh

Appendix B
Early Theatre Work
Stock, Vaudeville, Repertory

1918 Denham Stock Company, Denver, Colorado

Actor, director and producer O. D. Woodward was a well-established theatrical personage in the early twentieth century, particularly in stock cities like Kansas City, Missouri; Omaha, Nebraska; and Minneapolis, Minnesota. Woodward leased the Denham Theatre, at Eighteenth and California Streets in Denver, Colorado, in late 1913. Over the ensuing five years, he would offer dramas, comedies and musicals geared to be affordable to the general populace. The Denham Theatre was proscenium equipped and seated 1,732, with ticket prices ranging from 10 cents to a high of 75 cents. Woodward attempted to surround himself with quality performers and technicians, maintaining a reputation for both variety and realism. The Denham Players, however, were on the wane when Dwight Frye joined them in the latter stages of the 1917/18 stock season.

Under the direction of O. D. Woodward, the 1917/18 Denham Players, in addition to Frye, included: Emmett Vogan (leading man), Hazel Whitmore (leading lady), Ethel Tucker, Betty Garth, Ralph Lee, Clare Hatton, Richard Weight, "Billy" Jensen, Uncas Daniel, Si Condit, Lea Penman, Adele Bradford, Eugene Powers, Henry Crosby, Lillian Compton and Charles Beard.

June 16, 1918
The Man From Mexico
Farce in three acts by H. A. Du Souchet, from the French of Gondinet and Bisson.

Frye made his professional theatrical debut as Richard Daunton in *The Man From Mexico*, derived from a French farce. Billed by his given name, Dwight Fry, this was his only play prior to enrolling in the summer program of the University of Colorado at Boulder. Less than two months later, Frye received word from O. D. Woodward, via his mother Ella, that the Denham company juvenile had enlisted in the armed forces. Frye leapt at the opportunity to replace the juvenile, leaving college at once.

August 16, 1918
Turned Up
Farce in three acts by Mark Melford.

Frye portrayed Nod Stedham. "A new man appears in the cast. He is Dwight Frye, a Denver fellow and graduate of West Side high school" (unspecified clipping from Frye's pre-Broadway scrapbook). From this point on in his professional career, Dwight would spell his name "Frye."

August 25, 1918
Salomy Jane
Drama in four acts by Paul Armstrong.

In *Salomy Jane*, which has been erroneously reported as Frye's stage debut, Dwight played Rufe Waters. A Denver critic commented, "Dwight Frye showed a gain in mastery of his part this week and will no doubt in time lose the forced and unnatural eagerness which has marked his work thus far" (Frye's pre-Broadway scrapbook).

September 1, 1918
Cheating Cheaters

Play in four acts by Max Marcin.

As Antonio Verdi, Frye received the following review: "Dwight Frye also played up to the standard and his interpretation of Toni, the musical thief, was unusually good" (Frye's pre-Broadway scrapbook).

September 8, 1918
Upstairs and Down

Comedy in three acts by Frederic and Fanny Hatton.

As Louis Le Tour, O'Keefe's man, Frye was one of the "downstairs" characters in this comedy. In the role of Captain O'Keefe was Denham leading man Emmett Vogan, who would become a good friend of Dwight. In 1921, Vogan rejoined Frye and Woodward in stock in Spokane. Vogan and Frye later appeared together as Czech hostages in Fritz Lang's *Hangmen Also Die!* (1943).

September 15, 1918
Captain Rackett

Comedy in three acts by Charles Townsend.

As Hobson, a Denver reviewer noted, "Dwight Frye was cast in an inferior part, but his song of the 'Rainbow' brought a storm of applause" (Frye's pre-Broadway scrapbook). Frye's musical number is listed in the *Captain Rackett* program as "Florida Moon."

September 22, 1918
A Bachelor's Romance

Play in four acts by Martha Morton.

"Contrary to the theory that the farewell plays of a company are their worst, the play at the Denham Sunday was one of the best they have ever put on" (Frye's pre-Broadway scrapbook). *A Bachelor's Romance*, with Frye as Gerald Holmes, marked the conclusion of the Denham Players' five seasons in Denver. A critic stated, "Frye's acting was good. His boyish freshness takes well with the audience" (Frye's pre-Broadway scrapbook).

1918/19 Woodward—Arington Stock Company
Spokane, Washington

O. D. Woodward had enjoyed moderate success during his years in Denver, but, feeling it was time to move on, chose Spokane, Washington as the next base of operations for his stock company. His timing, however, was far from ideal. Spokane was in the midst of an influenza quarantine, part of the flu pandemic of 1918 that took so many lives.

Woodward leased the American Theatre, erected in 1910 at the intersection of Post Street and Trent Avenue, renaming it the Woodward Theatre. The Woodward-Arington Players in Spokane gave ten performances of a given play each week, including one show per night and matinees on Sunday, Wednesday and Saturday. Each Sunday, the bill of fare would change.

The 1918/19 Woodward-Arington Players of Spokane featured a number of transplanted Denham Players from Denver, including: Frye (the company juvenile), Hazel Whitmore (leading lady), Richard Weight, Clare Hatton, Ralph Lee, "Billy" Jensen, Lea Penman and Ethel Tucker. Emmett Vogan did not accompany the troupe from Denver as was originally planned, so Robert Brister was selected as leading man. Brister was in turn succeeded in this position by J. Burke Morgan and William Courneen. Other members of the 1918/19 Woodward-Arington

Players were: William Morse, Thomas Pawley, Josephine Genaro, Virginia Watkins, Edward Bickford, Joseph LaValliere, Lucile LaValliere, Mayme Arington, Carl Daintree, Walter Siegfried, Cliff Lancaster, Dorothy Bartley, Joycie Booth and Chester Meyer.

November 23, 1918
Cheating Cheaters
Play in four acts by Max Marcin.
The Woodward-Arington Players opened their 1918/19 season in Spokane with a play in which some of the company had been involved twelve weeks earlier in Denver. Frye played Antonio Verdi in *Cheating Cheaters*, as he had at the Denham Theatre. A Spokane clipping read, "Dwight Frye, the juvenile, was a particular favorite and contributed a piano solo" (Frye's pre-Broadway scrapbook).

December 1, 1918
Hit-the-Trail Holiday
Farce in four acts by George M. Cohan, suggested by George Middleton and Guy Bolton.
In this successful presentation of the Cohan comedy, Frye had a fairly small part as Joe, one of the barbers in the basement shop at the American Hotel.

December 8, 1918
Common Clay
Drama in four acts by Cleves Kinkead.
Frye played the clerk in the police court.

Dwight Frye did not appear in the Woodward production for the week of December 15, 1918: *Charley's Aunt.*

December 22, 1918
The Master Mind
Drama in four acts by Daniel D. Carter.
In this play wherein a brilliant criminal (played by William Morse) seeks vengeance upon the former district attorney (Robert Brister), Frye, as Walter Blount (alias "Diamond Willie"), was said to have "carried his part well." Another review added, "Dwight Frye has a somewhat similar double part, a victim of double fear, the law and the master mind in whose hands his life rests" (Frye's pre-Broadway scrapbook).

December 29, 1918
Mam'zelle
Comedy in three acts by Leo Stange.
Although not in the actual cast of *Mam'zelle*, Frye, along with other members of the company, provided "specialties" during the second act. A Spokane reviewer noted, "Dwight Frye did a pianologue at the grand piano and was encored, receiving a quintet of floral tributes" (Frye's pre-Broadway scrapbook).

January 5, 1919
Outcast
Comedy drama in four acts by Hubert Henry Davies.
"The depression of the first act," asserted a Spokane critic, "...is relieved by the ever-welcome Dwight Frye as Tony Hewlett." Another wrote, "Dwight Frye plays the youthful pal with lots of enthusiasm" (Frye's pre-Broadway scrapbook).

January 12, 1919
A Woman's Way

Farce comedy in three acts by Thompson Buchanan.

As Bob Livingstone, Frye played the brother of the wronged wife (Hazel Whitmore) involved in a scandal. According to one review, "Dwight Frye has a good bit as the juvenile stupid who is forever putting his foot in it," with a second notice claiming he "...gave an excellent delineation of the part" (Frye's pre-Broadway scrapbook).

January 19, 1919
Upstairs and Down

Comedy in three acts by Frederic and Fanny Hatton.

As he had in Denver, Frye played Louis Le Tour, O'Keefe's man, and helped "...provide the laughs which keep the audience merry" (Frye's pre-Broadway scrapbook).

January 26, 1919
Sis Hopkins

Farce comedy in three acts. Playwright unknown.

This rustic play, noted even in 1919 as being "somewhat out of date," included a "fine role" for Frye as Obadiah Odlum. A critic stated, "Dwight Frye outdoes himself in the comedy role of the village undertaker who looks for business everywhere" (Frye's pre-Broadway scrapbook).

February 2, 1919
The Cinderella Man

Romantic comedy in four acts by Edward Childs Carpenter.

In this tale of a struggling young author, J. Burke Morgan made his debut with the Woodward company, replacing Robert Brister as leading man. "Dwight Frye (in his role of Walter Nicholls) has a good scene in the first act, which he negotiates effectively," said a Spokane paper (Frye's pre-Broadway scrapbook).

February 9, 1919
The Thirteenth Chair

Drama in three acts by Bayard Veiller.

Hazel Whitmore, normally the leading lady, scored in this mystery play as the elderly spiritualist. The spiritualist helps reveal Philip Mason (played by Frye) as the murderer. The Spokane critics continued to take note of Frye's efforts: "Dwight Frye does a great bit of acting in the confession scene," and "Dwight Frye has his big opportunity in the act and rises to the occasion surprisingly" (Frye's pre-Broadway scrapbook).

February 16, 1919
Nothing But the Truth

Farce comedy in three acts by James Montgomery.

In Woodward's production of the play in which William Collier starred on Broadway for 332 performances, Frye portrayed Dick Donnelly.

February 23, 1919
Rebecca of Sunnybrook Farm

Play in four acts by Kate Douglas Wiggin and Charlotte Thompson.

Having played an aged medium in *The Thirteenth Chair* two weeks prior, Hazel Whitmore displayed her versatility assaying the youthful role of Rebecca. "Dwight Frye also makes the most of a small bit as Abijah Flagg, the captain of the fife and drum corps and village smart aleck," reported a critic (Frye's pre-Broadway scrapbook).

March 2, 1919
Nearly Married
Farce in three acts by Edgar Selwyn.

Frye played Richard Griffin in Selwyn's play, which reportedly was "...almost continuously comedy, rising sometimes to the speed and vigor of farce and descending once or twice to the vulgarity of burlesque" (Frye's pre-Broadway scrapbook).

March 9, 1919
Within the Law
Play in four acts by Bayard Veiller.

Within the Law had been a huge success on Broadway, opening in 1912 and running for almost two years. Veiller's drama gave Frye the substantial role of the heavy, Joe Garson, a forger. Reviewers found Frye's performance "creditable" and "cleverly portrayed" (Frye's pre-Broadway scrapbook).

After the closing of *Within the Law*, Frye left the Woodward company for a "short rest." He ventured to Tacoma, Washington; Vancouver, British Columbia; and, finally, California, before returning to Spokane. During this hiatus, Frye missed appearing in *What's Your Husband Doing?* (3/16/19) and *The Gentle Honeymoon* (3/23/19).

March 30, 1919
It Pays to Advertise
Farcical fact in three acts by Roi Cooper Megrue and Walter Hackett.

The Spokane press paid special attention to Frye's return performance as Ambrose Peale: "Dwight Frye, after an absence of several weeks, comes back strong in the cyclonic role of the press agent, and it is a role after his own heart, in which his peculiar ability to hurl words in a deluge with bombastic effect has free expression. Frye has done no better work with the stock company" (Frye's pre-Broadway scrapbook).

April 6, 1919
Sham
Play in three acts by Geraldine Bonner and Elmer Harris.

As J. Montague Buck, Frye played the rich young suitor to Hazel Whitmore. Although one critic found Frye's part an "odd bit," he added, "His work stands out in the evening's entertainment." Another penned "Dwight Frye, as the wealthy, but unpolished western lad, attacks the role with his usual enthusiasm and abandon" (Frye's pre-Broadway scrapbook).

April 13, 1919
The Blue Envelope
Farce in three acts by Frank Hatch and Robert E. Homans.

In this satirical comedy of errors set, in part, in a sanitarium, Frye played Richard Rowe, showing "himself to be an excellent comedian." "Dwight Frye is called upon for strenuous lines and scenes and acquits himself with his usual painstaking portrayal," reported a reviewer of Frye's final play of the 1918/19 season with the Woodward company in Spokane (Frye's pre-Broadway scrapbook).

August 14, 1919 — May 27, 1920
The Magic Glasses, Vaudeville
After leaving O. D. Woodward's stock company in Spokane, Washington, in mid-April 1919, Frye obtained work in vaudeville with the Cliff Dean Players and with George Dickham.

In August 1919, Frye embarked on a tour, primarily on the Keith circuit, with the vaudeville sketch *The Magic Glasses*. Written by Frances Nordstrom, *The Magic Glasses: A Speculation in Specs* starred Mary Johnson, the wife of entertainer Jack Norworth, who had written the lyrics for "Take Me Out to the Ballgame." *The Magic Glasses* was a four character short piece, usually featured in the latter portion of a vaudeville bill. The cast, which featured Frye as the "poor man," would present the sketch at least twice a day.

The Magic Glasses

Vaudeville sketch. Subtitled *A Speculation in Specs*. Written by Frances Nordstrom. CAST: The Doctor...Ray L. Royce; Poor Man...Dwight Frye; Rich Man...C. Elliot Griffin; The Girl...Mary Johnson

Time: Yesterday, To-day, To-morrow
Place: Just around the corner

Staged under the personal direction of Wm. Pinkham.

June 28 — July 9, 1920
Girls Will Be Girls, Vaudeville

Upon finishing with the long tour of *The Magic Glasses* in Norfolk, Virginia, in late May 1920, Frye returned home to Denver. The next booking he was able to secure was as a singing comedian in another vaudeville act, *Girls Will Be Girls*, on the Pantages circuit. Frye played Bob, a role originally slated for Johnny Sullivan, in this "20-minute musical tabloid with two principals and a chorus of four" (Frye's pre-Broadway scrapbook). Florence Loraine was Frye's co-star. The sketch included what critics called a "catchy number," "My Recipe for Love," as well as "some risqué gowns and a blonde that's easy to look at" (Frye's pre-Broadway scrapbook).

Girls Will Be Girls would not provide the steady employment of *The Magic Glasses*, instead lasting only two weeks. The itinerary for *Girls Will Be Girls* (as handwritten by Frye in his pre-Broadway Scrapbook):

June 28, 1920	Colorado Springs, Colorado
June 30, 1920	Pueblo, Colorado
July 2-4, 1920	El Paso, Texas
July 5-9, 1920	El Paso, Texas

August — October 1920
La, La, Lucille, Road Company

La, La, Lucille, A Musical Comedy
Book by Fred Jackson. Music by George Gershwin. Lyrics by Arthur J. Jackson and B. C. de Sylva. Staged by Herbert Gresham and Julian Alfred. Musical director, W. W. Lanthurn

CAST: Jonathan Jaynes, an Ex-Juggler...Frederic Hampton; Lucille Jaynes Smith, his daughter... Betty Burke; **John Smith, her husband...Dwight Frye**; Oyama, a Japanese butler...Donald Duff; Nicholas Grimsby, a lawyer...Bert J. Horton (1), John A. O'Brien (2); Thomas Brady... Paul Hamin; Mrs. Thomas Brady...Vivian Gill; Fanny, a janitress...Marion Langdon; Mlle. Victorine, a cabaret dancer...Gene Lane (1), Joan Davis (2); Britton Hughes, a Romeo from the South...Jules Saucier; Mrs. Britton Hughes, his Juliet (aka Peggy)...Mildred Chandler (1), Miriam Holland (2); Duffy, house detective...James D. Crowley (1), Frank Doane (2); Colonel

Marion, Peggy's father...James Anderson; Reginald Blackwood...George Ricard; Bell Boy...Elsie Roberts; Bill Collectors, Heiresses, etc....Edna Torrey, Dorothy Manley, Anna Hartmann, Lillian Davis, Helen Mason, Clara Wright

Specialty Dances by Gertrude Hatman

Frye replaced actor Leon Cunningham in the lead role of John Smith during rehearsals. Early reviews, like those from Stamford, Connecticut, wrongly credit Cunningham with Frye's performance. *La, La, Lucille* started poorly, with cast members criticized for not knowing their lines. The show apparently improved with time, as the company traveled to locations like Pottstown, Pennsylvania, and Portland, Maine. Frye remained with the road company of *La, La, Lucille* for either eight or ten weeks.

Later reviews of *La, La, Lucille* list other replacement cast members, including: Julia Gifford, Leila Tarsanen, Rena MacKenzie, Charles Fearing and Robert Livingstone.

October 1920—May 1921
Myrkle-Harder Repertory Company

Headed by leading lady Emma Myrkle, the Myrkle-Harder Repertory Company toured the Northeastern United States, playing small cities and towns like Corning and Oneonta, New York; Rutland, Vermont; and Easton, Pennsylvania. The company would remain for a week in each location, then travel to the next city on Sunday. While in a given town, the Myrkle-Harder Repertory Company would offer a different play each day, Monday through Saturday. There would be two performances of the same play, matinee and evening, on those days.

In addition to Emma Myrkle and Frye, who was the company juvenile, the Myrkle-Harder Repertory Company was comprised of: Alfred Swenson (leading man), William McCarthy, Charles F. Ward, R. E. Brady, Jack Lynch, Jere Taylor, Isabel McMinn, Lorle Palmer, Corda Davy, Frank Hawkins and Dorothy Bartley.

The Myrkle-Harder repertory lineup for part (if not all) of Frye's tenure with the company was:

DAY	PLAY	PLAYWRIGHT(S)
Monday	Polly With a Past	George Middleton and Guy Bolton
Tuesday	Civilian Clothes	Thompson Buchanan
Wednesday	Dawn O' the Mountains	DeWitt Newing
Thursday	39 East	Rachel Crothers
Friday	Blind Youth	Willard Mack and Lou Tellegen
Saturday	The Unkissed Bride	unknown

Frye's only known role in any of the above plays was Billy Arkwright in *Civilian Clothes*. He toured with the Myrkle-Harder Repertory Company for approximately thirty weeks, from October 1920 until May 1921. After leaving the company, Frye found work in New York City nightclubs, performing pianologues. Frye then signed with the Goldstein brothers to join the Colonial Players of Pittsfield, Massachusetts.

1921 Colonial Theatre, Pittsfield, Massachusetts

The Colonial Theatre in Pittsfield, Massachusetts, was built on South Street, part of Route 7, the main thoroughfare through the Berkshires, by John and James Sullivan. The Colonial opened on 9/28/03, with the Bostonians' production of the opera *Robin Hood*. Early in their careers, Ethel and John Barrymore appeared at the Colonial in 1906 in *Alice Sit-by-the-Fire*. Walter Damrosch conducted the New York Symphony at the Colonial on 2/24/11. The Pittsfield

Theatre Company, comprised of local businessmen, purchased the Colonial from the Sullivans, refitting the stage and reopening it in May 1912. Samuel and Nathan Goldstein next bought the Colonial in 1915. Pianist Ignace Jan Paderewski performed at the Colonial on 11/17/15. William Gillette was Sherlock Holmes there on 2/24/16. Sarah Bernhardt and her company also were seen at the Colonial on 9/28/17. When Dwight Frye joined the Colonial Players in 1921, Pittsfield reportedly was the smallest city, by population, in the United States with a resident stock company.

As with most stock companies, the Colonial Players were a mixture of individuals with varying levels of experience and degrees of talent. Frye was chosen to be the company juvenile, after signing on for the 1921 stock season. The leading man was Alfred Swenson (1883-1941), in the first of his two seasons in Pittsfield. Swenson had extensive stock experience and had appeared in silent films, such as *Hypocrisy* (1916) and *Strife* (1917). He would later be seen on Broadway in plays like *That Day* (10/3/22), *Wall Street* (4/20/27) and *The Great Power* (9/11/28), also being featured in the 1929 film version of the latter. Perhaps Swenson's greatest acting fame, however, came in radio, where he starred in *The Adventures of Captain Diamond* (1932) and was a regular on both *The O'Neills* (1934) and *Hilltop House* (1937). Ruth Amos was the leading lady for the 1921 Colonial Players. She would sporadically appear on Broadway over the years (*Slightly Delirious*—12/31/34; *Strange Bedfellows*—1/14/48; *A Tree Grows in Brooklyn*—4/19/51), while also being heard on radio and being seen in the early days of television. Other 1921 Colonial Players included: Character man Bob McClung, second man William Melville, ingenue Marie Hodgkins, character woman Lorle Palmer, William H. Murdock, Ida Molthen, Isabel McMinn, Eleanor Carleton, Byron C. Irving, Lola James and Kirwin Wilkinson. Walter S. Baldwin directed most of the 1921 Colonial stock offerings, while Albert Amend received plaudits for his creative set designs. Swenson, Palmer and McMinn had all formerly played together with Frye in the Myrkle-Harder Company.

May 23, 1921
Adam and Eva

Comedy in three acts by Guy Bolton and George Middleton.

Dwight Frye portrayed Clinton DeWitt, the husband of Julie (Ida Molthen) and son-in-law of wealthy James King (Bob McClung). *The Berkshire Eagle* (5/24/21, p. 2) found the roles of the DeWitts to be "...taken ably by Dwight Frye and Ida Molthen."

May 30, 1921
Turn to the Right

Drama in a prologue and three acts by Winchell Smith and John E. Hazzard.

Frye played Sam Martin, the "factotum" at the store of town skinflint Deacon Tillinger (William Murdock). Martin begs to be taken into the prospective peach jam syndicate that is at the core of the plot. "The rest of the company have fairly good roles, with Dwight Frye as an outstanding figure in the part of Sam Martin, a bright young lad with an eye to the future," wrote *The Berkshire Eagle* (5/31/21, p. 4).

June 6, 1921
The Sign on the Door

Melodrama in a prologue and three acts by Channing Pollock.

As Allan Churchill, Frye was engaged to spunky Helen Regan (Marie Hodgkins), the daughter of opinionated and puritanical Lafe Regan (Alfred Swenson).

June 13, 1921
Up in Mabel's Room
Farce in three acts by Wilson Collison and Otto Harback.

"Dwight Frye shines as Jimmy Larchmont" (*The Berkshire Eagle*, 6/14/21) in the Colonial's well-received presentation of this frivolous comedy. Another former Myrkle-Harder player, Isabel McMinn, played his wife, Alicia Larchmont.

June 20, 1921
The Only Girl
Musical comedy in three acts, with book by Henry Blossom and music by Victor Herbert.

Frye played lawyer John Ayre, known as "Fresh," and sang the solo "All by Myself." He also exhibited his song and dance skills in numbers like "Connubial Bliss" and "When You're Wearing the Ball and Chain."

June 27, 1921
Smilin' Through
Fantastic comedy in a prologue and three acts by Allan Langdon Martin (Jane Cowl and Jane Murfin).

John Carteret (Alfred Swenson) wishes for his ward Kathleen (Ruth Amos) to marry neighbor Willie Ainley (Dwight Frye), but she desires Kenneth Wayne (William Melville). Frye was said to be effective as the thrown-over suitor.

July 4, 1921
That Girl Patsy
Comedy in four acts by Sumner Nichols.

Frye played Fred Coulson, a friend of Bob (Alfred Swenson). *The Berkshire Eagle* (7/6/21, p. 4) reported, "Messrs. Swenson, McClung, Melville, Frye, Murdock, Baldwin, and Wilkinson are all seen to advantage."

July 11, 1921
The Acquittal
Drama in three acts by Rita Weiman.

In *The Acquittal*, which had been produced on Broadway by George M. Cohan, Frye had the minor role of Claflin, a reporter.

July 18, 1921
Pollyanna
Drama in four acts by Eleanor Porter, from the book of the same name by Catherine Chisholm Cushing.

Frye portrayed Jimmy Bean, "the poor orphan child."

July 25, 1921
The Girl in the Limousine
Farce in three acts by Wilson Collison and Avery Hopwood

Frye played Tony Hamilton. *The Berkshire Eagle* (7/26/21, p. 4) noted, "Dwight Frye as the unfortunate young man who was found by the burglars and robbed of even his clothes while he was unconscious, has many situations that call for quick action."

August 1, 1921
The Love of Su Shong

Melodrama in a prologue, three acts and epilogue by Dewitt Newing.

As Song Sing, Frye, in love with Su Shong (Ruth Amos), gives up his life to aid American Richard Taber (Alfred Swenson).

August 8, 1921
Scandal

Comedy in three acts by Cosmo Hamilton.

In his final 1921 stock role at the Colonial Theatre, Frye was Malcolm Fraser.

1921/22 The Woodward Players, Woodward Theatre, Spokane, Washington

The 1921/22 stock season was the fourth and final one for the Woodward Players in Spokane, Washington. Frye had been with the company early in his career for its 1918/19 season, a successful period for the troupe. By the 1921/22 campaign, however, critics were complaining about the choice of plays, casting and production values. Woodward felt that by bolstering his company with some of his former players, like Frye and Hazel Whitmore, he might infuse new life into his productions.

In addition to Frye, a significant member of the 1921/22 Woodward Players in Spokane was company ingenue Laura Lee (Laura Bullivant), whom Dwight would marry in August 1928. Rodney Hildebrand had been the original leading man for the company, but he was replaced in late October 1921 by Emmett Vogan. Hazel Whitmore, as she had earlier been for Woodward in Denver and Spokane, was the leading lady. Other Woodward Players from the 1921/22 Spokane company were: Margaret Robinson (character woman), William Dills (character man), Charles Fletcher, Virginia Brown, Smith Davies, Marguerite Klein, William T. Holden, Richard Mack, Glenmar Witt, Letta Brockman, William Jackson, Edward Russell, Mira McKinney, Clinton Tustin, Mary True and Jack Whittemore.

Frye remained with the Woodward Players in Spokane for 24 weeks, spanning August 27, 1921—February 12, 1922. In mid-February 1922, Frye and Whitmore were dispatched by Woodward to head a new company he was installing at the Woodward (formerly Levy's Orpheum) Theatre in Seattle, Washington.

(Note: Five plays [*Apartment K-12, Billy, Friendly Enemies, My Lady Friends* and *Pot Luck*] were performed by the Woodward Players during the weeks of 11/28/21, 12/5/21, 1/9/22, 1/16/22 and 1/23/22, but the correct matching of production with date is not known. These five shows have been referred to as (a), (b), (c), (d) and (e), and are described following the 24th week's production, *A Woman's Way* [2/6/22].)

August 27, 1921
Smilin' Through

Fantastic comedy in a prologue and three acts by Allan Langdon Martin (Jane Cowl and Jane Murfin).

The Spokane press noted, "Dwight Frye popular as ever," when he rejoined the Woodward Players as company juvenile after an absence of two stock seasons. As Willie Ainley, a role he had played at the Colonial, in *Smilin' Through*, a critic noted, "Dwight Frye was accorded much applause and carried his juvenile role in a very pleasing manner" (Frye's pre-Broadway scrapbook).

September 4, 1921
The Girl in the Limousine

Farce in three acts by Wilson Collison and Avery Hopwood.

Frye played Dr. Jimmie Galen, who fears he is suffering from temporary insanity. A review read, "Dwight Frye was particularly successful in the role of the young doctor bent on murdering the butler for alleged flirtations with his wife" (Frye's pre-Broadway scrapbook). Galen's wife was portrayed by an actress who, seven years later, would fill that role in Frye's own life—Laura Bullivant ("Miss Laura Lee [her stage name at the time] played her part with much ease and grace and was welcomed back to the Woodward cast last evening.").

September 11, 1921
Turn to the Right

Comedy in a prologue and three acts by Winchell Smith and John E. Hazzard.

In a different part than he had assayed in *Turn to the Right* at the Colonial, Frye was Muggs, one of the ex-convict pals of Joe Bascom (Rodney Hildebrand).

September 18, 1921
Widow by Proxy

Farcical comedy in three acts by Catherine Chisholm Cushing.

As Johnathan Pennington, Frye is presumed dead, with Hazel Whitmore attempting to help Laura Lee obtain the inheritance due from her late husband's estate. Chaos occurs, however, when "Jack" is "re-incarnated." "Dwight Frye has one scene in the last act as the exuberant young husband, suddenly rescued from the 'dead'" (Frye's pre-Broadway scrapbook).

September 25, 1921
A Tailor-Made Man

Comedy in four acts by Harry James Smith.

As Peter, the assistant to John Paul Bart, the tailor (Rodney Hildebrand), "Dwight Frye furnished a score of laughs with as many lines," stated one critic (Frye's pre-Broadway scrapbook).

October 2, 1921
Divorcons

Comedy in three acts, adapted by Margaret Mayo from the French of Victorien Sardou and Emile de Najac.

Frye's scrapbook indicates particular plaudits for his role of M. Adhemar de Gratignan. "Dwight Frye was delicious as Adhemar, the lover. He looked imposing in his uniform and foolish enough in his bedraggled evening clothes. He gave every line its touch of broad comedy." "Dwight Frye was the comedy hit of the drama. As the impetuous young French officer insanely in love with the wife (Hazel Whitmore) he kept the audience in constant twitters" (Frye's pre-Broadway scrapbook).

October 9, 1921
Merely Mary Ann

Comedy in four acts by Israel Zangwill.

In a tale set in an English boarding house, Frye was Lord Valentine Foxwell, "a gilded youth." A reviewer wrote, "Dwight Frye appears in the final scenes in an amusing comedy character" (Frye's pre-Broadway scrapbook).

October 16, 1921
Nightie Night

Farce in a prologue and three acts by Martha M. Stanley and Adelaide Matthews.

According to one Spokane critic, "Dwight Frye, as Phil Burton, Mrs. Moffat's brother, brings down potential disaster on the heads of all concerned when he innocently rents his sister's apartment to the itinerant widow (Hazel Whitmore)." Another said, "Dwight Frye has a sort of quiet-corner part, which he executes admirably" (Frye's pre-Broadway scrapbook).

Martha Stanley, the co-author of *Nightie Night*, would become a lifelong friend of the Frye family.

October 23, 1921
The Chorus Lady

Comedy in four acts by James Forbes.

"Dwight Frye doubles as a stable boy and a call boy for the chorus," noted a Spokane review (Frye's pre-Broadway scrapbook).

October 30, 1921
The Hottentot

Farce comedy in three acts by Victor Mapes and William Collier.

Emmett Vogan, who replaced Rodney Hildebrand as the Woodward Players' leading man in this show, received rave reviews. Frye played Alex Fairfax, the "horse enthusiastic" brother.

November 6, 1921
Scandal

Comedy in three acts by Cosmo Hamilton.

As Malcolm Fraser, a role he had already played at the Colonial, Frye did not receive his usual positive notices. A critic stated, "Dwight Frye is a bit cold and stiff as the mutual friend of the principals (Emmett Vogan and Hazel Whitmore)." (Frye's pre-Broadway scrapbook).

November 13, 1921
My Lady Friends

Farce in three acts by Emil Nyitray and Frank Mandel.

In this comedy adapted from the book *Oh, James* by May Edgington, Frye played the sulking Tom Trainor. One critic claimed, "Dwight Frye has a few stormy moments as the dejected suitor," while another reported "Laura Lee and Dwight Frye have a stormy love affair to finally "make up." (Frye's pre-Broadway scrapbook).

November 20, 1921
Not Tonight, Dearie

Farce. Playwright unknown.

This burlesque comedy was greeted by "rounds of laughter and applause" by Woodward audiences. Hazel Whitmore played an eloping young lady, "...with Dwight Frye as a charming and attentive young suitor." "Dwight Frye has a straight juvenile role and handles it neatly" (Frye's pre-Broadway scrapbook).

November 27, 1921
My Wife

Comedy in four acts by Michael Morton, from the French of Messrs. Gavault and Charvay.

Frye bounced back strongly, after a disappointing previous week. A Spokane writer claimed, "He is screamingly funny as the Hon. Gibson Gore and does some of his best acting of the season in the part" (Frye's pre-Broadway scrapbook).

December 4, 1921
Friendly Enemies
Comedy drama in three acts by Samuel Shipman and Aaron Hoffman.

Frye portrayed William Pfeifer, the soldier son of Karl Pfeifer (Emmett Vogan), in this story of German-Americans during World War I. A reviewer stated, "As the son, Dwight Frye has a manly, popular role, which he handles carefully." A second wrote, "Dwight Frye makes a fine soldier-officer type in smart uniform. He is a dashing, kissable hero, annexing all the kisses of the play and they are generally prolonged affairs for the most part" (Fryeís pre-Broadway scrapbook).

December 11, 1921
Kindling
Play in three acts by Charles Kenyon.

Playing Steve Bates, the offspring of an Irish washerwoman (Margaret Robinson), Frye again garnered strong reviews. One stated, "To Dwight Frye must go high personal honors for his role of the worthless son and Bowery crook" (Frye's pre-Broadway scrapbook).

December 18, 1921
Come Seven
Blackface comedy in three acts by Octavus Roy Cohen.

With the entire company playing in blackface, the Woodward Players "scored their biggest comedy hit of the season" with *Come Seven*. A reviewer wrote, "Dwight Frye, who really has the lead this week as Florian Slappey, the 'slick' Negro swell, also scores heavily in a specialty, singing 'Tucky Home' with numerous encores and playing the piano for Vogan. Frye has a sort of gingerbread finish and does fine work" (Frye's pre-Broadway scrapbook).

December 25, 1921
Three Live Ghosts
Comedy in three acts by Frederick Isham.

After the success of *Come Seven*, the Woodward Players were humbled by the poor critical reception for *Three Live Ghosts*. As Jimmie Gubbins, one of three British soldiers who have escaped from a German prison, Frye was found to be "listless" (Frye's pre-Broadway scrapbook).

January 1, 1922
The Love of Su Shong
Melodrama in a prologue, three acts and epilogue by Dewitt Newing.

Reprising his role of Song Sing from the Colonial Theatre production, Frye garnered accolades for his work in *The Love of Su Shong*. More than one critic drew comparisons between Frye's Oriental and that of Richard Barthelmess from D. W. Griffith's silent classic, *Broken Blossoms* (1919). "Particularly fine work is done by Dwight Frye as the young poetic Chinese lover, quite a Griffith type, and his work stands out this week with striking clearness." "Dwight Frye's portrayal of Song Sing, the lover of Su Shong, who gives up his life for his love, is one of the highlights of the play. Mr. Frye succeeds in embodying the true oriental atmosphere, and brings out the pathos of the part in a gripping manner." "Dwight Frye is a true Richard Barthelmess type this week and his characterization of Song Sing is another personal triumph for the juvenile." (all from Frye's pre-Broadway scrapbook)

January 8, 1922
Pot Luck
Comedy in three acts by Edward Childs Carpenter.

Frye had the juvenile role (name unknown) in this "rural crook play written as a comedy." A review related, "Dwight Frye begins as a handy 'kid' about the store, goes to the big town and returns in five months with a dinner jacket and a roll that would choke the proverbial horse" (Fryeís pre-Broadway scrapbook).

January 15, 1922
Billy
Comedy in three acts by George Cameron.

Again, Frye's part is uncertain, but Dwight was said to be "... genuinely amusing in his seasick scenes..." in this romance set on an ocean liner (Fryeís pre-Broadway scrapbook).

January 23, 1922
Apartment K-12
Farce in three acts by Lawrence Rising.

In this play, said to mix "bedroom farce" with "crook melodrama," a critic noted, "Dwight Frye rants divinely for the obvious reason that a man in his position doubtless would not" (Fryeís pre-Broadway scrapbook). Frye's exact role is unknown.

January 29, 1922
Moonlight and Honeysuckle
Comedy in three acts by George Scarborough.

Moonlight and Honeysuckle was found to be "brighter, cleverer and more wholesome than any offering at the Woodward theater in recent weeks." Frye's character is not known, but he was said to give "...his best efforts to an unsympathetic role and scores in its subtle speeches" (Frye's pre-Broadway scrapbook).

February 5, 1922
A Woman's Way
Comedy in three acts by Thompson Buchanan.

This play marked the Spokane farewell for Frye, Emmett Vogan and Hazel Whitmore. After the departure of these three Spokane favorites, the remainder of the 1921/22 season proved highly unsuccessful for O. D. Woodward and his company. Frye's role in *A Woman's Way* is not known.

1922 Woodward Theatre, Seattle, Washington

After performing with O. D. Woodward's company in Spokane, Washington for 24 weeks in 1921/22, Frye, along with Hazel Whitmore, left to form the core of a new company in Seattle, Washington. Woodward had leased Levy's Orpheum Theatre in Seattle and renamed in the Woodward Theatre. In addition to Frye and leading lady Whitmore, Woodward's Seattle company included: Leading man Alexis Luce (later to be Laura Frye's second husband and Dwight David Frye's stepfather after Dwight I. Frye's death), Ruth Saville, Arthur Allard, Babette Berneau, Erma Melville, William Wallace, Clinton Tustin, Jessie P. Mosier, Margaret Robinson, William Dills, William H. Bloom and Doreen O'Day.

Frye remained with the company for its entire eleven week season in Seattle, appearing in the following productions:

February 18, 1922
A Woman's Way
Comedy in three acts by Thompson Buchanan.
Frye's role is unknown.

February 26, 1922
The Rose of the Rancho
Play in three acts by David Belasco and Richard Walton Tully.
Frye played the lieutenant of the militia.

March 5, 1922
Scandal
Comedy in three acts by Cosmo Hamilton.
A Seattle critic wrote, "Dwight Frye is also good as Malcolm Fraser, Franklin's closest friend and Beatrix's fond admirer" (Frye's pre-Broadway scrapbook). Frye had previously played the same part in *Scandal* in both Pittsfield and Spokane.

March 12, 1922
The Marriage of William Ashe
Play in five acts by Margaret Mayo.
Frye played Eddie Helston and was said to furnish "continual amusement" (*The Seattle Union*).

March 19, 1922
Merely Mary Ann
Comedy in four acts by Israel Zangwill.
Frye portrayed Lord Foxwell, as he had in Spokane.

March 26, 1922
The Outrageous Mrs. Palmer
Comedy in four acts by Harry Wagstaff Gribble.
"Dwight Frye, in his first important role as Mrs. Palmer's son, proves worthy of the trust and he gained a high place in the estimation of yesterday's crowds," reported a Seattle newspaper (Frye's pre-Broadway scrapbook). Frye's character was Philip Michael Palmer.

April 2, 1922
Moonlight and Honeysuckle
Comedy in three acts by George Scarborough.
Although his part is uncertain, Frye had earlier done this play in Spokane.

April 9, 1922
My Wife

Comedy in four acts by Michael Morton, from the French of Messrs. Gavault and Charvay.

As the Honorable Gibson Gore, Frye recreated his Spokane success.

April 16, 1922
The Holy City

Play by Thomas W. Broadhurst.
Frye played Lazarus, who is raised from the dead.

April 23, 1922
The Hottentot

Farce comedy in three acts by Victor Mapes and William Collier.
Frye reprised another Spokane characterization as Alex Fairfax.

April 30, 1922
Stop Thief

Farce in three acts by Carlyle Moore.
Frye's role is unknown. Frye later acted with the playwright's son, Carlyle Moore, Jr., in Pauline Frederick's company in its 1933 cross country tour, performing *Her Majesty, the Widow* and *Amber*.

1922 Colonial Theatre, Pittsfield, Massachusetts

The composition of the 1922 Colonial Players was slightly different from the 1921 company. Bob McClung, William Melville, Marie Hodgkins and Albert Amend had moved to another Goldstein brother's troupe: The Victory Players of Holyoke, Massachusetts. Alfred Swenson was still the leading man, but Marguerite Fields had taken over for Ruth Amos as leading lady. Fields, however, lasted only four weeks in Pittsfield before being replaced by Edna Preston, a superior actress with a predominantly Canadian (Toronto, Montreal, Halifax) stock background. Eventually, Preston would enjoy a long performing career that included radio and television. Preston was prominent on Broadway in the 1950s (*Out West of Eighth*—9/20/51; *Tovarich*—5/14/52; *Mademoiselle Colombe*—1/6/54; *Fanny*—11/4/54), later appearing with the Lunts at the New York City Center in *The Visit* (3/8/60), shortly before Edna's death. According to Dwight David Frye, Ms. Preston remained good friends with his father, after their days at the Colonial, and eventually the rest of the Frye family, as well.

The character man for the 1922 Colonial Players was John "Jack" McCabe, who had served as a U.S. Army sergeant in the Philippines during the Spanish American War and later toured extensively with the legendary Otis Skinner. Phil Quin, the second man, was a member of Fritz Leiber's Shakespearean company both prior to and after his time at the Colonial Theatre. Barbara Bertrand, the ingenue, was, at a young age, already a veteran of the Blaney stock circuit (Brooklyn, Yorkville, Hoboken). Other members of the 1922 Colonial Players were: William H. Murdock, character woman Lorle Palmer, second woman Phyllis Gilmore, James B. Dean, Thomas Morrison, Harland Worley, Edward Averill, Ruth Conne, Ethel Downie and Arthur C. Morris, who also was the company stage manager. Carroll Daly and Willard Dashiell, the two directors, also appeared in some of their Colonial productions.

May 29, 1922
Cornered

Comedy drama in four acts by Dodson Mitchell.

As Nick Martin, in this play set in the Pekin Pleasure Palace, Hell's Kitchen, New York City, *The Berkshire Eagle* (5/30/22) reported that Frye "...came hurrying across the continent to be on hand for opening night. Dwight was the 'dope' of Dodson Mitchell's *Cornered*, the opening attraction, and in his every twist and turn and mannerism was the typical slave to the craving."

June 5, 1922
Three Wise Fools

Comedy in three acts by Austin Strong.

As Benjamin Suratt, aka "Benny the Duck," Frye was a convincing young crook in this comedy.

June 12, 1922
The Nightcap

Drama, with continuous action, by Guy Bolton and Max Marcin.
Frye played Fred Hammond.

June 19, 1922
Buddies

Musical comedy in two acts and an epilogue, with book by George V. Hobart and lyrics and music by B. C. Hilliam.

Set in Normandy just after the World War I armistice, *Buddies* was the first musical of the season for the 1922 Colonial Players. *Buddies* was the story of two doughboys: Sonny, who, though engaged to a girl in Brooklyn, agrees to protect Julie (Marguerite Fields) by posing as her husband; and Babe, enamored of Julie but too shy to tell her. A series of misunderstandings occur when Babe fails to understand Sonny's motive, and then Sonny's real fiancee (Phyllis Gilmore) arrives. Frye was originally slated to play Babe and Alfred Swenson, Sonny, but, because of Frye's more adept musical skills, the roles were switched during rehearsals. *The Berkshire Eagle* (6/20/22) claimed, "...Gilmore and Frye have a singing and dancing diversion that adds materially to the variety of the entertainment."

June 26, 1922
The Storm

Romantic melodrama in four acts by Langdon McCormack.

Frye was Maniteekwa, the Native American, in this play, set in the Pacific northwest and featuring a forest fire sequence using electrical effects from the New York production.

July 3, 1922
Twin Beds

Farce in three acts by Salisbury Fields and Margaret Mayo.

Twin Beds concerned the humorous difficulties faced by three couples in an apartment house. Frye was in good form as Andrew Larkin, a newlywed with a suspicious wife (Barbara Bertrand).

In response to the request of Mrs. John Hutton, Broadway producer Brock Pemberton took a train from New York City to Pittsfield to view Frye in *Twin Beds*, but missed the first act in which Dwight had his best scenes. Pemberton still saw enough to whet his interest, returning to the Colonial the following week to catch Frye in *The Broken Wing*.

July 10, 1922
The Broken Wing
Comedy in four acts by Paul Dickey and Charles W. Goddard.

In a tale concerning a flyer whose airplane crashes into the house of a Mexican girl, Frye portrayed American lawyer Sylvester Cross. *The Berkshire Eagle* (7/11/22) reported, "Dwight Frye affords many comedy touches in his rendering of the character of the oil operator."

July 17, 1922
Shavings
Drama in three acts by Pauline Phelps and Marion Short.

Shavings, based on Joseph C. Lincoln's story of Cape Cod life, included Frye as Leander Babbitt. Leander, the son of the village skinflint (William H. Murdock), falls in love with the daughter (Barbara Bertrand) of good-hearted Captain Hunniwell (Willard Dashiell).

July 24, 1922
The Net
Drama in three acts by Maravene Thompson.

Frye played artist John Royce, who tries to effect a reconciliation between his cousin Allayne (Edna Preston) and her brutish husband Bruce Norman (Phil Quin).

July 31, 1922
Nightie Night
Farce in a prologue and three acts by Martha M. Stanley and Adelaide Matthews.

Philip Burton (Frye), the brother-in-law of newlywed Billy Moffat (Alfred Swenson), causes chaos by inadvertently renting the apartment of his sister (Barbara Bertrand) to the widow Trixie Lorraine (Edna Preston), Billy's former lover.

August 7, 1922
The Little Millionaire
Musical comedy in three acts by George M. Cohan.

In the Colonial Players second musical of their 1922 stock season, Frye had the starring role of Robert Spooner, which Cohan himself had played on Broadway in 1906. Robert and his father Henry (John McCabe) are both obliged to be married in order to satisfy the conditions of the late Mrs. Spooner's will. Frye was the central figure in five musical numbers, three in the first act ("The Little Millionaire," "New Yorkers" and "The Old Flag") and two in the third act ("Wonderful Girl" and "Come to My Bungalow," the latter with Edna Preston). Frye sang "The Wedding," with McCabe, Preston, Phil Quin, Phyllis Gilmore and Lorle Palmer, and also appeared in the Finale.

August 14, 1922
The Love Bandit
Romantic drama in three acts by Charles E. Blaney and Norman Houston.

Set in the woods of Maine, *The Love Bandit* included Frye as Frederick Van Clayton, the gambling brother of Amy (Edna Preston), both descended from a formerly aristocratic family that has lost its fortune. To support his habit of playing the ponies, Frederick steals money belonging to lumber man Jim Blazes (Alfred Swenson), resulting in Amy offering to marry Jim to keep her brother out of prison.

After closing in *The Love Bandit* on August 18, 1922, Frye said his farewells to the Colonial Players, heading to New York to join producer Brock Pemberton, preparing for Dwight's Broadway debut. Of the thirteen offering of the 1922 Colonial stock season, *The Berkshire Eagle*

Dwight Frye's Last Laugh

(8/24/22, p. 4) noted, "*Slippy McGee* will also serve to introduce locally a new juvenile man, Harold Hutchinson, who replaces Dwight Frye."

1923 Colonial Theatre, Pittsfield, Massachusetts

After two successful stock seasons in 1921 and 1922 at the Colonial, directly leading to his Broadway debut, Frye, under the auspices of Brock Pemberton, hoped to show his gratitude to Pittsfield theatre patrons by this limited engagement. Pemberton gave special permission to produce *Rita Coventry*, which featured Frye's most significant Broadway performance as of that time. Pemberton even made a personal appearance at the Colonial during the run of *Rita Coventry*.

The 1923 Colonial Players included: Leading lady Ruth Amos (after a one year absence), new leading man Robert Hyman, Phil Quin, Jack McCabe, Bob McClung, Edith Bowers, Jane Manners, Glen Argoe and Frank Kitterick.

July 9, 1923
In Old Kentucky
Drama by Charles T. Dazey.

In the first play of his limited return engagement with the Colonial Players, Frye played the young moonshiner in this old stock staple, which featured a live horse race sequence on stage.

July 16, 1923
Rita Coventry
Comedy in three acts by Hubert Osborne.

Frye recreated his Broadway success as Patrick Delaney, the gifted young piano tuner and composer.

July 23, 1923
The Champion
Farce in three acts by A. E. Thomas and Thomas Louden.

Frye's final appearance during his 1923 engagement at the Colonial came in this boxing story, in which Grant Mitchell had starred on Broadway.

Dwight Frye and Katherine Alexander in *The Queen's Husband* (1928).

Dwight Frye's Last Laugh

Appendix C
Broadway Plays

The Plot Thickens

A comedy in three acts; Adapted by Thomas Beer, from the Italian *Quello Che Non T'Aspetti*, by Luigi Barzini and Arnaldo Fraccaroli; Produced by Brock Pemberton; Sets by Sheldon Viele and Ruby Ross Goodnow; Opened at the Booth Theatre, 222 W. 45th Street, September 5, 1922; Broadway run: 15 performances

CAST: Adonis Duckworth...Edwin Nicander; Joseph...Roy Cochrane; Olivetti...Jasper Mangione; Halliday...Fred House; Claudine Dupont...Miss Remy Carpen; Benjamin Playfair Jones...John Thorn; Bill...Albert Bannister; First Player...Russell Morrison; Second Player...Neil Quinlan; Third Player...John Saunders; Basil Fanshawe...Edward Lester; Mike Sheehan...Dallas Welford; **Mike Sheehan, Jr...Dwight Frye**; Grizzel McNab...Miss Janet Murdock; Police Commissioner... Joseph R. Mann; Dr. Maggs...John Amory

NOTES: Dwight Frye made his Broadway debut in this slapstick farce, of which critic Heywood Broun wrote:

> Fortunately, two exceedingly amusing characterizations serve to hold up the interest when the plot sickens. Dallas Welford is enormously amusing as a thief who carries on his business with the aid of a sedulously dutiful son... When young Sheehan breaks into a radical outburst against the fearfully high prices charged by profiteers his father rebukes him and remarks, "You've got to get over this habit of buying things." While this pair are engaged on another job the talk switches around to the future of the eldest Sheehan girl. The father wants her to get into the movies, but her brother thinks the chorus would be better on account of the bad reputation of Hollywood. The elder Sheehan almost drops the pearl necklace which he is filching, so much is he outraged by the remarks of the boy. He reminds him that "a girl who has been brought up in a good home will go straight anywhere." Dwight Frye plays the part of the younger Sheehan and gives Mr. Welford able assistance....

Frye proudly pasted notices of *The Plot Thickens* in his scrapbook. In a little over five years since he had made his stage debut in Denver, he was now a Broadway actor—and only 23 years old.

REVIEW

"...Dwight Frye, as the dutiful young robber, was delightfully true to character and he did a refreshingly clever bit of work..." —Charles Darnton, *The New York EveningWorld*

Six Characters in Search of An Author

Fantastic comedy in two acts by Luigi Pirandello; Translated from the Italian by Edward Storer; Produced and staged by Brock Pemberton; Settings by Cleon Throckmorton; Opened at the Princess Theatre, New York, on October 30, 1922; Broadway run: 137 performances

CAST: The Father...Moffat Johnston; The Mother...Margaret Wycherly; The Step-Daughter... Florence Eldridge; **The Son...Dwight Frye**; The Boy...Ashley Buck; The Little Girl...Constance Lusby; Madame Pace (Evoked)...Ida Fitzhugh; The Manager...Ernest Cossart; The Leading Man... Fred House; The Leading Lady...Eleanor Woodruff; The Juvenile...Elliot Cabot; The Ingenue... Kathleen Graham; The Character Woman...Maud Sinclair; The Third Actor...Jack Amory; The Fourth Actor...William T. Hays; The Third Actress...Leona Keefer; The Fourth Actress...Blanche Gervais; The Fifth Actress...Katherine Atkinson; The Stage Manager...Russell Morrison; The Property Man...John Saunders

NOTES: Luigi Pirandello (1867-1936), a major Italian dramatist, often played with the notion of the shifting boundary between illusion and reality. In *Six Characters in Search of An Author*, Pirandello mocks the medium of the theatre, citing its inadequacy for revealing the truth. Pirandello won the 1934 Nobel Prize for Literature and authored numerous plays, including *Sicilian Limes* (1910), *Each in His Own Way* (1924) and *Tonight We Improvise* (1930).

Frye received high critical acclaim for his portrayal of the Son in *Six Characters in Search of An Author*. The Son has nothing but contempt for the Father, who considers the young man a "cynical imbecile," while bemoaning his lack of affection upon the Son's return home. The Son begs the manager to "leave me out of it," as he relates the difficulty of having to adjust to a reunited family and three new half-siblings. Continuing to resist the idea of presenting the characters' story as a drama, the son exclaims:

> Yes, but haven't you yet perceived that it isn't pos-
> sible to live in front of a mirror which not only freezes
> us with the image of ourselves, but throws our likeness
> back at us with a horrible grimace?

The Son, the only legitimate child of the four, is indifferent toward the Mother and hostile to the Step-Daughter. The Father, however, bears the brunt of the Son's angry tirades:

> What does it mean, this madness you've got? Have
> you no decency, that you insist on showing everyone
> our shame? I won't do it! I won't! And I stand for the
> will of our author in this. He didn't want to put us on
> the stage, after all!

The Son, however, becomes the character that reveals how the two children died: The Little Girl by drowning and the Boy by a self-inflicted gunshot wound.

REVIEW

"Mr. Dwight Frye brought a convincing imaginative insight to the part of the son, whose life had been outraged by the contrast between his idea of parents, and his actual instance of them, and whose place in the whole situation was violently against his will and at the same time an inner necessity. Mr. Frye is a beginner with something very much beyond what the New York stage expects of its young men; he has talent and intelligence; though he should get his r's rightly placed—his "father" and "mirror" and "horror" come off with great travail so far—he should work on his English as Miss Woodruff must have done, whose whole tone and accent is better than last year." — Stark Young, *New Republic*

Rita Coventry

Comedy in three acts by Hubert Osborne, from the novel by Julian Street; Produced and staged by Brock Pemberton; Sets by Sheldon K. Viele; Incidental Music by Deems Taylor; Opened at the Bijou Theatre, New York, on February 19, 1923; Broadway run: 24 performances

CAST: Pierre, a footman at Coventry's...Hans Herbert; Mrs. Fernis, Coventry's companion...Grace Filkins; Larry Merrick, a young idler...Edward H. Wever; Busini, conductor at the opera...Luis Alberni; Paldowski, a famous pianist...G. Albert Smith; Eleanor, his American wife...Leopoldine Damrosch; Herman Krauss, a banker and patron of art...Eugene Powers; Rita Coventry...Dorothy Francis; Richard Parrish, a Wall Street broker...Charles Francis; Louis, a waiter at the Ritz... Auguste Aramini; Wetherall, assistant manager at the Ritz...Corbet Morris; **Patrick Delaney, a piano tuner...Dwight Frye**; Miss McSweeney, of Maison Beupre...Clare Weldon; Maggie, a delivery girl...Harriette Frazier; Johnson, press representative of the Ritz...Jay Fassett; Wolff, of the Associated Press...Curtis Karpe

NOTES: Prior to opening on Broadway, Brock Pemberton gave *Rita Coventry* an out-of-town tryout. *Rita Coventry* played Bristol, Connecticut, on January 30, 1923, and the Beechwood Theater, Scarborough-on-Hudson, February 1-3, 1923.

Dorothy Francis, the star of *Rita Coventry*, had been a member of the Chicago Opera Company before turning to the theatre. She had been seen in a revival of *The Merry Widow* (1921) and later appeared on Broadway in *The Love Song* (1925), *The Climax* (1926), *Criss Cross* (1926) and *Eye on the Sparrow* (1938). During the run of *Rita Coventry*, Francis sang two of Deems Taylor's compositions for the show on the radio. Frye accompanied Dorothy on piano for "Bonnie Doon" on that broadcast.

Luis Alberni (1887-1962), perhaps the most recognizable name in the cast of *Rita Coventry*, was a colorful and busy motion picture character actor in addition to his theatre work in *39 East* (1919), *The Checkerboard* (1920) and *What Price Glory?* (1924). The Spanish-born Alberni's film career began in the silent era with *Little Italy* (1921) and *The Man from Beyond* (1921), starring Harry Houdini. He appeared in numerous sound films, including *Svengali* (1931, as Gecko), *The Mad Genius* (1931), *The Sphinx* (1933), *The Black Cat* (1934), *Anthony Adverse* (1936), *A Bell for Adano* (1945) and *The Ten Commandments* (1956).

In Act II of *Rita Coventry*, set at the Ritz Hotel in Atlantic City, New Jersey, a piano tuner is dispatched to the suite of Rita Coventry (Dorothy Francis), the noted soprano. Patrick Delaney (Dwight Frye), the poorly dressed piano tuner, is soon revealed to be a gifted composer, as he tries out his works on her piano, playing "haunting phrases, marvelously executed." This undiscovered genius exhibits a "delightful touch of condescension... to all the arrived masters" (Heywood Broun), confident his talents are the equal of anyone. Delaney, not awed by Coventry's presence or reputation, is quick to point out defects in the soprano's vocal range. The opinionated young Irish American's major concern is that his mother (who was an O'Flannigan) might not keep supper waiting for him. Rita is impressed by both his creative ability and honesty, as she abandons her current lover (Charles Francis) and determines to make Delaney a major figure in the music world.

By the final act, Rita has already taken some of Delaney's compositions and had them published. As a result of residuals from sheet music and phonograph recordings, Patrick is sporting a new suit and money in his pocket. Rita decides, however, that this is just the beginning and arranges for Delaney to journey with her to Europe by steamer to further his musical education and development. Delaney counters that his mother would not approve of his traveling with

Rita under the present circumstances. "We can't go on merely keeping company," the innocent Patrick concludes. So, with three of Rita's former lovers still lingering, it appears Delaney is to be wed to Coventry, or, as one critic noted (from Frye's Broadway scrapbook), "...sacrificed to the vagaries of an egotistical and whimsical prima donna."

REVIEWS
"Dwight Frye gives an uncommonly good performance as Delaney, especially in his quiet, matter-of-fact suggestion of the piano tuner's aggressive honesty."—Charles Darnton, *New York World*

"Mr. Frye has a droll sense of humor and the knack of getting it over the footlights. He plays with a serious face, so that when he smiles his face lights up in a burst of luminosity that compels a response in like manner from the audience. Mr. Frye registered a solid hit and was the particular bright spot in the evening's entertainment."—Gordon Whyte

"Mr. Pemberton has gone off on another tack in casting the role of Delaney. It is probable that Dwight Frye, to whom the part falls, has never tuned a piano in his life, but he is an excellent actor which serves the purposes of the play much better. Indeed his performance is one to be underlined in red. It is delightful work in a most unusual role and brings out every value of the play."—Heywood Broun

The Love Habit
Farce in three acts from the French of Louis Verneuil; adapted by Gladys Unger; Produced and staged by Brock Pemberton; Sets by Ruby Ross Goodnow; Opened at the Bijou Theatre, New York, on March 14, 1923; Broadway run: 69 performances

CAST: The Young Man...James Rennie; Marie...Mary Kennedy; Nadine Morand...Florence Eldridge; Gustave Morand...Ernest Cossart; Rosette Pompon...Fania Marinoff; **Max Duvelleroy... Dwight Frye**

NOTES: Ernest Cossart and Florence Eldridge had both appeared with Frye earlier in the 1922/23 theatrical season in *Six Characters in Search of An Author*. James Rennie (1889-1965), the Young Man in *The Love Habit*, also was a veteran of stage and screen. Rennie appeared in *Wilson* (1944), which would have reunited him with Frye had Dwight lived to appear in it.

Toward the end of the run of *The Love Habit*, the show moved from the Bijou to the Princess Theatre, with two important cast changes. Frye, who had already played four different parts in 1922/23, replaced James Rennie as the Young Man, marking his fifth role of the season. Mary Kennedy took over for Florence Eldridge as Nadine Morand. Frye and Kennedy's characters were, in turn, assumed by G. Albert Smith (who had played Paldowski in *Rita Coventry*) and Julia McMahon.

REVIEWS
"At that moment of Dwight Frye's entrance in a role rather unimportant of itself, the piece took on an irresistible interest because, even though he soon departed, you knew he might enter again at any moment and illuminate the proceedings. We doubt if even the Moscow artists could do anything quite like the expression on his face when someone asked him if the letter he had seen—from Rosette to Morand—might cause trouble."—Julia West

"Dwight Frye gave another of his remarkably fine interpretations of a small bit."—James Craig.

"Once again Dwight Frye deserves honorable mention. He is cast for a character part which, even for farce, seems somewhat incredible, only his sound acting making it credible and unique."—*The Baa-Lamb*

Six Characters in Search of An Actor
(revival)

Revival of the play by Luigi Pirandello; Presented and staged by Brock Pemberton; Opened at the Forty-fourth Street Theater, New York, on February 6, 1924; Broadway Run: 17 performances

CAST: The Father...Moffat Johnston; The Mother...Margaret Wycherly; The Step-Daughter... Florence Eldridge; **The Son...Dwight Frye**; The Boy...Knox Kincaid; The Little Girl...Mildred Lusby; Madame Pace (Evoked)...Ida Fitzhugh; The Manager...Ernest Cossart; The Leading Man... Fred House; The Leading Lady...Ethel Jones; The Juvenile...Borden Harriman; The Ingenue... Kathleen Graham; The Character Woman...Maud Sinclair; The Third Actor...Jack Amory; The Fourth Actor...William T. Hays; The Third Actress...Leona Keefer; The Fourth Actress...Blanche Gervais; The Fifth Actress...Katherine Atkinson; The Stage Manager...Russell Morrison; The Property Man...John Saunders

NOTES: After the revival of *Six Characters in Search of An Author* opened at the 44th Street Theater in early February 1924, producer Brock Pemberton quickly assessed that a smaller house would better suit the play. Pemberton moved *Six Characters...* to the 299-seat Punch & Judy Theatre on 49th Street, where the revival would complete its run.

An uncredited clipping in Frye's Broadway scrapbook indicates that he only played The Son in the revival of *Six Characters in Search of An Author* for the two matinee performances each week. An unknown actor assumed the role for all the evening shows.

While backstage at the Punch & Judy Theatre, Frye mused about his part of The Son:

> I have almost returned to thinking parts in this, haven't I? The Son speaks only a couple of times. So, to even things up, I am contemplating a travesty where each of the six characters may do what he is never allowed to do in the play. The Son shall talk all the time and refuse to shut up. I shall constantly be interrupted by The Mother, and The Boy and The Girl shall cry loudly all the time. The Step-Daughter and The Father, who now never give any one else a chance to speak, shall be silenced for at least one performance. We should like to do one for the screen and have it made up of well known characters like "The Old Mother," "The Man," "The Pure Girl," "The Villain," etc. (Frye's Broadway scrapbook)

Shaking his head at the interviewer, Frye concluded that the public "...wouldn't get it."

So adept was Frye's interpretation of The Son in the two productions of *Six Characters in Search of An Author*, that it "...aroused in Pirandello himself, when he saw it, the greatest satisfaction and admiration"—Stark Young, *The New York Times*, 3/22/25.

Sitting Pretty

Musical comedy in two acts; Book by Guy Bolton, lyrics by P. G. Wodehouse and music by Jerome Kern; Produced by F. Ray Comstock and Morris Gest; Staged by Fred G. Latham and Julian Alfred; Choreography by Larry Ceballos; Musical director, Max Steiner; Orchestration by Robert Russell Bennett; Opened at the Fulton Theatre, New York, on April 8, 1924; Broadway run: 95 performances

CAST: Mrs. Wagstaff...Marjorie Eggleston; James...Albert Wyart; Roper...Harry Lilford; "Bill" Pennington...Rudolph Cameron; Judson Waters...Eugene Revere; Babe LaMarr...Myra Hampton; May Tolliver...Gertrude Bryan; Dixie...Queenie Smith; Jasper...Edward Finley; Wilhelmina... Jayne Chesney; Otis...George Sylvester; Wilhelmina...Marian Dickson; Mr. Pennington...George E. Mack; **Horace...Dwight Frye**; Joe...Frank McIntyre; Professor Appleby...George Spelvin; Bolt...George O'Donnell; Jane...Terry Blaine; Characters at the Ball: Jenny Lind...Wynthrope Wayne; Edgar Allan Poe...George Sylvester; Barbara Frietchie...Mariettea O'Brien; Stonewall Jackson...Edward Finley; Rachel...Marjorie Eggleston; Harriet Beecher Stowe...Frieda Fitzgerald; Louisa M. Alcott...May Clark; George Sand...Charlotte Wakefield; Florence Nightingale...Jayne Chesney; Empress Eugenie...Dorothy Janice

NOTES: Guy Bolton and P. G. Wodehouse had originally planned *Sitting Pretty* as a collaborative effort with Irving Berlin and a vehicle for the Duncan Sisters. When the Duncans became unavailable due to their stage success in *Topsy and Eva*, Berlin bowed out of the project. Jerome Kern, who had worked with Bolton and Wodehouse in previous musicals at the Princess Theatre, agreed to compose the music for *Sitting Pretty*.

Producers F. Ray Comstock and Morris Gest elected to premiere *Sitting Pretty* at Detroit's Shubert Theatre on March 23, 1924. Bolton, Wodehouse and Kern continued to fine tune the show, which moved on to Buffalo, New York, at the end of March. Two of Dwight Frye's numbers, "A Romantic Man" and "Ladies are Present" (Horace, with Bill and Dixie), were cut. The show's title song, "Sitting Pretty," sung by Horace (Frye) and Dixie (Queenie Smith), was surprisingly eliminated before the Broadway opening.

With six songs removed in all, the truncated *Sitting Pretty* arrived at the Fulton Theatre on April 8, 1924. Despite receiving decent reviews, the show, lasting 95 performances, was the only Bolton-Wodehouse-Kern collaboration not to run for at least an entire season.

Although Dwight Frye's appearance in a musical may have seemed a novelty to Broadway patrons and critics, theatergoers in Spokane and Pittsfield could testify that he was already well-versed in song and dance. As Horace Peabody, an uncouth young man from "the north side of Delancy Street," Frye is adopted by millionaire Mr. Pennington (George E. Mack), who has disinherited his actual relatives. In the first act, Frye's two main musical numbers were "Bongo on the Congo" sung by Horace, Uncle Joe and Judson Waters and "Mr. and Mrs. Roper," a duet with Dixie (Queenie Smith); in the second act, Frye joined Frank McIntyre in the show-stopping "Dear Old Fashioned Prison of Mine."

REVIEWS
"Dwight Frye, snatched from the legitimate stage, gives an unusual and delightful performance." — Heywood Broun
"... and there is the wide-eyed and astonishing Dwight Frye, late of Mr. Pemberton's sundry ventures." — Alexander Woollcott, *The Sun*

REVIVAL
In 1982, a trunk of Jerome Kern-related material, including the score for *Sitting Pretty*, was discovered at the Warner Brothers warehouse in Secaucus, New Jersey. Reassembling the musical from the source material, John McGlinn conducted a concert revival of *Sitting Pretty*, with five performances at the Weill Recital Hall at Carnegie Hall, April 13-16, 1989. Jason Graae, who sang the part of Horace in this revival, is a personal friend of Dwight David Frye. Other members of the concert cast included: Davis Gaines (Bill), Paige O'Hara (May), Kim Criswell (Dixie), Robert Nichols (Uncle Joe) and Richard Woods (Mr. Pennington).

New World Records released a CD (80387-2) of *Sitting Pretty* in 1990, providing theatre aficionados the opportunity to experience the score of this virtually forgotten musical.

So This is Politics (Strange Bedfellows)

Comedy in three acts by Barry Conners; Presented by Carl Reed; Staged by Henry Miller; Opened at the Henry Miller Theatre, New York, on June 16, 1924; Broadway run: 144 performances

CAST: **Willie Marsden...Dwight Frye**; Nina Buckmaster...Marjorie Gateson; Mrs. Cliff Collender...Lolita Robertson; Mrs. Lucretia Aswell...Florence Earle; Mrs. Amos Woodruff...Marion Dyer; Elizabeth Moore Madison...Alice Fleming; Mr. McKenna...William Courtleigh; John Buckmaster...Glenn Anders; Brooks Caldwell...John S. Morrissey

NOTES: On tour, prior to coming to Broadway, *So This is Politics* was called *The Clean-Up.* After two weeks at the Henry Miller Theatre, Miller, the director, and playwright Barry Conners decided on yet another name change, retitling the play *Strange Bedfellows.*

In *So This is Politics/Strange Bedfellows*, Frye played Willie Marsden, Nina's long-suffering, disagreeable brother, who helps about the house, works as a bank clerk and teaches Sunday school. During New York rehearsals, Frye astounded theatre legend Henry Miller, who staged the play, by requesting that his part of 38 sides be cut to 18 sides. According to the article, "Dwight Frye is a Specialist in Negative Roles" (*New York Herald Tribune*, 2/6/27):

> Mr. Frye complained that he was constantly popping on and off the stage and that he felt like a jack-in-the-box, instead of the character intended. He was talking so much that he had no chance to act. Needless to say, his unusual request was granted, and the part of the stubborn, unpleasant brother who disagreed with everything and everybody, became one of the memorable funny characters of the season, although there was not one really laughable line in the role.

REVIEWS

"Dwight Frye got some amusement out of the part of a weakling brother who taught Sunday school."—Leo A. Marsh

"Mr. Dwight Frye strives breathlessly to be noticeable in a minor role."—Percy Hammond, *New York Herald Tribune*

"Dwight Frye is generously amusing, as a character that our playwrights have cliched out of all resemblance to humanity."—*The New York Times*

Puppets

A play in three acts, by Frances Lightner; Produced by Brock Pemberton; Opened at the Selwyn Theatre, New York, March 9, 1925; Broadway run: 57 performances

CAST: Sandro Rubini, Nicki's assistant...Ralph J. Locke; Bruno Monte, Nicki's cousin...Fredric March; Rosa, wardrobe mistress...Michelette Burani; Joe Moretti, puppeteer...Frank McDonald; Mike, puppeteer...Remo Bufano; Luigi, puppeteer...Ascanio Spolidoro; Bianca, puppeteer...Florence Koehler; **Frank Mohacz, a piano player...Dwight Frye**; Nicola Riccobini, "Nicki"...C. Henry Gordon; Mamie O'Brien...Elizabeth Taylor; Angela Smith...Miriam Hopkins; A Messenger...Stanley Grand; McSweeney...Charles D. Brown; "Turkey" Abdullah...Alexis M. Polianov

NOTES: *Puppets* reached Broadway after two out-of-town tryouts. *The Marionette Man* had played Washington, D. C. and Stamford Connecticut in January of 1924; Claudette Colbert had been the original Angela, and Dwight had played Bruno. Just prior to its New York opening, the play (with the Broadway cast) played Providence, Rhode Island and New Haven, Connecticut under the title *The Knife in the Wall*. The old title referred to a dramatic (and phallic) bit of business in *Puppets*: Nicki stabbed a knife into a wall to remind Bruno that Angela was his wife—and not to be tempted while Nicki went off to war.

The actor who truly stole the spotlight in *Puppets*—an incredible feat, considering the presence of Fredric March (1897-1975) and Miriam Hopkins (1902-1972)—was Dwight. As Frank, the puppet show's evil pianist, luring young ladies into white slavery, lusting after the waif-like Hopkins, Dwight (as critic Charles A. Collins wrote) "takes everything in sight." The juicy role allowed him to show off his piano-playing talent, but it was his incredibly intense villainy that gave Broadway playgoers nightmares that season and won him critical raves as a brilliant young character actor.

Dwight reprised his performance as Frank at Chicago's La Salle Theatre in the spring of 1925. It was his final show for producer Brock Pemberton, and a personal triumph that led directly to full Broadway stardom in *A Man's Man* come the fall of 1925.

REVIEW
"Some day this young man is going to appear in a play worthy of his talent, and the resulting vibration will be felt west of Denver."—Charles A. Collins

FILM VERSION
Puppets: First National, 1926; Director: George Archainbaud; Screenplay: John F. Goodrich; CAST: Milton Sills (Nicki); Gertrude Olmstead (Angela); Francis McDonald (Bruno); Mathilde Comont (Rosa); Lucien Prival (Frank); William Ricciardi (Sandro); Nick Thompson (Joe)

A Man's Man
Comedy in three acts by Patrick Kearney; Produced by the Stagers; Staged by Edward Goodman; Setting by Cleon Throckmorton; Opened at the 52nd Street Theatre, New York, on October 13, 1925; Broadway run: 120 performances

CAST: Ma Tuttle...Margaret Love; Edie Tuttle...Josephine Hutchinson; Hazel Williams...Rita Romilly; **Melville Tuttle...Dwight Frye**; S. Barrett Blackstone...Arthur Hughes; Charlie Groff... Robert Gleckler; Mabel Plant...Olga Brent; Joe Plant...Jean Worth; Marjorie Tuttle...Marienne Francks; Herb Brown...Jerry Lynch; Eddie Eckles...Clarke Billings

NOTES: Subtitled "A comedy of life under the 'el'," *A Man's Man* was written by Patrick Kearney (1895-1933), who also dramatized Theodore Dreiser's *An American Tragedy* (1926) and Sinclair Lewis' *Elmer Gantry* (1928). Kearney co-authored *Old Man Murphy* (1931) with Harry Wagstaffe Gribble, and contributed to the screenplays for *Darkened Rooms* (1929) and *Fast Company* (1929). He also worked on Jules J. Leventhal's 1931 revival of *A Man's Man*, retitled *A Regular Guy*, with Glenn Hunter as Mel and Charlotte Wynters as Edie.

A Man's Man was the first production of the Stagers' second subscription season. After seven weeks at the 52nd Street Theatre, *A Man's Man* moved to the 49th Street Theatre. From there, the show moved to the Provincetown Playhouse in Greenwich Village, where Pat O'Brien (1899-1983) replaced Robert Gleckler (1890-1939) as the villain, Charlie Groff. In his autobiography, *The Wind at My Back*, O'Brien recalled, "I got through the play with no major disaster because Josephine Hutchinson and Dwight Frye were two firm supports in bringing me through my performance" (p. 70).

Shortly after the opening of *A Man's Man*, Frye was interviewed during a radio broadcast on WGBS (316 meters), a ten minute spot at 3:20 PM (exact date unknown). In a separate magazine interview, Frye commented on the play:

> If *A Man's Man* is a success, it is because it is human. The people in it are humble to the point of futility, but they are real, and the audiences seem to care about them—almost love them. For a play to be interesting, brilliant or diverting, is not enough. The audiences must care and there must be a glow or warmth on the stage, radiated by beings who succeed in being "just folks." Our audiences seem largely composed of people whose struggles we are depicting in the play. Fashionable audiences are curious about us, but we seem to hit hardest the people who vibrate in our play. It is the problem and nearness of Life that is convulsing people today and on the stage you had better give them something which they know intimately and feel poignantly. (Frye's Broadway Scrapbook)

REVIEWS

"As Mel Tuttle, the best part he has ever had, Dwight Frye gave a brilliant performance."—Stephen Rathbun, *The Sun*

"*A Man's Man*' was generally satisfactorily acted. Dwight Frye is an intelligent young man, and though I thought he fell down a bit when he heard of his wife's fall from grace, his work was good."—Alan Dale

FILM VERSION

A Man's Man; MGM, 1929; Director: James Cruze; Screenplay: Forrest Halsey; CAST: William Haines (Mel); Josephine Dunn (Peggy); Sam Hardy (Charlie); Mae Busch (Violet); Gloria Davenport; John Gilbert (himself); Greta Garbo (herself)

The film adaptation of *A Man's Man* took several liberties with Patrick Kearney's play. Peggy (rather than Edie) travels to Hollywood in the hope of breaking into films. She marries Mel, an affable but gullible soda jerk. Charlie, a discredited assistant director, makes a play for Peggy, promising her stardom, and sells Mel some worthless oil stock. After Charlie's true nature is discovered, Mel thrashes him in a fight and reconciles with Peggy.

The Goat Song

Play in five acts by Franz Werfel; Translated by Ruth Langner; Produced by the Theatre Guild; Staged by Jacob Ben-Ami; Sets and costumes by Lee Simonson; Opened at the Guild Theatre, New York, on January 25, 1926; Broadway run: 58 performances

CAST: Gospodar Stevan Milic...George Gaul; Gospodar Jevrem Vesilic...William Ingersoll; Mirko's Mother...Blanche Yurka; Stanja's Mother...Judith Lowry; Stanja...Lynn Fontanne; **Mirko...Dwight Frye**; Babka...Helen Westley; A Maid...Lorna McLean; Young Serving Man... Philip Loeb; Physician...Albert Bruning; Messenger...Bela Blau; Starsina...Erskine Sanford; Elder of Krasnokraj...Stanley G. Wood; Elder of Modrygor...Philip Loeb; Elder of Medejya...Anthony Andre; Clerk...Harold Clurman; The American...Edward Fielding; Teiterlik...Herbert Yost; Reb Feiwel...Edward G. Robinson; Bogoboj...Frank Reicher; Kruna...Zita Johann; Juvan...Alfred

Lunt; An Old Man...Anthony Andre; Innkeeper...Martin Wolfson; Priest...Erskine Sanford; Bashi Bazook...House Baker Jameson; The Hangman...William Ingersoll

NOTES: Franz Werfel (1898-1945), the Czech-born Austrian writer, captured the minds of European theatregoers with his *Bockgesang*, which the Theatre Guild presented in translated form as *The Goat Song*. The author of other plays, like *Juarez and Maximilian* (1925), *The Eternal Road* (1935) and *Jacobowsky and the Colonel* (1944), Werfel is perhaps best known for his novels, *The Forty Days of Musa Dagh* (1933) and *The Song of Bernadette* (1941).

Frye had a challenging role in Mirko, the timid son of Stevan Milic (George Gaul) and his wife (Blanche Yurka), who is not attuned to the social upheaval all around him. When Mirko's betrothed, Stanja (Lynn Fontanne), arrives, he questions her about past loves. Stanja, on the other hand, interrogates Mirko about the smokehouse, forcing him to consider a matter he has blocked out of consciousness for twenty years. Mirko relates:

> I do not know. Ever since I was a little child that was
> the forbidden place that we hurried by in fear, with
> downcast eyes.

Stanja and Mirko later confront the vagabonds, prompting criticism from young Milic: "They own nothing, they are dirty, they do not go to communion." At an inn, the couple meets Juvan (Alfred Lunt), with whom Mirko drinks. Juvan's attention to Stanja evokes Mirko's rage, challenging the student leader to a knife fight, which doesn't materialize.

Later, after learning that the monster is actually his brother, Mirko also realizes Stanja loves Juvan. He laments:

> For the second time we must flee from him, Stanja. The
> student is stronger than we. And... we bring no happiness
> for each other... I shall die without you... I release you.

Mirko takes half of a broken cross and hurls himself at Juvan. Instead, he lands on the outstretched blade of a guard, is impaled and dies.

REVIEWS

"Lynn Fontanne and Dwight Frye are well cast as the betrothed couple, Stanja and Mirko. That quality of buried treasure in Dwight Frye's voice of dreams unrealized, fits well into the part of Mirko, the boy who had lived in cloistered innocence." — Windsor P. Daggett, *The Spoken Word*

"In the part of that flabby-willed husband, Dwight Frye accents well the congenital weakness." — J. Brooks Atkinson, *The New York Times*

The Chief Thing

Comedy-drama in three acts by Nikolai Evreinov; Produced by the Theatre Guild; Staged by Philip Moeller; Sets and costumes by Serge Soudeikine; Opened at the Guild Theatre, New York, on March 22, 1926; Broadway run: 40 performances

CAST: Paraklete...McKay Morris; Lady With the Dog...Edith Meiser; Retired Government Clerk...Henry Travers; A Dancer...Estelle Winwood; An Actor Who Plays the Lover...C. Stafford Dickens; Landlady in a Rooming House...Alice Belmore Cliffe; Her Daughter...Esther Mitchell; **A Student...Dwight Frye**; The Manager of a Provincial Theatre...Stanley G. Wood;

A Stage Director...Edward G. Robinson; Electrician...William Griffith; Nero...Harold Clurman; Petronius...Romney Brent; Tigelin...Donald Angus; Lucian...House Baker Jameson; Popea Sabina...Peggy Conway; Ligia...Kate Lawson; Calvia Crispinilla...Mary True; Nigidia...Hildegard Holliday; A Prompter...Lee Strasberg; A Slave...Willard Tobias; A Comedian...Ernest Cossart; A School Teacher...Helen Westley; A Fallen Woman...Patricia Barron; A Deaf Mute...Hildegard Holliday; Masked Actors, and Actresses, Boarders and Guests: Wandeen Dole, Patricia Barron, Dorethea Chard, Serena Bari, Nora Krechun, Madeleine Galbraith, Margaret Harmon, Margaret Ellis, Edith Meiser, Kate Lawson, Mary True, H. Gordon Graham, James Norris, Willard Tobias, William S. Johnston, Harold Conklin, Henry Geiger, Harold Clurman, Lee Strasberg, Romney Brent, House Baker Jameson, Donald Angus

NOTES: Nikolai Evreinov (1879-1953), the author of *The Chief Thing*, was one of the innovators of the golden age of Russian theatre. *The Chief Thing* was first produced in Russia in 1921, with its American premiere in Yiddish at the Irving Place Theatre in 1923, featuring Muni Weisenfreund (Paul Muni) in the lead. The Theatre Guild version was from the translation of Evreinov by Herman Bernstein and Leo Randole.

As Fedya, the Student, Frye is first on stage in *The Chief Thing* accompanying his landlady (Alice Belmore Cliffe) and her daughter (Esther Mitchell) to see Paraklete (McKay Morris), who is in the guise of a fortuneteller. Almost stuttering, the student rebuffs the fortuneteller:

> No ...if you please. I only came to escort them to your
> chamber of horrors. That's all I intend to do.

Fedya's father (Henry Travers), a retired government clerk, has already established that his son tried to hang himself, failing because the hook did not hold the rope. The young man is carelessly dressed and nearsighted, with a shaggy mop of hair.

Back at the rooming house, the student sympathetically interacts with the new servant, Aniuta (Estelle Winwood), actually the dancer assigned to him by Paraklete. Fedya tells her he finds life "...not only sad, but unendurable," beginning to tell the dancer the truth about his brother, Volodya, but stops short of revelation. When the intrusive school teacher (Helen Westley) challenges Fedya about his suicide attempt, he defends himself with examples of famous people who have taken their own lives.

In the final act, Fedya's spirits are greatly improved and he again is playing chess with his father. He tells Aniuta that she inspired him to go to the office from which his father was discharged, where Fedya told off and knocked down the responsible official.

Fedya tells Aniuta that he has spent the last year shielding his father from news of his brother's death at sea. The student went so far as to fabricate letters, fearing his father would die if he knew the truth. The pressure led to his own suicide attempt. Later, Fedya finds great irony in the school teacher's botched suicide effort by swallowing "...a whole bottle of opium." "She used to laugh at me," Fedya muses, "and yet she followed my example." Nonetheless, Fedya helps nurse the teacher "...back to life," then participates in the harlequinade.

REVIEWS

"...the melancholy young student, played feelingly by Dwight Frye." — Gordon M. Leland

"...and Dwight Frye as the glum youth who worshipped at her (Estelle Winwood's) soiled though dimpled kneecaps." — Percy Hammond, *New York Herald Tribune*

"The cast includes such stalwarts as Ernest Cossart, Estelle Winwood, Edward G. Robinson, Esther Mitchell and Dwight Frye, who give such an excellent account of themselves with a versatility which ranges all the way from barefoot dances and minuets to hurling themselves bodily off the stage." — Frank Vreeland

The Devil in the Cheese

A comedy in three acts; Written by Tom Cushing; Staged and produced by Charles Hopkins; Sets by Norman Bel-Geddes; Opened at the Charles Hopkins Theatre, 153 West 49th Street, New York City, December 29, 1926; Broadway run: 165 performances

CAST: Jimmie Chard...Fredric March; **Dr. Pointell Jones...Dwight Frye**; Mr. Quigley...Robert McWade; Mrs. Quigley...Catherine Calhoun Doucet; Goldina Quigley...Linda Watkins; Chubbock...George Riddell; Father Petros...Bela Lugosi; Constantinos...Earl McDonald; Min...Brandon Peters; Some men friends, girl friends, monks, shepherds, a few cannibals, constituents, servants and a gorilla...Hassell Brooks, Fred Curtis, Gregory Deans, Joseph Downing, Betty Lee Carter, Zaidee de Becker, Louis Summers, Richard Perry, Archie Sayer, Robert Daggett, William Ramage, Joseph Hazel, Herbert Ellis, William Jones, Edmund Ray, Donald Lashley, Miriam Seeger, Alyne Szold, John Hilliard, Hooper Bunch

NOTES: *The Devil in the Cheese* had three-fold importance for Dwight Frye: it was one of his longest-running Broadway hits (165 performances), provided him with one of his most vivid comic characters—and put him onstage with future *Dracula* star, Bela Lugosi.

A clipping in Dwight's theatre scrapbook reports that he worked with the playwright in developing the role of Dr. Pointell Jones:

> I have a deep respect for the author and his words. He knows better than I do what he wants. But sometimes, when I start rehearsing a part, I find some lines that would belong more to the character if they were switched around a little. Mr. Cushing worked with me in twisting Dr. Pointell Jones' phrases to make them more and more indefinite until we now have him floundering beautifully in his speeches, until now I feel able to act the negative role confidently and positively.

For the future Dracula and Renfield of Hollywood, *The Devil in the Cheese* had been a very rewarding success.

REVIEW

"...an ingenious and unique combination of love tale, angry-father story, bedtime story, tale of adventure with brigands and an account of an eleventh-hour rescue... There are also Bela Longosi (sic) for the bandit chief and Dwight Frye for the doctor..." —E. W. Osborn

Ink

Satirical melodrama in three acts by Dana Watterson Greeley; Presented by Charles L. Wagner; Staged by T. Daniel Frawley; Sets by Albert Bliss; Opened at the Biltmore Theatre, New York, on November 1, 1927; Broadway run: 15 performances

CAST: Hester Trevelyan...Clara Blandick; Hal Somerset...Robert Hyman; Jack Davis...John H. Dilson; Franklin W. Jerome...Charles Richman; **Clarence Jerome...Dwight Frye**; Henrietta Scott...Clare Woodbury; Robert Buchanan...William Harrigan; Mrs. Jerome...Eleanor Woodruff; Jim Reynolds...Brandon Evans; "Bull" Taggart...Leo Kennedy; Jeanne Keenan...Kay Strozzi; Office Boy...Carlyle Moore

NOTES: *Ink* was actually written by William J. McNally, who derived the nom de plume of Dana Watterson Greeley from three major figures of journalism: Charles Dana, Henry Watterson and Horace Greeley.

Before opening on Broadway, *Ink* received out-of-town try-outs at the Stamford Theatre, Stamford, Connecticut (10/13/27), Werba's Brooklyn Theatre, Brooklyn, New York (10/17/27), and the Apollo Theatre in Harlem, New York.

There was no intermission between the second and third acts. Instead, a film was shown, depicting the path of a newspaper editorial from the typewriter, to the mechanical plant, through the delivery system and, finally, to the reader.

The top ticket price for *Ink* was $3.30.

William Harrigan (1886-1966), the star of *Ink* as managing editor Robert Buchanan, came from a well-known theatrical family. His father was Edward "Ned" Harrigan of "Harrigan and Hart" fame, while his mother was actress Annie Braham Harrigan, the daughter of composer David Braham. William's sister, Nedda Harrigan Logan, was a fine actress in her own right, featured in films like *Charlie Chan at the Opera* (1935) and *Thank You, Mr. Moto* (1937). As a young child, William Harrigan first appeared on stage with his father in shows like *Reilly and the 400*. After returning home a wounded hero from World War I, he resumed acting in plays like *Polly Preferred* (1923) with Edward Van Sloan. Harrigan received critical acclaim in the lead role of Eugene O'Neill's *The Great God Brown* (1926). Over the next thirty years, Harrigan remained active in both the theatre (e.g., the Captain in *Mr. Roberts*, 1948) and film (*G-Men*, 1935, *Flying Leathernecks*, 1951, etc.). Harrigan again was seen on Broadway with Frye in *Keeper of the Keys* (10/18/33), as well as in the movie *The Invisible Man* (1933).

It is difficult to ascertain why Frye, after a series of Broadway successes, would opt for a role like Clarence Jerome, the priggish assistant managing editor and son of the publisher (Charles Richman), in *Ink*. The critics were the least kind they had ever been to Frye during his tenure on Broadway. Even Alexander Woollcott, who usually sang Dwight's praises, labeled Frye's role "preposterous" and performance "terrible."

REVIEWS

"Dwight Frye as his (Richman's) son did everything he knew to make the ridiculous role even more clownish." — Percy Hammond, *New York Herald Tribune*

"Dwight Frye was badly directed as the idiot son." — Burns Mantle, *New York Daily News*

"Dwight Frye is unwisely chosen as the publisher's son and consequently the role is quite off-key with the rest of the production." — Gordon M. Leland

The Queen's Husband

Comedy in three acts by Robert Emmet Sherwood; Presented by William A. Brady, Jr., and Dwight Deere Wiman; Staged by John Cromwell; Sets by Livingston Platt; Opened at the Playhouse Theatre, New York, on January 25, 1928; Broadway run: 125 performances

CAST: Frederick Granton...Gyles Isham; Phipps...Edward Rigby; Lord Birten...Wallace Widdecombe; Petley...James H. Morrison; Princess Anne...Katherine Alexander; Queen Martha... Gladys Hanson; Lady-in-Waiting...Marguerite Taylor; Another Lady-in-Waiting...Helen Cromwell; General Northrup...Reginald Barlow; King Eric VIII...Roland Young; Major Blent...William Boren; Sergeant...John M. James; Dr. Fellman...Arthur Hughes; **Prince William of Greck... Dwight Frye**; Laker...Benedict MacQuarrie

NOTES: *The Queen's Husband* actually premiered out-of-town in Providence, Rhode Island, reportedly grossing $10,000 during its try-out period. At the Playhouse in New York, ticket prices for *The Queen's Husband* ranged from two to five dollars.

The Queen's Husband was the third effort of playwright Robert Emmet Sherwood (1896-1955), then editor of Life magazine, following the success of his initial production, The Road to Rome (1926). Sherwood, who also penned the compelling The Petrified Forest (1935), authored three Pulitzer Prize-winning plays: Idiot's Delight (1936), Abe Lincoln in Illinois (1938) and There Shall Be No Night (1940). He won a fourth Pulitzer for the biography Roosevelt and Hopkins (1948). Sherwood worked on many Hollywood screenplays, notably The Best Years of Our Lives (1946). Considered a romantic idealist, Sherwood, one of the founders of the Playwrights Company, steered away from the "realistic problems" featured in many of his works in the light and humorous The Queen's Husband.

Like most of Sherwood's plays, The Queen's Husband was published, in hardcover, by Charles Scribner's Sons (in 1928).

Roland Young (1887-1953), King Eric VIII in The Queen's Husband, enjoyed a long acting career on both stage and screen. Some of his noteworthy film roles were: George McWhirter Fotheringay in The Man Who Could Work Miracles (1936), Cosmo Topper in Topper (1937, and its two sequels) and William Blore in And Then There Were None (1945). Reginald Barlow (1867-1943), the villainous General Northrup of Sherwood's play, rarely had comparable parts in movies, instead being seen in briefer bits, like Dr. Phillips in Werewolf of London and Hans at the opening of Bride of Frankenstein (1935). Marguerite Taylor, daughter of stage legend Laurette Taylor, made her stage debut in The Queen's Husband as a lady-in-waiting.

As Prince William of Greck, the intended husband of Princess Anne (Katherine Alexander), Frye's appearance in The Queen's Husband was brief, but memorable. John Anderson noted in his article, "Some Actors Take the Easiest Exit Every Night":

> But the player most nearly approaching the dream of paid inactivity is Mr. Dwight Frye, who appears for about six minutes in the last act of The Queen's Husband, so that he is practically not annoyed by his job at all, except in shoehorning himself into a snow-white uniform, which feat probably comes under the head of acrobatics, and makes it worth anything.

J. Brooks Atkinson commented that Frye's character was "unspeakably supercilious," with most critics admiring Frye's work as Prince William.

REVIEWS

"... Dwight Frye made his Crown Prince a corking character bit. Frye was only on for a few moments. His sallow makeup, little mustache, Teutonic dialect, all went to make Prince William a real person." — Ibee., Variety

"Mr. Dwight Frye, lavished prodigally upon one act, plays a decadent Prince to complete effect." — John Anderson, New York Evening Journal

"Dwight Frye is put to considerable gold-fringed burlesquing of an imperial heir." — Gilbert Gabriel, New York Sun

FILM VERSION

The Royal Bed : RKO, 1931; Director: Lowell Sherman; Screenplay: J. Walter Ruben; Running Time: 72 minutes; CAST: Lowell Sherman (King Eric VIII); Mary Astor (Princess Anne); Anthony Bushell (Freddie Granton); Hugh Trevor (Prince William); Nance O'Neill (Queen Martha); Robert Warwick (Northrup); Gilbert Emery (Phipps); J. Carrol Naish (Laker); Alan Roscoe (Birten); Frederic Burt (Fellman); Desmond Roberts (Major Blent); Lita Chevret (Lady-in-Waiting); Nancy Lee Blaine (Lady-in-Waiting)

RADIO
A clipping (date unspecified) in Dwight Frye's Broadway scrapbook revealed the following:

> *The Queen's Husband*, with Roland Young, Gladys
> Hanson, Katherine Alexander, Reginald Barlow and
> Dwight Frye in the roles they portray on the stage, will
> be presented as the second in the Stardom of Broadway
> series by the National Broadcasting Company through
> WJZ, New York, next Friday afternoon at 3:30 o'clock.
> Robert E. Sherwood's comedy has been condensed
> and adapted for presentation before the microphone by
> Mortimer Stewart, who is in charge of the productions
> in this series of "broadcast matinees."

Mima

A play in three acts and twenty scenes; Adapted by David Belasco from *The Red Mill*, by
Ferenc Molnar; Music composed and conducted by Edwin Ludig; Choreography by Mme. Freda
Symon; Produced under the personal direction of David Belasco; Opened at the Belasco Theatre,
New York, December 12, 1928; Broadway run: 180 performances

CAST: Human Beings: The Schoolmaster...Philip Bishop; Etel, his Wife...Madeleine King;
Palmyra...Ruth Dayton; The Poet...Eugene Donovan; A Member of Parliament...William Boag;
Janos, a Forester...Sidney Blackmer; Ilonka, his Wife...Vivienne Glesen; Manikins: Mima...
Lenore Ulric; **Alfons...Dwight Frye**; The Husband...Arthur Stuart Hull; The Maid...Jane Fer-
rell; Vocal Soloist...Kitty Gray; Devils—Magister, an Inventor...A. E. Anson; Magister's Staff
of Engineers: Malacoda, Assistant to Magister...Romaine Callender; Rubicante, in Charge of the
Three Cylinders of the Machine...Lionel Braham; Draghignazzo, Chief Electrician...Anthony
J. Sansone; Alichino, At the Great Fly Wheel...Eduardo Abdo; Calcabrina, at the Reflectors...
Schuyler MacGuffin; Cagnazzo, in Charge of the Boilers...Jerome Jordan; Scarmiglione, in
Charge of the Dynamo...Arthur MacArthur; Libicocco, Controlling the Transmission...Richard
Lambart; Farfarello, in Charge of the Vocal Records...Allan Hale; Barbariccia, At the Valves...
Frank Lengel; Chief Stoker...Douglas F. Swanson; Green Imp...Fred Nelson; Satan and his Court:
His Majesty, the King of Hell...Reginald Carrington; The Adjutant...Lennox Pawle; Secretary to
the Adjutant...Harold Seton; The Prime Minister...Charles H. Martin; First Arch-Devil...George
Gardon; Second Arch-Devil...Ben Probst; Third Arch-Devil...Kraft Walton; Fourth Arch-Devil...
Normand Constantin; Fifth Arch-Devil...W. Gordon Craig; Sixth Arch-Devil...Frederick Ray-
mond; and "Baccarat players," "Monte Carlo characters," "Cabaret folk," "Imps," "Devilkins,"
"Standard bearers," "Guards," "Pages" and "Dancers of the Damned"

NOTES: *Mima* was super-showman Belasco's most spectacular show, a $325,000 fantasy epic,
which Belasco proclaimed (in a circular given to the first night audience) as "the play supreme."
He totally refashioned the interior of his Belasco Theatre to accommodate the Red Mill (which
blazed and exploded and toppled before the awestruck audience), and festooned it with an orchestra, dazzling costumes and a huge cast.
As Mima, Lenore Ulric had a grand showcase: she provided imitations of "a French street-
walker," "a Greek thief," "a Hungarian coffee house trollop," "a German beer saloon girl" and
"a Cockney street-walker," performed a strip, wore magnificent costumes and wigs and delivered
dialogue such as:

I want to hold an innocent man in my arms. You remind
me of a tiger... a big wild tiger looking for his first mate...
in a jungle spring... all passion and shivers... Oh, you...
you...you...

Miss Ulric was delivering this passionate dialogue to her real offstage fiance —
Sidney Blackmer, who played Janos, the Forester. Born in Salisbury, North Carolina on July
13, 1895, Blackmer had a background that included Shakespearean repertory, such early film
work as *Perils of Pauline* and serving as a lieutenant in WW I; he'd acted in such Broadway
plays as *The Thirteenth Chair* (1916), *The Mountain Man* (1921), *Scaramouche* (1923), *The
Moonflower* (1924) and *Springboard* (1927). His engagement to Miss Ulric (which *The New
York Times* announced on Christmas Eve of 1927) and their subsequent marriage titillated fans
of the Broadway stage.
As Mima herself, Lenore Ulric, said of her old mentor David Belasco:

All of us who were with him depended upon him so
much that we'd just flounder around and say, "What do
I do now?" He was a good soldier, a hard worker and
a great director.

As Alfons the Spider in the Satanic spectacle, Frye enjoyed a juicy role that was a harbinger
of his Hollywood horrors to come.

REVIEWS
"Mr. Belasco has staged his own adaptation of Ferenc Molnar's *The Red Mill* as no other play,
allegory or fantasy has ever before been staged within sight and sound of Broadway... Certainly
as a spectacle it is worth looking at... The display of Lenore Ulric's versatility, together with her
other charms, which I assume was also a determining factor in the decision to produce *Mima*, is
successfully accomplished. She is often very beautiful and as moving as a soulless heroine can
be. She is assisted by Sidney Blackmer, who is a little less successful in overcoming the play's
handicaps... Dwight Frye plays a spider effectively..." —Burns Mantle

Keeper of the Keys
Drama in three acts by Valentine Davies; Adapted from the novel of the same name by Earl
Derr Biggers; Produced and staged by Sigourney Thayer; Sets by Donald Oenslager; Opened at
the Fulton Theatre, New York, on October 18, 1933; Broadway run: 24 performances

CAST: Don Holt...Roy Roberts; Kathleen Ireland...Ruth Easton; Dr. Frederick Swan...Romaine
Callender; Inspector Charlie Chan...William Harrigan; **Ah Sing...Dwight Frye**; Dudley Ward...
Fleming Ward; Luis Romano...Aristides De Leoni; John Ryder...Howard St. John; Ellen Landini...
Roberta Beatty; Michael Ireland...Robert Lynn; Cash Shannon...Warren Parker; Seth Leahy...
Elwood K. Thomas

NOTES: *Keeper of the Keys* was tried out at the Hollis Street Theatre, Boston, Massachusetts
(late September 1933) and the Broad Street Theatre, Philadelphia, Pennsylvania (10/2/33), under
the title *Inspector Charlie Chan*. When the show arrived on Broadway at the Fulton Theatre, it
was renamed after the story from which it was adapted, *The Keeper of the Keys*, the final Charlie
Chan novel penned by Earl Derr Biggers before his death.
Existent theatre stills provide evidence of the extensive makeup Frye wore to be transformed
into the ancient, mysterious Ah Sing in *Keeper of the Keys*. Valentine Davies' play was never
published, but, if Ah Sing's dialogue from the novel is an indication, Frye must have had difficulty

presenting lines like, "What's mallah you? You clazy?," in a dignified manner. As the long-time servant of Dudley Ward and his family, noted for cooking huge bowls of rice with meat gravy, Ah Sing is central to the plot of *Keeper of the Keys*, in addition to being a major suspect.

Keeper of the Keys reunited Frye with William Harrigan, their having appeared together on Broadway in the ill-fated *Ink* in 1927. Both actors also were seen in Universal's *The Invisible Man* (1933). Frye, Harrigan and their respective families became lifelong friends.

Although Fox enjoyed a great deal of success with its Charlie Chan film series, *Keeper of the Keys*, the sole attempt to present Chan on stage, was met with poor reviews and closed after only 24 performances. Donald Oenslager's sets, however, received critical acclaim, noting a pleasant hunting lodge with fine balconies and a winter-in-the-mountains effect on the outside.

REVIEWS
"Dwight Frye as Ah Sing is the only other male personator of consequence (besides Harrigan)" — ABEL., *Variety*, October 24, 1933.

Queer People
A comedy in three acts and ten scenes by John Floyd, based on the novel of the same name by Carroll and Garrett Graham; Produced by Galen Bogue; Staged by Melville Burke; Sets by P. Dodd Ackerman; Opened at the National Theatre, New York, February 15, 1934; Broadway run: 13 performances

CAST: John Grew...Willard Dashiell; Mrs. Grew...Clara Palmer; Eunice Stair, "Miss Mississippi"... Colleen Cooper; Edward Worth...Frank Allworth; Rosie...Sylvia Manners; Gladys...Ruth Lee; Bellboy...James Fallon; Theodore Anthony White, "Whitey"...Hal Skelly; Jane Wilson...Gladys George; Henry McGinnis...Frank Otto; **Frank Carson...Dwight Frye**; Johnny Rocco...Walter Fenner; Ricardo Roque... "Peppy" d'Albrew; Mandu...Frank de Silva; Gilbert Vance...Arthur Pierson; Joe Greet...Leonard Lord; "Peanuts" Oliver...Milly June; Milton Hoffberger...Lawrence Keating; Albert Blynn...William Roselle; Louise Bagshaw...Edna Mears; Dorothy Irving...Helen Claire; Monica Mercedes...Kay Carlin; Reatha Clore...Nita Naldi; Bartender...Wesley Givens; Sammy Schmaltz...Jerry Hausner; "Pop" Schmaltz...Harry Vokes; Ruth Schmaltz...Marga Herden; Fanny...Billie Kemp; Madame Frankie Lee...Flavia Arcaro; Sol Snifkin...Herbert Heywood; Mr. Pappadoulous...J. Arthur Young; Fanna Wong Yong...Ming Soy; A policeman...Frank Allworth; A policeman...W. W. Shuttleworth; Turnkey...James Levers; Sheriff...Joseph Burton; Brady... Charles O'Connor; A hotel porter...Walter Kevan

NOTES: By 1934, Dwight Frye must have savored the idea of thumbing his nose at Hollywood, which already had typecast him via *Dracula, Frankenstein, The Vampire Bat* and *The Circus Queen Murder*, as the cinema's maddest lunatic. Backed by the fortunes of Howard Hughes (who also held the film rights), *Queer People* vowed to be the last word in lampoons of Hollywood. Ironically, the play was a disaster—the biggest flop in Dwight's Broadway career and his final job in the New York theatre.

As Percy Hammond described in his morning-after review:

> If the evidence of *Queer People* is to be relied upon,
> Hollywood is all that its detractors claim for it—a shrine
> of stale iniquity in which grotesque debauchees celebrate
> Vice and give Decorum the Bronx hoot. There, under
> summer skies and in a climate invented by the angels,
> girlish innocents from the East go to hell the hardest

way; and the cinematic Art is prostituted to the greed and
pleasure of a horde of amateur Babylonians...

It certainly sounded diverting, and the play had several things going for it. First of all, there was the exuberant star, Hal Skelly, starring as "Whitey," the boozehound newspaper reporter. (The program of *Queer People* even referred to Skelly's role—with some hyperbole—as "the lovable and immortal role of Whitey.") Skelly had triumphed in the hit Broadway show, *Burlesque*, and had starred in D. W. Griffith's last film, *The Struggle* (1931, with Zita Johann). Then there was the $40,000 worth of sets, including such spectacles as the observation platform of the Santa Fe Train "The Chief" en route west, the banquet hall of the Ambassador Hotel, a Santa Monica beach house patio and (most tantalizingly of all) "the reception room of Madame Frankie Lee's studio" —i.e., a "notorious" Hollywood brothel, where Skelly sang "Frankie and Johnny." In addition to the "bawdy-house" episode, *Queer People* offered two orgy sequences and a murder.

For a special splash of spoofy showmanship, producer Galen Bogue premiered *Queer People* at Broadway's National Theatre the night of February 15, 1934, a la a Hollywood premiere (floodlights, a red carpet, a microphone in the lobby, etc.). But it all boomeranged; critics axed the show, with John Mason Brown judging of *Queer People*:

> Though it is intended as a laughing tirade against the
> movies, Hollywood will doubtless recover from its
> onslaughts without realizing they were ever made. But
> some of us who sat the play out last night will need a
> longer time.

Queer People came down in such flames (only 13 performances—the shortest run of any of Dwight Frye's Broadway plays) that Howard Hughes tossed the film rights. The script was never published—making it tough to research Dwight's performance. Based on the novel, his character of Frank Carson was a heartsick husband, tormented by a wife who had ascended to stardom and left him behind. In the novel—and, presumably, the play—he commits suicide.

Leading lady of *Queer People* was Gladys George, best-remembered for her movie performances in *Valiant is the Word for Carrie* (1936), *Madame X* (1937) and *The Roaring Twenties* (1939). Dwight admired her greatly, and remained friends with her for the rest of his life; she died in Hollywood in 1954 from a barbiturate overdose. Also curiously in the cast was Nita Naldi, who had played Gina, the bad girl in John Barrymore's 1920 film of *Dr. Jekyll and Mr. Hyde*, as well as Valentino's temptress in *A Sainted Devil* and *Blood and Sand*. Since Miss Naldi (a talkie casualty who died in 1961) spent the rest of her life dreaming of a movie comeback ("Oh, Gawd, just one more chance!" she reportedly pleaded on radio in the 1950s), one suspects she—like Dwight—had her own ax to grind with Hollywood.

Queer People let everyone down. Although Dwight Frye probably didn't realize it at the time, *Queer People* was a tawdry ending to a brilliant Broadway career.

REVIEWS
"...Mr. Skelly is no glib wit. He is a trouping comic... (the play) offers Gladys George in a rosy part, Helen Claire as a comely ingenue, Frank Otto as a hardened sinner, Dwight Frye as a tragic husband, and a host of Hollywood profligates. But the dramatization is feebly theatrical."—Brooks Atkinson, *The New York Times*

Dwight Frye's Unrealized Broadway Projects

Meet the Wife

Comedy in three acts by Lynn Starling; Opened at the Klaw Theater, New York, on November 26, 1923; Cast: Mary Boland, Clifton Webb, Humphrey Bogart, Ernest Lawford, Eleanor Griffith; Broadway Run: 261 performances

Dwight Frye had toured with the show, then known as *Underwrite Your Husband*, during its out-of-town pre-Broadway tryout. Clifton Webb replaced Frye as Victor Staunton prior to the Broadway opening.

Beggar on Horseback

Fantastic comedy in two parts by George S. Kaufman and Marc Connelly; Opened at the Broadhurst Theater, New York, on February 12, 1924; Cast: Roland Young, Kay Johnson, Osgood Perkins, Spring Byington, George W. Barbier; Broadway Run: 224 performances

A late 1923 newspaper clipping from Frye's Broadway scrapbook listed Dwight among the preliminary cast of *Beggar on Horseback,* about to go into rehearsals. For whatever reason, Frye and Lois Meredith, also announced, did not appear in this successful comedy.

57 Bowery

Comedy in three acts by Edward Locke; Opened at Wallack's Theatre, New York, on January 26, 1928; Cast: Hyman Adler, John D. Seymour, Robert Brister, Joan Blair, Renee Rush. Broadway Run: 57 performances

After the closing of *Ink*, Frye was hired to appear in *57 Bowery*, which went into rehearsals under the direction of Edward Elsner in December 1927. Frye, however, departed early in the show's development, accepting a smaller role in what would be a far more successful production: *The Queen's Husband*.

The Patriots

Historical drama in a prologue and three acts by Sidney Kingsley; Opened at the National Theatre, New York, on January 29, 1943; Cast: Raymond Edward Johnson, House Jameson, Madge Evans, Frances Reid, Cecil Humphreys, John Souther, Juano Hernandez; Broadway Run: 172 performances

In late 1942, Frye auditioned for and virtually won the substantial role of Alexander Hamilton in *The Patriots*. Frye's hesitance to be away from his wife and son, his involvement with the war effort at the aircraft plant and his obsession with being readily available for even the slightest film part all contributed to his turning down the opportunity to be in this production. *The Patriots*, centering on the conflicted relationship between Thomas Jefferson and Alexander Hamilton during the early days of the Republic, featured skillful, provocative writing by Pulitzer Prize winner (for *Men in White*) Sidney Kingsley. House Jameson assumed the complex role of Hamilton, which might have reestablished Frye's Broadway career had Dwight chosen to play the part.

Criminal At Large (1933): Inspector Tanner (Crane Wilbur) glances toward Lady Lebanon (Pauline Frederick), while the disturbed Lord Lebanon (Dwight Frye) pensively sits.

Appendix D
Regional Theatre (1923-1941)

Underwrite Your Husband
Comedy in three acts by Lynn Starling; Staged by Bert French; Presented in Washington, D. C., Stamford, Connecticut, and Worcester, Massachusetts, among other locations, as the out-of-town tryout for the show which opened on Broadway as *Meet the Wife* on November 26, 1923

CAST: Gertrude Lennox...Mary Boland; Harvey Lennox...Charles Dalton; Doris Bellamy...Faire Binney; **Victor Staunton...Dwight Frye**; Gregory Brown...Humphrey Bogart; Philip Lord... Ernest Lawford; Alice...Patricia Clavert; William...Charles Bloomer

NOTES: All of the above-listed cast, with the exception of Frye and Faire Binney, stayed with the company for the Broadway opening of the retitled *Meet the Wife*. Frye was replaced as Victor Staunton by Clifton Webb, while Eleanor Griffith succeeded Binney in the role of Doris Bellamy.

Dwight Frye's Broadway scrapbook includes a number of out-of-town reviews for *Underwrite Your Husband*, generally being favorable regarding his interpretation of Staunton, "an asthmatic, flat-footed person with a flair for house decorations." Critical comments from the scrapbook included:

"Mr. Frye is delightful in a role that supplies much of the fun in the play."

"Dwight Frye, remembered for his striking performance in *Six Characters in Search of An Author*... is faultlessly cast... as Victor Staunton—the Village's prize asininity."

"Dwight Frye carried off his comedy scene in the last act with telling effect."

"Dwight Frye as the fortune hunter does some wonderful character work that stamps him as a real artist."

Despite Frye's fine notices, it is assumed that the producers of *Meet the Wife* determined that Clifton Webb's epicene appearance and more extensive comedy experience made him a better choice as Victor Staunton.

The Marionette Man
Melodrama in three acts by Frances Lightner; Staged by Brock Pemberton; Opened at the Stamford Theatre, Stamford, Connecticut, on January 18, 1924

CAST: Sandro Rubini, Toni's assistant...R. M. D'Angelo; Carlotta, Rosa's daughter...Miriam Battista; **Bruno Riccoboni...Dwight Frye**; Angela, Toni's wife...Claudette Colbert; Frank Baracca, Rosa's nephew...Hal Crane; Mrs. McCartney, a widow...Claire Weldon; Antonio Riccoboni, "Toni"...Ullrich Haupt; Rosa, wardrobe mistress for the Marionettes...Michelette Burani; McSweeny, a policeman...Park Callahan; Rossi, a detective...C. Porter Hall; Adolpho, a boy of the theatre...Emanuel Schrader; Meyers, an electrician...John Parker; Rogers, a police captain... Edmund Soraghan

NOTES: Brock Pemberton gave Frances Lightner's *The Marionette Man* out-of-town tryouts in Stamford, Connecticut, and Washington, D. C., before determining the play was not ready for Broadway. It would resurface in early 1925 as *The Knife in the Wall*, later retitled *Puppets*, eventually opening on Broadway on March 9, 1925. By that time, there had been substantial revisions to the plot, as well as changes in characters. A superior cast had been assembled, with only Dwight Frye and Michelette Burani, as Rosa, making the transition from *The Marionette Man* to *Puppets*.

In *Puppets*, Frye would portray Frank Mohacz, a villain more insidious than the character of Frank Baracca in *The Marionette Man*. Bruno, in *Puppets*, would no longer be the brother of Toni (now "Nicki"), but rather his cousin. The role of Bruno, that Frye vacated to play the heavy in *Puppets*, would fall to Fredric March.

Frye, however, had done a fine job portraying Bruno Riccoboni in *The Marionette Man*, as Betty Green's review of the Stamford production would indicate:

"Dwight Frye, who has the knack of living the part he plays and of spreading an atmosphere of tragedy about him, makes Bruno a pitiful young man, in whom love is the one absorbing fire. To get Angela he commits murder, and then self preservation accuating him, he lies about the whole affair and allows Toni to be incriminated. In the sleep walking scene he reminded us of another Lady Macbeth, confessing his guilt in spite of himself." — (Frye's Broadway scrapbook)

The cast of *The Marionette Man*, perhaps not as talented as that of *Puppets*, still featured some interesting players. The most prominent member was Claudette Colbert, at the time in the embryonic stage of a long and celebrated acting career. C. Porter Hall (1888-1953) appeared in numerous films from 1931-through-1954, including *Bulldog Drummond's Peril* (1938) and *Miracle on 34th Street* (1947). Ullrich Haupt's film career, which encompassed roles in *The Tempest* (1928), *The Rogue Song* (1930) and *The Unholy Garden* (1931), was cut short by his untimely death in a hunting accident on August 5, 1931.

A Man's Man

Comedy in three acts by Patrick Kearney; Staged by Edward Goodman; Toured the Midwest in the Spring of 1928, opening at: The Colonial Theatre, Cleveland, Ohio, on April 29, 1928; the Cass Theater, Detroit, Michigan, on May 6, 1928 and the Adelphi Theatre, Chicago, Illinois, on May 13, 1928

CAST: Ma Tuttle...Edee Von Buelow; Edie Tuttle...Charlotte Wynters; Hazel Williams...Dorothy Randall; **Melville Tuttle...Dwight Frye**; S. Barrett Blackstone...James La Curto; Charlie Groff... Pat O'Brien; Mabel Plant...Eleanor Andrus; Joe Plant...Kenneth Dana; Margery Tuttle...Dorothy Mary Smith; Herb Brown...Jerry Lynch; Eddie Elkins...Eddie Casey

NOTES: When Edward Goodman, who had directed Frye in the 1925 Broadway production of Patrick Kearney's play, decided to take *A Man's Man* on the road in the spring of 1928, he was unable to find an actor to his liking for the lead role of Melville Tuttle. Goodman attempted to persuade Frye to leave the Broadway company of *The Queen's Husband* and recreate his portrayal of Mel on tour. After much discussion, Frye agreed to join *A Man's Man*, leaving New York after the final curtain of *The Queen's Husband* on Saturday night, April 28, 1928. The following day, without benefit of a rehearsal, Frye opened in *A Man's Man* at the Colonial Theatre in Cleveland.

A Man's Man played for one week each in Cleveland, Detroit and Chicago. Jerry Lynch, who played Herb Brown, was the only player, other than Frye, from the original Broadway cast in the tour company. Pat O'Brien, who had replaced Robert Gleckler as the heavy, Charlie Groff, during the New York run, was also reunited with Dwight in this production. Charlotte Wynters, fated to appear with Frye in the opening sequence of the film *Sinners in Paradise* (1938), received favorable reviews in the Josephine Hutchinson-created part of Edie Tuttle.

Broken in both body and spirit, Mel Tuttle (Dwight Frye) removes his treasured correspondence school diploma as he threatens to leave his wife in *A Man's Man*.

Here is a sampling of Frye's critical notices from the tour:

"By his excellent acting Dwight Frye makes the simple-minded Mel Tuttle quite believable. There is a furtive eagerness, an almost childish faith to his work in the earlier scenes, a half-hearted attempt to assert himself later, when confronted by the truth, that is highly effective." —Detroit, (Frye's Broadway scrapbook)

"There is a young chap named Dwight Frye in this play who is simply tremendous, acting a struggling clerk whose consuming ambition is to become an Elk and win the favor of his employer. He cudgels his brain over books he can not understand, and is a gull for every fake correspondence course in character building." —Chicago, (Frye's Broadway scrapbook)

Other critics found Frye "...superb as the clerk," "perfect as Melville Tuttle" and having given "...a splendid interpretation." It is a shame Dwight was not able to play Mel Tuttle on film. MGM brought *A Man's Man* to the screen in 1929, with William Haines in the lead role. Frye would assay the part of Mel one final time, opposite Kayo Tortoni as Edie, in a 1930 West Coast production of *A Man's Man*.

Yellow

Melodrama in seven acts by Margaret Vernon; Directed by Charles Schofield; Presented by the Edward F. Albee Stock Company at the Albee Theater, Providence, Rhode Island, the week of September 10, 1928

CAST: Porter...Frank S. Peck; **Val Parker...Dwight Frye**; Polly Parker...Jean Oliver; Waiter... Albert Bushee; Jack Crompton...Wilfred Lytell; Daisy Lingard...Helen Gilmore; Jenny Wilkes... Flora Maud Gade; Jimmy Wilkes...Day Manson; Thomas Sayre...John Winthrop; Mrs. Sayre... Louise Gerald Huntington; Donaldson...Mal Kelly; Carrie...Mabel Woolsey; Welles...Malcolm Arthur; Inspector Graney...Charles Schofield; Louis...Albert Bushee; Popsy...Malcolm Arthur; Starter...William Finneran; Officer...James G. Robertson

NOTES: *Yellow* had been staged by George M. Cohan on Broadway, opening at the National Theatre on September 21, 1926. Chester Morris played Val Parker, the immoral young architect interpreted by Frye in the Albee production. Spencer Tracy, portraying Jimmy Wilkes, was in the original Broadway company of *Yellow*.

Frye had just returned from his honeymoon in Bermuda when he signed with the Albee Stock Company to co-star with Helen Gilmore in *Yellow*. Val Parker was a meaty, villainous role for Frye: charming and confident on the outside, but manipulative, insolent and uncaring underneath. The Providence critics heaped praise upon Frye's performance in *Yellow*:

"It would be well-nigh impossible to conceive a more contemptible being than that of Val Parker, as he is drawn by the author and played by Dwight Frye, a new member of the Albee Company. As devoid of courage as he is of morality, he assumes at times like a cornered rat, a bravado which serves only to accentuate his all-pervading yellowness and the girl whom he betrayed and deserted manifests even in her degradation a nobility of soul which lifts her immeasurably above him." — (Frye's Broadway scrapbook)

"Mr. Frye had his lines in hand every minute..." — (Frye's Broadway scrapbook)

"Mr. Lytell and Mr. Frye made a striking contrast in the respective characters of avenger and villain. The one, dark and relentless, the other light, evasive and defiant. Their difference in stature emphasized dominance and enforced calm of the two parts. They were extremely intelligent performances." — (Frye's Broadway scrapbook)

Although Frye supposedly signed for the remainder of the Albee Company's 1928 summer stock season, there is no current evidence that he appeared in their three remaining productions.

Rope's End
Melodrama in three acts by Patrick Hamilton; Directed by Arthur Greville Collins; Opened at the Vine Street Theater, Los Angeles, California, in late Fall 1929, running for six weeks before moving to San Francisco, California

CAST: Wyndham Brandon...Hugh Huntley; **Charles Granillo...Dwight Frye**; Rupert Cadell...Noel Madison; with: Brenda Forbes; Susanne Leach; Alfred Jenkin; Peter Shaw; Vesey O'Davoren

NOTES: Based on the Leopold-Loeb murder case, Patrick Hamilton's *Rope's End* caused a sensation in London. It also enjoyed a 100-performance run on Broadway at the Theatre Masque, commencing September 19, 1929. Ivan Brandt played Frye's role of Charles Granillo in the Broadway company.

Frye received strong praise from the critics for his portrayal of the cowardly Charles, one of two Oxford students who kill a boy and flaunt their foul deed. Doris Denbo wrote:

"Dwight Frye as the fear crazed, weaker member of the pair, has a most difficult role to play and rises to great dramatic heights during the unfolding of the weird plot." — (Frye's Broadway scrapbook)

Both Frye and Noel Madison, the son of actor Maurice Moscovitch, were signed by Warners to appear in *The Doorway to Hell* (1930) as a result of having been observed in *Rope's End*.

Alfred Hitchcock brought *Rope's End* to the screen in 1948 as *Rope*. Farley Granger enacted the role of the more neurotic, spineless student, renamed Philip, in the film.

Criminal at Large

Mystery play in three acts by Edgar Wallace; Directed by Russell Fillmore; Produced by Henry Duffy; Presented on tour in 1933, commencing at the Alcazar Theatre, San Francisco, California, on February 22, 1933; playing the El Capitan Theatre, Hollywood, California, in March 1933; eventually concluding at the Tremont Theatre, Boston, Massachusetts, in late April 1933

CAST: Chief Detective Inspector Tanner...Crane Wilbur; **Lord Lebanon...Dwight Frye**; Lady Lebanon...Pauline Frederick; Isla...Kay Hammond; Sergeant Totty...Donald Stuart; Kelver, the butler...Boyd Irwin; with: Eric Snowden; Hugh Huntley; Kernan Cripps; Ray Ripley

NOTES: Noted mystery writer Edgar Wallace, who had many of his stories turned into films (*The Terror, Chamber of Horrors* and *The Human Monster,* among others), delivered a clever play with an interesting denouement. *Criminal at Large* had been produced by Guthrie McClintic on Broadway, opening at the Belasco Theatre on October 10, 1932. Emlyn Williams enacted the role of Lord Lebanon in the Broadway production. Frye would later play another Emlyn Williams-originated role as Dan, in the Federal Theatre version of *Night Must Fall* in 1938.

Crane Wilbur, who played Inspector Tanner in *Criminal at Large*, had a long career both as an actor, beginning in the silent era, and screenwriter, penning fantasy genre films like *House of Wax* and *The Mad Magician.* Pauline Frederick, who excelled as Lady Lebanon, would become a life-long friend of Dwight Frye and his family. Dwight and Laura Frye both toured with her later in 1933 in *Her Majesty, the Widow* and *Amber.*

Frye received very good notices as Lord Lebanon, who is revealed to be the psychotic murderer. *The Los Angeles Examiner* found his "...third-act scene... powerful in its drama and quick in its emotional transitions." George C. Warren, in the *San Francisco Chronicle* (2/23/33), wrote, "The role (Lord Lebanon) is a superb one to act and Mr. Frye does it full justice. His final speech, a monologue of his life, is wonderfully well read."

Her Majesty, the Widow

Comedy in three acts by John Charles Brownell; Directed by Edward Elsner; Opened at the Biltmore Theatre, Los Angeles, California, on May 8, 1933; Presented by Pauline Frederick's company, in tandem with *Amber*, on a cross country tour, Spring and Summer of 1933

CAST: Sarah...Grayce Hampton; Jane Seymour...Pauline Frederick; Judge Coolidge...Richard Tucker; **Robert Seymour...Dwight Frye**; "Bunny" Williams...Carlyle Moore, Jr.; Veronica Day... Isabel Withers; Elsie Reynolds...Laurette Bullivant; Peter Stuyvesant...Boyd Irwin

NOTES: Having already toured with Pauline Frederick as her son in *Criminal at Large*, Frye was chosen to play a role with the same relationship to the star in *Her Majesty, the Widow.* An added bonus was that Laura Frye, under her stage name of Laurette Bullivant, played Elsie Reynolds, Dwight's character's former love, who wins back his affections at the end. Both Dwight and Laura received favorable reviews after the Los Angeles opening of *Her Majesty, the Widow.* Tom Geraghty wrote:

"Dwight Frye made two laughs grow where there should have been one. Laurette Bullivant, a very clever ingenue, dynamited laughs into her part with personality and some very expert work."

In addition to Pauline Frederick, other members of the company became good friends of the Frye family as a result of the cross country tour of *Her Majesty, the Widow* and *Amber.* In particular, Grayce Hampton, who played Sarah, the domineering maid, Isabel Withers, Carlyle Moore, Jr. and Frederick Bell (*Amber* only) remained in contact with the Fryes for many years.

Pauline Frederick was finally able to present *Her Majesty, the Widow* on Broadway, opening at the Ritz Theatre on June 18, 1934, running for 32 performances. Ms. Frederick, Laura Frye, Hampton and Withers all repeated their roles from the tour, but the four male characters were all played by different actors. Thomas Beck portrayed Robert Seymour, the role Frye had assayed on the tour.

Amber

Drama in three acts by Martin Brown; Directed by Edward Elsner; Opened at the Biltmore Theatre, Los Angeles, California, on May 11, 1933; From there, on tour to San Francisco, California; the Pacific Northwest; Netcong, New Jersey; and other locations

CAST: Clara...Marjorie Ashton (1), Maude Scheerer (2); Madame Delambre...Pauline Frederick; **Peter Lawton...Dwight Frye**; Attilio...Joseph McGuire; Christina...Grayce Hampton; Freddy Disart...Carlyle Moore, Jr. (1), Frederick Bell (2); Daisy...Isabel Withers; Tony, a Duke...Richard Tucker (1), Roland Drew (2); Phyllis...Laurette Bullivant; Candelsee...Boyd Irwin (1), Herbert Warren (2)

NOTES: Pauline Frederick chose Martin Brown's *Amber*, a combination of melodrama and English comedy, to present alternately with *Her Majesty, the Widow* during her second cross country tour of 1933. *Criminal at Large* had been her vehicle for the first tour.

As Peter Lawton, Frye failed to elicit favorable notices. *Variety* reported, "Her (Frederick's) son's part is essayed by Dwight Frye, an excellent character actor but sadly miscast in his present assignment, failing to get the sympathy the role calls for." Another review of the Los Angeles production noted, "Dwight Frye again appears as her son and struggles with a role to which he isn't suited."

Frye apparently fared better as Robert Seymour in *Her Majesty, the Widow* than he did as Peter Lawton in *Amber*. Neither role provided Dwight with the opportunity to display his dramatic range as did Lord Lebanon in *Criminal at Large*. The fact that Frye played Pauline Frederick's son in all three productions indicates the regard in which this fine actress held Dwight's talents. As a result of working closely with her on these three plays, Dwight and Laura Frye formed a deep friendship with Pauline Frederick, interrupted only by her unfortunate death on September 19, 1938.

The Play's the Thing

Comedy in three acts by Ferenc Molnar; Adapted by P. G. Wodehouse; Produced by Irving A. Isaacs, under the supervision of Arthur Casey. Opened at the Tremont Theatre, Boston, Massachusetts, on December 25, 1933

CAST: Sandor Turai...Guy Bates Post; **Albert Adam...Dwight Frye**; (For this production, the other members of the company, in the roles of Mansky, Johann Dwornitschek, Almady, Ilona Szabo, and the lackeys, are unknown.)

NOTES: *The Play's the Thing* was first produced on Broadway at the Henry Miller Theatre on November 3, 1926. It starred Holbrook Blinn, Reginald Owen and Catherine Dale Owen, with Edward Crandall in Frye's role of the young composer Albert Adam. *The Play's the Thing* was not Frye's initial contact with a Molnar opus, of course. He previously appeared in *Mima*, David Belasco's adaptation of Molnar's *The Red Mill*.

While being interviewed during rehearsals for *The Play's the Thing*, Frye commented, "This is the first time I've been allowed to smile since 1923..." Explaining Dwight's statement, the interviewer noted, "You see, it's been a long time since he appeared as an ordinary sort of individual, a really decent fellow one would like to make friends with!"

The Second Man

Comedy in three acts by S. N. Behrman; Directed by Edward Hartford; Opened at the Broad Street Theatre, Philadelphia, Pennsylvania, on April 30, 1934

CAST: Mrs. Kendall Frayne...Rosalind Russell; Clark Storey...Bert Lytell; **Austin Lowe...Dwight Frye**; Monica Grey...Lora Baxter; Albert...Don Arbury

NOTES: *The Second Man*, S. N. Behrman's first play, had been produced on Broadway by the Theatre Guild in 1927. Alfred Lunt and Lynn Fontanne starred in the roles played in this production by Bert Lytell and Rosalind Russell. Frye's character, the dull but sincere suitor Austin Lowe, was portrayed on Broadway by Earle Larimore.

"W.R.M." in *The Public Ledger* (5/1/34) wrote of Frye's performance in *The Second Man*:

"Dwight Frye, once seen here as the spider-catching neurotic of *Dracula*, does a finely etched job as the other man. He has some marvelous intonations in his voice, which convey comedy through their solemnity."

Frye had played the Broad Street Theatre six months earlier as Ah Sing in *Inspector Charlie Chan*, which would be renamed *Keeper of the Keys* for its Broadway opening.

The Pursuit of Happiness

Comedy in three acts by Lawrence Langner and Armina Marshall; Presented on tour in the summer and fall of 1934; Among other locations, opened at the Hopatcong Theatre, Netcong, New Jersey, under the direction of E. J. Blunkall, on August 20, 1934; and the Hollis Street Theatre, Boston, Massachusetts, under the direction of Seth Arnold, on November 12, 1934 (running at the Hollis until November 24, 1934)

CAST: Meg, a servant...Eidell Heidt (1). Marjorie Cameron (2); Mose, a servant...Donald Melborne (1), Sidney Easton (2); Captain Aaron Kirkland...Harry Fischer (1), Frank Camp (2); Colonel Mortimer Sherwood...Richard S. Bishop (1), John Boyd (2); Prudence Kirkland, Aaron's daughter...Laurette Bullivant; Comfort Kirkland, Aaron's wife...Valerie Begere (1), Ruth Gates (2); **Max Christmann, a Hessian...Dwight Frye**; Thaddues Jennings, a sheriff...Edward Nannary (1), Albert Bergh (2); Two Sons of Liberty...George Spelvin, Robert Noack (1), Peter Harris (2); Reverend Lyman Banks...Herbert Warren (1), John F. Hamilton (2)

NOTES: Lawrence Langner and his wife, Armina Marshall, both of Theatre Guild fame, wrote *The Pursuit of Happiness* under the pseudonyms of Alan Child and Isabelle Loudon. The play opened on Broadway at the Avon Theatre on October 9, 1933. Tonio Selwart was featured as Max Christmann in the Broadway production.

The Pursuit of Happiness had just closed on Broadway three months prior to Dwight and Laura taking the show on tour in the summer of 1934.   The Fryes, including young "Buddy," traveled with the comedy for about three months, playing locales as small as Netcong, New Jersey, and as large as Boston, Massachusetts. Various members of the cast came and went during the tour, but Dwight and Laura were constants as Max and Prudence, the young lovers.

Elinor Hughes, in her review of the Boston production at the Hollis Street Theatre, wrote, "Dwight Frye played the innocent-faced, polite and bewildered young Hessian in a pleasant fashion," adding that Laurette Bullivant was "a demure Prudence" who "ably seconded" her husband.

Night Must Fall

Drama in three acts by Emlyn Williams; Directed by O. D. Woodward; Presented at the Mason Opera House, Los Angeles, California, as part of the W. P. A. Federal Theatre, opening on May 3, 1938

CAST: The Lord Chief Justice...Millard Vincent; Mrs. Bramson...Adelaide Melnotte; Olivia Grayne, her niece...Winifred Nimo; Hubert Laurie...Pat O'Hara; Nurse Libby...Viola Haynes; Mrs. Terence, Mrs. Bramson's cook...Florence Hymes; Dora Parkoe, her maid...Ann Morgan; Inspector Belsize...William Felts; **Dan...Dwight Frye**

NOTES: The plum role of the murderous, devious bellboy Dan had been portrayed by playwright Emlyn Williams, himself, when the drama opened on Broadway at the Ethel Barrymore Theatre on September 28, 1936. For this production at the Mason Opera House, Frye was secured to play Dan by O. D. Woodward, his old mentor from Dwight's early stock days in Denver, Spokane and Seattle. The Federal Theatre, which staged this production of *Night Must Fall*, was an arm of the Works Progress Administration, created by the federal government during the Depression.

When MGM produced the screen version of *Night Must Fall* in 1937, they chose Robert Montgomery to interpret the role of Dan (and he did so with considerable relish). Although Frye had not been considered for the film, one can only conjecture what a role like Dan in a major studio production would have done for his sagging career.

Other Regional Theatre Credits of Dwight Frye

Dumb Luck
Comedy in three acts by Earl Simmons and John Bohn; Opened at the Stamford Theatre, Stamford, Connecticut, on August 11, 1927; Moved to the Lyceum (location unknown), August 12-13, 1927

Dumb Luck, advertised as "One jump ahead of the Sheriff" and "The 'Flying Fool' of Comedies," received an out-of-town tryout in August 1927. Frye and his wife-to-be, Laurette Bullivant, played the leading roles. Playwright John Bohn may have been the same person who played the buried-alive rival of Erich von Stroheim in *The Crime of Doctor Crespi* (1935).

Rip Van Winkle
Play in two acts, adapted by Dion Boucicault from the folk legend in *Washington Irving's Sketch Book*; Opened at the Colonial Theatre, Pittsfield, Massachusetts, on July 22, 1929, playing for one week

CAST: **Derrick Van Beekman...Dwight Frye**; Rip Van Winkle...Donald Meek

Rip Van Winkle was the last play in which Frye appeared before leaving for the West Coast in the summer of 1929. It also represented his final role at Pittsfield's Colonial Theatre, where he had first come to the attention of producer Brock Pemberton during the 1922 stock season.

A Man's Man
Comedy in three acts by Patrick Kearney; Opened at the Figueroa Playhouse, Los Angeles, California, on June 5, 1930

Frye again revived his successful role of Melville Tuttle in a West Coast production of *A Man's Man*, which reopened the Figueroa Playhouse. Kayo Tortoni played Edie.

Squaring the Circle
Comedy in three acts by Valentine Katayev, adapted by Dmitri Ostrov from a translation by Charles Malamuth and Eugene Lyons; Opened at the John H. Hessel Memorial Hall, Woodmere, Long Island, New York, on July 16, 1934

This Long Island production of *Squaring the Circle* was the American premiere for the Soviet comedy/drama. In addition to Dwight Frye, the cast included Frank Shannon, of *Flash Gordon* notoriety, and Ray Miller. The following year, *Squaring the Circle* opened on Broadway on October 3, 1935 at the Lyceum Theatre, where it ran for 108 performances. Albert Dekker was in the Broadway company.

The Country Wife
A newspaper clipping (*New York Daily News*, 6/7/35) stated Frye had been added to the cast of a revival of William Wycherley's *The Country Wife*. This news item declared *The Country Wife* was scheduled to open on July 1, 1935, at the Westport Country Playhouse, Westport, Connecticut. Subsequent research, however, has not yielded any evidence of Frye appearing in this production.

Dracula
Play in three acts, dramatized by Hamilton Deane and John Balderston from Bram Stoker's novel, *Dracula*; Produced at the Beaux Arts Playhouse, Los Angeles, California, in 1941 (exact dates unknown).

Dwight Frye repeated his noted film characterization of Renfield on the California stage. According to Dwight David Frye, who witnessed his father in this production, Frederick Pymm "wasn't very scary" as Count Dracula.

BIBLIOGRAPHY

American Film Institute Catalog of Feature Films, 1921-1930: Edited by Kenneth Munden, New York: R. R. Bowker Co., 1971

American Film Institute Catalog of Feature Films, 1931-1940: Edited by Patricia King Hanson, Berkeley and Los Angeles, CA: University of California Press, 1993

American Theatre Companies 1888-1930: Edited by Weldon B. Durham, Westport, CT. Greenwood Press, 1987

Antosiewicz, John, and Rizzo, Charlie: "Dementia's Son: Dwight Frye, Jr. Speaks," *Midnight Marquee* #29, October 1980, pp. 39-42

Best Plays of and Year Book of the Drama in America: 1909-1919: Edited by Burns Mantle and Garrison P. Sherwood; 1919-1920 to 1943-44, New York: Dodd, Mead and Co., various

The Biographical Encyclopedia and Who's Who of the American Theatre: Edited by Walter Rigden, New York: James H. Heineman, Inc., 1965

Bojarski, Richard: "Dwight Frye, the Mighty Midget of Menace" *For Monsters Only* #8, 1969, pp. 26-35

Bolton, Guy; Wodehouse, P. G., and Kern, Jerome: *Sitting Pretty*, Unpublished script, 1924

Bordman, Gerald: *Jerome Kern: His Life and Music*, New York: Oxford University Press, 1980

Bordman, Gerald: *The Oxford Companion to the American Theatre*, New York: Oxford University Press, 1984

Botto, Louis: *At This Theatre*, New York: Dodd, Mead and Company, 1984

Bowman, David: "Dwight Frye: The Man With the 2000 Watt Stare," *Filmfax* #35, Oct./Nov. 1992, pp. 73-79

Bronner, Edwin J.: *The Encyclopedia of the American Theatre 1900-1975*, San Diego, CA, A. S. Barnes & Company, Inc., 1980

Brunas, Michael; Brunas, John, and Weaver, Tom: *Universal Horrors: The Studio's Classic Films, 1931-1946*, Jefferson, NC: McFarland & Co., Inc., 1990

Coughlin, James T.: "Dwight Frye," *Film Fan Monthly* #154, April 1974, pp. 3-11

Coughlin, James T.: "Dwight Frye," In *The Real Stars* (Leonard Maltin, editor), New York: Popular Library, 1979, pp. 171-189

Curtis, James: *James Whale*, Metuchen, NJ: The Scarecrow Press, Inc., 1982

Cushing, Tom: *The Devil in the Cheese*, New York: Samuel French, 1927

Dorst, Gary D.: "Dwight Frye: Gone and Forgotten," *Gore Creatures* #19 , April 1971, pp. 8-13

Elwood, Muriel: *Pauline Frederick: On and Off the Stage*, Chicago, IL: A. Kroch, 1940

Everson, William K.: *The Detective in Film*, Secaucus, NJ: The Citadel Press, 1972

Evreinoff, Nikolas: *The Chief Thing*, Garden City, NY: Doubleday, Page & Company, 1926

Ford, Ron: "The Next Generation Speaks: Dwight D. Frye, the Son of Dracula's Servant," *Filmfax* #35, Oct./Nov. 1992, pp. 78-79, 82

Frye, Dwight I. Pre-Broadway Scrapbook: 1914-1922

Frye, Dwight I. Broadway Scrapbook: 1922-1929

Hanke, Ken: *Charlie Chan at the Movies: History, Filmography, and Criticism*, Jefferson, NC: McFarland and Company, Inc., 1989

Kearney, Patrick: *A Man's Man*, New York: Brentano's, 1925

Maltin, Leonard: *The Great Movie Shorts*, New York: Bonanza Books, 1972

Mank, Gregory William: *It's Alive! The Classic Cinema Saga of Frankenstein*, New York: A. S. Barnes & Company, Inc., 1981

Mank, Gregory William: *The Hollywood Hissables*, Metuchen, NJ: The Scarecrow Press, Inc., 1989

Mank, Gregory William: *Karloff and Lugosi: The Story of a Haunting Collaboration*, Jefferson, NC: McFarland and Company, Inc., 1990

Mank, Greg: "Dwight Frye: His Life and Career," *Scarlet Street* #16, Fall 1994, pp.39-48, 110-113

Molnar, Ferenc: *Mima*; In *The Plays of Ferenc Molnar*, New York: The Vanguard Press, 1929

The Motion Picture Guide (12 volumes): Edited/published by Jay Robert Nash and Stanley Ralph Ross, Evanston, IL: Cinebooks, 1985

O'Brien, Pat: *The Wind at My Back: The Life and Times of Pat O'Brien*, Garden City, NY: Doubleday & Co., Inc., 1964

Pirandello, Luigi: *Six Characters in Search of An Author*, In *Three Plays*, New York: E.P. Dutton & Co., Inc., 1922

Pitts, Michael R.: "Dwight Frye," In *Horror Film Stars*, Jefferson, NC: McFarland and Company, Inc., 1981, pp. 234-239

Scherl, Bob: "Dracula's Disciple - 'Renfield'!" *Famous Monsters of Filmland* #126, July 1976, pp. 22-31

Seymour, Blackie: "Dwight Frye: The Ultimate Villager," *Classic Images* #252, June 1996, pp. 18-19

Sherwood, Robert E.: *The Queen's Husband*, New York: Charles Scribner's Sons, 1928

Skal, David J.: *Hollywood Gothic: The Tangled Web of Dracula from Novel to Stage to Screen*, New York: W. W. Norton and Co., 1990

Skal, David J.: *The Monster Show: A Cultural History of Horror*, New York: W.W. Norton and Co., 1993

Turner, George E., and Price, Michael H.: *Forgotten Horrors: Early Talkie Chillers from Poverty Row*, New York: A. S. Barnes & Company, Inc., 1979

Weaver, Tom: *Poverty Row Horrors! Monogram, PRC and Republic Horror Films of the Forties*, Jefferson, NC: McFarland and Company, Inc., 1993

Weaver, Tom: "Monster Sidekicks: The Good, The Bad, The Ugly," *Monsters from the Vault* #1, Summer 1995, pp. 11-18

Werfel, Franz: *The Goat Song*, Garden City, NY: Doubleday, Page & Company, 1926

Van Hoogstraten, Nicholas: *Lost Broadway Theatres*, New York: Princeton Architectural Press, 1991

Young, Stark: "Creative Criticism," *New Republic*, March 28, 1923

Young, Stark: "Dwight Frye and Acting," *The New York Times*, March 22, 1925

Dwight Frye as Karl in Universal's sequel to *Frankenstein*, *Bride of Frankenstein*.

Dwight Frye's Last Laugh

ACKNOWLEDGMENTS

The authors would like to thank the following individuals and organizations for providing various assistance with the research and development of this project:

The Berkshire Athenaeum (Local History Collection); The Billy Rose Theatre Collection, Library of the Performing Arts, New York Public Library (especially Donald Madison); the Museum of the City of New York; SUNY College at Purchase Library (mainly Robert Evans); University of Wisconsin Center for Film and Theater Research. Thanks (as always) to curator extraordinaire Ned Comstock, of the Performing Arts Library of the University of Southern California, for unfailing help and high spirits.

John Abrassart; John Antosiewicz; Dr. Dave Baldwin; Buddy Barnett (and Cinema Collectors Shop, Hollywood); Richard Bojarski; Ronald Borst; the late Barry Brown; John Brunas; Michael Brunas; John Cocchi; Frank Coghlan, Jr.; the late Randye Cohen; Jane Coughlin; Marianne Coughlin; Maryann DeGiacomo; Dr. Ron Delehanty; Marta Dobrovitz; Gary D. Dorst; Eddie Brandt's Saturday Matinee (Claire Brandt); Catherine Hagele Elmore; Bob Esposito; the late William K. Everson; Film Favorites; Jan Garfield; Denis Gifford; Eve Golden; Ron Harvey; Charles Heard; Tom Johnson; the late Patric Knowles; Larry Edmunds Bookshop (Mike Hawks); Kenneth G. Lawrence; Marc Lawrence; Leonard Maltin; Darwin Maurer; Doug McClelland; Linda Miller; Cyndi Mobley; Movie Star News (Paula Klaw, Ira Kramer, the late Jack Kramer); Joan Naumann; Doug Norwine; Barbara Rhodes; Gary Don Rhodes; Eli Savada; Robert Scherl; Richard Scrivani; Blackie Seymour; David J. Skal; John Skillin; John Soister; Elliot Stein; Richard Stoddard; Susan Sutter; Tony Timpone (Editor, *Fangoria*); Linda J. Walter; Bill Warren; the redoubtable Tom Weaver; Scott Wilson; Steven and Nathalie Yafet; and Dave Zimmerman.

We are indebted to Donald Maurer, the original Dwight Frye fan, for his suggestions, memories and the loan of materials from his collection.

Greg would like to add his particular appreciation to:

Special thanks to Josephine Hutchinson for her friendship, hospitality and vivid memories of starring with Dwight Frye in Broadway's 1925 *A Man's Man*; also for her reminiscences re: *Son of Frankenstein*.

Much gratitude to all those who have discussed their classic horror films in interviews with me over the years, and whose memories contribute so much to the background of this book: David Manners; the late Mae Clarke; Marilyn ("little Maria") Harris; Pauline Moore; the late Elsa Lanchester; Valerie Hobson; Curt Siodmak and to the various horror stars' family members, who have kindly given me so many insights: Sara Karloff; Bela Lugosi, Jr.; the late Lillian Lugosi Donlevy and Mrs. George Zucco.

Jessie Lilley (Publisher) and Richard Valley (Editor) of *Scarlet Street* Magazine, which ran his tribute to Dwight Frye (No. 16, Fall, 1994)—sections of which are reprinted here.

And, as always, thanks and much love to Barbara, Jessica and Christopher Mank. All have become experts at graciously ignoring the fact that I temporarily take on the tragic aspects of whomever I'm researching. Love all!
—GWM

Jim's love and gratitude go out to his wife, Mary Quinn, and children, Kerry and Brian Quinn Coughlin, for their caring, patience and support during the research and production of this book.

—JTC

A salute to Gary and Susan Svehla of Midnight Marquee Press for championing the project.

Finally, our sincere gratitude to Dwight David Frye for entrusting us with the task of telling his father's life story in an honest, forthright and complete-as-possible manner, while making available all surviving family materials and being a patient, generous collaborator.

Jim Coughlin, Dwight Frye, Jr. and Gregory Mank at a book signing for the first edition of *Dwight Frye's Last Laugh*.

AUTHORS

Gregory William Mank

    Writer/actor/teacher, Greg Mank is the author of the books *It's Alive! The Classic Cinema Saga of Frankenstein*, *The Hollywood Hissables*, *Karloff and Lugosi* and *Hollywood Cauldron*. He wrote the production histories for 11 MagicImage books (licensed by Universal); co-authored the James Robert Parish books *The Best of MGM*, *The Hollywood Reliables*, *The Hollywood Beauties* and *The Funsters*; contributed to the anthologies *Boris Karloff, Bela Lugosi, Bitches, Bimbos, and Virgins*, *Magill's Survey of Cinema* and *The Real Stars*; and writes periodically for the following magazines: *American Cinematographer*, *Cinefantastique*, *Cult Movies*, *Filmfax*, *Films in Review*, *Fangoria*, *Midnight Marquee*, *Movie Club*, *Monsters from the Vault*, *Starlog*, *Scarlet Street* and *Video Watchdog*. He appeared on *Entertainment Tonight* and *Rivals!* (discussing the topic of Karloff and Lugosi). Greg received the FANEX Award from The Horror and Fantasy Film Society for his "Outstanding Contribution to Film Literature."

He acted in over 90 stage productions in such roles as Prof. Harold Hill in *The Music Man*, "Il Stupendo" in *Lend Me a Tenor* and the evil Barnaby in *Babes in Toyland* (which he played for 13 seasons with Baltimore Actors Theatre).

Greg teaches English on the high school and college level. His specialty is Shakespeare. He has an MLA degree from Johns Hopkins University and a BA degree from Mount St. Mary's College, Maryland.

He lives with his wife of twenty-five years, Barbara, who is completely understanding of his filmic obsessions and with his children Christopher and Jessica in Delta, Pennsylvania.

James T. Coughlin

James Thomas Coughlin has a life-long affection for the colorful supporting actors and actresses associated with horror films, as evidenced by his ongoing "Forgotten Faces of Fantastic Films" articles appearing in *Midnight Marquee*. Born in Rye, New York, Jim was raised on the grounds of Playland Amusement Park, where his late father was superintendent. Jim studied to be an electrical engineer prior to making a career switch, obtaining a Masters and Doctorate in clinical psychology from Fordham University. Currently a consultant for a residential treatment facility in Westchester County, Jim also maintains a private psychotherapy practice. He is married to Mary Quinn, a clinical psychologist. Jim and Mary reside in Carmel, New York, with their daughter Kerry and son Brian.

In addition to *Midnight Marquee*, Jim's writing has appeared in Leonard Maltin's *Film Fan Monthly* and *The Real Stars*. With the late actor Barry Brown, Jim co-authored the unpublished *Unsung Heroes of the Horrors*.

Dwight D. Frye

Dwight David Frye was born in Spokane, Washington the day after Christmas, 1930—less than two months before the official release date of *Dracula*. With show business in his "blood," so to speak, he made his acting debut at the age of six in a film with his father. Following college, an Army stint in Europe and eight years of professional acting in Los Angeles, San Francisco and New York, he has spent the past 32 years in all areas of the professional theatre. Twenty-one years as assistant to Broadway director Albert Marre on such hits as *Man of La Mancha* have been interwoven with two years as business manager of The Repertory Theatre of Lincoln Center and nine years as associate to Broadway producer Frederick Brisson. In addition, Dwight has co-produced several original cast and studio cast recordings, including *Do Black Patent Leather Shoes Really Reflect Up?*, *The Secret Garden*, *Rags*, *Magdalena*, *Nymph Errant* and *Eating Raoul*. He has lived in New York City since 1961.Dwight D. Frye passed away in New York city on March 27, 2003.

Dwight Frye's Last Laugh

Made in the USA
San Bernardino, CA
25 November 2019